T0094252

Software Engineering

Software engineering is as much about teamwork as it is about technology. This introductory textbook covers both. For courses featuring a team project, it offers tips and templates for aligning classroom concepts with the needs of the students' projects. Students will learn how software is developed in industry by adopting agile methods, discovering requirements, designing modular systems, selecting effective tests, and using metrics to track progress. The book also covers the why's behind the how-to's, to prepare students for advances in industry practices. The chapters explore ways of eliciting what users really want, how clean architecture divides and conquers the inherent complexity of software systems, how test coverage is essential for detecting the inevitable defects in code, and much more. Ravi Sethi provides real-life case studies and examples to demonstrate practical applications of the concepts. Online resources include sample project materials for students, and lecture slides for instructors.

Ravi Sethi is Laureate Professor of Computer Science at the University of Arizona, USA, and is an ACM fellow. He co-authored *Compilers: Principles, Techniques, and Tools*, popularly known as the "dragon" book, and launched Avaya Labs.

Software Engineering

Basic Principles and Best Practices

RAVI SETHI

University of Arizona

CAMBRIDGE
UNIVERSITY PRESS

CAMBRIDGE
UNIVERSITY PRESS

Shaftesbury Road, Cambridge CB2 8EA, United Kingdom

One Liberty Plaza, 20th Floor, New York, NY 10006, USA

477 Williamstown Road, Port Melbourne, VIC 3207, Australia

314–321, 3rd Floor, Plot 3, Splendor Forum, Jasola District Centre, New Delhi – 110025, India

103 Penang Road, #05–06/07, Visioncrest Commercial, Singapore 238467

Cambridge University Press is part of Cambridge University Press & Assessment, a department of the University of Cambridge.

We share the University's mission to contribute to society through the pursuit of education, learning and research at the highest international levels of excellence.

www.cambridge.org
Information on this title: www.cambridge.org/highereducation/isbn/9781316511947
DOI: 10.1017/9781009051811

First published 2023

Printed in the United Kingdom by TJ Books Limited, Padstow Cornwall 2023

A catalogue record for this publication is available from the British Library.

Library of Congress Cataloging-in-Publication Data
Names: Sethi, Ravi Mohan, 1947-author.
Title: Software engineering : basic principles and best practices /
    Ravi Sethi, University of Arizona.
Description: Cambridge, United Kingdom ; New York, NY : Cambridge
    University Press, 2023. | Includes bibliographical references and index.
Identifiers: LCCN 2022034132 (print) | LCCN 2022034133 (ebook) |
    ISBN 9781316511947 (hardback) | ISBN 9781009051811 (epub)
Subjects: LCSH: Software engineering.
Classification: LCC QA76.758 .S45834 2023 (print) | LCC QA76.758 (ebook) |
    DDC 005.1–dc23/eng/20220822
LC record available at https://lccn.loc.gov/2022034132
LC ebook record available at https://lccn.loc.gov/2022034133

ISBN 978-1-316-51194-7 Hardback

Additional resources for this publication at www.cambridge.org/sethi.

Brief Contents

Contents

Preface

The selection of content for this book was guided by the following question: What do software engineers really need to know about the subject to be productive today and relevant tomorrow? The discipline continues to evolve, driven by new applications, technologies, and development methods. There is every indication that the evolution will continue during an engineer's career. The IEEE-ACM software engineering curriculum guidelines stress continual learning:

Because so much of what is learned will change over a student's professional career and only a small fraction of what could be learned will be taught and learned at university, it is of paramount importance that students develop the habit of continually expanding their knowledge.[1]

This book therefore focuses on basic principles and best practices. The emphasis is not only on what works, but on why it works. The book includes real-world examples and case studies, where possible. Some classic examples are included for perspective.

Principles endure while practices evolve as the assumptions behind them are reexamined. The principles in the book relate to the intrinsic properties of software and human nature: software is complex, requirements change, defects are inevitable, teams need coordination. Assumptions about how to deal with these intrinsic properties have been tested over the years. Must testing follow coding? Not with test-driven development. The distinction between development and maintenance blurs with an evolving software code base. All assumptions have to be questioned to enable the pace of continuous deployment. What does not change is that design and architecture are the key to managing complexity, iterative agile methods accommodate requirements changes, validation and verification reduce defects, and a healthy balance of structure and flexibility motivates teams and improves performance.

Content Organization and Coverage

This book is intended for a junior- or senior-level introductory course in software engineering. Students are expected to have enough programming maturity to engage in a team project. They are not expected to have any prior team experience.

The ACM-IEEE guidelines strongly recommend the inclusion of a significant project in a software engineering course. First, systematic engineering methods are intended for problems of complexity and scale. With a significant project, students get to experience the benefits of engineering concepts and methods. Second, users and teams bring a human dimension to the discipline. Working with a real customer on a project suitable for a team of, say, four provides students with a team experience. Appendix A addresses the challenge of organizing a course with dual tracks for concepts and a project. See also the brief comments in the following paragraphs.

The chapters in this book can be grouped as follows: getting started, what to build, design and architecture, software quality, and metrics.

Getting Started: Chapters 1–2 Chapter 1 introduces key topics that are explored in the rest of the book: requirements, software architecture, and testing. The chapter also has a section on social responsibility and professional conduct.

Chapter 2 deals with processes, which orchestrate team activities. A team's culture and values guide activities that are not covered by the rules of a process. Process models tend to focus on specific activities, leaving the rest to the team: Scrum focuses on planning and review events, XP on development practices, V processes on testing, and the Spiral Framework on risk reduction. The chapter discusses how a team can combine best practices from these process models for its project.

What to Build? Chapters 3–5 Requirements development is iterative, with both agile and plan-driven methods. The difference is that agile methods favor working software to validate what to build, whereas plan-driven methods validate a specification document. Chapter 3 deals with elicitation (discovery) of the wants and goals that users communicate through their words, actions, and emotions. What users say can differ from what they do and feel. To help clarify user goals, the chapter introduces three classes of questions, aimed at identifying user motivations, solution options, and goal quantification. User requirements can be recorded as user stories, system features, or user-experience scenarios. Goal refinement techniques, covered with requirements, also apply to security (attack trees) and measurement (metrics).

The requirements prioritization techniques in Chapter 4 include MoSCoW (must-should-could-won't), value-cost balancing, value-cost-risk assessment, and Kano analysis. Kano analysis is based not only on what satisfies customers, but on what dissatisfies them. The chapter also includes estimation techniques based on story points for agile methods and on Cocomo formal models for plan-driven methods. Anchoring, which can bias estimates, is a phenomenon to be avoided during both individual and group estimation.

Chapter 5 covers use cases. Use cases can be lightweight if they are developed incrementally, starting with user goals, then adding basic flows, and finally alternative flows as needed.

Design and Architecture: Chapters 6–7 Architecture is a subset of design, so the following comments carry over to design. Software architecture, Chapter 6, is key to managing the complexity of software. A modular system is built up from units such as classes, so the chapter introduces UML (Unified Modeling Language) class diagrams and includes guidelines for designing modular systems. For system architecture, the chapter introduces views and how to describe a system in terms of key view(s).

A pattern outlines a solution to a problem that occurs over and over again. Chapter 7 covers the following architectural patterns: layering, shared data, observer, publish-subscribe, model-view-controller, client-server, and broker. Client–server architectures enable new software to be deployed to a production system: a load balancer directs some of the incoming traffic to the new software on a trial basis, until the new software is ready to go into production. The ability to add new software to a production system is needed for continuous deployment.

Software Quality: Chapters 8–10   The combination of reviews (architecture and code), static analysis, and testing is much more effective for defect detection than any of these techniques by themselves. Chapter 8 discusses reviews and static analysis. The focus of the chapter is on static or compile-time techniques.

Chapter 9 is on testing, which is done by running code on specific test inputs. A test set is considered good enough if it meets the desired coverage criteria. For code coverage, the chapter includes statement, branch (decision), and MC/DC coverage. For input-domain coverage, the chapter includes equivalence partitioning and combinatorial testing.

The quality theme continues into Chapter 10, which applies metrics and measurement to the goal of quality assessment and improvement. The chapter introduces six forms of quality: functional, process, product, operations (ops), aesthetics, and customer satisfaction. Ops quality refers to quality after a system is installed at a customer site.

Metrics: Chapter 10   An alternative long title for this chapter is "the design and use of metrics and measurement, with applications to software quality." The chapter has roughly three parts. The first part introduces the measurement process, the design of useful metrics, and the graphical display of data sets. The second part deals with metrics for product and ops quality. The third part introduces statistical techniques. Boxplots, histograms, variance, and standard deviation summarize the dispersion of values in data sets. The last two sections on confidence intervals and simple linear regression are mathematical.

A Team Project: Appendix A   The main challenge in a course with a concepts track and a project track is that the two tracks have somewhat different objectives; for example, the concepts track typically covers multiple process models, while a project embraces a single process. In general, each of the two tracks has its own pace: the concepts track takes many weeks to cover the what, why, and how of processes, requirements, design, and testing, whereas some knowledge of all of these topics is needed early, during the first iteration of a project.

The appendix discusses a hybrid approach, which aligns the tracks initially, while teams are formed and projects are launched. Once the students have enough to start their projects, the coupling between the tracks can be loosened so each track can proceed at its own pace.

Acknowledgments

My trial-by-software came when Harry Huskey handed me a full box of cards with the assembly code for a compiler for HH-1, his Algol-like language. The code was the only description for either the language or the compiler. Harry then left for a long trip, after giving me free rein to see what I could do. Hello, summer job! The job was at the end of my first year as an undergraduate at IIT Kanpur. At the time, the sum total of my experience was a few short Fortran and assembly programs for the IBM 1620. I spent a formative summer tracing through the code and doing peephole optimization. In retrospect, it would have helped if I had clarified Harry's requirements, tested after every change, asked for a view of the system architecture, and so on.

Fast forward a dozen years to Bell Labs in New Jersey, where I had the good fortune to join Doug McIlroy's department in the Computer Science Research Center. In the Center, Unix was about to be ported from one machine to another for the first time. As a user, I came to appreciate the Unix tools culture, quick iterations, and continual refinement of tools through user feedback. Steve Johnson once lamented "the inability of users to see things" his way and added that "invariably, they were right!"

I also came to appreciate the challenges faced by the Switching business unit in building 99.999 percent reliable telephone switches: each phone call was handled by a concurrent process at each end. Their existing approach had a cast of thousands using variants of waterfall processes. They managed the risks of waterfall methods by freezing requirements and by rigorous continuous validation and verification.

In 2000, Avaya was spun off as a separate company and I went with it to build up Avaya Labs Research. Half of the research staff came from Bell Labs, David Weiss among them. David built up the software technology research department, together with a small group called the Avaya Resource Center (ARC), which served as a bridge to the R&D community in the business units. The mission for the department and the ARC was to "Improve the state of software in Avaya and know it." After David retired, I got a chance to work directly with Randy Hackbarth and John Palframan from the ARC and with Audris Mockus and Jenny Li from the research department. These were the people behind the quality improvement effort described in Section 10.5. I am grateful to them for their briefings and insights about software.

When I joined the University of Arizona in 2014, David generously shared the materials from his software engineering course at Iowa State University. At Arizona, I want to thank Todd Proebsting and David Lowenthal for the opportunity to teach the senior and graduate-level software engineering courses.

For this book, I would like to single out Jon Bentley, Audris Mockus, and Joann Ordille for their insights, encouragement, and comments. Thanks also to the many students in the software engineering courses. The Cambridge University Press team has been most thorough. My thanks to the editors, Emily Watton and Lauren Cowles. Emily's ongoing suggestions have greatly improved the book. Most of all, I want to thank Dianne and Alexandra. Alexandra took over the figures when I could no longer do them.

1   Introduction

Software engineering is the application of engineering methods to software development and evolution. Its principles and practices address three fundamental goals: discover user requirements, manage software complexity, and build quality products and services. This chapter introduces the goals, their associated challenges, and how to deal with the challenges.

The main requirements goal is to pin down what users really want, so developers know what to implement. The main complexity goal is to overcome the intrinsic complexity of software, primarily through the design of modular systems. The main quality goal is to build dependable systems, despite the inevitability of defects. Defects are detected and removed by software checking and testing.

These software engineering goals are met by using systematic quantitative methods (processes) to organize development teams and their activities; see Chapter 2 for processes. Teams must balance the scope (functionality) they deliver against budget, schedule, and other external constraints. This chapter concludes with a brief discussion of professional conduct and social responsibility.

This introductory chapter will enable the reader to:

- Describe approaches to addressing the fundamental software engineering goals/challenges of identifying user requirements, managing software complexity, and achieving product quality.
- Explain the elements of the ACM/IEEE Software Engineering Code of Ethics and Professional Practice (short version).

1.1   What Is Software Engineering?

Most definitions of software engineering are variations on the theme of applying engineering to software. In other words, they focus on the application of systematic processes to create and maintain software products. Left unstated in most definitions is the fact that engineering projects have customers (users) and face business and regulatory constraints. As we shall see, customers and constraints are major driving forces (drivers) for projects. The definition in this section includes them explicitly.

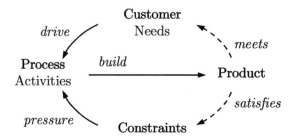

Figure 1.1 The arrows represent relationships between four pervasive drivers of software projects: Customers, Processes, Products, and Constraints.

The definition therefore includes four key drivers: customers, processes, products, and constraints.

This book uses the term *development* broadly to extend past initial development to changes after a product is created. Initial development spills over into evolution/maintenance because products continue to be updated long after they are first deployed. The distinction between development and evolution disappears with the practice known as continuous deployment; see Example 1.1.

1.1.1   Definition of Software Engineering

Software engineering is the application of systematic, quantifiable processes to the development and evolution of software products for customers, subject to cost, schedule, and regulatory constraints.[1]

The arrows in Fig. 1.1 illustrate the relationships between the four key drivers in the preceding definition. Customer needs are at the top in the figure – without them, there would be no project. Customer needs drive the process activities that build the product. Once built, the product must meet customer needs and satisfy any constraints on the product, the process, or the project.

Driving Forces on Software Projects
The four key drivers in Fig. 1.1 are representative of the many forces that a project must balance. The four key drivers appear in boldface in Fig. 1.2.

Customers and users belong in the same grouping of forces. In popular usage, the target audience for a product is called "the customer" or "the user." Both roles drive requirements for what to build. We therefore use the two terms interchangeably, unless there is a need to be specific about a role.

Processes and teams are closely tied, since processes organize teams and their activities. Team skills belong in the same grouping.

Product is a convenient term for any deliverable from a software project. Examples of products include software systems, services delivered from the cloud, test suites,

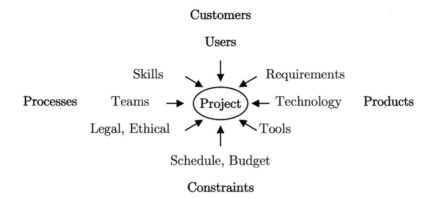

Figure 1.2 Some of the many drivers that projects must balance. Key drivers are in bold.

and documentation. A deliverable can also be an event, such as a live demo at a conference.

Products and technology are a natural fit. Technology takes two forms: (a) it is delivered in the form of products, and (b) it is used in the form of tools to build products.

Constraints are external forces from the context of a project. For example, European Union regulations prohibit products from exporting personal data. Cost, time, and legal constraints are mentioned explicitly in the definition of software engineering. Projects must also deal with ethical and social norms.

Box 1.1 Origins of the Term Software Engineering

Software engineering emerged as a distinct branch of engineering in the 1960s. The term "software engineering" dates back to (at least) 1963–64. Margaret Hamilton, who was with the Apollo space program, began using it to distinguish software engineering from hardware and other forms of engineering. At the time, hardware was precious: an hour of computer time cost hundreds of times as much as an hour of a programmer's time.[2] Code clarity and maintainability were often sacrificed in the name of efficiency. As the complexity and size of computer applications grew, so did the importance of software.

Software engineering was more of a dream than a reality when the term was chosen as the title of a 1968 NATO conference. The organizers, especially Fritz Bauer, chose the title to be

provocative, in implying the need for software manufacture to be based on the types of theoretical foundations and practical disciplines, that are traditional in the established branches of engineering.[3]

Since then, much has changed. On November 22, 2016, Margaret Hamilton was awarded the Presidential Medal of Freedom for her (software) work leading up to the Apollo missions.

1.1.2   A Tale of Two Companies

The key drivers – customers, processes, products, and constraints – are pervasive in the sense that a significant change in any one of them can affect every aspect of a project. The two examples that follow illustrate the far-reaching effects of forces related to customer needs and regulatory constraints. The examples illustrate how different situations drive dramatically differing decisions, as measured by the pace of the projects. One company chooses continuous deployment, the other chooses semiannual releases.

Example: Rapid Response to Customer Needs

In the following example, a technology company wants to respond rapidly to any change in customer needs. This goal drives every aspect of the company, from the development process to product design to organization structure to the reward system for employees.

Example 1.1   In order to respond rapidly to customer suggestions and feedback, a tech company updates its software frequently: it makes hundreds of changes a day to the software on its main servers. Each change is small, but the practically "continuous" small updates add up.

Each change is made by a small team that is responsible for "everything" about the change: design, coding, testing, and then deploying the software directly on customer-facing servers. The change cycle from concept to deployment takes just a few days. There are multiple teams, working in parallel. Together, they make hundreds of updates a day.

The cost of a misstep is low, since the company can trial an update with a few customers and quickly roll back the update if there is a hitch. After a short trial period, the updated software can be put into production for the entire customer base.

Every aspect of the preceding description is driven by the company's desire to respond rapidly to its customers. Rapid response implies that the cycle time from concept to deployment must be very short. Developers are responsible for making and deploying their changes directly onto live production servers, since there is no time for a handoff to a separate operations team. The short cycle time also means that changes are small, so work is broken down into small pieces that can be developed in parallel. Management support is essential, especially if something goes wrong and an update has to be rolled back.

In short, the company's whole culture is geared to its responsiveness to customer needs.   □

Example: Regulations and the Pace of Deployment

In the following example, strict regulations on large banks ripple through the banks to their suppliers. The cost of a misstep is high, so both the banks and their suppliers do extensive testing. The time and cost of testing influence software release schedules.

Example 1.2 A supplier of business software releases software semiannually, on a schedule that is set by its large customers, including highly regulated investment banks. Some of the bigger customers conduct their own rigorous acceptance tests in a lab, before they deploy any software from a supplier. The trial-deploy cycle takes time and resources, so the customers do not want small updates as soon as they are available; they prefer semiannual releases.

The supplier's development projects are geared to the customers' preferred release cycle. Since releases are relatively infrequent, they include more functionality to be included and tested. Dedicated product managers stay in close touch with major customers to ensure that a release includes what they want. □

Assessment: The Impact of a Change

What can we learn from Examples 1.1 and 1.2? Using the pace of release/deployment as a measure, the examples illustrate the range of projects that software engineering can handle. Both the tech company and the supplier of business software chose solutions that were best for their specific situations.

Based on his experience with large-scale software systems at Google, Jeff Dean advises that a tenfold change in any aspect of a project is a time to revisit the existing solution: it may no longer work as well, or it may no longer work at all due to the change. A hundredfold change may require an entirely new solution approach, perhaps even a new organizational structure.[4] There is well over a thousandfold difference in the pace at which the companies in Examples 1.1 and 1.2 release/deploy software.

1.2   The Requirements Challenge

Consider the following scenario. A development team talks to customers to identify their needs for a product. The developers then build a product to meet those needs, only to find that the completed product does not meet customer expectations. What went wrong? Customer needs "changed" while the developers were building the product. With respect to Fig. 1.3, needs identified at the beginning of a cycle can differ from needs at the end of the cycle.

A *user requirement* is a description of a customer/user need or want for a product. The *requirements challenge* is to define a coherent set of requirements that meets user expectations. There are two aspects to the challenge:

- Identify and prioritize user requirements that truly reflect user needs. The challenges include multiple users with differing needs and communication gaps between users and developers.
- Accommodate changes in user requirements. Users can change their minds, either because they are uncertain or because of some unexpected external event.

The requirements challenge is also referred to as the problem of *changing requirements*.

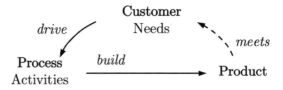

Figure 1.3 The cycle represents the iterative nature of product development based on customer needs.

1.2.1   Identifying Users and Requirements

To identify the requirements for a product, we can begin with the following questions:

- Who is the customer? There will likely be multiple classes of users, each with their own needs and goals.
- What do users really want? There can be gaps between what users are willing and able to communicate and what developers are able to grasp.
- Are there any external factors? Changes in external conditions can have repercussions on the project.

Any one of these situations can result in a mismatch between customer expectations and a snapshot of needs at the start of a project.

Who Is the Customer?

Different users can have different, perhaps conflicting, needs and goals for a project. These differences have to be identified, reconciled, and prioritized into a coherent set of requirements. If any class of users is missed or inadequately represented, the requirements will not match the needs and goals of the user community. The mismatch can result in later changes to the requirements. Part of the problem is that it may not be possible to satisfy all users.

Example 1.3   The makers of a speech-therapy app found a creative way of meeting the differing needs of two classes of users: parents and children. What was the problem? Market testing with a prototype revealed that parents really wanted the program for their children, but found it frustratingly hard to use. Children, meanwhile, had no trouble using the program but could not be bothered with it. They found it annoyingly like a lesson.

The two classes of users were therefore frustrated parents and annoyed children. Their differing needs were addressed by changing the program so it was easier to use for parents and was more like a game for children.[5]   □

The term "stakeholder" is sometimes applied to a class of users. In general, a *stakeholder* is anyone with a stake in a project. Stakeholders include developers and marketers. For requirements, the focus is on users and their needs.

What Do Users Really Want?

What customers say they want can differ from what will satisfy them. There may also be needs that they are unable to articulate. Even if they did know their needs, they may have only a general "I'll know it when I see it" sense of how a product can help them.

Example 1.4 Netflix is known for its video and on-demand services. Their experience with their recommender system is as follows:

Good businesses pay attention to what their customers have to say. But what customers ask for (as much choice as possible, comprehensive search and navigation tools, and more) and what actually works (a few compelling choices simply presented) are very different.[6]   □

Uncertainty about user needs is a known unknown, which means that we know that there is a requirement, but have yet to converge on exactly what it is. Uncertainty can be anticipated when proposing a solution or design.

Unexpected Requirements Changes

Unexpected changes are unknown unknowns: we do not even know whether there will be a change. Here are some examples:

- A competitor suddenly introduces an exciting new product that raises customer expectations.
- The customer's organization changes business direction, which prompts changes in user requirements.
- Design and implementation issues during development lead to a reevaluation of the project.
- The delivered product does what customers asked for, but it does not have the performance that they need.

Requirements changes due to external factors can lead to a project being redirected or even canceled.

1.2.2   Dealing with Requirements Changes

Changes in customer needs and requirements have repercussions for the development process and for the product, because of the relationships shown in Fig. 1.3. We have no control over changes in customer needs, but there are two things we can do.

1. Do as good a job as possible of identifying and analyzing user requirements. Requirements development is a subject in its own right; see Chapter 3.
2. Use a development process that accommodates requirements changes during development. In effect, iterative and agile processes go through the cycle in Fig. 1.3 repeatedly, evolving the product incrementally. Each iteration revisits customer needs to keep the product on track to meeting customer expectations when it is completed.

1.3   Software Is Intrinsically Complex

Let us call a piece of software *complex* if it is hard to understand, debug, and modify. Complexity due to poorly written code is *incidental* to the problem that the code is supposed to address. Meanwhile, if well-written code is hard to understand, its complexity is due to the algorithm behind the code. This algorithmic complexity will remain even if we rewrite the code or use another programming language, because it is *intrinsic* to the problem; that is, it is due to the nature of the problem.[7]

We focus on intrinsic complexity. Architecture is a primary tool for managing software complexity. A software architecture partitions a problem into simpler subproblems. Layered architectures are used often enough that we introduce them in this section.

1.3.1   Sources of Complexity

The two main sources of complexity are scale and the structure/behavior distinction.

- **Scale** Program size is an indicator of the scale of a problem. A large software system can have tens of millions of lines of code. Sheer size can make a system hard to understand.
- **Structure versus Behavior** Here, structure refers to the organization of the code for a system. Behavior refers to what the code does when it is run. The challenge is that behavior is invisible, so we do not deal directly with it. We read and write code and have to imagine and predict how the code will behave when the code is run.

Example 1.5   As a toy example of the distinction between structure and behavior, consider the following line from a sorting program:

```
do i = i+1; while ( a[i] < v );
```

In order to understand the behavior of this loop, we need to build a mental model of the flow of control through the loop at run time. The behavior depends on the values of i, the elements of the array a, and v when the loop is reached. Control flows some number of times through the loop before going on to the next line. If any of these values changes, the number of executions of the loop could change.

The structure of this loop identifies the loop body and the condition for staying in the loop. The behavior of the loop is characterized by the set of all possible ways that control can flow through the loop.   □

The single well-structured do-while loop in the preceding example was convenient for introducing the distinction between program structure and run-time behavior. Complexity grows rapidly as we consider larger pieces of code; it grows rapidly as decisions are added, as objects are defined, as messages flow between parts of a program, and so on.

To summarize, scale and the predictability of run-time behavior are significant contributors to software complexity.

1.3.2   Architecture: Dealing with Program Complexity

Informally, a *software architecture* defines the parts and the relationships among the parts of a system. In effect, an architecture partitions a system into simpler parts that can be studied individually, separately from the rest of the system. (See Chapter 6 for a more precise definition of architecture.)

In this section, the parts are *modules*, where each module has a specific responsibility and a well-defined interface. Modules interact with each other only through their interfaces. The complexity of understanding the whole system is therefore reduced to that of understanding the modules and their interactions. For the interactions, it is enough to know the responsibilities of the modules and their interfaces. The implementation of the responsibilities can be studied separately, as needed.

What is inside a module? The program elements in a module implement its responsibility and services. As long as its interface remains the same, the internal code for the module can be modified without touching the rest of the system. A module can be anything from the equivalent of a single class to a collection of related classes, methods, values, types, and other program elements. This concept of module is language independent. (Modules are closer to packages in Java than they are to classes.)

For more information about modules, see Chapter 6. In particular, modules can be nested; that is, a module can have submodules. For example, a user-interface module may have submodules for handling text, images, audio, and video – these are all needed for a user interface.

Layered Architectures

For examples, let us turn from a general discussion of architecture to a specific form: layered architectures, which are widely used. In a *layered architecture*, modules are grouped into sets called *layers*. The layers are typically shown stacked, one on top of the other. A key property of layered architectures is that modules in an upper layer may use modules in the layer immediately below. Modules in a lower layer know nothing about modules in the layers above them.

Example 1.6   The layered architecture in Fig. 1.4 is a simplified version of the architecture of many apps. At the top of the diagram is the Presentation layer, which manages the user interface. Below it is the Domain layer, which handles the business of the app. In a ride-sharing app, the Domain layer would contain the rules for matching riders and drivers. Next is the Service Access layer, which accesses all the persistent data related to the app; for example, customer profiles and preferences. At the bottom, the Platform layer is for the frameworks and the operating system that support the app.

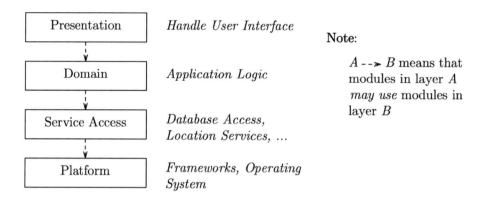

Figure 1.4 A simplified version of the layered architecture of many apps. Boxes represent layers containing modules, and dashed arrows represent potential dependencies between modules in an upper layer on modules in a layer just below.

The dashed arrows represent the may-use relation. Modules in the Presentation layer may use modules in the Domain layer, but not vice versa; that is, modules in the Domain layer may not use modules in the Presentation layer. Similar comments apply to the other layers. By design, all the arrows are down arrows from one layer to the layer immediately below it..   □

The arrows in Fig. 1.4 are included simply to make the may-use relationships explicit. Vertical stacking of layers can convey the same information implicitly. From now on, such down arrows will be dropped from layered diagrams. By convention, if layer A is immediately above layer B in a diagram, modules in the upper layer A may use modules in the lower layer B.

Example: Modules from an App

The next example is about the modules in a specific app that has a layered architecture like the one in Fig. 1.4.

Example 1.7   A local pool-service company has technicians who go to customer homes to maintain their swimming pools.[8] Each technician has an assigned route that changes by day of the week. At each home along their route, the technicians jot down notes for future reference. The company wants to replace its current paper-based system with a software system that will support a mobile app for technicians and a web interface for managers. Managers would use the web interface to set and assign routes to technicians. Technicians would use the mobile app for individualized route information, data about each pool along the route, and some customer account information.

The main modules in the solution correspond to the layers in Fig. 1.4.

- **Presentation Module** The presentation module has submodules for the mobile app and the web interface.
- **Mobile Interface Module** Provides technicians with the data they need along their assigned route; for example, customer account information and pool-service history. Also supports note-taking.
- **Web Interface Module** Supports route management, work assignments, access to pool service history, and customer services.
- **Domain Module** Serves as an intermediary between the user interfaces and the data repository.
- **Data Access Module** Supports create, read, update, and delete operations related to customers, routes, technicians, and pool-service history. The database schema is private to this module, as is the nature of the data repository, which happens to be in the cloud.   □

1.4   Defects Are Inevitable

In a series of experiments, the psychologist George A. Miller found that people can accurately "receive, process, and remember" about seven chunks or units of information. The units in his experiments included bits, words, colors, tones, and tastes.[9] Beyond about seven chunks, confusion and errors set in. Software involves much larger numbers of statements, variables, functions, messages, objects, control-flow paths, and more. Hence the assertion that defects are inevitable.

Miller's experiments also have implications for how to deal with complexity: design software systems in chunks that a developer can understand in relative isolation from the rest of the system. Such chunks correspond to modules; see Section 1.3.

Testing for defects is a very important part of software development. By testing after every change, developers can catch and fix errors early, thereby increasing confidence in the correctness of the change. Testing early and often can actually shorten overall development time. Regrettably, testing does not always get the priority it deserves. In the rush to complete coding, developers put off thorough testing until later. Later, as a deadline looms, time runs out before testing is complete.

1.4.1   Fix Faults to Avoid Failures

Defect, fault, bug. Failure, malfunction, crash. These are all terms to indicate that something is wrong with a program.

Defect and fault are synonyms: *fault* refers to something that is wrong in the program text (source code), the documentation, or some other system artifact. The term fault also applies to any deviations from programming style guidelines. Typically, fault refers to a flaw in the static program text.

Failure refers to unexpected behavior when a program is run. The incorrect behavior may occur only some of the time, under certain conditions, or on certain inputs.

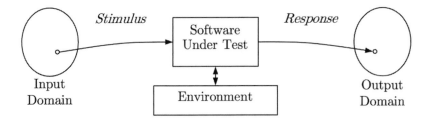

Figure 1.5 Software can be tested by applying an input stimulus and evaluating the output response.

Saying, "programs have faults, their computations have failures," is equivalent to saying, "code can have faults, its runs can have failures." A *computation* is the sequence of actions that occur when a program is run on given inputs. The next example illustrates the distinction between faults and failures. It also illustrates the distinction between programs and their computations.

Example 1.8   There had been 300 successful trial runs of the airborne guidance system for NASA's Atlas rocket. Then, an Atlas Athena rocket was launched, carrying Mariner 1, an unmanned probe to the planet Venus. Shortly after launch, signal contact with the ground was lost. The rocket wobbled astray and was destroyed by the safety officer 293 seconds after launch.

The developers had planned for loss of signal contact, but the code had a fault. The airborne guidance system was supposed to behave as follows:

if not in contact with the ground **then**
do **not** accept course correction

Due to a programming error, the **not** was missing. The guidance system blindly steered the rocket off course, until the rocket was destroyed.

The missing **not** was a fault in the source code. This fault lay undetected through 300 successful trial runs. During these trials, the fault did not trigger a failure. The failure occurred when contact with the ground was lost and control reached the fault in the code. Stated differently, the program had a fault; 300 computations did not trigger a failure.[10]   □

1.4.2   Introduction to Testing

Software testing refers to running a program in a controlled environment to check whether its computations behave as expected. A test input *fails* if its computation fails. If a test fails, then the source code must have a fault.

This introduction to testing is in terms of the four main elements in Fig. 1.5:

- **Software under Test** The software under test can be a code fragment, a module, a subsystem, a self-contained program, or a complete hardware-software system.
- **Input Domain** The input domain is the set of possible test inputs. A test input is more than a value for a single variable. A test input provides values for all the relevant input variables for the software under test. The input need not be numeric; for example, it could be a click on a web page or a signal from a sensor.
- **Output Domain** The output domain is the set of possible output responses or observable behaviors by the software under test. Examples of behaviors include the following: produce text outputs; display an image on a screen; send a request for a web page.
- **Environment** Typically, the software under test is not self contained, so an environment is needed to provide the context for running the software. For example, the software under test may use a package or call a function external to the software. The role of the environment is to provide a (possibly dummy) package or external function.

The following questions capture the main issues that arise during testing:[11]

- How to set up and stabilize the environment to make tests repeatable?
- How to select test inputs?
- How to evaluate the response to a test input?
- How to decide when to stop testing?

The main barrier to testing is test selection. Once tests are selected, automated tools make it convenient to rerun all tests after every change to the program. See Chapter 9.

1.4.3   Black-Box and White-Box Testing

During test selection, we can either treat the software under test as a black box or we can look inside the box at the source code. Testing that depends only on the software's interface is called *black-box testing*. Testing that is based on knowledge of the source code is called *white-box testing*.

Typically, white-box testing is used for smaller units of software and black-box testing is used for larger segments that are built up from the units. Black-box testing is the only option if the source code is not available and all we have is an executable version of the software. Chapter 9 has more information on testing.

1.5   Balancing Constraints: The Iron Triangle

All projects balance competing priorities and constraints. The *Iron Triangle* (also known as the *Project Management Triangle*) illustrates the typical resource constraints faced by projects: scope, time, and cost; see Fig. 1.6. Looking ahead, variants of the Iron Triangle will be used in Section 2.1.2 to illustrate the contrasting priorities of traditional and agile methods.[12]

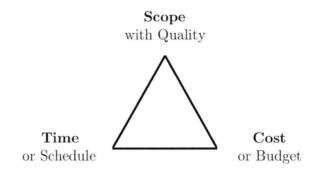

Figure 1.6 The Project Management Triangle, with constraints at the vertices. The Iron Triangle is sometimes drawn with constraints attached to the edges instead of the vertices.

1.5.1   Scope. Cost. Time. Pick Any Two!

A *project* is a set of activities with a start, a finish, and deliverables. The deliverables can be an artifact or an event; for example, a product like an app, a demo at a conference, a service delivered from the cloud, or an assessment report. *Project management* consists of planning, organizing, tracking, and controlling a project from initial concept through final delivery.[13]

In the Iron Triangle, *scope* refers to two things: (a) the functionality to be delivered or the customer requirements to be met by the project, and (b) the quality of the product that is delivered. Quality is interpreted broadly to include not only free of defects, but also attributes of the product such as security, performance, and availability. The two vertices at the base of the triangle represent time (schedule) and cost (budget) constraints.

The edges of the triangle represent the connections between the constraints. For example, if scope increases, then time and/or cost are bound to be affected. Similarly, if time or cost is reduced, then scope is bound to be affected. Schedule overruns have typically been accompanied by cost overruns or scope reductions.

In practice, there is rarely enough time or budget to deliver the full scope with quality. The challenge of meeting the triple constraints simultaneously accounts for the quip, "Fast. Cheap. Good. Pick any two!"

Example 1.9   The Iron Triangle is convenient for illustrating the experience of a company that will remain nameless. In a rush to get new products to market, the executives of Company X pressed the development teams for a 15 percent reduction in project schedules, compared to similar past projects. The budget remained the same. The teams responded by spending fewer days, on average, on every activity: design, coding, testing.

Once the new products were released, it became evident that functionality and quality had suffered. Early customers complained about missing features and product defects. The company reacted to the trouble reports by issuing upgrades to improve the products that had already been delivered. Eventually, the problems with the products did get fixed, but the company's reputation had been tarnished.

In a bid to repair its reputation, the company prioritized quality over schedule for its next set of products.   ☐

The discussion of the Iron Triangle in this section touches on a small part of a big subject. To a large extent, the entire book is relevant to software project management since a project manager needs to know about software development in order to manage it.

1.6 Social Responsibility

Software engineering decisions can have consequences, intended or unintended. This section uses two cases to illustrate this point. In the Volkswagen case, the misuse of software by the company eroded public trust and had severe financial repercussions on the company. In the Therac-25 case, the medical-device supplier's software decisions had unintended consequences: a patient died due to a software malfunction.

1.6.1 Case Study: The Volkswagen Emissions Scandal

Between 2009 and 2015, Volkswagen (VW) won several environmental awards for cars it called "Clean Diesels." The company sold 11 million of them worldwide, 50,000 of them in the USA.[14]

On September 3, 2015, VW admitted that it had misused software to mislead regulators and the public about emissions. The software was designed to engage emissions controls only while a car was being tested for emissions. The designers knew how the test would be conducted, and they programmed the software to detect whether the car was being tested. The car passed the Environmental Protection Agency's (EPA's) emissions test with flying colors. During normal real-world driving, the software disengaged the emissions controls. NO_x emissions were 40 times higher during real-world driving than they were during a test.

When news of the deception became public, VW stock lost a third of its market value in two trading days. The company's reputation was damaged. Lawsuits were filed around the world. Between the April 2016 $18.32 billion recall campaign and the January 2017 $4.3 billion EPA fine, the monetary cost to the company was in excess of $22 billion for these two charges alone. Meanwhile, lawsuits continued in countries across the world.

1.6.2 The ACM Code

To guide decisions related to software, the Association for Computing Machinery (ACM) has published a Software Engineering Code of Ethics and Professional

Practice. The Code begins with the strong recommendation that software engineers act in the public interest, in the best interests of clients and employers, and maintain integrity and independence in their professional judgment.

The short version of the Code appears in Box 1.2. The preamble to the short version warns that its aspirational principles are to be taken with the examples and details in the full version of the Code. Neither the aspirations nor the details stand on their own:

Without the aspirations, the details can become legalistic and tedious; without the details, the aspirations can become high sounding but empty; together, the aspirations and the details form a cohesive code.

The issue of social responsibility is very much with us. The Code does not deal with true ethical dilemmas; for example, if an accident seems inevitable, should a self-driving car prioritize the life of the driver or the life of a pedestrian? The Code does apply to negligence and misconduct; for example, to malware.

1.6.3 Case Study: The Therac-25 Accidents

When the patient came to the East Texas Cancer Center for his ninth treatment on March 21, 1986, more than 500 patients had been treated on the Therac-25 radiation therapy machine, over a period of two years. The planned dose was 180 rads. Nobody realized that the patient had actually received between 16,500 and 25,000 rads over a concentrated area, in less than 1 second. He died five months later due to complications from the massive radiation overdose.

The East Texas Cancer Center accident was one of six known accidents with the device. The patient death is the first known case of a software-related fatality. Based on a thorough investigation by Nancy Leveson and Clark Turner, basic software engineering principles had apparently been violated during the development of the software.[15]

Box 1.2 ACM Code of Ethics and Professional Practice (Short Version)

1. PUBLIC. Software engineers shall act consistently with the public interest.
2. CLIENT AND EMPLOYER. Software engineers shall act in a manner that is in the best interests of their client and employer consistent with the public interest.
3. PRODUCT. Software engineers shall ensure that their products and related modifications meet the highest professional standards possible.
4. JUDGMENT. Software engineers shall maintain integrity and independence in their professional judgment.
5. MANAGEMENT. Software engineering managers and leaders shall subscribe to and promote an ethical approach to the management of software development and maintenance.
6. PROFESSION. Software engineers shall advance the integrity and reputation of the profession consistent with the public interest.
7. COLLEAGUES. Software engineers shall be fair to and supportive of their colleagues.

8. SELF. Software engineers shall participate in lifelong learning regarding the practice of their profession and shall promote an ethical approach to the practice of the profession.

See www.acm.org/code-of-ethics.

Copyright © 2018 by the Association for Computing Machinery. This Code may be published without permission as long as it is not changed in any way and it carries the copyright notice.

What Is Malfunction 54?

On March 21, when the technician pressed the key for treatment, the machine shut down with an error message: "Malfunction 54," which was a "dose input 2" error, according to the only documentation available. The machine's monitor showed that a substantial underdose had been delivered, instead of the actual overdose. The machine was shut down for testing, but no problems were found and Malfunction 54 could not be reproduced. The machine was put back in service within a couple of weeks.

Four days after the machine was put back in service, the Therac-25 shut down again with Malfunction 54 after having delivered an overdose to another patient, who died three weeks later. An autopsy revealed an acute high-dose radiation injury.

Synchronization Problems and Coding Errors

After the second malfunction, the physicist at the East Texas Cancer Center took the Therac-25 out of service. Carefully retracing the steps by the technician in both accidents, the physicist and the technician were eventually able to reproduce Malfunction 54 at will. If patient treatment data was entered rapidly enough, the machine malfunctioned and delivered an overdose. With experience, the technician had become faster at data entry, until she became fast enough to encounter the malfunction.

The accidents in Texas were later connected with prior accidents with Therac-25, for a total of six known accidents between 1985 and 1987. After the 1985 accidents, the manufacturer made some improvements and declared the machine fit to be put back into service. The improvements were unrelated to the synchronization problems that led to the malfunctions in Texas in 1986.

On January 17, 1987, a different software problem led to an overdose at the Yakima Valley Memorial Hospital. The Yakima problem was due to a coding error in the software.

1.6.4   Lessons for Software Projects

The following discussion explores what software projects can do right, not just what went wrong with Therac-25. The idea is to highlight a few clauses from the Code of Ethics and Professional Practice that are relevant for any project. Note that the clauses in the Code are not meant to be applied individually, in isolation. The Code provides fundamental principles for guiding thoughtful consideration of the merits of a situation. "The Code is not a simple ethical algorithm that generates ethical decisions."

Act in the Public Interest

The full version of the Code includes the following section.

1.03. [Software engineers shall, as appropriate] approve software only if they have a well-founded belief that it is safe, meets specifications, passes appropriate tests, and does not diminish quality of life, diminish privacy or harm the environment. The ultimate effect of the work should be to the public good.

With Therac-25, before the massive overdose in the East Texas Cancer Center, there were reports of unexpected behavior from other sites. Each time, the manufacturer focused narrowly on specific design issues, without getting at the root cause of the problem or the overall safety of the medical device.

Lesson Act in the public interest at every stage of a software project, from require-ments, to design, to coding and testing, even to maintenance. The software needs to be safe not only when it is first delivered, but also whenever it is modified. Get to the root cause of any problem.

Design Defensively

The product principle of the Code begins as follows:

3. Software engineers shall ensure that their products and related modifications meet the highest professional standards possible.

Could the accidents in East Texas have been prevented? Possibly. Therac-25 did not have a hardware interlock to prevent an accidental overdose due to a software problem. The software was reused from an earlier machine, called Therac-20. A related software problem existed with Therac-20, but that earlier machine had a hardware interlock to guard against an overdose.

Lesson Design for fault tolerance, so a failure in one part of the system is contained rather than cascaded.

Test the System in its Environment

The product section of the Code includes

3.10. Ensure adequate testing, debugging, and review of software and related documents on which they work.

For Therac-25, testing was inadequate. Documentation was lacking. The first safety analysis did not include software.

The failure in Texas was due to an interaction between the human technician and the machine. Specifically, the Therac-25 software had concurrent tasks and Malfunc-tion 54 was due to a task synchronization problem. The malfunction occurred only when the technician entered data fast enough.

Lesson A system can fail due to interaction between its components or between the system and its environment. Test the system in its environment.

1.7   Conclusion

Key Drivers of Software Engineering Projects   Software engineering is the application of engineering processes to the building of software products. Engineering projects have customers; their needs drive what is built. Projects also have constraints, such as budget, schedule, business, legal, and social/ethical constraints. Customers, processes, products, and constraints are therefore key drivers of software projects.

Ground Truths about Software   One measure of the wide diversity of software projects is development interval, which is the time between initial concept and final delivery or deployment of a product. Development intervals can range from a few months to a few days, depending on a project's unique situation. Tech companies that have control over their servers typically have short development intervals, measured in days. Regulated companies, on the other hand, may set longer development intervals, measured in months, to allow for extensive lab trials prior to deployment. The development interval influences everything about a project, from level of automation to organizational structure.

Given the diversity of projects, we might well ask: what are the underlying principles or ground truths that apply across projects? A ground truth is a statement that is generally true, based on empirical evidence. This chapter explores the following ground truths:

- Requirements change during the life of a project.
- Software systems are intrinsically complex.
- Defects are inevitable.
- Scope. Cost. Time. Pick any two! (You can't simultaneously control a project's functionality, budget, and schedule, so pick any two to fix – the other will vary.)

Requirements Changes   User requirements change for three reasons. First, there may be multiple users with diverging or conflicting needs. Second, users may not know what they want until they experience a working version of the product. Third, conditions can change, with external factors then leading to a reappraisal of user needs. In any of these cases, a product built to the initial requirements may fail to meet customer expectations upon delivery. From a developer's perspective, requirements will have changed. The way to deal with changing requirements is to use an iterative process that incorporates ongoing customer feedback.

Software Complexity   The distinction between a program and its behavior adds to the complexity of software. Program text is visible, but understanding is based on behavior, which is invisible – behavior refers to actions that occur inside a machine at run time. The separation between programs and computations has implications for both program design and testing. Modular designs partition a program into subprograms that are easier to understand; see the discussion of software architecture in Chapter 6.

Defect Removal People make mistakes that lead to defects in programs. Mistakes occur because software complexity outstrips our limited human ability to deal with complexity. Defects are therefore inevitable.

Testing is a key technique for finding and removing defects; see Chapter 9. Testing by itself is not enough to ensure product quality. The combination of testing with reviews and static analysis (Chapter 8) is very effective for defect removal.

Resource Constraints A project has a start, a finish, and deliverables. In practice, there is never enough time or budget to deliver the full product functionality, with quality (the scope). The Iron Triangle, also known as the Project Management Triangle, has scope, time, and cost at its three vertices. The message is that a project can control any two, but cannot simultaneously control all three: scope, cost, and time.

Social Responsibility Finally, software engineers have a social and ethical responsibility to act professionally and do no harm. The first known software-related fatalities were due to a malfunction in a medical device called Therac-25; the device delivered fatal doses of radiation. A careful investigation concluded that the makers of the device did not follow generally accepted software engineering practices.

Further Reading

- Fred Brooks's insightful essay, "No Silver Bullet," discusses the nature of software [38].
- The IEEE Guide to the Software Engineering Body of Knowledge, SWEBOK 3.0 [36], is a starting point for exploring the subject.
- For history buffs, the 1968 NATO conference was a defining event for the field of software engineering. The papers and discussions from the conference make for fascinating reading [143]; see also the report on the NATO conference in 1969 [40].

Exercises for Chapter 1

Exercise 1.1   Most definitions of software engineering boil down to the application of engineering methods to software. For each of the following definitions answer the questions:

- What is the counterpart of "engineering methods" in the definition?
- What is that counterpart applied to?
- Does the definition have any elements that are not covered by the preceding questions? If so, what is it and how would you summarize its role?

The definitions are as follows.[16]

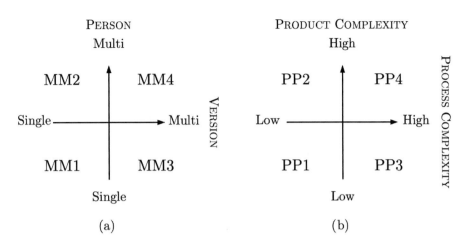

Figure 1.7 Diagrams for Exercise 1.2.

a) **Bauer**: "The establishment and use of sound engineering principles in order to obtain economically software that is reliable and works on real machines."
b) **SEI**: "Engineering is the systematic application of scientific knowledge in creating and building cost-effective solutions to practical problems in the service of mankind. Software engineering is that form of engineering that applies the principles of computer science and mathematics to achieving cost-effective solutions to software problems."
c) **IEEE**: Software engineering is the "application of a systematic, disciplined, quantifiable approach to the development, operation, and maintenance of software; that is, the application of engineering to software."

Exercise 1.2   This exercise explores the distinction between simply programming and software engineering. Consider the following variant of a characterization by Brian Randell:

Software engineering is multi-person or multi-version development of software.[17]

By contrast, programming by itself is single-person development of single-version programs; see Fig. 1.7(a). Assume that "multi-version" implies that the versions are built one after the other, and that each version builds on the last.

a) Relate the diagram in Fig. 1.7(a) to the diagram of product versus process complexity in Fig. 1.7(b). Use the MM and PP labels to briefly describe the relationships, if any, between the quadrants in the two diagrams.
b) Give examples to illustrate your answer to part (a).

Exercise 1.3   For each of the following sixteen driving forces on software projects, choose the "best fit" with the four key drivers in Fig. 1.1: Customers, Processes, Products, and Constraints. The drivers are listed in priority order. If a force seems to fit under more than one driver, choose the earliest driver in the priority order.Briefly justify your grouping of each force under a key driver.[18] (The forces are in alphabetical order.)

Compatibility	Functionality
Complexity	Legal
Context	Mission
Cost	Performance
Deployment	Reliability
Development	Safety
Ethical	Schedule
Evolution	Security

Exercise 1.4   This exercise deals with the distinction between programs and computations. The program is the following C code for rearranging the elements of an array:

```
int partition(int i, int j) {
    int pivot, x;
    pivot = a[(i+j)/2];
    for(;;) {
        while( a[i] < pivot ) i = i+1;
        while( a[j] >= pivot ) j = j-1;
        if( i >= j ) break;
        x = a[i]; a[i] = a[j]; a[j] = x;
    }
}
```

Consider the function call partition(0,4), where the relevant array elements are as shown in the following list. A *computation path* through a program is the sequence of actions that occur during an execution of the program. In each case, what are the computation paths through the function body?

a) 53, 53, 53, 53, 53.
b) 53, 58, 53, 84, 59.

Exercise 1.5   The Python code in this exercise is deliberately complex. It computes 24, the factorial of 4, but it does so in a way that can be hard to understand. How does it work?[19]

```
def f(g, m):
    if m == 0:
        return 1
    else:
        return m*g(g,m-1)

def main():
    print f(f,4)
```

Exercise 1.6   The pool-service company in Example 1.7 has two user interfaces: a mobile interface for technicians and a web interface for managers. Both technicians and managers also rely on an external map service to display routes. Modify the architecture diagram in Fig. 1.4 to show the two user interfaces and both an external data repository and a mapping service.

Exercise 1.7   An investigation of the Therac-25 accidents concluded that the following software engineering practices were violated (see Section 1.6.3):

- Specifications and documentation should not be an afterthought.
- Establish rigorous software quality assurance practices and standards.
- Keep designs simple, and avoid dangerous coding practices.
- Design audit trails and error detection into the system from the start.
- Conduct extensive tests at the module and software level.
- System tests are not enough.
- Perform regression tests on all software changes.
- Carefully design user interfaces, error messages, and documentation.

How would each of these practices have helped avoid the Therac-25 accidents? Provide two or three bullet items per practice.

2   Software Development Processes

The selection of a development process is one of the earliest decisions in the life of a software project. A process orchestrates the workings of a team: it guides what each role does and when in order to define and build a product. This chapter introduces the two main groupings of processes: agile and plan-driven. Agile processes are designed to accommodate requirements changes. Plan-driven processes emphasize careful up-front design. Each process class within these groupings addresses some, but not all, of the challenges faced by projects. Teams therefore customize their processes by borrowing best practices as needed. For example, all teams benefit from essentially the same testing practices.

The main learning objectives of this chapter are to enable the reader to do the following:

- Describe the strengths and caveats associated with the agile methods Scrum and Extreme Programming (XP); the plan-driven methods Waterfall and V processes; and the Spiral risk-reduction framework.
- Use a combination of Scrum and XP for a software project.
- Select best practices from agile and plan-driven methods to customize a process for the software system they will build.

2.1   Processes and Values Guide Development

In simple terms, a process provides rules and guidelines for "who will do what by when and why" to achieve a goal.[1] A development team's values and culture can be as important for a project's success as "who does what." Values guide decisions that are not covered explicitly by a process. Values and processes complement each other.

The "right" process for a project depends on the project's challenges, such as the stability and complexity of the goal. For example, if user needs change, we need a process that accommodates goal changes gracefully.

2.1.1 What Is a Process?

A *process* is a systematic method for meeting a goal by doing the following:

- Identify and organize a set of *activities* to achieve the goal.
- Define the *artifacts* (deliverables) produced by each activity.
- Determine the *roles* and skills needed to perform the activities.
- Set *criteria* for progressing from one activity to another.
- Specify *events* for planning and tracking progress.

Processes can be defined for any aspect of software development, ranging from building an entire product to conducting a code review, to deploying a system update.

Example 2.1   The goal in this example is test-driven development. The process has four activities, represented by the boxes in Fig. 2.1. The ordering of the activities is represented by the arrows. The process starts at the top of the diagram, with the selection of items for development work. The next activity is to write tests for the selected items. Coding comes after tests are written. With the addition of the new code, the resulting code base may need to be cleaned up. After cleanup, there is a choice between delivering the code base and continuing the process with more work items.

The artifacts in this example are work items, tests, and code. There is only one role: developer. The criterion for progression is the same for all activities: it is the completion of the activity. The only event is the delivery of the code base.   □

A specific actionable description of an activity is called a *practice*. "Test after every change" is a practice that catches bugs early. It tells a developer when to test and implies that the thing to test is the change. In Example 2.1, the activities are written as practices. The description "Write code to pass tests" is specific and actionable.

By definition, a process "identifies" activities. They need not be written as practices. Most process descriptions identify activities at a high level; for example, Design, Coding, Testing.

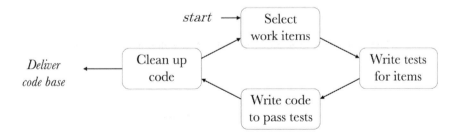

Figure 2.1 A process for test-driven development. Boxes represent activities. Lines represent the progression from one activity to the next. The process has one event: deliver the code base.

In practice, processes provide rules for only some elements of a process, giving developers the flexibility to choose how they fill in the rest. Often, only the activities and their ordering are specified. Of the process classes in this chapter, Scrum alone specifies artifacts, roles, and events. Scrum lets developers choose their development practices; see Section 2.2. Developers choose practices, guided by their values and culture. The discussion of values and culture continues in Section 2.1.3.

Terminology: Models, Frameworks, Values, Culture

A class of processes is called a *model*; for example, "iterative model" for the class of iterative processes, introduced in what follows. A *framework* is a partial specification of a process class. Frameworks provide the core of a process, as opposed to providing a complete process. The core can serve as a starting point for customizing a process for a project. Scrum bills itself as a framework.

Values are the principles that guide individual and group decisions. *Culture* refers to group norms, such as the practices that are commonly used by a team or group. Values and culture go together during software development.

In practice, *method* is a general term for a specific process, a model, a framework, or a combination of process and values. Unless otherwise stated, "process" by itself refers to developing and delivering a product to a customer. Postdelivery maintenance to fix customer-found defects can be treated as a separate project, with its own process.

2.1.2   Two Development Cultures: Plan versus Grow

The processes in this chapter take one of two cultural approaches to software development. These approaches can be described succinctly as (a) plan and build, and (b) iterate and evolve (grow). Once dominant, the rigidity of plan and build led to the rise of the more flexible iterate and evolve.

Plan and Build   Processes that plan and build are called *plan-driven*. They include waterfall processes (Section 2.4) and V processes (Section 2.5). Plan-driven processes are characterized by two phases:

1. A planning phase produces a detailed specification for what to build. The specification may be accompanied by an initial design approach.
2. A build phase that faithfully implements the specification and initial design. A key point is that the requirements for what to build are captured once and for all by the specification produced during the planning phase.

Plan-driven processes are orderly and were a big improvement over the ad hoc code and fix methods of the 1950s. Plan and build became the dominant culture in the 1970s. That dominance is illustrated by the following example.

Example 2.2 The NASA Space Shuttle team viewed plan and build as being the "ideal." But, they could not use it.

From an idealistic viewpoint, software should be developed from a concise set of requirements that are defined, documented, and established before implementation begins. The requirements on the Shuttle program, however, evolved during the software development process.[2]

An iterate and evolve approach allowed the team to accommodate the more than 2,000 requirements changes made by NASA and its contractors between 1975 and the first flight of the Shuttle in 1981.   □

A rigid plan then build approach does not allow for requirements changes after the planning phase. This inability to handle changes is a major limitation.

Iterate and Evolve Processes that iterate and evolve a product are called *iterative*. As a rule, agile methods are iterative. Both Scrum and Extreme Programming (XP) (Section 2.3) are iterative. Iterative processes evolve a product as follows:

1. A sequence of iterations develops increasingly functional versions of the product.
2. Customer feedback during each iteration guides the evolutionary development of the product.

Iterative software development dates back to the 1950s. The concept came through NASA to IBM, a federal contractor, where it was applied to software.[3] Both the Unix and agile cultures discussed in Section 2.1.3 stress iterative development.

Contrasting Plan-Driven and Agile Development

The contrast between plan-driven and iterative processes extends to how they prioritize the scope (requirements), time, and cost of a project. The two variants of the Iron Triangle in Fig. 2.2 illustrate the differing priorities. The triangle in Fig. 2.2(a) is for a traditional plan-driven process. It fixes the scope and allows the time and cost to vary. Such a project is run until the full scope can be delivered, even if there are schedule and cost overruns.

The inverted triangle in Fig. 2.2(b) is for a time-boxed iterative/agile process. With *time-boxed* iterations, time and cost are fixed; scope varies. Such a project drops lower-priority features that cannot be completed within the allotted time. Customers participate in the prioritization process, so they help select the features to be completed and the features to be dropped.

Conclusion The contrast between plan-driven and iterative/agile methods is as much about culture as it is about practices.

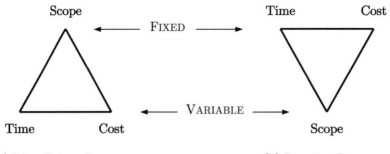

Figure 2.2 Project Management (Iron) Triangles for traditional plan-driven and time-boxed iterative processes. Note that agile processes are iterative, so the inverted triangle applies to them as well.

2.1.3   Role Models: Unix Culture and Agile Values

The Unix and agile cultures are presented here as models for a new team to emulate. Both stress working software that evolves based on user feedback.

The Unix Tools Culture

Culture and values, rather than processes, guided the group that created Unix and its related software tools. Practices like the following were part of the culture:

- "Design and build software, even operating systems, to be tried early, ideally within weeks."
- Refactor: "Don't hesitate to throw away the clumsy parts and rebuild them."
- Make every program do one thing well.
- Expect programs to be used in combination with others; for example, in pipelines, where the output of one becomes the input of another.[4]

   The group valued working software and the refinement of tools through early user feedback. Echoes of the Unix values resonate in agile values, discussed in what follows. The idea of stringing tools in a pipeline leads directly into dataflow networks (Section 7.4).

Box 2.1 The Agile Manifesto

We are uncovering better ways of developing software by doing it and helping others do it. Through this work we have come to value:

Individuals and interactions	*over*	processes and tools
Working software	*over*	comprehensive documentation
Customer collaboration	*over*	contract negotiation
Responding to change	*over*	following a plan

That is, while there is value in the items on the right, we value the items on the left more. See https://agilemanifesto.org.

Reproduced by permission; see Note 5 in the "Notes for Chapter 2" section at the end of the book.

Agile Methods Rely on Values

The valued items in the Agile Manifesto (see Box 2.1) can serve as an example of a set of values for software developers. They can also serve as a starting point for defining a set of shared values for a project team.

The term *agile* was coined by a group of self-described "independent thinkers about software development." They met in 2001 to explore "an alternative to document driven, heavyweight processes." The group included proponents of a range of existing methods, including Scrum and XP. They were all technical people with extensive development experience.

The group found common ground in a set of values embodied in the Agile Manifesto.[5] The group put "Individuals and interactions" first: the team comes first, before process and technology. The underlying assumption is that the team consists of "good" people, who value technical excellence and work together on a human level.

The point is, the team doing work decides how to do it. That is a fundamental agile principle. That even means if the team doesn't want to work in an agile way, then agile probably isn't appropriate in that context, [not using agile] is the most agile way they can do things.[6]

Pre-Manifesto Agile Methods

It is a myth that agile methods started with the Agile Manifesto. As the Agile Alliance notes,

A lot of people peg the start of Agile software development, and to some extent Agile in general, to a meeting that occurred in 2001 when the term Agile software development was coined.
    However, people started working in an Agile fashion prior to that 2001 meeting.[7]

Let the term *agile method* apply to any software development method that conforms with the values in the Agile Manifesto and the principles behind it.[8] Thus, agile methods are characterized by the following:

- The teams are skilled and self-organizing.
- They satisfy customers through collaboration.
- They deliver working software frequently, in weeks, not months.
- They accommodate requirements changes during development.
- They value simplicity and technical excellence.

This characterization covers all of the processes that were represented when the Manifesto was created; for example, Scrum and XP, which date back to the mid-1990s. It also allows for other pre-Manifesto agile projects; that is, projects that we would now call agile.

Values and Culture for a Team

Working software and customer collaboration are values that are critical for all teams, whether the team considers itself agile or not. Requirements changes are outside a development team's control. Requirements changes are a fact of life, so we might as well accept them cheerfully. The flexibility to choose how to do the work is desirable, and not entirely within a team's control. Note that flexibility does not relieve the team from accountability. The team remains responsible for getting the work done.

The teams in the next two examples share these values. Both teams are successful. Their practices and cultures differ, however, because their situations differ.

Example 2.3   The App team is a small well-knit team that specializes in building custom smartphone apps. They know from experience that small screens can lead to surprises when clients see a working app on a smartphone. It can take a few iterations to converge on the final product.

They choose how they do the work. They collaborate closely with clients and expect requirements to change. They rely heavily on working software.   □

Example 2.4   The Corporate team is part of a supplier to large, stable, highly regulated customers who want semiannual releases. The customers run extensive tests in their own labs before putting any software into production. The Corporate team has a dozen people, including a product manager, who represents customer interests, a project manager to organize the project, and developers in different time zones.

Within their corporate approval and review structure, the developers can choose their own practices. The product is complex and the team is geographically distributed, so they have chosen to carefully document design decisions, including what not to change.

The team values working software. While they deliver semiannually to customers, they have their own internal mini-deliveries of working software. The product manager knows the customer's business inside out and has good contacts in the customer organization. Requirements are relatively stable, since big changes tend to wait for the next release. Nevertheless, nondisclosure (confidentiality) agreements allow the product manager to review the team's progress, to keep the project on track to meeting customer needs.   □

2.1.4   Selecting a Process Model

If we know a project's challenges or risks, we can select a process model to manage the risks. The decision tree in Fig. 2.3 makes process recommendations based on two kinds of risk factors: the design complexity of the product and the stability of the

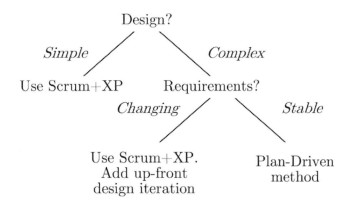

Figure 2.3 Decision tree for selecting a process model for a project. The decisions in this tree are based on design complexity and requirements stability.

requirements. A third key factor, product quality, is not included in the decision tree because high product quality is desirable for all projects; see Section 2.5 for testing practices. For additional project risks, see Section 2.6.

Simple Design

With a simple design, there is no need for a significant up-front design effort. If requirements might change, a team needs to use an agile (iterative) method. Even if requirements are expected to be stable, unexpected events could still result in changes.

With a simple design, the decision tree therefore recommends a combination of Scrum and XP. As we shall see, the Scrum Framework lets developers choose how they build a product. Extreme Programming provides an approach to development. The combination of Scrum and XP is discussed in Section 2.3.

Example 2.5   The App team from Example 2.3 has been retained by an airline to build a flight-reservations app. The basic features of the app have been outlined: it will enable passengers to choose a flight, select seats, and pay by credit card or frequent-flier miles.

The team specializes in apps, so they already have a design in mind. They therefore take the left branch at the root of the decision tree (for simple designs). The decision tree takes them to using a combination of Scrum and XP. This agile approach will be helpful because the team members expect changes to the requirements.   □

Complex Design, Changing Requirements

With a complex design and changing requirements, the decision tree recommends an agile method. A complex design demands some up-front design to set the direction for the project. The decision tree recommends a Scrum+XP combination with an initial design iteration. See also the discussion of up-front design and XP in Section 2.3.

Complex Design, Stable Requirements

In this case, the decision tree notes that a plan-driven approach can be used. An up-front design phase is needed to handle design complexity. The design effort will not be wasted because requirements are stable.

Example 2.6   The Corporate team from Example 2.4 has been tasked with the redesign of an existing product to incorporate new technology. The requirements for the project have been frozen. The team knows the product well and expects significant design complexity.

From the root of the decision tree, the team follows the *Complex* design branch and then the *Stable* requirements branch. The team chooses a plan-driven method. Even with frozen requirements, to be on the safe side, the product manager stays in close contact with customers during the build phase.   □

2.2   Structuring Teamwork: The Scrum Framework

Scrum has relatively short iterations, called *sprints*, that take no more than a month. A product grows in increments, with each sprint resulting in a potentially deliverable version of the product. What differentiates Scrum from other process models is its focus on planning and review events for keeping a project on track. Scrum's rules specify three things: events during a sprint, roles for team members, and artifacts related to product development. Scrum does not specify how the product is built and how requirements are elicited. Developers are free to choose their development practices. Techniques for eliciting requirements are discussed in Chapter 3.

Scrum is by far the most widely practiced of all agile methods. Surveys of agile projects have shown that over half of all projects use Scrum by itself. Another 25 percent use a hybrid of Scrum with another method.[9]

Scrum is the work of Ken Schwaber and Jeff Sutherland. At different companies, they independently devised similar approaches to product development. In 1995, they combined their approaches and created Scrum. The name Scrum comes from the sport of rugby, where a scrum is called to regroup and restart play. Both Schwaber and Sutherland participated in the 2001 meeting where the term agile was coined.[10]

2.2.1   Overview of Scrum

The diagram in Fig. 2.4 represents the specified events that occur during a sprint with its specified artifacts and events. Arrows represent the flow of events. A sprint begins at the left, with the current *product backlog* of potential work items. Think of the product backlog as a "wish list" of requirements items.

The first event is sprint planning. The purpose of *sprint planning* is twofold: (a) to craft a goal for the work to be done during the sprint; and (b) to select work items

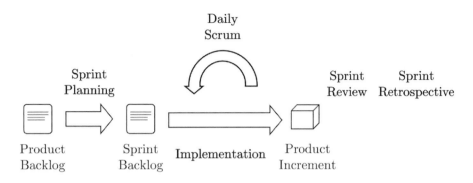

Figure 2.4 Elements of Scrum. The diagram shows the events during a sprint and the artifacts related to planning and review.

for implementation during the sprint. The work items are selected from the product backlog. The selected items are called the *sprint backlog*.

The arrow labeled implement represents the work to develop the sprint backlog. The circular arrow represents an event called a daily scrum. A *daily scrum* is a brief (15-minute) review of the work being done by the developers. During the event, developers review what was done the previous day and what is planned for the given day.

The output from the development work is called a *product increment*; it consists of the functionality completed in this sprint. The product increment is inspected during a *sprint review* with stakeholders. The sprint ends with a *sprint retrospective* to explore process improvements, in readiness for the next sprint.

Scrum: Structure and Flexibility

Scrum is a framework, not a complete process. A framework specifies some aspects of a process and leaves other aspects to be filled in for a given project. Scrum specifies events and lets developers decide how they implement work items in a sprint backlog.

In other words, Scrum provides a combination of structure and flexibility: sprints, events, roles, and artifacts structure team interaction; and developers have the flexibility to choose how they design and build work items. To keep a project on track, development work is reviewed regularly, during daily scrums, sprint reviews, and sprint retrospectives.

About 10 percent of agile projects use a Scrum/XP hybrid, which integrates team structure from Scrum with development practices from XP. Extreme Programming is discussed in Section 2.3. Individual Scrum practices, such as daily scrums, have been widely adopted by agile projects.

Example 2.7   For their project with stable requirements and a complex product, the Corporate team in Example 2.6 chose a plan-driven approach. They like the idea of a daily scrum, so they decide to adopt the practice for their team. The other Scrum events do not fit with their plan-driven approach.

Quick daily reviews with peers will provide some structure and will help the geographically distributed team members stay informed about the team's progress. One of the senior developers will act as moderator. With ten developers, the team is a little large for a 15-minute review, but they intend to stay within the time limit.   □

2.2.2   Scrum Roles

Scrum defines three roles: product owner, developer, and scrum master. Together, they form a *scrum team*.

Example 2.8   The team experience is not the same as a social experience. One project team of four students started the semester with,

"We're good friends. We see each other every day. We're all equals. We don't need roles and a [development] process."

At the end of the first iteration, they chose roles: product owner, scrum master, developers. Why? Because they were well behind both the other teams and their own plans.   □

Product Owner   The *product owner* is responsible for the content of the product. The owner must be a single person; ownership is not to be spread across team members. In all team events, the product owner serves as the voice of the customer and sets priorities for what the team implements.

Developers   *Developers* have sole responsibility for implementation. The development team comes up with estimates for the time and effort needed to implement a work item.

Scrum Master   The *scrum master* acts as coach, facilitator, and moderator, responsible for arranging all events and for keeping them focused and on time. The scrum master guides people by highlighting the purpose and ground rules of an event, not by telling people how to do their jobs. An additional responsibility is to remove any external impediments for the team.

Example 2.9   As an example of an impediment, a developer discovered a bug in a video subsystem from an outside supplier. The scrum master took responsibility for working with the purchasing manager to negotiate the date for a fix.   □

2.2.3   Scrum Events

Scrum defines four kinds of time-boxed events: sprint planning, daily scrums, sprint reviews, and sprint retrospectives. *Time-boxed* means that the time interval of each

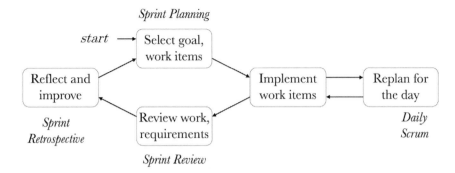

Figure 2.5 A process diagram for Scrum. Boxes represent the activities associated with the Scrum events.

event is fixed. All of these events occur during a sprint; see Fig. 2.4. One purpose of Scrum events is to plan, review, and steer development work. The boxes in Fig. 2.5 show the activities associated with the events. Another reason for specified or scheduled events is to foster communication within the scrum team. The events are time-limited, to keep down the time spent in meetings.

Sprint Planning The purpose of *sprint planning* is to set a sprint goal and to select a sprint backlog. The product owner represents customer needs and priorities. The development team provides estimates for what it can accomplish during the sprint. See Sections 4.2–4.4 for estimation and prioritization of work items.

Sprint planning is time-limited to eight hours or less for a one-month sprint. The attendees are the entire scrum team.

- **Sprint Goal** The product owner proposes a goal for the functionality to be implemented during the sprint. The owner leads the entire scrum team in converging on the *sprint goal*. Once set, the sprint goal may not be changed during the sprint.
- **Sprint Backlog** Given the sprint goal, the development team has sole responsibility for selecting product-backlog items to achieve the goal. The developers are accountable for explaining how completion of the selected items during the sprint will achieve the sprint goal. During a sprint, the developers may renegotiate with the product owner what they can accomplish.

Daily Scrum During a sprint, a *daily scrum* is a short 15-minute meeting to regroup and replan development work for the day. The attendees are the scrum master and the development team. The scrum master facilitates the meeting. Each developer addresses three questions:

- What did I do yesterday toward the sprint goal?
- What will I do today?
- Are there any impediments to progress?

These questions keep the whole development team informed about the current status and work that remains to be done in the sprint. The scrum master takes responsibility for addressing any impediments that are external to the scrum team.

Daily scrums are also known as *daily stand-ups* because the attendees sometimes stand (to encourage observance of the 15-minute time limit). The 15-minute time limit works for small teams. The process can be scaled to larger teams by creating smaller subteams responsible for subsystems. The daily scrum for the larger team is then a *scrum of scrums*, with representatives from the subteams. The representatives are typically the scrum masters of the subteams.

Sprint Review A *sprint review* is an at most four-hour meeting at the end of a one-month sprint. The purpose of the review is to close the current sprint and prepare for the next. The review includes stakeholders and the whole scrum team.

Closing the current sprint includes a discussion of what was accomplished, what went well, and what did not go well during the sprint. The development team describes the implemented functionality and possibly gives a demo of the new functionality.

A sprint review sets the stage for the planning meeting for the next sprint. Preparing for the next sprint is like starting a new project, building on the current working software. The product owner updates the product backlog based on the latest understanding of customer needs, schedule, budget, and progress by the development team. The group revisits the priorities for the project and explores what to do next.

Sprint Retrospective A *sprint retrospective* is an at most three-hour meeting for a one-month sprint. In the spirit of continuous improvement, the purpose of the retrospective is for the scrum team to reflect on the current sprint and identify improvements that can be put in place for the next sprint. The improvements may relate to the product under development, the tools used by the team, the workings of the team within the rules of Scrum, or the interactions between team members.

Example 2.10   At the end of their first sprint, student teams often identify communication among team members as an area for improvement.   □

2.2.4   Scrum Artifacts

Scrum specifies three artifacts: product backlog, sprint backlog, and product increment. The artifacts are visible to all team members to ensure that everyone has access to all available information.

Product Backlog The *product backlog* is an evolving prioritized list of items to be implemented. It is maintained by the product owner. It represents the requirements for the product, based on stakeholder needs, market conditions, and the functionality that has been implemented during previous sprints. At the end of each sprint, the product backlog may be updated, during the sprint review with stakeholders.

Sprint Backlog A *sprint backlog* consists of the work items to be implemented during the current sprint. The work items are selected from the product backlog during sprint planning, by the development team.

The sprint goal drives the selection of work items for the sprint backlog. The goal cannot be changed during the sprint. The sprint backlog may, however, be changed during a sprint. Based on progress on the work items and any new information that comes to light, the developers may renegotiate the sprint backlog. Only the developers may change the sprint backlog, and the changes must preserve the sprint backlog's focus on the sprint goal. Any requirements changes have to wait until the next sprint planning event.

Product Increment As with any iterative process, the product evolves with every sprint. The deliverable from a sprint is called a *product increment*. The added functionality in the product increment is driven by the sprint goal.

The product increment is reviewed with stakeholders during the sprint review. The intent is to have a potentially releasable product at the end of each sprint.

2.2.5 Summary

- **Highlights** Scrum takes an iterative approach to product development; iterations are called sprints. Scrum's focus is on planning and review events to coordinate and structure development work. Developers are free to choose how they implement the goal for a sprint.
- **Strengths** Scrum's rules coordinate teams and maintain a project's momentum. Iterations (sprints) address the risks related to requirements changes.
- **Caveats** Since developers choose their development practices, risks related to design, coding, and testing depend on the chosen practices.

Scrum is recommended for all teams contemplating iterative/agile development. The next section deals with development practices, which Scrum leaves unspecified. For teams considering plan-driven development, Scrum's careful specification of roles and time-boxed events can serve as a model for adding roles and review events to plan-driven process. Plan-driven teams have been known to adopt daily scrums. Reviews and retrospectives can be added upon completion of a "chunk" or a subsystem.

2.3 Agile Development: Extreme Programming

With Extreme Programming (XP), values drive iterative development. The development cycle in Fig. 2.6 is a form of test-driven development. The cycle reflects advice such as the following:

- Listen to what customers need from the system.
- Make testing central to development.
- Write simple, readable code.
- Refactor to keep designs modular and focused on just what is needed.

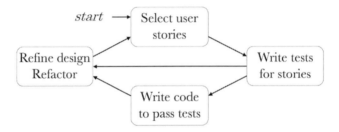

Figure 2.6 Software development using XP.

This advice and the boxes in the development cycle correspond to the four main XP activities: listening, testing, coding, and design, respectively.

Kent Beck defined XP while he led a payroll project for Chrysler, starting in 1996. The name comes from taking best practices to the extreme; for example,

If design is good, we'll make it part of everybody's daily business (refactoring).[11]

Extreme Programming was refined in the years following the Chrysler project. There are now XP values, principles, activities, and practices.

This section focuses on the activities. It explores the XP way of practicing the activities in the development cycle; see also Example 2.1. The section concludes with how Scrum and XP can be combined into a unified agile development method. Specifically, the section includes a diagram that combines Scrum events and XP activities into one process.

Agile Development Practices Extreme Programming's practices and development cycle are representative of agile development in general. What is of interest is how the practices work together. Most of the individual practices predate XP, in some cases by decades. Test-driven development dates back to NASA's Project Mercury in the 1960s.

2.3.1   Listening to Customers: User Stories

Extreme Programming invites customers into the development process. The cycle in Fig. 2.6 begins with listening to customers to identify and understand their needs and wants. The needs are recorded as user stories, which represent bits of functionality that can be implemented in days. The identification of user needs is a topic in its own right; see Chapter 3.

User stories are key part of agile development, so they are introduced here; the main coverage of user stories is in Section 3.4. *User stories* have three properties:

- **Brief Description** In simple language, a user story contains a brief testable description of a user need. A user story is written from the user's perspective.
- **Acceptance Tests** Each user story is accompanied by one or more acceptance tests to validate the implementation of the story.
- **Estimates** A rough estimate of the development effort for a user story is essential for cost-benefit trade-offs across stories. Estimates are provided by the

development team. The rough estimate could be just a low-medium-high estimate; see Section 4.2.

A user story is meant to be a brief, not a complete, description of a user requirement. The acronym *3C* highlights the intent of a user story. 3C stands for Card, Conversation, and Confirmation: fit on a 3×5 index card; spark a conversation; confirm understanding through an executable acceptance test.[12] A software product of any size may have dozens or perhaps hundreds of user stories.

The description part of a user story is typically written by using the following template:

As a ⟨*role*⟩ **I want to** ⟨*task*⟩ **so that** ⟨*benefit*⟩

The angle brackets ⟨ and ⟩ enclose placeholders for text.

Example 2.11   A ride-sharing app has at least two classes of stakeholders: riders who want rides and drivers who provide rides. Here are some examples of user stories for riders:

- As a rider, I want flexible on-demand transportation so that I can get to my destination whenever I want.
- As a rider, I want a trustworthy driver, so that I will feel safe getting into the driver's vehicle.
- As a rider, I want the app to remember my preferred drivers so that I can request their services in the future.

The number of stories will grow as additional needs are identified.   □

Returning to the development cycle in Fig. 2.6, customers participate in the selection of user stories for an iteration. Selection is done by balancing the customer-perceived benefit of a story with the developer-estimated cost. For prioritization, see Section 4.4.

2.3.2   Testing: Make It Central to Development

Extreme Programming promotes working software all the time, not just at the end of an iteration. Two forms of testing play an essential role in maintaining a state of clean working software: automated tests and continuous integration. Test-driven development is covered in what follows, under "Coding: Write Simple Readable Code."

The combination of constant unobtrusive automated testing and periodic refactoring increases confidence in new code and in changes to existing code. By extension, the combination increases confidence in the overall system under development. The combination therefore promotes the creation of correct code from the outset, instead of accumulation of untested code that will later be fixed. This shift in approach represents a cultural change in how software is developed, whether or not customer needs are expressed as user stories and whether or not tests are written before code.

Automated Regression Testing   With any change to a system, there is a risk that the change will break something that was working. The risk of breakage can be significantly reduced by ensuring that the system continues to pass all tests that it used to pass. This process of running all tests is called *regression testing*.

The burden of regression testing can be lifted by automating it. Automated regression testing provides a safety net while developers are making changes. The more complete the regression tests, the greater the safety net provided by automated tests.

Continuous Integration The goal of working software applies to the overall system, not just to the modules. Continuous integration means that overall system integration is done several times a day; say, every couple of hours.

System integration includes a complete set of system tests. If a change causes system tests to fail, then the change is rolled back and reassessed. The complete set of tests must pass before proceeding.

Coding: Write Simple Readable Code

In the development cycle, coding comes after tests are written. This activity is guided by the XP emphasis on simplicity: use the simplest solution that could possibly work. Coding is also the setting for XP's controversial practice of pair programming; see Box 2.2.

Test-Driven Development Test-driven coding assumes that a story is fully implemented if the implementation passes all of the acceptance tests for the story. In other words, the tests are assumed to characterize the functionality represented by the user story. It is enough therefore enough for the developers to write just enough code to pass the acceptance tests. In addition to acceptance tests, developers may write their own tests that are relevant to the implementation.

Box 2.2 Pair Programming

Pair programming is perhaps the most controversial aspect of XP. *Pair programming* is the practice of two developers working together on one task, typically in front of the same screen. The claimed benefit of pair programming is that it produces better software more effectively. Two people can share ideas, discuss design alternatives, review each others' work, and keep each other on task. As a side benefit, two people know the code, which helps spread knowledge within the team. So, if one person leaves or is not available, there is likely someone else on the team who knows the code.

One of the concerns with pair programming is that having two people working on the same task could potentially double the cost of development. An early study with undergraduate students reported that pair programming added 15 percent to the cost, not 100 percent. Further, the 15 percent added cost was balanced by 15 percent fewer defects in the code produced by a pair of students. Do these findings carry over to software development at large? The controversy over pair programming remains.[13]

Before any code is written, the new tests should fail. Furthermore, the tests should fail for the expected reasons. If, however, the tests pass, then either the feature already exists, or the tests are too weak to find bugs.

Once there is an adequate set of tests, the idea is to make only the code changes that are necessary; that is, to modify the software just enough so it passes all tests.

Regression testing acts as a safety net during coding, since it runs all tests to verify that the new code did not break some existing feature.

Coding is not the time to restructure the code to gracefully accommodate the new functionality. Cleanup belongs in the next activity: refactoring.

Designing and Refactoring

Extreme Programming treats refactoring as a form of designing: it keeps the design clean. Each iteration therefore includes some designing. There is more to designing than refactoring, however, as we shall see in what follows.

Periodic Refactoring *Refactoring* consists of a sequence of correctness-preserving changes to clean up the code. Correctness-preserving means that the external behavior of the system stays the same. Each change is typically small. After each change, all tests are run to verify the external behavior of the system.

Without refactoring, the design and code of the system can drift with the accumulation of incremental changes. The drift can result in a system that is hard to change, which undermines the goal of working software.

2.3.3   When to Design?

Best practices such as early customer feedback, daily scrums, and testing after every change have become part of the culture of software development. Designing, however, involves trade-offs. What to do is not clear-cut:

- **Wasted Effort** Too much designing too early may lead to wasted effort on planning for something that will not be needed.
- **Brittle Architecture** Too little design too late may result in an unwieldy architecture that does not scale or has to be reworked to accommodate new requirements.

Kent Beck's Advice In the early days of agile development, some teams deferred design until the last possible moment and ended up with "brittle poorly designed systems." They cited the acronym *yagni*, which comes from "you aren't going to need it."[14] Yagni came to mean don't anticipate, don't implement any functionality until you need it.

However, yagni does not have to mean no design up front. On design, Kent Beck's advice to XP teams

is not to minimize design investment over the short run, but to keep the design investment in proportion to the needs of the system so far. The question is not whether or not to design, the question is when to design.[15]

		Stable	Changing
Product	*Complex*	Design in quality attributes; e.g., reliability	Use a modifiable modular design
	Simple	Minimal design to set direction	Defer major decisions until needed

Stable   Changing

Requirements

Figure 2.7 Guidelines for designers. Product complexity pushes for early design work. Requirements volatility (changeability) pushes for deferring design work.

He recommends deferring design until the last "responsible" moment. The last responsible moment depends on the project.

Some Guidelines In addressing the question of when to design, we must contend with at least two competing forces: product complexity and requirements volatility. Product complexity pushes for up-front design: we run the risk of too little design too late. Requirements volatility or changeability pushes for deferring design activities: we run the risk of too much design too soon.

The guidelines in Fig. 2.7 group projects into four categories, based on product complexity and requirements stability. The guidelines look ahead to the coverage of design and architecture in Chapters 6 and 7.

The top left box in the figure is for complex products with stable requirements. With stable requirements, we can go ahead with early design efforts to address product complexity. System properties, such as scale, performance, reliability, security, and so on, have to be designed into a system from the start. They are hard to retrofit. Products in this category can be designed up front to meet performance, or reliability, or other goals. See Chapter 7 for architectural patterns, which carry ideas from previous solutions to recurring problems.

Proceeding clockwise, the top right box is for complex products with changing requirements. Here, complexity and requirements are opposing forces. Complexity pushes for early design, but early design efforts might be wasted if requirements change. The recommendation in this case is to invest some design effort up front, in a modifiable design, based on what we do know. For example, a product with stringent reliability requirements is likely to continue to have stringent reliability requirements. And, for reliability, we would need primary and backup versions. A modular system isolates design decisions in modules so they can be changed without affecting the rest of the system; see Section 6.2. In short, for products in this category, the idea is to do some up-front design and to isolate and defer design decisions that can be deferred.

The bottom-right category is for simple products with changing requirements. For a simple product, we can get started with minimal up-front design effort. Since

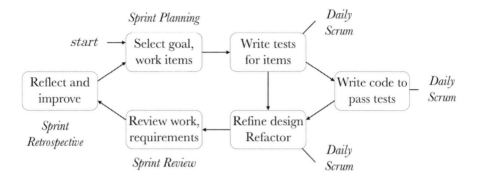

Figure 2.8 A Scrum+XP hybrid that unifies Scrum events/activities, Fig. 2.5, and the XP development cycle, Fig. 2.6.

the product is simple, we can adapt the design readily to keep up with changing requirements.

Finally, the bottom-left box is for simple products with stable requirements. Stable requirements allow us to do design work whenever it is most convenient. The recommendation is to defer design work until it is needed, on the off chance of an unexpected change in requirements.

2.3.4   A Scrum+XP Hybrid

Scrum and XP have compatible values and complementary process, so they can be readily unified into a single agile method. Scrum concentrates on time-boxed planning and review events; see Fig. 2.5 for the events and their associated activities. Extreme Programming concentrates on development practices.

The process diagram in Fig. 2.8 unifies Scrum and XP. Let us use Scrum terminology for the unified process: iterations are sprints, user stories are work items, and collections of user stories form a backlog. For convenience let us use the terms event and Scrum activity interchangeably to refer to an event and its activity.

The activities of the unified process are as follows:

0. **Start**. (Not shown in the diagram.) Initialize the product backlog with work items (user stories) based on customer needs.
1. **Sprint Planning**. Select work items for the sprint backlog of work items for this sprint. This activity is formed by merging Scrum sprint planning and XP iteration planning (the first activity in the development cycle in Fig. 2.6).
2. **Test Planning**. Write tests based on the work items in the sprint backlog. With this activity, the hybrid process switches to XP for development. In the hybrid, the XP development activities incorporate daily scrum events.
3. **Coding**. Write just enough code to pass the tests.
4. **Design and Refactoring**. Clean up the code base. After this activity, the hybrid process switches to Scrum.

5. **Sprint Review**. Review the work completed in this sprint with customers. Update the product backlog, as appropriate.
6. **Sprint Retrospective**. Reflect on the current sprint and make process improvements, as appropriate.

For further information about activities 1, 5, and 6, see Scrum. For activities 2–4, see XP.

Note Scrum and XP differ slightly in their handling of user requirements. With Scrum, needs are identified, and the product backlog updated, during the sprint review with stakeholders. With XP, the natural place to identify customer needs is iteration planning, the first activity in the development cycle. Either way, the product backlog is updated before work items are selected. The hybrid process follows Scrum.

2.3.5   Summary

- **Highlights** The premise of XP is "an always-deployable system to which features, chosen by the customer, are added and automatically tested on a fixed heartbeat."[16]
- **Strengths** Extreme Programming's iterative development cycle accommodates requirements changes. It emphasizes testing and refactoring to increase the quality of the code. Extreme Programming values simple, modular, readable code.
- **Caveats** Extreme Programming's focus on simplicity and on deferring design until needed has to interpreted as "appropriate simplicity" and as "deferring design until the last responsible moment." Too literal an interpretation of simplicity can lead to unwieldy brittle systems.

A combination of Scrum and XP is recommended for teams interested in agile software development. The process diagram in Fig. 2.8 shows how Scrum events can be unified with the XP development cycle. Variants of the hybrid process can be created by tweaking the development activities. Keep the Scrum events as they are, however.

The XP development cycle does not include an explicit up-front design activity. All projects need some up-front design: more for complex products, less for simpler ones. For a simple product, up-front design may be cursory, just enough to set direction with a solution approach and initialize the development cycle. See Fig. 2.7 for some guidelines.

2.4   Limitations of Waterfall Processes

A *waterfall* process is a plan-driven process, in which all activities are done sequentially: one activity completes before the next one begins. Waterfall processes provide two useful lessons in what not to do. First, they lack customer involvement after requirements are documented up front, before implementation begins. Second, a working product emerges with a big bang near the end.

Customer collaboration has already been stressed in the discussion of agile processes. This section explores some of the consequences of deferring testing until

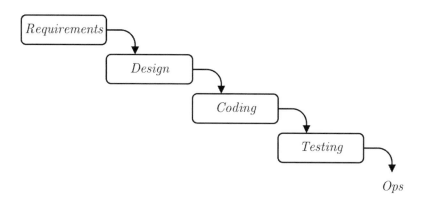

Figure 2.9 A waterfall process. Boxes represent activities.

the end. Problems related to late-stage testing continue to trip up software projects; `healthcare.gov` is a 2013 example. This section concludes with notes on how major projects managed the risks associated with waterfall processes.

The name waterfall comes from diagrams like the one in Fig. 2.9. In the diagram, the sequential flow from one activity to the next looks a little like water streaming over a series of drops in a waterfall. The name "waterfall" was applied to this process model in the 1970s. The first known published example is the 1956 paper on the SAGE air-defense system; see Section 2.5.[17]

2.4.1 The Perils of Big-Bang Integration and Testing

Waterfall processes were supposed to make software development orderly and predictable. The implicit assumption behind them is that everything will go according to plan. In other words, we can specify what a system must do before we design it; that we can fully design it before we code it; that we can code it before we test it; and that there will be no serious issues along the way. This assumption is very risky.

Testing that is deferred until the end of a project is called *big-bang testing*. With it, design and coding issues are typically discovered late in a project's life. Design issues include system properties such as security and scalability.

In practice, late discovery of major issues has resulted in replanning and rework, leading to significant cost and schedule overruns. Late projects can also suffer from quality problems. When projects run late, testing can get squeezed. Inadequate testing can result in the delivery of projects with defects.

There continue to be cases of testing getting squeezed when software projects run late. The public project in the next example had problems that were due, in part, to big-bang integration and testing of components from multiple contractors.

Example 2.12 The Affordable Care Act has enabled millions of people in the United States to get healthcare coverage. The software system to implement the law was the result of a two-year project, with components built by several contractors. The system includes a website, `healthcare.gov`, for people to enroll for health insurance.

The October 1, 2013 launch of the website did not go well. Integration and testing came at the tail end of the rollout of the site, too late to address usability and performance issues.

The chairman of the oversight committee opened a congressional hearing on October 24 as follows:

> Today the Energy and Commerce Committee continues our ongoing oversight of the healthcare law as we examine the many problems, crashes, glitches, system failures that have defined open enrollment [for health insurance].

When questioned, one of the contractors admitted that integration testing for the website began two weeks before launch. Another contractor admitted that full end-to-end system testing did not occur until "the couple of days leading up to the launch."

At the time, $118 million had already been spent on the website alone.[18]   □

2.4.2   The Waterfall Cost-of-Change Curve

We expect the cost of making a software change to rise as a project progresses and the product takes shape. For waterfall processes, the cost of a change rises exponentially. There is data to back up the intuition that the later the fix, the greater the cost.

A Proxy for the Cost of a Change

The data that is available is for the cost of fixing a defect. Making a change and fixing a defect are closely related, since both require an understanding of the code for a system. Let us therefore use defect data to support conclusions about the cost of a change.

The curves in Fig. 2.10 show changes to the cost of fixing a severe defect as a waterfall project progresses. The cost is lowest during the requirements and design phases. The solid curve is based on a chart published in 1976 by Barry Boehm. The underlying data was from three companies: GTE, IBM, and TRW. Boehm added data from smaller software projects in a 2006 version of the chart.[19]

For large projects, the relative cost of fixing a severe defect rises by a factor of 100 between the initial requirements and design phases and the final phase where the system has been delivered and put into operation. The cost jumps by a factor of 10 between requirements and coding and jumps by another factor of 10 between coding and operation.

The dashed curve for smaller projects is much flatter: the cost of a fix during operation is seven times the cost of a fix during the requirements phase. For non-severe defects, the ratio may be 2:1 instead of the 100:1 ratio for severe defects.

The following table summarizes the preceding discussion comparing the cost of late fixes (during operation, after delivery) to the cost of early fixes (during initial requirements and design):

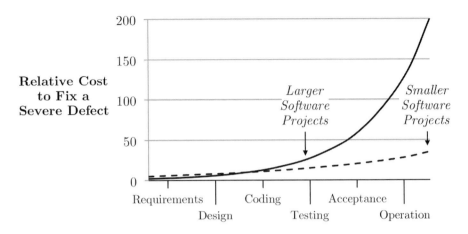

Figure 2.10 For severe defects, the later the fix, the greater the cost. (The original diagram had a log scale for the relative cost.)

PROJECT SIZE	DEFECT SEVERITY	RATIO
Large	Severe	~ 100 : 1
Small	Severe	~ 7 : 1
Large	Non-severe	~ 2 : 1

(The symbol "~" stands for "roughly.")

Similar ratios were reported during a 2002 workshop by projects from IBM Rochester, Toshiba's software factory, and others.[20]

2.4.3 Managing the Risks of Waterfall Processes

With all its limitations, how did waterfall become the dominant process model for over two decades, into the 1990s?[21] So far in this section, we have looked to this process model for lessons on what not to do. What can we learn from projects that used waterfall processes to build successful products?

This is the main lesson: for successful use of a process, we must set up its preconditions and adopt practices that manage its risks. A precondition applies to a factor outside a team's control. A practice is a specific activity that is within the team's control. For the waterfall model, a key precondition is requirements stability, and a key risk is product quality, due to big-bang testing. The limitations/risks of the model were overcome by essentially freezing requirements, fully understanding the design, and testing early and often.

Note To repeat, the waterfall model is not recommended for current projects. Freezing requirements is an uneasy compromise: customers who want new features may have to wait until the features are implemented in the next release. Use an iterative rather than a waterfall method.

Example 2.13 The data in Fig. 2.11 is for multiple releases of the 5ESS switching system.[22] The switches handle telephone calls across the world. About half of US telephone central offices rely on them.

The Releases (Projects) The data in the figure is for the time period 1985–1996. The upper half of the figure is for releases I1–I15 for international markets. The lower half is for releases D1–D11 for domestic US markets. Development of the releases overlapped. The histograms in each row show the number of developers on that release in that time period. Each release was carefully planned and built using a waterfall variant.

Requirements Were Frozen The teams managed the risk of requirements changes by essentially freezing the requirements during the implementation of a release. Product managers stayed in close contact with customers and maintained a backlog of requirements items. Items that were easy to include were added to the current release. Major changes were queued for the next release. Frozen requirements contributed to the success of the projects, but it left both customers and developers wishing for a better way of accommodating new features.

High 99.999 Percent Reliability The releases aimed for and achieved "five nines (99.999%)" reliability in terms of up time. This stringent requirement had implications

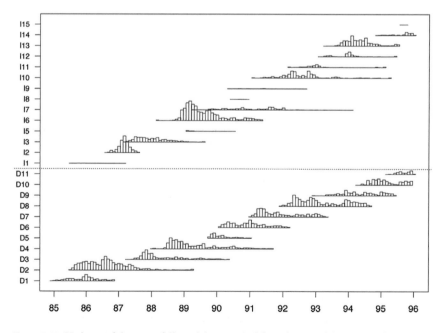

Figure 2.11 Variants of the waterfall model were used for releases of the successful AT&T/Lucent 5ESS switching system. The rows show releases between 1985 and 1996. The histograms display effort levels. Diagram by Harvey Siy. Used by permission.

for both design and testing. For design, the teams relied on seasoned architects with significant domain knowledge. Testing began early – as soon as there was code to test – and continued long past the end of coding. Thus, unlike pure waterfall processes, where testing comes at the end, the 5ESS teams used a variant, where testing coding and testing were done in parallel.

Conclusion This example deals with 5ESS releases between 1985 and 1996. Careful up-front planning and design helped the teams meet stringent performance, scalability, and reliability requirements. The teams avoided the problems associated with big-bang testing by starting module testing as soon as there was code to test. Strong testing contributed to high quality and high 99.999 percent reliability. On requirements, the record is mixed. Requirements were frozen after the planning phase, so major new features had to wait until the next release. The long 24-month development cycle from project start to product delivery was an equal contributor to the time lag for major new features. Overall, the releases were a technical and business success. □

2.4.4 Summary

- **Highlights** Waterfall processes break software development into a linear sequence of phases, one following the other. The early phases identify requirements and plan what to build. The later phases build according to the plan.
- **Strengths** Product complexity can be handled by up-front planning, provided requirements remain stable. Waterfall processes offer lessons in what not to do; see "Caveats."
- **Caveats** Waterfall processes are very risky, for two reasons. First, requirements often change while a product is being built to the original plan. Second, the cost of fixing a defect rises exponentially as a project progresses, so late-stage testing can result in costly rework and project delays.

Waterfall projects typically took months rather than weeks. Some of the time went into careful up-front planning and documentation. Some of it went into extensive testing at the end to root out defects. Successful projects often froze requirements for months, which led to long waits for new product features. Successful projects also customized their processes to start testing early, so they used a waterfall variant rather than a purely sequential process.

2.5 Levels of Design and Testing: V Processes

By specifying what to test and when to test it, a process can provide a development team with a testing strategy. All teams need a strategy because testing is such an important part of software development. We know from waterfall processes that big-bang testing at the end is a bad idea. The XP strategy is to write tests before writing code to pass the tests. A process does not tell us how to test; testing is covered in Chapter 9.

V processes introduce the concept of testing at various levels of granularity, down to smaller and smaller parts, until we get to units of implementation. Specifically, V processes introduce the concepts of unit, functional, integration, system, and acceptance testing. These terms are now part of the software engineering vocabulary. These concepts can be adopted by any team using any of the processes in this chapter.

V processes are based on the development process for the SAGE air defense system, built in the 1950s. SAGE (Semi-Automated Ground Environment) was an ambitious distributed system that grew to 24 radar data collection centers and three combat centers spread across the United States.[23]

2.5.1   Overview of V Processes

A *V process* has levels of paired specification/design and testing activities. The higher the level, the larger the software under design and test. The number of levels varies from project to project. An example of a five-level V process appears in Fig. 2.12.

Diagrams for V processes resemble the letter V. The design phases are drawn going down and to the right. Coding and any testing that occurs during coding are at the bottom. The testing phases are drawn going up and to the right. The dashed arrows in Fig. 2.12 link a specification (design) phase with its corresponding testing phase. Design and testing are thus paired, like opening and closing parentheses, surrounding a coding phase.

At each level, the result of the design activity is a specification of what to build and test at that level. The testing activity at each level checks that its corresponding specification is implemented correctly.

Test planning can begin in the down part of the V, before coding begins. In the SAGE project, test planning was done in parallel with coding. Test execution must follow coding, so test execution is in the up part of the V. Including relevant tests with a specification strengthens the specification.

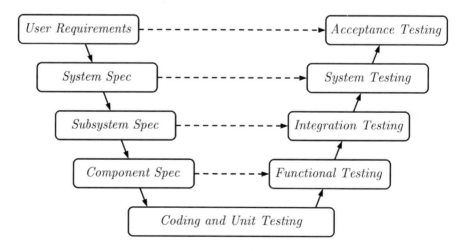

Figure 2.12 A V process with five levels of specification and testing.

V processes are essentially waterfall processes. Note that the solid arrows in Fig. 2.12 trace the sequential flow from customer requirements to acceptance testing. A specific V process may have different levels of specification and testing.

2.5.2 Levels of Testing, from Unit to Acceptance

The upper levels of a V process focus on validation, and the lower levels focus on verification, as described in what follows. Both validation and verification refer to forms of error checking:

> *Validation*: "Am I building the right product?"
> *Verification*: "Am I building the product right?"

Validation testing checks whether a product has the correct functionality. Verification testing checks for implementation defects. See Chapter 8 for more on validation and verification.[24]

The following are typical levels of testing; see Fig. 2.12:

- *Acceptance Testing* Performed by customers to ensure that the system meets their requirements.
- *System Testing* Done by developers to check the functionality and performance of the system as a whole.
- *Integration Testing* Done by developers to verify that the modules worked together.
- *Functional Testing* Black box testing to verify the design of the modules. Testing for functionality also occurs during system testing.
- *Unit Testing* Primarily white-box testing of modules or units, where *unit* is short for unit of implementation.

For more on these levels of testing, see Chapter 9.

2.5.3 Summary

- **Highlights** V processes emphasize testing. They pair specification and testing at multiple levels of granularity, from the whole system down to individual units of implementation. The testing phases check that the corresponding specification was implemented correctly.
- **Strengths** Thorough testing addresses the risk of defects in the design and implementation of a system.
- **Caveats** V processes are a form of waterfall processes, so they remain subject to requirements-related risks.

Levels of testing – unit, functional, integration, system, acceptance – came with V processes in the 1950s. These levels of testing are now widely used, independent of the process model used by a team.

2.6 Additional Project Risks

This section continues the discussion of process selection in Section 2.1.4. In Section 2.1.4 the selection of a process model was based on two factors: requirements

Customers

Changing Requirements

Inadequate User Involvement

Process   **Product**

Lack of Team Coordination   Design and Quality Issues

Staff and Skills Shortfalls   Immature Tools

Constraints

Unrealistic Schedules and Budgets

Lack of Management Commitment

Figure 2.13 Sample project risks. Processes can be customized to reduce known risks.

stability and product complexity. Once a process model is selected, it can be adjusted to manage additional risks. A quick rough risk assessment can highlight potential risk factors. For a sampling of project risks, see Fig. 2.13.

The pair of case studies in this section illustrate that a process reduces, but does not eliminate risks. The first project was very successful. The second project, by the same team using the same process, failed to live up to expectations. It faced many challenges, related to requirements, its code base, new technology, and staff shortfalls.

Example 2.14   This example illustrates a process adjustment to manage a potential project risk. For their complex product with stable requirements, the Corporate team chose a plan-driven approach in Example 2.6. In Example 2.7, the team added daily scrums.

The addition of daily scrums is an adjustment to a plan-driven process. Now, the team has identified performance as a potential risk for the proposed design. The developers consider three options for adjusting their process to manage the performance risk:

- Add a design review.
- Add a prototyping step.
- Add a formal modeling step.

The team decides to add a two-day design review by a panel of external experts. The expert reviewers will meet with the team on the afternoon of the first day. The next morning, the reviewers will present their feedback. Depending on the feedback, the team will decide whether to add a prototyping or a modeling step.   □

> **Box 2.3** Quantifying Risk as a Cost
>
> Risk factors such as the ones in Fig. 2.13 can be quantified and compared by treating each risk as a cost: it is the cost of something going wrong. For example, there is a potential cost associated with missing a deadline or with having to rework a design. Let us refer to something going wrong as an event. The risk of an event is:
>
> $$Risk \text{ of event} = (Probability \text{ of event}) \times (Cost \text{ of handling event})$$
>
> For a predictable or known event, its probability can be estimated, based on intuition and experience with similar projects. Unforeseen or unknown events can be accounted for by building in a margin of error, again guided by experience.

2.6.1   Rough Risk Assessment

An intuitive high-medium-low notion of risk will suffice, as in Section 2.1.4. If desired, risk can be quantified as a cost; see Box 2.3. Here is an approach for assessing and reducing risk:

1. Identify potential risk factors. Any aspect of a project is subject to risk. The sample risks in Fig. 2.13 provide a starting point.
2. For each risk factor, ask questions to classify the risk as high, medium, or low. See the following for examples of questions.
3. Define actions, such as process adjustments, to address all high risks.
4. Examine each medium risk to decide whether to accept the risk or to reduce it.

Sample Questions
Here are some sample questions to help with a quick risk assessment:

- How critical is the application: high, medium, or low? With critical projects, design, quality, and regulations merit special attention.
- How experienced is the team? If the code base has just been handed to a green team, the team risk may be high. If the team has years of experience with different projects, the team risk is low.
- Is any external technology unsupported, somewhat supported, or well supported?
- Does the project lack management support, have some support, or have a corporate commitment? Management support can be a key risk factor.

2.6.2   Netscape 3.0: A Successful Iterative Project

The iterative process employed to build the wildly successful Netscape 3.0 web browser relied on short iterations and continuing user feedback. Today, we would call their process agile. The Firefox code base descends from the Netscape project.

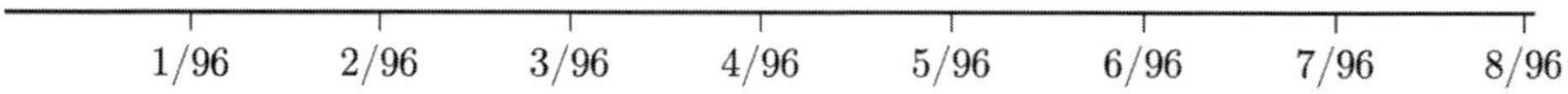

```
     1/96      2/96      3/96      4/96      5/96      6/96      7/96      8/96
```

Figure 2.14 An iterative process was used to build the Netscape Navigator 3.0 web browser. Each iteration produced a beta release. The timeline shows the dates of the releases.

In the early days of the Web, Netscape Navigator was the dominant browser, with 70 percent market share. Microsoft appeared to have missed the Internet "Tidal Wave" until it unveiled its Internet strategy on December 7, 1995. The company compared itself to a sleeping giant that had been awakened, and launched an all-out effort to build a competing browser, Internet Explorer 3.0.[25]

Example 2.15 In the race with Microsoft, time to market was paramount for the Navigator 3.0 project. The development process emphasized quick iterations; see the timeline in Fig. 2.14, where each date represents a release at the end of an iteration. There were six beta releases between the start of the project in January 1996 and the final release of the product in August.

The requirements challenges included both user uncertainty and a competitive threat:

- The initial requirements were based on extensive interactions with customers; however, there was uncertainty about whether customers would like the design and usability of the features.[26]
- The team carefully monitored beta releases of Microsoft's Explorer 3.0, ready to change requirements dynamically to keep Navigator 3.0 competitive.[27]

The Navigator 3.0 project began with a prototype that was released internally within the company as Beta 0. The prototype was followed by quick design-build-test iterations. Each iteration led to an external beta release, available for public download. The beta releases elicited valuable user feedback that guided the content of the next beta version.

Navigator 3.0 and Explorer 3.0 both hit the market in August 1996.   □

The takeaway from this example is that their iterative process enabled the team to rapidly evolve a prototype into a successful product. The initial requirements came from internal users within the company. The requirements were updated based on user feedback and the competitive threat from Microsoft. Beneath the surface, there was a lurking issue with the code base. In the rush to market, it had not been adequately refactored to clean up the code.

2.6.3   Netscape 4.0: A Troubled Project

Netscape 4.0 illustrates that there are limits to what a process can do to accommodate requirements changes. Iterative and agile methods are not a silver bullet. Besides requirements, projects can succumb to other challenges; for example, related to design, technology, and staff shortages.

Example 2.16 The Netscape Communicator 4.0 project had the same iterative process, the same team, and the same code base as the 3.0 project. But 4.0 faced multiple challenges.

Users and Requirements With 4.0, Netscape shifted its business strategy from focusing on individual consumers to selling to enterprises – enterprises include businesses, nonprofits, and government organizations. The senior engineering executive later described the shift as "a complete right turn to become an airtight software company." Enterprises have much higher expectations for product quality.[28]

The team took on new features, including email and groupware. Well into the 4.0 project, the requirements for the mailer changed significantly: the company changed the competitive benchmark. As the engineering executive put it, "Now that's an entire shift!"

The groupware features were unproven. Three-quarters of the way through the project, a major new feature was added.

Design and Technology The project had issues with the design of the code for the product and with the tools to build the system. Communicator 4.0 was built on the existing code base from Navigator 3.0. The existing code base needed to be re-architected to accept the new features, but the schedule did not permit a redesign.

As for tools, the team chose to use Java, so the same Java code would run on Windows, MacOS, and Unix. Java was relatively new at the time and did not provide the desired product performance. (Since then, Java compilers have improved significantly.)

Staff Shortages With multiple platforms to support – Windows, MacOS, Unix – the team did not have enough testers.

Conclusion When Communicator 4.0 was released in June 1997, it fell far short of expectations. The product had quality problems. Customers did not embrace the groupware features.

The takeaways from the 4.0 project are twofold. First, significant requirements changes, especially late in the project, were a challenge, even with an iterative process. The changes can result in redesign and rework. Second, an iterative process cannot help if the code base is brittle and needs to be redesigned, if the tools are inadequate, or if there are not enough developers.   □

2.7   Risk Reduction: The Spiral Framework

The *Spiral Framework* is a cyclic approach to risk reduction during software development. Conceptually, with each cycle, risk shrinks and the product grows. Each cycle is like a mini-project that revisits all of the numbered activities in Fig. 2.15. It identifies the next level of stakeholders, their requirements, and the current project risks. Developers then choose how they will build the next level of product deliverables. The cycle ends with a review and a decision about whether to commit to another cycle. The developers are free to choose agile development for one cycle and plan-driven development for the next.

Barry Boehm introduced the Spiral Framework in the 1980s.[29] The framework has been used to reduce the risk and cost of government contracts.

2.7.1   Overview of the Spiral Framework

The "Spiral" in the name comes from the increasing (spiraling) level of investment in a project with each cycle. This increasing investment and commitment is depicted by the widening cycles in Fig. 2.15. The first cycle is at the center.

The framework scales from small to very large projects. A small project may have just one cycle. Within that cycle, some of the activities in Fig. 2.15 may be combined. For a complex project, a more formal approach with more cycles might be helpful.

Example 2.17   Spiral cycles were used to incrementally select the winner of a large contract for a system to control remotely piloted vehicles (drones). The three cycles were as follows:

1. For the first cycle, four teams were selected to conduct feasibility studies.
2. For the second cycle, three of the teams were selected to build a scaled-down version of the system.
3. For the final cycle, one team was selected to build a viable system.

Each of the competing teams was free to choose its own process for a given cycle. The investment level increased with each cycle. Example 2.19 provides more

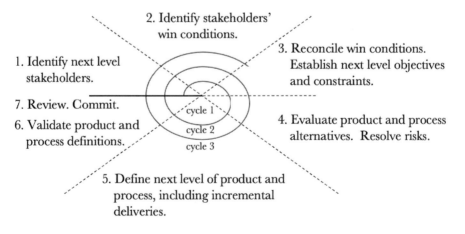

Figure 2.15 Spiral Risk-Reduction Framework.

information about the project and the benefits of an incremental spiral approach to awarding a large contract.   ☐

A Spiral Cycle

Each spiral cycle has two main parts, represented by the upper and lower halves of Fig. 2.15. The upper half defines the problem to be addressed in this cycle. The lower half develops a solution to the problem.

a) **Problem Definition**. Activity 1 identifies the stakeholders for this cycle. Win conditions in activity 2 correspond to requirements from the various stakeholders. These requirements are prioritized into a coherent set, which we call the problem definition for this cycle. The problem definition is accompanied by an assessment of the current risks.

b) **Solution Development**. Based on the problem definition and the current risks, activity 4 explores alternative solutions. For the chosen solution, activities 5–6 customize a process and then build using that process. Activity 7 reviews progress and decides the level of commitment, if any, for the next cycle.

Although the actions are numbered, they are expected to be concurrent, where possible.

The framework accommodates any methods or processes for carrying out the activities listed in Fig. 2.15. For example, risk resolution in activity 4 can be through analysis, prototyping, or by building an increment to the system. In activity 5, the chosen development process can be different from the process used during the previous cycle.

Example 2.18   In retrospect, a spiral approach was used to build the software for the SAGE air defense system in the 1950s. There were two cycles. Benington added in 1983 that the team first built an experimental prototype:

The experimental prototype ... performed all the bare-bones functions of air defense. Twenty people understood in detail the performance of those 35,000 instructions; they knew what each module would do, they understood the interfaces, and they understood the performance requirements.[30]

The prototype reduced the design and performance risk. In the second cycle, the team used a V process, with its levels of testing, to reduce quality risk.   ☐

Case Study: Incremental Commitment

In the following case study, a spiral approach led to a much better outcome, compared to the alternative, measured in both dollars and months. The case study expands on Example 2.17.

Example 2.19   This example contrasts two approaches to awarding a very large contract, called the Total and the Incremental (spiral) approaches. The Total approach cost $3B (billion) and took 80 months. For the same outcome, the Incremental approach cost $1B and took 42 months.[31]

The challenge was to improve productivity for remotely piloting a drone by a factor of eight, from two pilots for one drone (2:1) to one pilot for four drones (1:4). The Total approach awarded the total contract all at once. The winning bidder of the Total approach promised the desired 1:4 ratio in 40 months for $1B, but delivered only twofold improvement to 1:1 in 80 months for $3B.

The Incremental approach achieved the same two pilots for one drone (2:1) in 42 months for an overall investment of $1B, in three spiral cycles:

1. $25M for feasibility studies by four teams awarded $5M each, with $5M for evaluating the feasibility results. The review at the end of the first cycle concluded that the original goal of one pilot for four drones (1:4) was not realistic, but that some improvement was possible.
2. $75M for scaled-down versions by three of the teams, awarded $20M each, with $15M for evaluation.
3. A final third cycle where one of the teams was selected to build a viable version. This team achieved 1:1. Productivity improvement: twofold. Overall investment: $1B. Overall elapsed time: 42 months.

The spiral approach achieved the same improvement for a third of the investment, in roughly half the time.   □

2.7.2   Summary

- **Highlights** The Spiral Framework organizes software development as a sequence of risk-reduction cycles. In each cycle, the team revisits stakeholders, requirements, and risks. They then choose a suitable development process for continuing the evolution of the software under development. Commitment to the project increases with each cycle.
- **Strength** The Framework gives teams the freedom to choose how they will do the activities in a cycle; for example, how to identify risks and whether to do agile or plan-driven development. The Framework scales from small to very large complex systems.
- **Caveats** The Spiral Framework is often misinterpreted as either an iterative process or as a sequence of waterfall projects. Instead, it is a framework with placeholders for requirements, risk management, and implementation practices.

2.8   Conclusion

A software development team's decisions about "who will do what" are based on a combination of processes and values. Processes provide rules and guidelines, values provide principles that guide decisions. Plan-driven methods have traditionally relied more on processes than on values. Agile methods favor values: the Agile Manifesto puts individuals and interactions over "processes and tools."

Values So, where do we start when we organize a new project? Start with values. The purpose of a project is to build working software that will meet customer needs upon delivery. This purpose motivates the following agile values:

- Collaborate with customers. After all, the project is for their benefit.
- Welcome changing requirements. Let us accept that requirements (needs) can be a moving target,
- Deliver working software frequently. We can build more confidently and productively by aiming for working software at all times.

The conclusion is that agile values are a good starting point for defining a set of values for a team.

Process What about the development process? How do we choose one? The "right" process for a project depends on the nature and complexity of the project. Alternatively, process selection depends on a project's challenges or risks.

For an off-the-shelf process, start with Scrum. It is iterative, so it addresses the risk of requirements changes. It carefully defines roles for team members. To keep a project on track, it defines planning and review events. For each event, it defines the agenda, the participants, their responsibilities, and the allotted time. What it does not specify is how the product is built: developers are free to choose their development practices.

For a close to off-the-shelf agile method, consider the combination of Scrum and XP. Specifically, consider Scrum roles and events, together with XP development practices. Building on agile values, XP brings an emphasis on testing, simplicity, and clean code/design. The XP development cycle is test driven. Scrum and XP work well together; see Fig. 2.8 for a Scrum+XP process diagram.

Customizing a Process Early XP teams did no up-front design and ended up with poorly designed systems. Particularly with system properties like scale and performance, enough up-front design is needed to ensure that the completed system will have the desired properties. Such system properties are hard to retrofit. In effect, some up-front planning is needed, even with agile methods.

Experienced teams customize their processes to suit their projects. The process in Fig. 2.16 unifies best practices from both agile and plan-driven methods.

The process begins with an up-front planning phase to explore the problem and possible solutions. The leftmost two boxes represent this up-front exploration. The process then switches to Scrum. The boxes in the middle of the diagram represent sprints. Each sprint delivers code and unit tests. To enhance quality, the process includes multiple levels of testing from V processes. (Functional and acceptance tests are not shown.)

Spiral Risk Reduction The Spiral Framework takes an incremental cyclic approach to reducing risk during software development. Each cycle is essentially a mini-project.

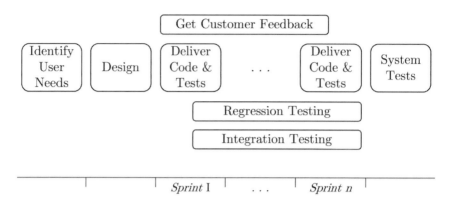

Figure 2.16 A unified process that combines up-front planning with Scrum. It has multiple levels of testing, as in V processes. This hybrid process is based loosely on a project at Avaya.

The lessons and artifacts from a cycle build up to a solution to the problem on hand. Each cycle addresses a level of risks. Ideally, risk goes down and commitment to the project increases with each cycle. Within a cycle, the team is free to choose its methods.

Further Reading

- Schwaber and Sutherland's [167] concise definitive guide to Scrum is available for download.
- For XP, see Beck's early paper [16] or the updated account in the book by Beck and Andres [17].
- Boehm [29] describes experience with the spiral framework.
- Larman and Basili [121] review iterative processes.
- For a sweeping view of changes in software development methods over the decades, see Boehm's retrospective [30].
- For a historical perspective on waterfall and V processes, see the republished version of Benington's original paper; the new foreword puts the project in context.

Exercises for Chapter 2

Exercise 2.1   Answer the following review questions about Scrum:

a) For a one-month sprint, what are the durations of the four Scrum events?
b) Who are the attendees for each of the Scrum events?
c) How is requirements identification integrated into a Scrum process?
d) How are work items selected for a sprint?
e) Who has responsibility for each of the Scrum artifacts?

Exercise 2.2   For each of the following statements, answer whether it is generally true or generally false. Briefly explain your answer.

a) With an iterative process, each iteration builds on the last.

b) Agile processes came after the Agile Manifesto.

c) With agile processes, project timelines can be hard to predict.

d) Agile processes are great for when you are not sure of the details of what to build.

e) Sprint planning is essentially the same as iteration planning.

f) The Scrum Master sets priorities for the product backlog.

g) Pair programming doubles the staff costs of a project.

h) Very few projects have been successful using waterfall processes.

i) With a waterfall process, testing comes very late in the process.

j) Plan-driven processes call for careful up-front planning so there are few errors in the product.

Exercise 2.3   A usage survey identified the following as the top five agile practices.[32] For each practice, describe

- its purpose or role, and
- how it is practiced.

The top five practices are

a) Daily Standup

b) Retrospectives

c) Iteration Planning

d) Iteration Review

e) Short Iterations

Exercise 2.4   In practice, processes do not always run smoothly. For each of the situations listed in this exercise, briefly answer the following questions:

- Is there a potential violation of a Scrum rule or an agile value? If so, which one(s)?
- How would you resolve the situation?

The situations are as follows:

a) The product owner challenges developer estimates for the time and effort needed for work items. The product owner is convinced that the developers are inflating their estimates.

b) It appears that, for lack of time, some essential product backlog items will have to be dropped entirely from the project.

c) Pressured by a loud stakeholder, a product owner comes to a daily scrum and pushes for the acceleration of work on certain items.

Exercise 2.5   The process in Fig. 2.17 is a variant of Infosys's development process, circa 1996.[33] Compare the process in Fig. 2.17 with each of the following. In each case, discuss any similarities and differences.

a) Waterfall processes

b) V processes

c) Iterative processes

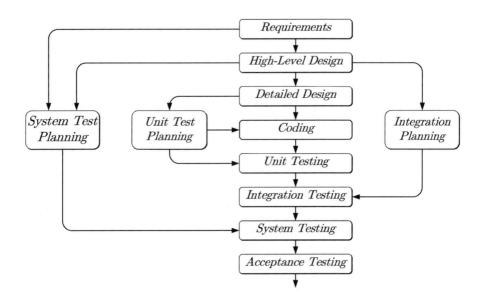

Figure 2.17 A variant of the Infosys development process, circa 1996.

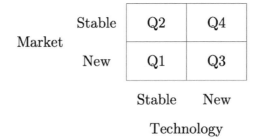

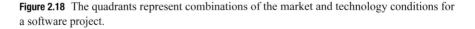

Figure 2.18 The quadrants represent combinations of the market and technology conditions for a software project.

Exercise 2.6   On a low-medium-high scale, how much would you invest in up-front design in each of the following kinds of software-development projects? Briefly describe your choice.

a) Create a website.
b) Develop software for a medical device.
c) Add a feature that maintains a list of the ten most requested songs. The input to the feature is a stream of customer requests for songs.
d) Build a billing system for a global music-streaming service with millions of customers.

Exercise 2.7   For each of the four quadrants in Fig. 2.18, classify the following risks as low or high. The quadrants represent combinations of the market and technology conditions for a software project. Briefly explain your classification.

a) Requirements-related risk
b) Design-related risk
c) Quality-related risk

Here, *New* refers to a market or technology that is new to the world, and *Stable* stands for well known to the world. There can be surprises with either new technology or new markets, and there are no surprises left with either stable technology or stable markets.

Exercise 2.8   For each of the quadrants in Fig. 2.18, how would you address the requirements, design, and quality risks identified in Exercise 2.7 if you are using

a) an agile process?
b) a plan-driven process?

3   User Requirements

All software projects face the twin questions of what users want and what to build to address those wants. These are related, but logically distinct questions. *Requirements elicitation* is the process of discovering user wants and writing them down as user requirements. *Requirements analysis* is the process of prioritizing user requirements from various sources and defining what to build as a product. In practice, elicitation and analysis are entwined: the same user–developer conversation can touch on a user goal, its priority, and acceptance tests for it.

This chapter deals with elicitation. It begins with an overview of requirements and requirements development. It then explores the elicitation and clarification of user needs and goals. Chapter 5 introduces use cases, which describe user–system interactions to accomplish user goals. Chapter 4 provides techniques for requirements analysis.

This chapter will enable the reader to:

- Describe requirements development and how it fits into overall agile or plan-driven software development.
- Elicit the needs and goals conveyed by users through their words, actions, and sentiments.
- Record user requirements as user stories, system features, and user-experience scenarios.
- Refine high-level goals into specific measurable goals and actions, by asking clarifying questions.

3.1   What Is a Requirement?

A *requirement* is a description of a business or user goal, a product behavior, a product attribute, or a product or process constraint.[1] Thus, we can have business requirements, product requirements, and so on. This section introduces the many kinds of requirements and the activities that produce them. Requirements are developed iteratively, with both agile and plan-driven methods. Iteration allows a collection of requirements to be refined until it is complete, unambiguous, and consistent.

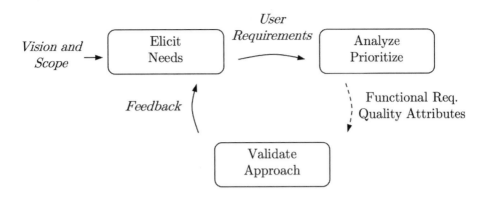

Figure 3.1 The basic elicit-analyze-validate requirements cycle. The boxes represent activities. The edges are labeled with the requirements produced by the activities. In practice, the activities may blur into each other.

Requirements can come from any stakeholder, where a *stakeholder* is anyone with a stake in a project, including both users and developers. Bowing to popular usage, we use the term stakeholder to refer to a class of users, unless developers are clearly included. Developers can contribute requirements; for example, about attributes of a product such as performance.

3.1.1   The Basic Requirements Cycle

The basic requirements cycle has three main logically distinct activities: elicitation of user needs, analysis and prioritization of requirements, and validation of the project's direction. The diagram in Fig. 3.1 illustrates the elicit-analyze-validate cycle. The edge from analysis to validation is dashed because there are other software development activities between analysis and validation, as we shall see in Section 3.2.

The edges in the figure are labeled with requirements produced by the activities. This chapter includes techniques for eliciting and clarifying user requirements. Overviews of the various kinds of requirements appear later in this section.

To elicit means to draw out a response. Requirements *elicitation* is the identification of the various stakeholders and the discovery and description of user motivations, goals, needs, and wants for a project. Section 3.3 discusses how to interact with users to uncover their needs.

During *analysis*, the output from elicitation is clarified, reconciled, and prioritized. Analysis produces a definition of the desired behavior, functionality, and attributes of a product. The product definition consists of a coherent set of specific requirements. Section 3.6 introduces techniques for clarifying requirements. Chapter 4 discusses prioritization.

To *validate* is to confirm with users that the right product is being built. Agile methods validate working software at the end of each iteration. Plan-driven methods validate detailed specification documents and high-level designs. See Section 3.2 for the handling of requirements during software development. Validation techniques include reviews and acceptance tests. See Chapter 8 for software-architecture reviews.

In practice, the boundaries between the activities in Fig. 3.1 are fluid. A single conversation with users can elicit a need and prompt a discussion about its priority (for use during analysis). The same conversation can then turn to possible acceptance tests for validating the need.

The activities have been teased apart in the basic cycle because each has its own bag of tricks and techniques. For a small project, some of the activities may be combined or skipped. For a large project, each activity can be a process in its own right.

3.1.2   Case Study: Requirements Challenges

The three leading causes of requirements challenges are (a) multiple stakeholders with differing and possibly conflicting goals, (b) incomplete or inadequate requirements, and (c) changes over time. In the next example, the developers cited changing requirements as their biggest challenge. The root cause may, however, have been that the project prioritized technology over user needs and goals.

Example 3.1   In May 2013, the British Broadcasting Corporation (BBC) canceled its Digital Media Initiative, writing off an investment of £98.4 million over six years.[2] What went wrong? The chief technology officer, who was subsequently dismissed, was reported to have said,

"Throughout the project, the team informed me that the biggest single challenge facing the project was the changes to requirements requested by the business."

Inconsistent Goals   The project was initiated by the Director of BBC Technology to standardize television production across the BBC. Standardization was not something users asked for. It implied a significant cultural shift in user behavior: production teams in some of the main BBC divisions would have to give up their existing tools and business practices in favor of the new integrated system. Thus, the business goal of standardization was not a user goal.

The original intent of the Initiative was to create a fully integrated archiving and production system for audio and video content. The archive is extensive: the BBC began radio broadcasts in the 1920s and television broadcasts in the 1930s. The project would have allowed BBC staff and partners to access the archive and create, manage, and share content from their desktops.

Incomplete Requirements   Unfortunately, the project began before detailed user requirements were fully established. The initial requirements focused on the technology, not on how receptive users would be to the technology. In other words, the requirements were not fully elicited and validated with users.

Project Delays   The project got off to a bad start. Funding was approved in January 2008 and a vendor was selected in February, but the contract to build a system was terminated by mutual agreement in July 2009. A year and a half after it started, the project was back to square one, with nothing to show.

The BBC then decided in September 2009 to bring the project in-house. They gave the IT organization the responsibility for building and delivering the system.

Changing Requirements The project was never completed. An inquiry by the UK National Audit Office noted that repeated delays and technical difficulties contributed to users losing confidence in the project. They relied on alternative tools to get their jobs done. According to news reports, the chief technology officer cited the following example of changing requirements:

Users wanted a function to produce a "rough cut" of video output, which was subsequently developed, only to be told that those users now wanted to use an off-the-shelf product from Adobe instead. Once the IT team had integrated that Adobe product into the Digital Media Initiative software, users then said they wanted to use a different Adobe product altogether.

□

The BBC project had multiple requirements-related problems. The project focused on technology standardization, not on users: its success depended on a major shift in user behavior. The project began before requirements were fully developed. Repeated delays meant that users turned to alternative tools and practices. If there is a single lesson from such projects, it is this: prioritize value for users and the business over improvements in technology and infrastructure.

3.1.3   Kinds of Requirements

The rest of this section introduces the various kinds of requirements shown along the edges in Fig. 3.1. The amount of documentation varies from project to project. Agile methods work primarily with user requirements; for example, with user stories. Plan-driven methods typically have detailed documentation.

Business Requirements The vision and scope of a project lay out the expectations for the value the project will provide for the customer. The expectations are the starting point for the project; see the top left of Fig. 3.1. Let us call the vision and scope the *business goals* or the *business requirements*. Here are some common categories of business goals:

- Improve customer satisfaction for the business's customers.
- Increase revenues.
- Reduce costs.
- Improve operations (business processes, technology, or infrastructure).

The goal of improving operations, by itself, gets less executive support, since it represents a cost, without a direct measurable benefit to the business.

Example 3.2   The BBC technology standardization project in Example 3.1 was presented as an improvement in operations. Besides the monetary cost to the BBC, the cost to the staff and partners (users) would be the inconvenience of giving up their existing tools and practices. The project would make the archive readily available, but would it improve television programming, and hence customer satisfaction? The only stated goal was technology standardization.   □

User Requirements   A *user requirement* for a product is a description of an elicited user goal, need, or want. This chapter includes three techniques for writing user requirements: features, user stories, and scenarios.

Example 3.3   Looking ahead to the pseudo-English syntax for writing features in Section 3.4, the following feature is for a notification system:

When the flight schedule changes, the system **shall** send a notification by text or email, based on the traveler's contact preferences.

The boldface words are keywords.

  User stories are written from the user's perspective; see Section 3.4. The preceding feature can be rewritten as the following user story:

> **As a**   traveler,
> **I want** to be notified of changes to the flight schedule,
> **so that** I can get to the flight at the right time.

  Scenarios describe a user's desired overall experience, including the user's emotions; see Section 3.5.   □

Product and Process Requirements   A *product requirement* influences or constrains the product's functionality or attributes. The development team defines product requirements by analyzing user requirements. Analysis is represented by the top-right box in Fig. 3.1.

  A *process requirement* constrains or influences how a product is developed; that is, it influences the development process. For decades, US defense contracts promoted the use of waterfall processes through standards such as Military Standard MIL-STD-1521B, dated June 4, 1985.

Example 3.4   Projects that build safety-critical software typically face process constraints. The US Federal Aviation Administration (FAA) imposes testing constraints on airborne software systems; see MC/DC testing in Section 9.5.   □

Functional Requirements and Quality Attributes   Product requirements can be grouped into two categories: functional requirements and quality attributes. A *functional requirement* relates to the job to be done. If the product can be described in terms of inputs and outputs, its functional requirements define the mapping from inputs to outputs. Similarly, if a product can be described in terms of user actions and system responses, its functional requirements define the action-response behavior of the product. Chapter 5 introduces use cases, which describe user actions and system responses in pursuit of a user goal.

Example 3.5   A user's experience with a shopping site can be described as a sequence of user actions and system responses. When the user visits the site, the system presents a welcome screen with a menu of options; for example, search for a product or log into the site. The user's action determines the system's next move. The interaction continues until the user goal for visiting the site is achieved. Examples of goals include searching for a product or purchasing a product.   □

A *quality attribute*, also known as a *nonfunctional requirement*, relates to how well a product must do its job. Quality attributes include properties such as scale, performance, and reliability. For example, the requirements for a shopping site would include how many million simultaneous users it must support (scale) and the number of milliseconds for responding to a product search (performance).

Quality attribute is a better name than "nonfunctional requirement." We not only want the product to function, we want it to function well.

3.2   Developing Requirements and Software

With agile methods, the elicit-analyze-validate requirements cycle is an integral part of overall software development. The product is developed during a series of elicit-analyze-build-validate iterations; see Fig. 3.2. Validation is done with working software.

With plan-driven methods, the requirements cycle is part of the planning phase, prior to the build phase. Requirements development consists of a series of elicit-analyze-specify-validate iterations; see Fig. 3.3. The output from the iterations is a document called a Software Requirements Specification (SRS). An SRS specifies what to build. Validation is done with specification documents and high-level designs.

3.2.1   Agile Methods Validate Working Software

The description of Scrum in Section 2.2 highlights roles, events, and artifacts. The description of XP in Section 2.3 highlights development practices. Both Scrum and XP iterations include requirements activities, but they occur in the background.

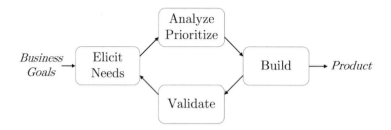

Figure 3.2 Requirements development is an integral part of agile software development. This diagram adds a build activity between analyze and validate in Fig. 3.1.

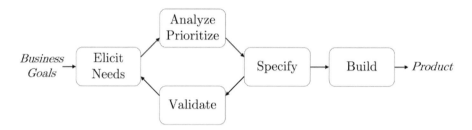

Figure 3.3 Requirements development is completed before the build phase, during plan-driven development. This diagram adds a specify activity between analyze and validate in Fig. 3.1.

Requirements Activities during a Sprint

Table 3.1 points out the requirements activities that occur during Scrum events. Scrum does not specify how the product backlog is initialized, so the table adds an implicit initialization event on Line 0. Sprint planning is a form of requirements analysis. Product backlog items are prioritized and the highest-priority items are selected for the sprint backlog. There are no requirements activities while the sprint backlog is being implemented or during daily scrums.

Sprint reviews are repeated on Lines 4 and 5 to separate out two key activities during a sprint review: (a) review the product increment (the implemented sprint backlog) and (b) update the product backlog based on user feedback. The review of the increment is a validation activity. The update to the product backlog is an elicitation activity. Sprint retrospectives are for process improvement, so there is no direct requirements activity.

With XP, the writing of user stories is an elicitation activity; see Section 3.4 for guidelines for writing user stories. The writing of tests for stories supports validation. It is left as an exercise to the reader to create a counterpart of Table 3.1 for XP.

3.2.2   Case Study: An Agile Emphasis on Requirements

The Fast Feedback process in Fig. 3.4 is based on Scenario-Focused Engineering, which has been used within Microsoft.[3] It highlights customer interactions during software development. The balance tips from mostly requirements development during

Table 3.1 Requirements activities during a Scrum sprint. The parenthesized events on Lines 0 and 2 are not "official" Scrum events. They highlight activities that occur during a sprint.

LINE	SCRUM EVENT	REQUIREMENTS ACTIVITY
0.	(Initialize Product Backlog)	Elicit backlog items
1.	Sprint Planning	Prioritize work items
2.	(Build Sprint Backlog)	
3.	Daily Scrum	
4.	Sprint Review (of Increment)	Validate
5.	Sprint Review (update Backlog)	Elicit backlog items
6.	Sprint Retrospective	

early iterations to mostly software development in later iterations. The Fast Feedback process complements Scrum and XP. Its requirements activities can be used together with the team events of Scrum and the development practices of XP.

Example 3.6 Starting at the top left of Fig. 3.4, the four activities of the Fast Feedback process correspond to elicitation, analysis, design, and build/validation. The focus of elicitation is on unmet needs and goals, not on product features and capabilities. The output from elicitation is a set of stories that represent product opportunities. The various opportunities could well pull the project in different directions.

Moving right, the next activity is to analyze the stories (user requirements) and frame or define a problem to be solved by a product. Collectively, developers and users sift through and prioritize the user requirements. Their task is to converge on the specific problem to be addressed.

For the distinction between eliciting needs and framing the problem, consider the need to listen to music on the go. This need can be met in at least three distinct ways:

> **Customer Need:**   Listen to music
>
> **Problem Definition 1**: Offer songs for purchase and download
> **Problem Definition 2**: Offer a free streaming service with ads
> **Problem Definition 3**: Offer paid subscriptions without ads

In general, there are multiple ways of addressing a user need. It may take several discussions to narrow down the possible problem definitions. The developers might even do quick prototypes of more than one approach.

The lower half of Fig. 3.4 represents implementation-related activities. The development team brainstorms about potential designs and then builds something to get user feedback. As the iterations continue, the solution is refined into a deliverable product. ☐

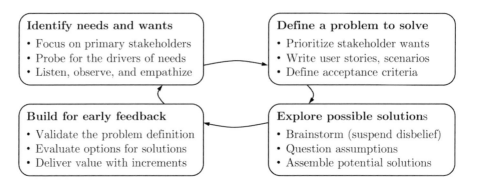

Figure 3.4 The agile Fast Feedback process emphasizes the identification and analysis of customer needs.

3.2.3   Plan-Driven Methods Validate a Specification

This high-level discussion masks the fact that each of the activities in Fig. 3.3 can be a process in its own right. With plan-driven methods, requirements development is a major phase, to the point that it is called *requirements engineering*, and treated as a branch of software engineering. The purpose of requirements engineering is to produce a specification of the product to be built.

SRS: Software Requirements Specifications A *specification* is a complete, precise, verifiable description of a product or of an aspect of a product. An SRS document serves as a agreement between users, designers, implementers, and testers about the product. IEEE Standard 830-1998 (reaffirmed in 2009) provides recommendations for writing an SRS: "There is no one optimal organization for all systems." According to the standard, a good SRS has the following characteristics:[4]

- **Correct** The SRS must truly reflect user needs and must agree with other relevant documentation about the project.
- **Unambiguous** Natural language descriptions can be ambiguous, so care is needed to ensure that the descriptions in the SRS permit only one interpretation. See also the suggested syntax for writing features in Section 3.4.2
- **Complete** It must cover all requirements and define the product behavior for both valid and invalid data and events.
- **Consistent** The individual requirements within an SRS must agree, and occurrences of the same behavior must be described using the same terminology.
- **Ranked** The description must include the priorities of the different requirements.
- **Verifiable** All requirements must be testable.
- **Modifiable** The requirements in the SRS can be easily modified without violating the preceding properties, such as consistency and completeness.

- **Traceable** Every requirement can be traced or connected with a user requirement (*backward traceability*). Furthermore, the requirement has a reference to any documents that depend upon it (*forward traceability*).
- **Usable for Maintenance** The operations and maintenance staff are typically different from the development team. The SRS must meet the needs of the operations and maintenance staff.

Documents created during requirements development need to be managed and maintained to keep up with requirements changes. Keeping documents current must be balanced, however, with actually producing working software.

3.3   Eliciting User Needs

What users say corresponds to just the level of needs in the model in Fig. 3.5. From left to right, the figure shows four levels of needs, how users exhibit the needs, and how developers can elicit what users exhibit. Here exhibit refers to what users communicate through their behavior; that is, through their words, actions, and emotions. Thus, articulated needs are exhibited through words and can be elicited by listening. The main message of this section is this: to elicit the full range of user needs, developers must attend to what users do and how they feel as well as to what they say. For example, user frustrations with the current situation can provide valuable insights for new product requirements.

3.3.1   A Classification of Needs

The classification of needs in Fig. 3.5 has four levels:[5]

- *Articulated* needs relate to what people say and think. They are what people want us to hear. By listening, we can elicit articulated needs.

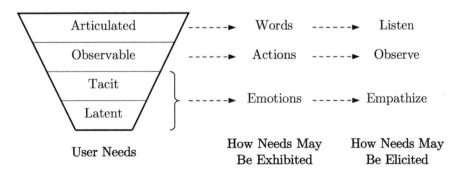

Figure 3.5 A classification of user needs. The dashed arrows represent how needs translate into behaviors and how user behaviors can be elicited by developers.

- *Observable* needs relate to what people do and use. They are made visible by actions and usage patterns. Through direct observations and examination of usage data we can elicit observable needs.
- *Tacit* needs are conscious needs that people cannot readily express. They relate to what people feel and believe. By empathizing and trading places – walking in someone else's shoes – we can elicit tacit needs.
- *Latent* needs are not conscious or are not recognized by people. Through empathy and intuition we might make hypotheses about latent needs.

Example 3.7 Disconnects between what people say and what they do are not new. Faced with a string of product failures in the 1990s, Scott Cook, the founder of Intuit, resolved that "for future new product development, Intuit should rely on customer actions, not words."[6]   □

Example 3.8 Let us apply the model in Fig. 3.5 to the user behavior of Netflix's recommendation system for videos. The articulated user need is for maximal choice and comprehensive search. Their usage patterns, however, exhibit the opposite: an observable need for a few compelling choices, simply presented.   □

Example 3.9 The user's articulated request was for an app that would send a notification when the temperature in the Lunar Greenhouse wandered outside a narrow range. The developers met the request, and the story does not end there. Once the developers learned the motivation for the request, they extended the app to meet a latent need that made life easier for the user.

The Lunar Greenhouse is part of a study of what it would take to grow vegetables on the moon or on a long space voyage.[7] Water will be a scarce resource. The temperature in the greenhouse was therefore strictly controlled: warm enough to grow plants, but not too warm, to limit water loss due to evaporation. Without notifications, the user, a graduate student, had to regularly visit the greenhouse to personally check growing conditions.

The development team created a notification app to meet the articulated need. They got a feed from sensors in the greenhouse and sent notifications to the user's phone. The app eliminated regular trips to the greenhouse for temperature checks.

There is more to the story. Every time the temperature went out of range, the graduate student would jump on a bicycle to go to check the greenhouse. Sometimes, all was well and the temperature returned to normal, without intervention. The developers set up a video surveillance camera in the greenhouse and enhanced the app to provide a live video feed to the user's phone, on demand. Now, the graduate student needed to go to the Lunar Greenhouse only when manual intervention was warranted.

In summary, the articulated user need was for a notification system. The latent need for video monitoring emerged out of the close collaboration between the user and the developers. The developers discovered the latent need by relating to the user's motivations and frustrations.   □

3.3.2   Accessing User Needs

When two people communicate, the receiver may not fully grasp or may misinterpret the message from the sender. Thus, there can be communication gaps when developers elicit user needs and write user requirements. The purpose of the following general tips is to reduce gaps and inaccuracies in user requirements. After the tips, we consider techniques for eliciting articulated and observable needs.

- Listen, observe, and empathize. The case study (Example 3.10) illustrates the use of all these modes of communication.
- Record user behaviors faithfully, without interpretation. In particular, record user words verbatim, without rephrasing or summarizing.
- Clarify and confirm that the written requirements capture the user's intent, to their satisfaction. To repeat, users must be satisfied with the written user requirements.
- Keep the focus on the user in the current conversation. Inconsistencies with requirements from other users are detected and ironed out later, during requirements analysis.

It is a skill that can be learned through practice. It involves attention not only to the technical content of what the other person is saying, but also to their sentiments toward the subject of the communication. In Example 3.9, how frustrated was the user about unnecessary trips to the Lunar Greenhouse, simply to check the temperature? The answer has implications for whether or not to enhance the app to eliminate unnecessary trips. The frustration level must have been high enough, because the developers chose to do video monitoring.

Box 3.1 Listening with Understanding and Empathy

True listening is listening with understanding and empathy. It can potentially elicit the full range of user needs. In a classic paper on communication, Carl Rogers notes that

True listening "means seeing the expressed idea and attitude from the other person's point of view, sensing how it feels to the person, achieving his or her frame of reference about the subject being discussed."[8]

Rogers is going well beyond passive attention to a person's words. Attending to attitude includes attending to sentiments and emotions. True listening is helpful for writing user-experience scenarios; see Section 3.5. User-experience scenarios are written from the user's point of view. They include the user's expected emotional reaction to a product.

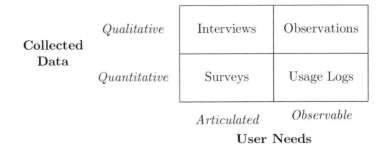

Figure 3.6 Techniques for eliciting articulated and observable needs.

The advice to developers is to hear the other person out before asking a question or changing the direction of the conversation. Words and phrases are important to people, so resist the urge to paraphrase or reword what users day. Marketers use the term *Voice of the Customer* for a statement "in the customer's own words, of the benefit to be fulfilled by the product or service."[9]

Listening and Observing

The qualitative and quantitative techniques in Fig. 3.6 can be used for eliciting articulated and observable needs. The left column in the figure is for articulated needs. Interviews are qualitative; that is, interview findings cannot be readily measured. Surveys, meanwhile, are quantitative, especially if the questions are multiple choice or on a numeric scale. Observation of customer behavior and analysis of usage logs are techniques for eliciting observable needs; see the right column in Fig. 3.6. Observations are qualitative; usage logs are quantitative.

3.3.3   Case Study: Intuit's Design for Delight

Intuit's Design for Delight process promotes the use of all modes of communication (listening, observing, empathizing) to elicit the full range of user needs (articulated, observable, tacit, and latent). Intuit is not alone. A similar process, called Scenario-Focused Engineering, has been used within Microsoft. The agile requirements process in Example 3.6 is based on Scenario-Focused Engineering. See also user-experience scenarios in Section 3.5.

Intuit's Design for Delight has three steps:[10]

1. Develop deep empathy with customers through understanding what really matters to them and what frustrates them.
2. Offer a broad range of options before settling on a choice.
3. Use working prototypes and rapid iterations to get customer feedback.

Example 3.10   The intended users for Intuit's QuickBooks app for the iPad were one-person business owners who spent most of their time out of the office, serving their customers.[11] The business owners wanted to manage all aspects of their business while mobile. For example, they wanted to provide professional estimates and invoices on the spot, at a customer site, rather than waiting until they got back to the office. Without the ability to manage their business while mobile, work was piling up and they were spending evenings and weekends catching up.

The Intuit team used interviews, observations, and empathy to relate to user goals, frustrations, and needs. The team came up with an initial list of requirements, which they evolved based on user feedback. User requirements were captured as user stories that were implemented using agile methods. The app was instrumented to provide usage data. During iteration planning, prioritization of stories was based on both observations and analysis of usage data.

Careful observations and empathy guided the design of the user experience. As an example, the team discovered that users held their tablets differently while they were mobile and while they were at home. On the go, they favored portrait mode, while at home they favored landscape mode. Why? The task mix on the go was different from the mix at home. At home, they dealt with more complex transactions and landscape mode allowed them to display more data on a line.   □

Once a project is underway, further needs can surface as (a) the developers establish rapport with stakeholders, and (b) as working software becomes available for user feedback. In the preceding example, it was through the working prototype that the developers learned how users held their iPads: in portrait mode in the field, and in landscape mode in the office/home. This insight influenced the evolution of the user experiences supported by the app.

3.4 Writing Requirements: Stories and Features

Having considered how to interact with users to discover their needs, we turn now to how to write user needs as user requirements. The approach in this section is to write them as snippets of functionality, called *features*. The bulk of the section deals with user stories, which describe a user want for a feature together with the expected benefit to the user. The section also more briefly considers system features, which describe some functionality the system "shall" provide. Another approach to writing user requirements is to write them as larger end-to-end scenarios. User-experience scenarios are considered in Section 3.5; see also use cases in Chapter 5.

3.4.1 Guidelines for Effective User Stories

User stories are typically written using the following template from Section 2.3:

As a ⟨*role*⟩ **I want to** ⟨*task*⟩ **so that** ⟨*benefit*⟩

Here, ⟨*role*⟩, ⟨*task*⟩, and ⟨*benefit*⟩ are placeholders for English phrases. Any task a user wants to accomplish is equivalent to a user goal, as discussed in Section 3.6. We therefore treat ⟨*task*⟩ as a user goal that may require clarification.

What is a good user story? Above all, a story is about a user need; it is not about the technology for addressing the need. Stories must therefore be written so that users can understand them and relate to them. At the same time, stories must be written so that developers can implement them and test for them. It may take multiple conversations to outline and refine the initial set of user stories for a project.

SMART Stories

Good user stories are *SMART*, where SMART stands for specific, measurable, achievable, relevant, and time-bound.

- A story is *specific* if it is a precise and unambiguous enough that acceptance tests can be defined for it.
- It is *measurable* if success criteria are defined for it.
- It is *achievable* if the developers are capable of implementing it within the allotted time.
- It is *relevant* if the ⟨task⟩ in the story contributes to the ⟨benefit⟩, and the ⟨benefit⟩ provides business value for the stakeholder.
- It is *time-bound* if it can be implemented in one iteration.

If one of these criteria is not met, then the story has to be refined until it is SMART. (SMART criteria can be applied to any goal; see Section 3.6.)

Example 3.11 The first draft of a user story may not meet all the SMART criteria. Consider the payroll story from Example 3.11:

> **As a**   payroll manager
> **I want to** produce a simple paycheck
> **so that**   the company can pay an employee

In this story, what does "simple paycheck" mean? Paychecks can be very complicated, between various forms of compensation (e.g., salary overtime, bonuses) and various deductions (e.g., taxes, savings, medical insurance).

The following refinement of the payroll story is specific about compensation and taxes:

> **As a**   payroll manager
>
> **I want to** produce a paycheck that accounts
>   for monthly wages and federal taxes
>
> **so that**   the company can
>   pay an employee and withhold federal taxes

□

How Much Detail?

When is a story SMART enough that we can stop refining it? A more fundamental question is: who decides whether a story is SMART enough? The story's developers make that decision. A story is SMART enough if the developers can write tests for it (which implies that they can implement the story).

Example 3.12 Consider the refined story in Example 3.11:

As a	payroll manager
I want to	produce a paycheck that accounts for monthly wages and federal taxes
so that	the company can pay an employee and withhold federal taxes

The developers decide that his story is SMART enough. The amount for monthly wages is an input. The story does not need to specify how taxes are calculated from wages. The developers know that tax calculations are specified separately by the Internal Revenue Service. The information in the story is enough for the developers to write tests for it. □

The takeaway from the preceding example is that a story does not have to include all the information needed to implement it. It needs to include enough for developers to write tests for the story.

INVEST in Stories

The INVEST acronym provides a checklist for writing good user stories. The acronym stands for Independent, Negotiable, Valuable, Estimable, Small, and Testable.[12]

- *Independent* A good collection of stories avoids duplication of functionality across stories.
- *Negotiable* Stories are developed in collaborations or negotiations between users and developers. They summarize functionality; they are not contracts that spell out all the details.
- *Valuable* A good story provides value for some stakeholder.
- *Estimable* A good story is specific enough that developers can estimate the time and effort needed to implement it.
- *Small* A good story is small enough that it can be implemented in one iteration. Split compound or complex stories into simpler stories. See also the discussion of estimation in Section 4.2.
- *Testable* A good story can be measured and tested.

Clarifying the Benefit

The **As-a-I-want-to-so-that** template contains both some functionality (the want) and the benefit that drives the want. Clear benefits help developers make implementation decisions.

If the functionality in a user story does not contribute to the stated benefit, then either the functionality is not relevant, or there may be a missing story. Stories that are not relevant can be dropped. Clear benefits can also help avoid *gold plating*, which refers to continuing to work on a project beyond the point of meeting all the stakeholder needs.

When clarifying benefits, ask "Why?" Why does a stakeholder want something? "Why" questions tend to elicit cause and relevance; see Section 3.6. Respectfully continuing to ask *Why* questions can surface an underlying need that has higher priority for the user than the starting point. The *Why* questions may either be posed explicitly or explored through other modes of communication, such as surveys and observations.

Acceptance Tests

User stories are accompanied by acceptance tests that characterize the behavior to be implemented. Acceptance tests are part of the conversation between users and developers about user wants.

The following template for writing acceptance tests addresses three questions from Section 1.4:

- How to set up the environment (the conditions) for running a test?
- What is the test input or stimulus?
- What is the expected response to the input?

The template is:[13]

> **Given** ⟨*a precondition*⟩
> **when** ⟨*an event occurs*⟩
> **then** ⟨*ensure some outcome*⟩

The precondition sets up the environment, the event is the input stimulus, and the output is the response.

Example 3.13   The payroll user story might be accompanied by a test of the form:

> **Given** an employee is on the payroll and is single
> **when** the paycheck is created
> **then** use the federal tax tables for singles to compute the tax

□

Acceptance tests must be written using language that is meaningful for both users and developers. They must focus on the desired functionality or behavior, not on whether the implementation matches its specification.

3.4.2   Guidelines for System Features

Plan-driven requirements are written in plain English (or some other natural language) to make them accessible to both users and developers. Free-form English can be

Table 3.2 Structured English constructions for plan-driven requirements.

---

1. The ⟨*system*⟩ **shall** ⟨*response*⟩
2. **If** ⟨*preconditions*⟩ **then** the ⟨*system*⟩ **shall** ⟨*response*⟩
3. **When** ⟨*trigger*⟩ the ⟨*system*⟩ **shall** ⟨*response*⟩
4. **If** ⟨*preconditions*⟩ **when** ⟨*trigger*⟩ the ⟨*system*⟩ **shall** ⟨*response*⟩
5. **While** ⟨*state*⟩ the ⟨*system*⟩ **shall** ⟨*response*⟩
6. **Where** ⟨*feature*⟩ is enabled the ⟨*system*⟩ **shall** ⟨*response*⟩

---

imprecise and ambiguous, so the requirements follow style guidelines to keep them focused. A typical description of a system property has the following form:

The system shall have a certain property.

Meanwhile, here is a description of a system response to an event:

When event x occurs the system shall respond by doing y.

The rules in Table 3.2 go a step further than style guidelines: they introduce keywords and some syntax for writing system features. The keywords in bold are required words. Angle brackets, ⟨ and ⟩, enclose placeholders for English phrases. A study at Rolls-Royce Control Systems found that the rules handled a wide range of requirements.[14]

Example 3.14   Let us apply the rules in Table 3.2 to write some system features. The features describe a notification system for an airline.

The first rule is for a system capability or property:

The system **shall** support notifications by text message, email, and phone.

Events can trigger system responses:

When a flight's schedule changes, the system **shall** send a notification using the communication mode specified in the traveler's contact preferences.

The next requirement illustrates the use of state information. In this case, the traveler can be in one of two states: "in transit" with the airline, between source and destination, or "not traveling" with the airline.

While the traveler is in transit, the system **shall** send notifications about gate change information using the communication mode in the traveler's contact preferences.

The syntactic rules in Table 3.2 are offered as an illustrative set, not as a complete set for all situations. Note also that a realistic notification system might have separate sets of requirements for (a) a subsystem that decides what and when to send as a notification and (b) another subsystem to handle modes for contacting a traveler.   □

3.4.3   Perspective on User Stories

User stories are recommended for writing requirements that describe individual snippets of functionality. The main reason is that stories are written from the user's point of view. Stories also include the benefit of the functionality for a given role. A story therefore not only tells developers what to implement, it gives them a feel for the significance and relevance of its functionality to the user, and hence to the product.

Stories do have limitations, however, which stem from their focus on bits of functionality. They do not convey the "big picture," and it is hard to tell if a collection of stories is a complete description of a product. System features share these limitations because they too focus on bits of functionality.

Big Picture? As the number of stories increases, it is easy to lose sight of the big picture overview of a product. The big picture can be helpful during product design and implementation. User-experience scenarios in Section 3.5 and use cases in Chapter 5 are at the level of an overall user experience, so they do provide a larger context. They show how individual features contribute to the user experience.

Stories and use cases complement each other: use cases provide context and stories provide specific functionality.

Completeness? Completeness is another issue with user stories: there is no guarantee that a collection of stories describes all aspects of a product. A stakeholder may have been missed. Or, a stakeholder may have forgotten or neglected to mention something. Users often do not think of mentioning something that they take for granted, something that "everybody knows" in their environment.

Example 3.15   In Example 3.1, BBC staff worked with outside partners on video production. The partners were therefore stakeholders. Outside partners can be missed when individual stories are written – say, about editing or accessing the archive, in the BBC case.

With an end-to-end experience, however, all the steps need to be described, so overall experiences are more likely to identify all the needed functionality.   □

Note Quality attributes (nonfunctional requirements) such as performance and privacy are often overlooked. They may not have been discussed in the conversations between users and developers.

Deeper Needs? Conversations, interviews, and surveys are well suited to identifying articulated needs, which users are able or willing to speak about. The **I want to** phrasing in the user story template is also suited to articulated needs. From Section 3.3, users may have additional "deeper" needs. A skilled development team can uncover additional needs through observation, intuition, and empathy.

User-experience scenarios do include a primary user's emotional state. The **I want** in a story does not touch the user's emotional state, so latent needs are likely to remain latent.

3.5   Writing User-Experience Scenarios

A *user-experience scenario*, or *UX scenario*, is a narrative about a primary user's end-to-end experience. In plain language, the narrative seeks to bring to life the user, their situation, their frustrations, their delights, and emotional state before and after the product. A UX scenario can lead to insights into the full range of a user's needs and wants. A scenario can help to immerse developers in the user's experience so they will relate to the user as they define and build a product.[15]

3.5.1   Guidelines for User-Experience Scenarios

A UX scenario identifies the following:

- The primary user.
- What the user wants to experience or accomplish.
- The proposed benefit to the user.
- How the proposed benefit contributes to their overall experience.
- The user's emotional response in the overall experience.

Note that the proposed product is part of a larger overall experience. Looking ahead, the medical app in Example 3.16 is just part of a child's overall experience with doctors and hospitals. The app is not the sole focus for children and their parents.

A Template for UX Scenarios A UX scenario is a narrative or a story, not a checklist of items. As a helpful suggestion, consider the following elements when writing a UX scenario:

1. **Title** A descriptive title.
2. **Introduction** An introduction to the primary user; their motivation; what they might be thinking, doing, and feeling; and their emotional state – that is, whether they are mad, glad, sad, or scared.
3. **Situation** A brief description of the real-world situation and the need or opportunity to be addressed by the product. The description puts the need in the context of an overall experience.
4. **Outcome** The outcome for the user, including success metrics and what it would take for the solution to delight the user.

Together, the introduction and situation in a UX scenario correspond to the current state. The outcome corresponds to the desired state. What a UX scenario must not include is any premature commitment to a potential implementation, to how to get from the current to the desired state.

A Checklist for UX Scenarios The acronym SPICIER provides a checklist for writing a good UX scenario:

S: tells the beginning and end of a *story*

P: includes *personal* details

I: is *implementation-free*

C: it's the *customer's* story, not a product story

I: reveals deep *insight* about user needs

E: includes *emotions* and *environment*

R: is based on *research*

3.5.2   Case Study: A Medical Scenario

The scenario in the following example is prompted by a doctor's request for an app to provide reliable information for seriously ill children and their parents. From the start, the doctor described the motivation for the request (the current state) and her vision for an app (the desired state). On her own, the doctor outlined a UX scenario during the first two or three meetings. She did not have a list of features. She and her colleague were focused on the overall experience for parents and kids. The desired outcome drove the iterative development of the prototype for the children's hospital.

Example 3.16   The narrative in this example has two paragraphs: one for the introduction and situation, and another paragraph for the outcome.[16]

Title: A Medical-Information App for Kids and their Parents

Introduction Alice and Bob are worried about their six-year-old, Chris, who is seriously ill. The parents have scoured the Internet for Chris's condition, and that has left them more confused and worried than ever. They don't know who to trust. Chris has been a trooper, cheerfully engaging with the doctors and nurses. Now, Chris is scheduled for further tests and scans in the hospital. Alice and Bob are concerned about Chris being frightened at having to lie still, surrounded by big, unfamiliar, whirring machines.

Outcome Alice and Bob have one less thing to worry about. An app provided by the children's hospital gives them reliable information about Chris's specific condition. The app works on both smartphones and tablets, so they can sit down with Chris and go over content created specifically for kids. Chris has seen the video of the scanning machine several times. Alice and Bob also go over the graphic from the last visit to the doctor, where the doctor had used the touch screen on the tablet to highlight where sensors would be placed during the upcoming scan. Chris's biggest concern is now which playlist to choose for music during the upcoming scan.

Applying the SPICIER checklist to the preceding scenario, we get

S: **Story** The narrative begins with Alice and Bob worried not only about their child's health, but by the confusing information they are getting from the Internet. They are also worried about Chris's upcoming tests and scan in the hospital. The scenario ends with them having a reliable source of information.

P: **Personal** The personal details include parents' worries about the health of their six-year-old child.

I: **Implementation-Free** The focus of the scenario is on the experience. It does not go into the specifics of the user interface.

C: **Customer's Story** The scenario is about Alice and Bob and their six-year-old.

I: **Insight** The scenario includes key insights into who will use the app and what the app must provide to support their desired experiences. The primary users are parents, who want reliable information. Then come children. The app needs to support a separate kid-friendly experience. Where does the content come from? If doctors add and edit content, they will need their own interface. The outcome could be taken apart, sentence by sentence, for follow-up conversations about requirements.

E: **Emotions and Environment** The scenario is specific about the environment (a hospital). The scenario starts with the parents being worried. A key purpose of the app is to prepare children so they are not frightened when they are surrounded by big, unfamiliar medical equipment. The scenario ends with six-year-old Chris being more concerned about the music during a test than about the prospect of the test.

R: **Research** The scenario is based on interactions with doctors at a children's hospital.

□

3.6 Clarifying User Goals

Conversations with users about their needs often begin with goals that express intent, goals that need to be clarified and refined before they can implemented. For example, the conversation with two doctors about the medical app in Example 3.16 began with

We want an app that provides seriously ill children and their parents with reliable medical information.

This goal is soft, where *soft* means that it fails one or more of the SMART criteria. Recall that SMART stands for specific, measurable, achievable, relevant, and time-bound. These criteria apply broadly to goals, requirements, questions, actions, and so on. SMART goals can be readily implemented and tested.[17]

Soft goals arise naturally during requirements development. This section phrases user needs and requirements as goals and asks clarifying questions to refine soft goals into SMART subgoals and actions. In practice, goal refinement is an iterative process. The refinement of the initial goal for the medical app (presented at the beginning of this section) was spread across two or three sessions with the doctors. The term "reliable information" was refined into (a) content created by the doctors and their colleagues, and (b) links to text, images, and videos approved by the doctors.

A single initial soft goal can be refined into multiple subgoals. To keep track of subgoals that arise during requirements development, this section introduces goal hierarchies, with the initial goal(s) at the top (root) of a hierarchy. The children of a node represent subgoals.

3.6.1   Properties of Goals

Anything a user wants to accomplish can be viewed as a user goal. The want in the user story

> As a ... **I want to** get rides from trusted drivers **so that** ...

can be restated as the goal

> My goal is to get rides from trusted drivers.

System features also have corresponding user goals. The feature

> **The system shall** send notifications by text, email, or phone,
> based on the user's contact preferences.

has a corresponding goal from a user perspective:

> **My goal is to** receive notifications by text, email, or phone,
> based on my contact preferences.

Soft goals arise naturally in conversations with users about their requirements. Conversations often start out with high-level soft goals such as the following:

- (I want to) upgrade the payroll system.
- (I want to) get rides from trusted drivers.
- (I want to) manage inventories so we keep popular items in stock.

Each of these goals fails one or more of the SMART criteria. How specifically does the payroll system need to be upgraded, and by when? How do we identify a "trusted" driver? How much inventory do we need to keep a popular item in stock? How is popular defined? As we shall see, simple "How?" questions can be a powerful tool for clarifying user goals.

Example 3.17   For a small example of goal refinement, consider the soft business goal:

> Improve customer satisfaction

This soft goal is an aspiration. How will customer satisfaction be measured? The following refinement is specific and measurable:

> Increase Net Promoter Score by 20 percent

The refinement is specific because Net Promoter Score (NPS) is an accepted measure of customer satisfaction. The refined goal is measurable because it includes a target, 20 percent. The refinement is not yet SMART, because we do not know how it can be achieved. Nor do we know the time frame for achieving the target.   □

A Temporal Classification of Goals

User goals and requirements frequently fall into one of three categories: What do users want to achieve? Maintain? Optimize? This classification can serve as a checklist during requirements elicitation to probe for missing goals.[18]

- *Achieve/Cease* goals eventually get to a desired state; for example, send a notificaion.
- *Maintain/Avoid* goals keep a property invariant; for example, keep the shopping site up 24 hours a day, 7 days a week.
- *Optimize* goals involve a comparison between the current state and the desired state; for example, increase Net Promoter Score by 20 percent.

Example 3.18   In Example 3.9, keeping the lunar greenhouse temperature within a given range is a maintain goal. Checking (determining) the temperature at a given time is an achieve goal.   □

3.6.2   Asking Clarifying Questions

Some simple questions, respectfully asked, can be very helpful for discovering and clarifying user requirements. This section introduces three classes of questions to provide guidance on what to ask. The questions probe for (a) motivation, (b) options, and (c) quantification. They will be illustrated by asking questions in pseudo-English to avoid the ambiguities and multiple meanings of words in a natural language. Put motivation, options, and quantification questions in your own words to fit a conversation.[19]

Motivation Questions: Why? Why Not?

A *motivation* question explores the context, cause, constraints, or considerations for a goal. Motivation questions are of two kinds: *Why* and *Why Not*. *Why* questions tend to be motivation questions. The pseudo-English form for such questions is:

Why do you want to ⟨*goal*⟩?

The short form of the question is "**Why** ⟨*goal*⟩?" or simply "**Why**?" if the goal is clear from the context.

Example 3.19   In the lunar-greenhouse example, the user's initial goal was to get notifications about the temperature in the greenhouse. The relevant motivation question is

Why do you want to get notifications about the temperature?

This question would likely have elicited the response:

Because I want to maintain the temperature within a range.

Maintaining the temperature is a higher goal than the initial goal. Maintaining provides the motivation for checking the temperature.   □

Example 3.20   Consider a conversation about providing contractors with mobile access to their business data. (This example is based loosely on Example 3.10.) The conversation might begin as follows:

Developer. "Help me understand. **Why do you want to** have mobile access to business data?
Contractor. "So I can produce invoices on the spot, at the customer site."

The conversation can then turn to what else contractors need to produce invoices. Perhaps there is additional functionality related to invoices that the app could provide.   □

Why Not questions are motivation questions that explore constraints or conditions on a goal or a task. They can elicit constraints that users neglect to mention; for example, because the constraints are taken for granted. A *Why Not* question has either of the following forms:

> **Why not** ⟨*goal*⟩?
> **What stops us from** ⟨*goal*⟩?

Example 3.21   This is a real example of a *Why-Not* question:

> **Why not** add these features to the current release?
> Because the customer-support teams won't be ready.

Even if some features are easy to develop and included in a product, a company may choose to withhold them, if the support structure for the product is not in place.   □

Options and Quantification Questions

Options questions explore possible solution approaches or implementation options. They explore subgoals or subtasks that contribute to the success of a goal. Options questions are of two kinds: *How* and *How Else*. Their pseudo-English forms are:

> **How can we** ⟨*goal*⟩?
> **How else can we** ⟨*goal*⟩?

How Else questions tend to elicit alternatives. If the goal is clear from the context, the simple forms are "**How?**" and "**How else?**".

   Quantification questions explore metrics and criteria for determining whether an optimize goal has been accomplished. They are of two kinds: *How Much* and *How Many*.

Example 3.22   Consider a brainstorming session with users about their interest in listening to music on the go. The following conversation illustrates the use of options questions:

How can we provide music while mobile? Download media to a portable personal device.

How else can we provide music while mobile? Stream music to a device over the network.   □

During elicitation, clarifying questions can uncover information that users may not have thought to share earlier. Users tend to neglect information that "everybody knows" in their environment. Respectful motivation and options questions can help developers overcome this barrier to communication.

When using clarifying questions, focus on the intent of the question; that is, on whether it is a motivation, options, or quantification question. Rephrase the pseudo-English so the wording fits naturally into the conversation. Keep conversations informal.

3.6.3   Organizing Goals into Hierarchies

Goal analysis is the process of clarifying starting or top-level goals until SMART subgoals are reached. As clarified subgoals are identified, it is helpful to organize goals and subgoals into a hierarchy. A goal is higher in the hierarchy than its subgoals. More precisely, a *goal hierarchy* has nodes representing goals and edges representing relationships between goals; see Fig. 3.7 for an example. The nodes in a hierarchy are of two kinds:

- An *and* node represents a goal G with subgoals $G_1, G_2, \ldots, G_k$, where every one of $G_1, G_2, \ldots, G_k$ must be satisfied for goal G to be satisfied. For example, the goal in Fig. 3.8(a) of beating a competitor is satisfied only if both of the following are satisfied: release the product by August, and deliver a superior product.

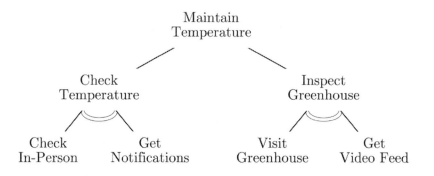

Figure 3.7 A goal hierarchy for the lunar greenhouse, Example 3.9.

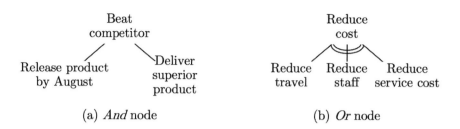

(a) *And* node   (b) *Or* node

Figure 3.8 Examples of *and* and *or* nodes in a goal hierarchy.

- An *or* node represents a goal G with subgoals $G_1, G_2, \ldots, G_k$, where goal G can be satisfied by satisfying any one of $G_1, G_2, \ldots, G_k$. For example, the goal in Fig. 3.8(b) of reducing costs can be satisfied by doing any combination of the following: reduce travel costs, reduce staff, or reduce the cost of service after delivery.

  An *or* node will be identified by a double arc connecting the edges between the goal node and its child nodes.

The hierarchy in Fig. 3.7 is a tree, but, in general, a subgoal may be shared by more than one higher goal.

Example 3.23   In Example 3.9, the user's initial request was for help with checking the temperature in the lunar greenhouse on a regular basis. This initial goal is represented by the first (left) child of the root in Fig. 3.7. The two children of this *or* node represent alternatives for satisfying the goal:

> **How can we** check the temperature?
> Check in-person, by going to the greenhouse.
> **How else**?
> Check automatically, and get notifications of exceptions.

The developers built an app to check the temperature automatically. But, that was not the end of the story. Checking the temperature is part of a larger context, elicited by a motivation question:

> **Why** check the temperature?
> To maintain the temperature within a range.

The higher goal is to maintain the greenhouse in a range that is warm enough to grow plants, but not too warm to avoid unnecessary water loss through evaporation.

This higher goal is the top (root) goal in Fig. 3.7. Another options question elicits what can be done to meet the top goal:

> **How can we** maintain the temperature within the range?
> Inspect the greenhouse visually, and adjust the controls, if needed.

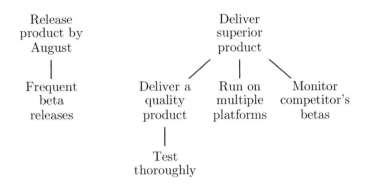

Figure 3.9 A goal hierarchy. See Fig. 3.10 for the contributing and conflicting goals in this hierarchy.

The root is an *and* node. To maintain the temperature, the user needs both the ability to both check it (left) and to inspect the greenhouse if it is outside the given range. The check subgoal is at the left child and the inspect goal is at the right child. The inspect subgoal is an *or* node. A visual inspection can be conducted in-person or by video.

The developers chose to provide a video feed. Adjustments still had to be made manually, since the app had read-only access to sensor and video feeds from the greenhouse, but it did not have permission to touch the controls. The user was happy because, with the app, a trip to the greenhouse was needed only when adjustments had to be made.   □

Example 3.23 ties together several of the concepts in this section: express user needs as goals; classify them as achieve, maintain, or optimize goals; use motivation and options questions to clarify and refine goals; and then use hierarchies to organize the proliferation of goals and subgoals. The top-level (root) goal in the hierarchy in Fig. 3.7 is a maintain goal. The other goals at the nodes are achieve goals. The articulated user need for an app to check the temperature corresponds to the goal for checking the temperature. Clarifying questions elicit the underlying motivation (Need) to maintain the temperature. Further questions uncover the latent need for a video feed from the greenhouse. This latent need corresponds to the goal at the bottom right of the hierarchy.

3.6.4 Contributing and Conflicting Goals

Informally, two user requirements conflict, if we cannot simultaneously satisfy them both. For example, "Add testers" to improve product quality potentially conflicts with "Reducing staff" to lower cost. If we add testers, we are adding, not reducing staff. Goal analysis gives us crisp SMART subgoals to check for conflicts.

Goal G_1 *conflicts* with goal G_2 if satisfaction of G_1 hinders the satisfaction of G_2. Goal G_1 *contributes* to goal G_2 if satisfaction of G_1 aids the satisfaction of G_2. For example, "Add testers" contributes to "Improve product quality."

The conflicts and contributes relationships will be depicted by adding directed edges to a hierarchy. An edge is marked ++ for a strong contribution, + for a weak contribution, -- for a strong conflict, and - for a weak conflict. For clarity, edges representing weak contributions or weak conflicts will be dashed.

Example 3.24   This example begins with the goal hierarchy in Fig. 3.9. The contributing and conflicting goals in this hierarchy are highlighted in Fig. 3.10. The hierarchy is motivated by the browser wars between Netscape and Microsoft; see Section 2.6.2. The hierarchy refines Netscape's two top-level goals:

- Release a product by August.
- Deliver a superior product.

There is only one goal in the hierarchy with more than one subgoal. It is the top-level goal of delivering a superior product. This goal has an *and* node, so, for it to be satisfied, all three of its subgoals must be satisfied. Netscape's strategy for a superior browser was to run on multiple operating systems. Microsoft's browser ran only on Windows, at the time. Netscape also closely monitored beta releases from Microsoft to ensure that its browser would have competitive features.

The graph in Fig. 3.10 shows the contributes and conflicts relations for the hierarchy in Fig. 3.9. Since subgoals contribute to higher goals, there are directed edges from subgoals (child nodes) to higher goals (parent nodes). As an example, the goal at the top right, "Deliver superior product," has three edges coming into it. Two of the edges are for strong contributions, so they are shown as solid edges. The third edge is for a weak contribution from "Monitor competitor's betas," so it is dashed.

There are two edges for conflicts, both to "Test thoroughly." At Netscape, the number of testers was fixed, so more platforms (operating systems) to test meant more work for the same testers. Furthermore, every beta release had to be fully tested, so more frequent betas also meant additional work for the same testers. Hence the conflicts

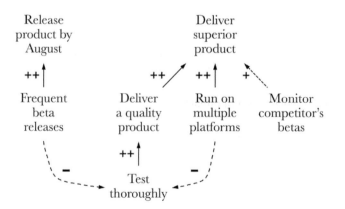

Figure 3.10 Contributing and conflicting goals for the hierarchy in Fig. 3.9.

edges from "Frequent beta releases" and "Run on multiple platforms" to "Test thoroughly."   □

The goal hierarchies in this section illustrate how soft high-level goals can be refined into more specific subgoals. The hierarchies grow down from higher goals to subgoals. This process of goal refinement can stop when SMART goals are reached. Here, SMART means that developers know how to implement them.

Example 3.25 Consider the following refinement of "Run on multiple platforms":

> How many platforms does the browser need to run on?
> Three: Windows, MacOS, and Unix.

No further refinement is needed, since the last goal of running on the three platforms tells the developers what they need to know to implement this requirement.   □

3.7   Identifying Security Attacks

The goal analysis techniques of Section 3.6.3 can be applied to defend against potential security attacks. The idea is to think like an adversary intent on attacking a system. Goal analysis can then be used to identify ways in which an attacker can achieve the goal of breaking into the system. Once security vulnerabilities are identified, defensive actions can be taken to foil possible attacks.[20]

3.7.1   Attack Trees: Think Like an Attacker

How might an attacker break into a system? An *attack tree* is a goal hierarchy, where the top-level goal is the attacker's goal of breaking into a system. The idea is to think like an attacker and identify security holes, so corrective actions can be taken to close them.

While building an attack tree, it is better to brainstorm and include ways that are later dismissed as impossible. Hackers typically launch attacks in ways that the system designers never anticipated. Therefore, it pays to make an attack tree as complete as possible. Security threats can be social as well as technical. Social threats include phishing attacks, bribery, deception, and so on. The attack tree in Fig. 3.11 includes a representative set of threats.

3.7.2   Finding Possible Attacks

Once an attack tree is built, possible attacks can be identified by marking possible nodes, starting with the leaves.

1. **At the Leaves** Mark each leaf p if that leaf is possible; that is, the goal at the leaf is achievable. Otherwise, mark it i for impossible.

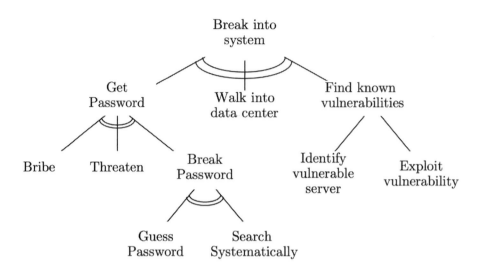

Figure 3.11 An attack tree. For simplicity, this tree includes a representative rather than a complete set of security threats.

2. **Bottom-Up** Mark each *or*-node *p* if one or more of its children is marked *p*. Mark each *and*-node *p* if all of its children are marked *p*. Otherwise, mark a node *i* for impossible. Continue until all nodes are marked.
3. **At the Root** If the root is marked *i*, no attack is possible, according to this attack tree. Otherwise, start identifying an attack by selecting the root.
4. **Top-Down**. For each selected *or*-node, select one of its possible children. For each *and*-node, select all of its children. Continue while there are new nodes that can be selected.
5. The selected nodes represent an attack.

Example 3.26 With the attack tree in Fig. 3.11, suppose that the following leaf goals are impossible:

- Threaten or blackmail a system administrator into revealing the password for the system.
- Walk into the data center and get physical access to the system.
- "Identify vulnerable server" is short for "Identify a server with a known vulnerability." Suppose that all servers have been fully updated to close all known vulnerabilities. (In practice, this is a risky assumption, because some server somewhere may have been overlooked.)

The corresponding leaves are marked *i* in Fig. 3.12; the other leaves are marked *p*, for possible.

Working bottom-up, "Threaten" is one of three children of an *or*-node. The other two children are marked possible, so "Get password" is possible.

Meanwhile, "Identify vulnerable server" is at a child of an *and*-node. Since we have assumed that this leaf goal is impossible, its parent goal, "Find known vulnerabilities," is impossible.

The root is an *or*-node, with three children. The first child, "Get password," is possible, so the root is marked possible. The other two children of the root are impossible. The marked attack tree appears in Fig. 3.12.

The root is marked *p*, so an attack is possible. To identify an attack, start by selecting the root and work top down. Since the root is an *or*-node, for an *or*-node, we need only one child to be possible. Let us select "Get password," an *or*-node. It has a child, "Break password," marked *p*, so let us select it. That leaves us with a choice between guessing the password and systematically searching for it.

The conclusion is that a hacker could break into the system by guessing the password or systematically searching for it. The countermeasure is to choose a strong password that is not easily guessed.   □

Estimating the Cost of an Attack

Cost information can be used to do a more granular analysis of security threats than doing a binary analysis of possible and impossible threats. The idea is to begin by associating cost estimates with the leaf goals in an attack tree. The estimates can then be propagated bottom-up to the root to estimate the minimum cost of an attack. With this approach, domain expertise is required for making the initial cost estimates for the leaf goals.

3.8   Conclusion

It can take several conversations to elicit (discover) what users really want. Why? There are three main reasons or factors:

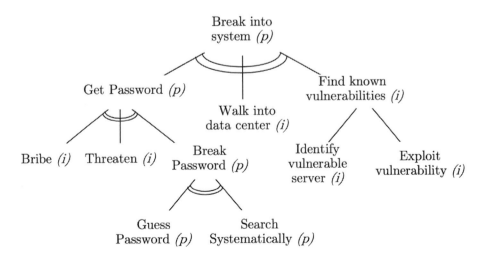

Figure 3.12 The result of marking nodes *p* for possible or *i* for impossible.

- **Levels of Needs** Needs can be classified as articulated observable, tacit, and latent, which they exhibit through their words, actions, and sentiments. Interviews and surveys tend to access just the first of these levels, the needs they articulate.
- **Multiple Goals** Users do not speak with one voice; that is, they can have differing goals and priorities. It may not be possible to simultaneously satisfy them all.
- **Changes over Time** User wants can change over time, as new needs emerge, and there are changes in the users' business and the marketplace.

For these reasons, requirements development is an iterative process, with both agile and plan-driven methods. The basic iterative cycle has three logically distinct activities: elicitation, analysis, and validation. Elicitation consists of the discovery of user needs, which are recorded as user stories, system features, or scenarios. Analysis consists of refining and prioritizing raw user requirements into a coherent set of product and process requirements. Validation consists of confirming that the project is on the right track.

Agile methods validate with working software. Each iteration combines requirements and implementation activities, so each iteration is essentially an elicit-analyze-build-validate cycle. From Section 2.2, each Scrum sprint begins with an elicited product backlog, which is analyzed during sprint planning. The result of analysis, the sprint backlog, is then built and validated during the sprint review with stakeholders. The review also elicits user requirements for the next iteration.

Plan-driven methods validate with specifications and paper designs. Requirements development is part of the plan phase, prior to implementation. the plan for a product includes a detailed validated software requirements specification (SRS). Each requirements iteration is an elicit-analyze-specify-validate cycle.

The preceding description of requirements activities has touched on several kinds of requirements. Elicitation begins with business goals (a kind of requirement) and produces un-prioritized user requirements, which describe user needs. Analysis then produces a product definition, in the form of functional requirements and quality attributes. Quality attributes are also known as nonfunctional requirements. Quality attributes are system properties, such as scale and security. Plan-driven methods create a software requirements specification.

User requirements are written in two main ways: at the feature level, as separate bits of functionality; or at the scenario level, as end-to-end experiences or interactions. As their names imply, user stories describe something that benefits a user and system features describe a system capability. Both are at the feature level. With feature-level requirements, it can be hard to tell if a collection of user requirements is complete. Scenarios, meanwhile, are end-to-end descriptions, so they convey the big picture of a system. User-experience (UX) scenarios seek to bring a user to life, including what frustrates them and what would delight them. Developers can then have a "real" person in mind, while they make design and implementation decisions. Use cases (Chapter 5) characterize system behavior through user–system interactions.

Goal analysis is the clarification and refinement of user needs and goals. Clarification and refinement are helpful during both requirements elicitation and analysis.

How and *Why* questions are helpful for eliciting specific, measurable, achievable, relevant, and time-bound (SMART) user requirements. The questions and goal analysis can also be applied during requirements analysis to organize goals and identify conflicting goals. Goal analysis is a general technique that has applications well beyond requirements. Attack trees, which model security attacks, are goal hierarchies where the top-level goal is the attacker's goal of breaking into a system. Once attacks are identified, we can strengthen defenses against them.

Further Reading

- For an overview of requirements development and engineering, see SWEBOK 3.0 [36].
- The book on Scenario-Focused Engineering by De Bonte and Fletcher describes user-experience scenarios and agile development with an emphasis on requirements. It also introduces levels of needs.
- For modeling security attacks and how to defend against them, see Schneier [165].
- See also the "Notes for Chapter 3: User Requirements" section.

Exercises for Chapter 3

Exercise 3.1   In your own words, summarize the issues that led to the failure of the BBC Digital Media Initiative, described in Example 3.1.

Exercise 3.2   The two diagrams in Fig. 3.13 are for agile software-development processes. The Fast Feedback Process (left) highlights requirements-related activities. Assume that the output of "Identify Needs" is a set of user stories. XP (right) highlights implementation-related activities.

Draw a diagram for a unified process that combines the two agile processes. Your diagram must highlight both requirements-related and implementation-related activities. Avoid duplication of activities in the unified process.

Exercise 3.3   Come up with your own examples of:

a) Articulated needs.
b) Observable needs.
c) Tacit needs.
d) Latent needs.

The examples need not be from the same software project. For each example, address the following questions: What is the underlying need in the example? How is the need exhibited? How is it accessed, in terms of listening, observing, and/or empathizing?

Exercise 3.4   Write user stories for the pool-service application in Example 1.7. Include stories from both a technician's and a manager's perspective.

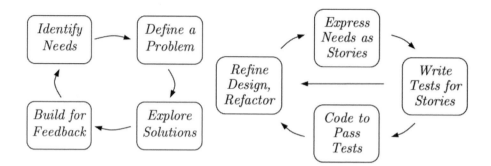

Figure 3.13 Two agile development processes.

Exercise 3.5 Use the pseudo-English syntax in Table 3.2 to write a set of features for the pool-service application in Example 1.7. Is the set of features complete? Briefly justify your answer.

Exercise 3.6 Consider a pet-adoption service that matches current pet owners with potential adopters.

a) What is your problem definition for such a service?
b) Use the pseudo-English syntax in Table 3.2 to write a set of features for the adoption service.
c) Is your set of features unambiguous, verifiable, ranked, and complete? Briefly explain your answers.

Exercise 3.7 Write a UX scenario based on the needs of the user in Example 3.9; the example deals with the Lunar Greenhouse. Give the user a name and use your imagination to fill in details, so your scenario conforms with the SPICIER guidelines.

Exercise 3.8 Write a UX scenario for a frequent traveler who wants an app to help deal with busy airports, flight delays, gate changes, tight connections, and the like. Put yourself in the shoes of the frequent traveler. What are your needs and desired end-to-end experience? What is your emotional state? Include details, in line with the SPICIER guidelines.

Exercise 3.9 Write four user stories based on the following scenario. Let these be the highest priority user stories, based on perceived business value for the client.

Your team is doing a project for a nationwide insurance company that prides itself on its personalized customer service. Each customer has a designated insurance agent, who is familiar with the customer's situation and preferences. The company has engaged you to create an application that will route customer phone calls and text messages to the designated agent.

And there may be times when the designated agent is not available. If so, the caller needs to speak to an agent – say, to report an accident – then, as a backup, the auto-mated application must offer to connect the caller with another agent at the local branch (preferred) or at the regional support center, which is staffed 24 hours a day, 7 days a week. The regional center will be able to help the caller because the application will simultaneously send both the phone call and the relevant customer information to the regional agent's computer.

At any choice point, callers will be able to choose to leave a voice message or request a callback.

Exercise 3.10   The goals for the San Francisco Bay Area Rapid Transit System (BART) included the following:[21]

- Serve more passengers.
- Minimize costs.
- Improve train safety.

Apply goal analysis to refine these top-level goals into SMART goals.

a) Show the questions that you use for refining goals into subgoals. Briefly explain the rationale for each question.
b) Draw the goal hierarchy.
c) Identify the contributing and conflicting goals.
d) Briefly explain why your leaf goals are SMART.

4   Requirements Analysis

Once user needs and goals are recorded as user requirements, the emphasis shifts to requirements analysis. User requirements, even specific and measurable ones, correspond to wish lists from the various stakeholders. Requirements analysis prioritizes these wish lists to define precisely what to build as a product; see Fig. 4.1. To prioritize, we must answer three questions. First, what properties of the product will prioritization be based on? Examples of properties include not only cost and functionality, but usefulness, usability, and desirability. Second, how will the properties be quantified? Quantification involves classification into ranked categories; for example, must-have, should-have, could-have, won't have. Third, how do we rank order requirements based on a combination of properties, such as benefit, cost, and perhaps risk?

This chapter considers a range of prioritization techniques: checklists, group consensus, heuristic. The chapter concludes with formal models that relate development effort and program size.

This chapter will enable the reader to:

- Do agile iteration planning, including estimation of development effort for work items and the selection of the highest-priority items for implementation during an iteration.
- Classify requirements by using MoSCoW prioritization and by balancing expected benefit, estimated cost, and potential risk.
- Use Kano prioritization of requirements, driven by what satisfies users and what dissatisfies them.
- Describe the Cocomo models for estimating development effort as a function of program size.

4.1   A Checklist Approach

For a simple project, some checklist questions may be enough to steer the project. The purpose of the questions is to define how a proposed product would contribute to the primary stakeholder's goals. Ideally, the proposed produce would be useful, usable, and desirable for delivering the stakeholder's overall experience in accomplishing the goal.[1]

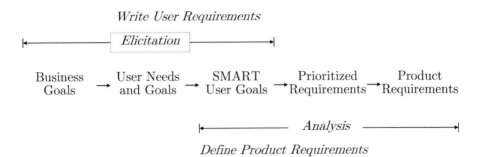

Figure 4.1 A view of requirements development. Clarification and refinement of user needs and goals into SMART user goals begins during elicitation and continues into requirements analysis. For simplicity, this figure shows only product requirements.

Example 4.1   Let us apply the useful, usable, desirable criteria to the initial and redesigned versions of the speech-therapy app of Example 1.3. The app had two main stakeholders: parents and their children. Parents bought the initial version because they felt it would be useful for their children. But, they were frustrated because they found it too hard to use. Thus, for parents, the app was desirable and useful, but not usable. Children, meanwhile, had no trouble using the initial version but were bored because it was like a lesson. Thus, for children, the initial version was usable but neither desirable nor useful (for entertaining them).

   The makers of the product found a creative way of redesigning it to remove usability as a pain point for parents and to make the app desirable and useful for children. They simplified the user interface for parents and made the app more like a game for children.

□

Checklist Questions

The following list of questions is offered as a starting point for creating a checklist for a project.

- Who is the primary stakeholder?
- Who are the secondary stakeholders?

While the needs of all stakeholders must be addressed, it helps to focus on a class of primary stakeholders. We can then begin by focusing on a product that really works for "the primary customer." Once we have an initial product proposal, it can be adapted or redefined to meet the requirements of other stakeholders. For example, products that have been designed for accessibility have benefited all users.

- What is the primary stakeholder's expected end-to-end experience?

The end-to-end experience provides the context for the stakeholder's use of the product. The question can expose any gaps between the proposed product and the stakeholder's desired role for the product in the overall experience. User-experience (UX) scenarios are designed to expose such gaps; see Section 3.5.

• Will the product be useful?

A *useful* product serves a need. This question relates to the product's functionality – a product that does not provide required functionality is not very useful. Instead of a yes-no answer, we can quantify usefulness by the degree to which the product provides the desired functionality.

• Will the product be easy to use?
• Will it do its job well?

A *usable* product is both easy to use and does its job well. Such products can either be used immediately or can be readily learned. The question about doing a job well opens the door for a discussion of quality attributes such as scale, performance, and reliability. For example, a product that has bugs and fails frequently is not very usable.

• Will the product be desirable?
• Will customers consider it "worth what paid for"?

A *desirable* product is one that customers really want and consider well worth the price that they paid for it. "Worth what paid for" is a measure of customer satisfaction. Desirable therefore touches on both aesthetic value and value as in cost/benefit.

Useful, Usable, and Desirable Are Independent

Useful, usable, and desirable are shown at vertices of a triangle in Fig. 4.2 to emphasize that they relate to the same product but are independent properties:

• A product can be useful and desirable, but not usable; for example, a product with a complex interface that is hard to use. Apple is known for its great products; however, after one of its product announcements, the news headline was "Innovative, but Uninviting." Why? Because "using the features is not always easy."[2]
• A product can be usable and desirable, but not useful; for example, fashionable apps that are downloaded, but rarely used.

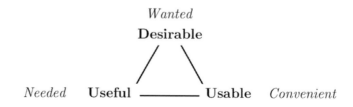

Figure 4.2 Key product attributes. Great products address needs, wants, and ease of use.

- A product can be useful and usable, but not desirable; for example, an application that gets treated as a commodity or is not purchased at all. Section 4.5 explores useful features that are taken for granted if they are implemented, but cause dissatisfaction if they do not live up to expectations.

4.2   Relative Estimation: Iteration Planning

Agile iteration planning is a form of incremental requirements analysis, in which the highest-priority user stories are selected for implementation during that iteration. Lower-priority requirements remain on the wish list and may eventually be dropped if time runs out. Iteration planning involves both prioritization and estimation: prioritization to rank order and select user stories, and estimation to determine how much the development team can implement during an iteration.

To *prioritize* a set of items is to rank order or linearly order the items, without needing to quantify them. To *estimate* is to quantify some property of an item; for example, the development effort for implementing a user story. People tend to be better at prioritizing (comparing) than they are at estimating (measuring).

This section begins with the phenomenon of anchoring, which can lead to biased estimates. Avoid anchoring! The section then considers the estimation of development effort during iterative planning.

4.2.1   Anchoring Can Bias Decisions

Cognitive bias is the human tendency to make systematic errors in judgment under uncertainty. *Anchoring* occurs when people make estimates by adjusting a starting value, which is called an *anchor value*. The anchor value introduces cognitive bias because new estimates tend to be skewed toward it (the anchor value).[3]

In order to get unbiased estimates from developers, avoid telling them about customer or management expectations about effort, schedule, or budgets.

Example 4.2   A single number in pages of documentation was enough to anchor estimates in a case study by Jorge Aranda and Steve Easterbrook. The participants were asked to estimate the time it would take to deliver a software application.[4] Each participant was given a 10-page requirements document and a three-page "project-setting" document. The project-setting document had two kinds of information: (1) a brief description of the client organization, including quotes from interviews; and (2) background about the development team that would implement the application, including the skills, experience, and culture of the developers.

The 23 participants were divided into three groups. The only difference between the instructions given to the three groups was a quote on the second page of the project-setting document, supposedly from a middle manager; see Table 4.1.

The results confirmed the phenomenon of anchoring. The mean development time estimates from the three groups were 8.3 months for the control group, 6.8 months for

Table 4.1 In a case study of the effect of anchoring on software effort estimation, three groups were given instructions that differed only in a single comment from a manager, shown here.

- **Group 1** Their quote had no mention of time.
- – "I admit I have no experience estimating."

- **Group 2** Their quote mentioned two months.
- – "I admit I have no experience with software projects, but I guess this will take about two months to finish."

- **Group 3** Their quote mentioned 20 months.
- – "I admit I have no experience with software projects, but I guess this will take about 20 months to finish."

the 2-month group, and 17.4 months for the 20-month group. The mean estimates from the experienced participants in the three groups were 9 months, 7.8 months, and 17.8 months, respectively. Further studies would be needed to explain the small differences between the control group and the low-anchor group.   □

4.2.2   Agile Story Points

Agile iteration planning relies on two kinds of estimates. (1) Users assess the expected benefit to them of a user story. They assign each story a priority, typically on a scale of 1–3. (2) Developers estimate the complexity or work effort for implementing a story by assigning *story points*, where the simplest story gets 1 point. This section considers two scales for story points: 1–3 and the Fibonacci numbers. Both the user priority and the story points are recorded when the story is written; see the user story template in Fig. 4.3.

Story points estimates of size and effort follow from the observation that people are better at prioritization than estimation; that is, at predicting relative, rather than absolute magnitude. Given work items A and B, it is easier to estimate whether A requires more or less effort than B, or whether A is simpler or more complex than B. It is harder to estimate the code size of an implementation of either A or B.

Point Values 1, 2, 3
The simplest scale for story points has point values 1, 2, and 3, corresponding to easy, medium, and hard. For example, the developers might assign points as follows:

- 1 *point* for a story that the team knows how to do and could do quickly (where the team defines quickly).
- 2 *points* for a story that the team knows how to do, but the implementation of the story would take some work.

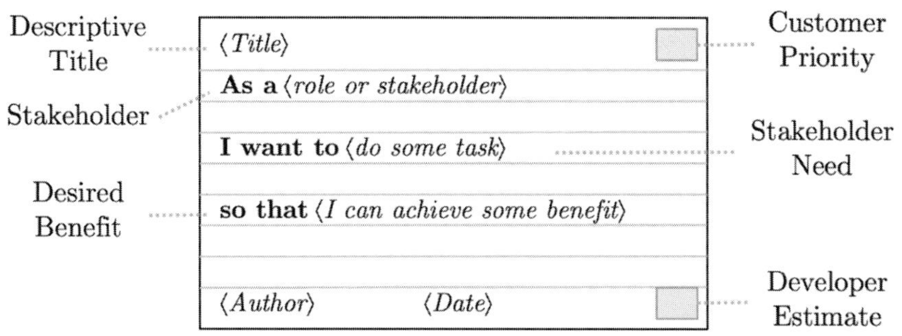

Figure 4.3 Connextra's index card template for a user story. The card includes fields for a user-assigned priority for benefit and a developer estimate of the work effort. Connextra was a London startup that, sadly, did not make it.

- 3 *points* for a story that the team would need to figure out how to implement.

Hard or 3-point stories are candidates for splitting into simpler stories.

Example 4.3   A development team assigns 1 point to the following story because they can readily extract and count words from a document, even if they have to strip out LaTeX formatting commands:

- **1 point. As a** book editor, **I want to** count words by section and subsection, **so that** I can compare the sizes of the sections.

  The team assigns 2 points to the following story because they know how to implement it, but it will take some work to hook up with the sensor feed from the greenhouse and send notifications:

- **2 points. As a** researcher studying plant growth during a space voyage, **I want to** get notifications when the temperature goes out of range, **so that** I can tightly control the climate in the Lunar Greenhouse.

The team assigns 3 points to the following story because they are not sure how to do color matching of images; for example, floral prints and geometric designs.

- **3 points. As an** interior designer, **I want to** color match wallpapers and curtain fabrics, **so that** I can offer a wider selection to my clients.

  □

Fibonacci Story Points

With experience, as the team gets better at assigning points to stories, they can go beyond an easy-medium-hard or three-value scale. A Fibonacci scale uses the point values $1, 2, 3, 5, 8, \ldots$ The reason for a Fibonacci rather than a linear $1, 2, 3, 4, 5, \ldots$ scale is that points are rough estimates and it is easier to assign points if there are some

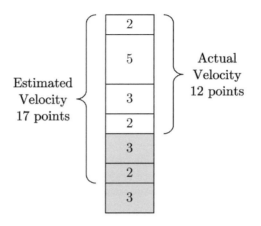

Figure 4.4 Estimated and actual velocity for an iteration. The team planned 17 points worth of work, but completed only 12 points worth.

gaps in the scale. The gaps leave room for a new story to be slotted in, based on its relative complexity.

4.2.3   Velocity of Work

Agile methods like Scrum do not specify how users and developers prioritize stories during iteration planning. They leave it to developers and users to jointly exercise their judgment in selecting the stories that will be implemented during an iteration. In addition to properties of stories, such as user benefit and development effort, the selection is based on how much the developers can implement in an iteration.

With any point scale, a team's *velocity* is the number of story points the team can complete in an iteration. A key assumption behind this definition is that a story point is a unit of work; for example, a 2-point story takes twice as much effort as a 1-point story. While this assumption does not always hold, velocity is still a useful measure.

Example 4.4   In Fig. 4.4, the team's estimated velocity was 17, but it only completed 12 points worth of stories in an iteration. For the next iteration, the team can adjust its estimated velocity based on its actual velocity from recent iterations. One possible approach is to use the average velocity for the past few, say three, iterations.   □

4.3   Structured Group Consensus Estimates

Unbiased consensus estimates from groups can be more accurate than individual estimates from members of a group. This observation dates back to Aristotle, who noted that, together, many perspectives from ordinary people were very likely to be better than those from a few experts.[5] The group estimation techniques in this section are variations on the theme of collecting rounds of independent estimates until consensus is reached. At the end of each round, group members get some information about the estimates from other group members.

Example 4.5 Consider the experience of the retailer Best Buy in estimating the number of gift cards they would sell around Christmas. The estimates from the internal experts proved to be 95 percent accurate. The consensus estimates from 100 randomly chosen employees proved to be 99.9 percent accurate. Both groups began with the actual sales number from the prior year.[6] □

Example 4.6 "How many lines of code will your team collectively write this semester?" Students were asked this question about halfway into their semester-long team projects. Each student wrote down an independent estimate, which they later shared with their team members.

The students were surprised at the wide range of estimates within each team of four students. As a representative example, the estimates ranged between 2,000 and 5,000 lines. After consulting with each other, they arrived at a consensus estimate of between 2,500 and 3,000 lines. □

4.3.1 Wideband Delphi and Planning Poker

The group estimation techniques in this section originated with the Delphi forecasting method, designed at RAND Corporation in the 1950s. The designers of the method were concerned that simply bringing a group together for a roundtable discussion would not work.[7] They experimented with how they addressed two key issues:

- **Avoiding Cognitive Bias** Groups are subject to anchoring and groupthink, where some members are swayed and adapt to the group instead of giving their own opinion.
- **Converging on Consensus** How can the individual forecasts be combined into a consensus forecast?

The Delphi method structures group interactions to arrive at a consensus forecast. The method begins with each group member independently supplying an initial forecast. The individual forecasts are then combined to provide feedback for the members. The feedback consists of the range of the forecasts, and some summary information, such as the median forecast. The forecast-feedback steps are repeated until the group converges on either a single forecast or a range of forecasts. The group members never meet.

---

repeat
    Participants anonymously submit individual estimates
    if the estimates have converged enough
        done
    else
        The moderator convenes a group meeting to discuss outliers

---

Figure 4.5 The Wideband Delphi method.

Wideband Delphi

For software projects, group discussion can lead to valuable insights that can be useful during design, coding, and testing. Any concerns that surface during the discussions can be recorded and addressed later. Pitfalls can hopefully be avoided. Such insights are missed if group members are kept apart to soften cognitive bias. Perhaps the benefits of group discussion outweigh the risks of bias.

The *Wideband Delphi* method, outlined in Fig. 4.5, combines rounds of private individual estimates with group discussion between rounds. The members have a chance to explain the reasoning behind their estimates. The method has been used successfully for both up-front and agile planning.[8]

Planning Poker

A variant of the Wideband Delphi method, called *Planning Poker* is used for estimation during agile iteration planning. In Planning Poker, participants are given cards marked with Fibonacci story points $1, 2, 3, 5, 8, \ldots$ Each developer independently and privately picks a card, representing their estimate for the user story under discussion. All developers then reveal their cards simultaneously. If the individual estimates are close to each other, consensus has been reached. More likely, there will be some high cards and some low cards, with the others in the middle.

The discussion begins with the developers with the high and low cards. Do they know something that the others don't? Or, are they missing something? The only way to find out is through group discussion. The process then repeats for further rounds of individual card selection and group discussion until consensus is reached.

A moderator captures key comments from the group discussion of a story, so that the comments can be addressed during implementation and testing.[9]

4.3.2   The Original Delphi Method

With the original Delphi method, the group members were kept apart and anonymous. Instead of direct contact with each other, they were provided with feedback about where their estimate stood, relative to the others. Consensus was achieved by having several rounds of estimates and feedback.

	Round 1	2	3	4
Expert 1	1,000	525	332	349
2	200	256	300	292
3	300	250	250	276
4	150	184	200	206
5	125	158	166	167

Figure 4.6 An application of the Delphi method with five experts. The same data appears in both tabular and graphical form.

Example 4.7 The data in Fig. 4.6 is for four rounds of forecasts by a group of five experts. The same data appears in tabular and graphical form.

The first round forecasts range from a low of 125 to a high of 1,000. The median forecast for the first round is 200. In the second round, the range of forecasts narrows to 158–525. The ranges for the third and fourth rounds are close: 166–332 and 167–349, respectively.

Note that the group is converging on a range, not on a single forecast. With forecasts, it is not unusual for experts to have differences of opinion. □

In different forecasting exercises, the designers experimented with different forms of feedback between rounds; for example, the median of the group estimates, a weighted average, the range (with outliers dropped), or some combination of these. In practice, a majority of applications of the Delphi method achieved group consensus. Even in cases where the rounds were stopped before the group's opinions had converged, the method was helpful in clarifying the issues and highlighting the sources of disagreement, leading to better decisions.

Box 4.1 Three-Point Estimation

Estimates can be improved by taking the weighted average of the best, worst, and most likely cases. A *Three-Point Estimate* is the weighted average

$$estimate = (b + 4m + w)/6$$

of three values:

b the best-case estimate
m the most likely case estimate
w the worst-case estimate

In practice, this weighted-average formula is good enough, even though the assumptions behind it do not fully hold. The formula is derived from on a theoretical model, based on the following assumptions:[10]

- Estimates b, m, and w for a work item can be made without considering the other work items in the project.
- Estimates b, m, and w are independent of schedule, budget, resource, or other project constraints. Furthermore, the estimates are assumed to be free of cognitive bias.
- Technically, the best case b is assumed to be the 95th percentile case and the worst case w is assumed to be the 5th percentile case.

4.4   Balancing Priorities

The prioritization techniques in this section progress from one factor to three. Cost (development effort), value (user benefit), and risk are examples of factors. The section begins with the MoSCoW priority levels for a single factor. The levels range from must-have down to won't-have requirements. We then consider how to balance two factors: cost and value. Finally, we consider three factors: value, cost, and risk.

Multiple factors involve trade-offs. Requirement A may take more development effort than requirement B, but if B provides much greater value to users, then B may merit a higher overall priority. That is, B may have a higher benefit-to-cost ratio than A. Early in a project, we typically do not have reliable data about cost, value, and risk, so the techniques in what follows use scales such as high-medium-low.

Example 4.8   As an example of the lack of reliable data, consider how an executive priced a risky new-to-the-world component for a communications system. He said, "I had no idea what the eventual cost would be. I then picked up my phone and thought that the component would be like a basic phone (not a smartphone). So, I used that to come up with a price." The executive adjusted for the fact that a phone is a consumer device that enjoys economies of scale, whereas he was pricing a much lower-volume component.   □

4.4.1   Must-Should-Could-Won't (MoSCoW) Prioritization

The *MoSCoW* approach classifies requirements into the following four categories, listed in order of decreasing priority: must-have, should-have, could-have, and won't-have. The initial letters in the names of these categories appear capitalized in MoSCoW. Note that the order of the capitalized letters in MoSCoW matches the priority order of the categories. Here are some suggestions for classifying requirements:[11]

1. *Must-have* requirements are essential to the viability of a product and have to be designed and built in for the project to be successful.
2. *Should-have* requirements are important, but are lower in priority than must-have requirements. For example, there may be alternative ways of meeting the needs addressed by should-have requirements.
3. *Could-have* requirements are nice to have. They contribute to the overall user experience with a product; however, user needs can be met without them.
4. *Won't-have* requirements can be dropped.

The MoSCoW prioritization approach relies on a shared understanding between users and developers on how to classify into the preceding categories. What if users undervalue some requirements that the development team considers essential to the success of the product? For example, customers often take for granted quality attributes such as reliability and performance. Such requirements can be classified as should-have, if they do not make it into the must-have category. Some companies, Avaya for example, have internal standards that require product teams to give priority to a range of quality attributes. (See also Section 4.5, where the classification of requirements is based on both customer satisfiers and dissatisfiers.)

MoSCoW prioritization can be combined with other prioritization methods. For example, we could start by assigning a high priority to must-have requirements and then apply another method to the rest.

4.4.2 Balancing Value and Cost

Rough cost-value prioritization of user requirements can be done by classifying them as high or low in value and high or low in cost; see Fig. 4.7(a). Here, value classification is done by users, based on their expected benefit from the requirement. Development effort can serve as a proxy for cost. The cost-value analysis will be refined below to balance value, cost, and risk.

For maximizing value while minimizing cost, prioritize the requirements as follows:

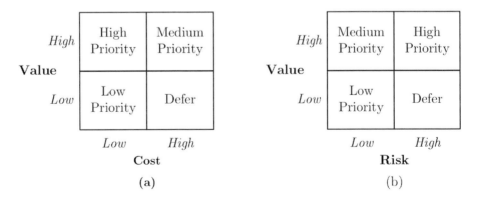

Figure 4.7 Prioritize first by value and cost and then by value and risk.

1. *High priority* for high-value, low-cost requirements.
2. *Medium priority* for high-value, high-cost requirements.
3. *Low priority* for low-value, low-cost requirements.
4. The low-value, high-cost requirements can potentially be deferred or dropped entirely.

4.4.3   Balancing Value, Cost, and Risk

Let us now refine the preceding value and cost prioritization to minimize risk as well as cost. The following is a value-cost-risk approach:[12]

a) Prioritize first by value and cost, as summarized in Fig. 4.7(a). The four categories in the figure are high-value, low-cost; high-value, high-cost; low-value, low-cost; and low-value, high-cost.
b) Within each category from Step(a), prioritize the requirements as follows (see Fig. 4.7(b)):

    1. *High priority* for high-value high-risk requirements.
    2. *Medium priority* for high-value low-risk requirements.
    3. *Low priority* for low-value low-risk requirements.
    4. The low-value, high-risk requirements can potentially be deferred or dropped.

In Step (b), it may seem counter-intuitive to rank high-value high-risk requirements ahead of high-value low-risk. All high-value requirements must presumably be implemented sooner or later. Tackling high-risk requirements early allows the development team more time to address the risks. For example, if risk resolution involves discussion and renegotiation with customers, it is better to surface issues earlier rather than later.

Assessing Risk The overall risk of a requirement can depend on a combination of risk factors.

Example 4.9   The Netscape 4.0 project in Example 2.16 tackled features that faced both market risk and technology risk. The groupware features involved market risk. They were unproven when they were added to the requirements for the product and were not embraced by users when the product was released. The technology risk was due in part to a brittle code base that was inherited from the 3.0 project and had not been refactored. The code base was not designed for the new features. Ultimately, the 4.0 project failed to live up to expectations.   □

The following approach to risk assessment considers two factors: requirements stability and technology familiarity. The less stable the requirements, the greater the risk. The less familiar the team is with the technology, the greater the risk. In

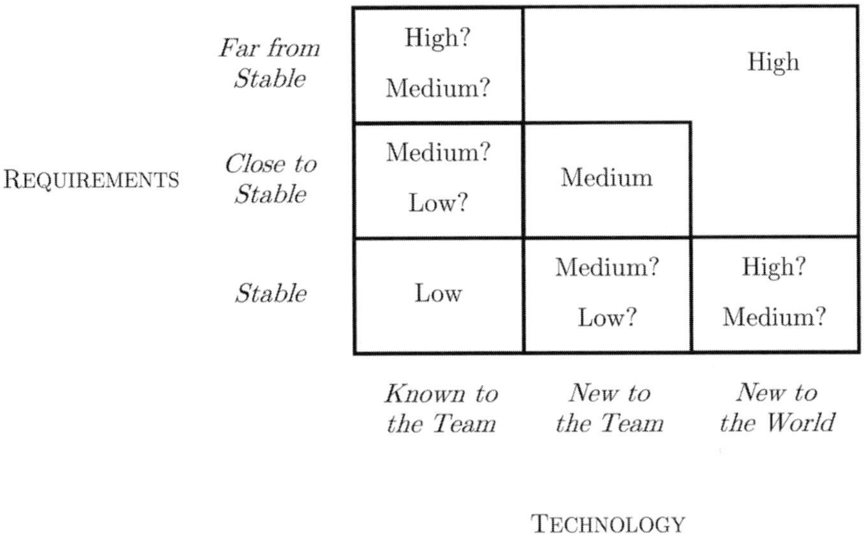

Figure 4.8 Combined risk based on two factors: requirements stability and technology familiarity. Risk increases as requirements become less stable and as the team becomes less familiar with the technology. In each box, the default is to go with the higher risk, unless the team has special knowledge that lowers the risk.

Fig. 4.8, requirements stability increases from top to bottom and technology familiarity decreases from left to right.

- *Low* risk if requirements are stable and the technology is known to the team.
- *Medium* risk is the default if either the requirements are close to but not yet stable or the technology is not known to the team, but known to the world.
  The risk may be lowered to *Low* for an experienced team if either the requirements risk is low (they are stable) or the technology risk is low (it is known to the team).
- *High* risk is the default if either the requirements are far from stable or if the technology is new to the world.
  The risk may be lowered to *Medium* for a team with special skills and experience, if either the requirements risk is low (they are stable) or if the technology risk is low (it is known to the team).

4.5   Customer Satisfiers and Dissatisfiers

What makes one product or feature desirable and another taken for granted until it malfunctions? An analysis of satisfiers and dissatisfiers is helpful for answering this question. The classification of features in this section can also be used for prioritization. Features are classified into the following categories: key, attractors, expected, neutral, and reverse. Key features correspond roughly to must-haves, expected to should-haves, and reverse to won't-haves. Attractor features are the ones to watch. They can surface latent needs – needs that users did not know that they had. Attractors can be the differentiator that turns a product into a best seller.

4.5.1   Kano Analysis

Noriaki Kano and his colleagues carried the distinction between job satisfiers and dissatisfiers over to customer satisfiers and dissatisfiers.[13] *Kano analysis* assesses the significance of product features by considering the effect on customer satisfaction of (a) building a feature and (b) not building the feature. Kano analysis has been applied to user stories and work items in software development.[14]

Paired Questions
Kano et al. used questionnaires with paired positive and negative questions about product features. The paired questions were of the following form:

- If the product **has** this feature . . .
- If the product **does not have** this feature . . .

For example, consider the following positive and negative forms of a question:

- If this product **can** be recycled . . .
- If this product **cannot** be recycled . . .

With each form, positive, and negative, they offered five options:

a) I'd like it
b) I'd expect it
c) I'm neutral

Box 4.2 Job Satisfiers and Dissatisfiers

The factors that lead to job satisfaction are different from the factors that lead to job dissatisfaction, as Frederick Herzberg and his colleagues discovered in the 1950s:[15]

- *Job satisfaction* is tied to the work, to what people do: "job content, achievement on a task, recognition for task achievement, the nature of the task, responsibility for a task and professional advancement."
- *Job dissatisfaction* is tied to "an entirely different set of factors." It is tied to the situation in which the work is done: supervision, interpersonal relationships, working conditions, and salary.

Improving working conditions alone reduces dissatisfaction, but it does not increase job satisfaction because the nature of the work does not change. Similarly, improving the nature of the work alone does not reduce job dissatisfaction, because working conditions and salary do not change.

	Satisfied		Attractor	Key
Feature is Built	*Neutral*	Reverse	Indifferent	Expected
	Dissatisfied	Reverse	Reverse	

| | *Satisfied* | *Neutral* | *Dissatisfied* |

Feature is Not Built

Figure 4.9 Classification of features.

d) I can accept it
e) I'd dislike it

4.5.2 Classification of Features

The results from paired positive and negative questions were classified using a grid such as the one in Fig. 4.9. For simplicity, Kano et al. used the nine-box grid in the figure, with the following three options instead of five:

a) I'd be satisfied
b) I'm neutral
c) I'd be dissatisfied

The rows in the nine-box grid correspond to the cases where a feature is built. The columns are for the cases where the feature is not built. Note the ordering of the rows and columns: with rows, satisfaction decreases from top to bottom; with columns, satisfaction decreases from left to right.

Key Features

The top-right box in Fig. 4.9 is for the case where customers are satisfied if the feature is built and would be dissatisfied if it is not built. With key features, the more the better, subject to the project's schedule and budget constraints. For example, with time-boxed iterations, a constraint would be the number of features that the team can build in an iteration.

Reverse Features

The box to the bottom left is for the case where customers would be dissatisfied if the feature is built and satisfied if it is not built. The two adjacent boxes are also marked Reverse. With reverse features, the fewer that are built, the better.

Example 4.10   Features that customers do not want are examples of reverse features. Clippy, an "intelligent" Microsoft Office assistant would pop up when least expected to cheerily ask something like, "I see that you're writing a letter. Would you like help?" The pop-up interrupted the flow of work, so it caused dissatisfaction.

Clippy was so unpopular that an anti-Clippy website got about 22 million hits in its first few months.[16]   □

The following is a modest example of a reverse feature.

Example 4.11   Users complain when there are changes in user interfaces. Out of the pages and pages of changes in the 4.** series of versions of TeXShop, the change that generated the most email was a formatting change in the default indentation of source text. Richard Cox, the coordinator and original author of TeXShop, writes:

I learned an important lesson. When a new feature is introduced which changes the appearance of the source code, the default value should make no change.

The change in formatting behavior in 4.08 was undone in 4.13 by resetting the default value.[17]

Disclosure This book was created using TeXShop.   □

Attractor Features

The box in the middle of the top row in Fig. 4.9 is for the case where customers would be satisfied if the feature is built and neutral if it is not. This box represents features that can differentiate a product from its competition. Features that address latent needs are likely to show up as attractors.

Example 4.12   Mobile phones with web and email access were a novelty around the year 2000. Kano analysis in Japan revealed that young people, including students, were very enthusiastic about the inclusion of the new features, but were neutral about their exclusion. These features were therefore attractors.

Indeed, such phones with web and email access rapidly gained popularity.   □

Expected Features

The box in the middle of the right column in Fig. 4.9 is for the case where customers would be neutral if the feature is built and dissatisfied if it is not built. Features customers take for granted fit in this box. For example, if a feature does not meet the

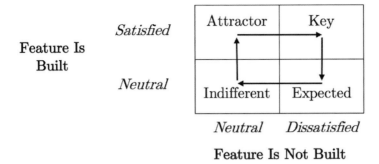

Figure 4.10 Over time, a feature can go from being indifferent to attractor to key to expected.

desired performance threshold – that is, if performance is not built in – customers would be dissatisfied. But if performance is built in, then customers may not even notice it.

Indifferent Features
The middle box in Fig. 4.9 is for the case where customers would be neither satisfied nor dissatisfied if the feature were built. Features that customers consider unimportant would also fit in this box.

4.5.3   Life Cycles of Attractiveness

The attractiveness of features can potentially vary over time. The progression in Fig. 4.10 shows a possible trajectory: from indifferent to attractor to key to expected. The table in the figure is from the top right of the nine-box grid in Fig. 4.9.

Example 4.13   Consider again mobile phones with features for web and email access. From Example 4.12, these features were attractors when they were introduced in Japan. Web and email access soon became key features that everyone wanted. Now, web and email access are expected: they are taken for granted since practically every phone has them.   □

In more detail, the progression in Fig. 4.10 is as follows:

1. **Indifferent** When an entirely new feature is introduced, people may be indifferent because they do not understand its significance.
2. **Attractor** As awareness of the new feature grows, it becomes an attractor, a delight to have, but people who do not have it are neutral.
3. **Key** As usage of the feature grows, people come to rely on it and are dissatisfied if they do not have it.
4. **Expected** Eventually, as adoption of the feature grows, it is taken for granted if it is present and people are dissatisfied if it is not present.

Table 4.2 Conceptually, increasing the degree of sufficiency of an attractor increases customer satisfaction from a neutral start. Meanwhile, increasing the degree of an expected feature moves customers from dissatisfied to at best neutral.

	INSUFFICIENT	SUFFICIENT
Attractor	*Neutral*	*Satisfied*
Expected	*Dissatisfied*	*Neutral*

The preceding progression is not the only possible one. A fashionable feature may rise from indifferent to key and fade back to indifferent as it goes out of fashion.

4.5.4 Degrees of Sufficiency

The classification of features in Fig. 4.9 is based on a binary choice: either a feature is built or it is not built. A sliding scale, from insufficient to sufficient, is more appropriate for features such as response time and scale.

Table 4.2 summarizes the likely effect on customer satisfaction of increasing the sufficiency of features. The rows in the table are for attractors and expected features. The columns are for two states: insufficient and sufficient. Insufficient corresponds to the feature being inadequately built or not built at all. Conversely, sufficient corresponds to the feature being usable or built.

The concept of attractors carries over from the binary "built or not" case to degrees of sufficiency. For attractors, customers start out neutral if the degree of the feature is insufficient. As the degree of sufficiency increases, customer satisfaction increases from neutral to satisfied. Conversely, for expected features, customers start out dissatisfied. As the feature's sufficiency increases, customer dissatisfaction decreases, eventually reaching neutral.

Example 4.14   Response time is an expected feature that is measured on a sliding scale. Let us measure it in milliseconds. Users are dissatisfied if it takes too long for an application to respond to a user action. In other words, users are dissatisfied if response time is insufficient.

As response time improves, it becomes fast enough, user dissatisfaction goes away. In other words, as response time becomes sufficient, users become neutral.   □

4.6   Plan-Driven Estimation Models

A software project has a cost and schedule overrun if the initial development effort estimates are too low. The state of the art of effort estimation can be summarized as follows:[18]

- Most estimation techniques ultimately rely to a lesser or greater extent on expert judgment.

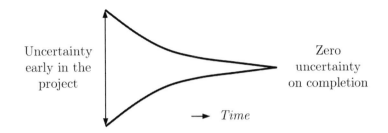

Figure 4.11 The Cone of Uncertainty is a conceptual diagram that illustrates the intuition that estimation uncertainty decreases as a project progresses.

- Historical data about similar past projects is a good predictor for current projects.
- Estimation accuracy can be improved by combining independent estimates from a group of experts.
- Simple models tailored to the local work environment can be at least, if not more accurate than advanced statistical models.
- There is no one best estimation model or method.

Estimation Uncertainty

Estimation uncertainty decreases as a project progresses and more information becomes available. This intuition motivates the conceptual diagram in Fig. 4.11. Let *estimation uncertainty* be the range between a pair of upper and lower bounds on estimates. The solid lines represent upper and lower bounds, so uncertainty at a given point in the project is the distance between the solid lines.

The diagram in Fig. 4.11 has been dubbed the *Cone of Uncertainty*, after the shape enclosed by the solid lines. Similar diagrams were in use in the 1950s for cost estimation for chemical manufacturing.[19]

4.6.1   How Are Size and Effort Related?

The "cost" of a work item can be represented by either the estimated program size or the estimated development effort for the item. Size and effort are related, but they are not the same. As size increases, effort increases, but by how much?

The challenge is that, for programs of the same size, development effort can vary widely, depending on factors such as team productivity, problem domain, and system architecture. Team productivity can vary by an order of magnitude.[20] Critical applications require more effort than casual ones. Effort increases gradually with a loosely coupled architecture; it rises sharply with tight coupling.

Project managers can compensate for some of these factors, further complicating the relationship between size and effort. Experienced project managers can address productivity variations when they form teams; say, by pairing a novice developer with someone more skilled. Estimation can be improved by relying on past data from the same problem domain; for example, smartphone apps can be compared with smartphone apps, embedded systems with embedded systems, and so on. Design guidelines and reviews can lead to cleaner architectures, where effort scales gracefully with size.

The relationship between size and effort is therefore context dependent. Within a given context, however, historical data can be used to make helpful predictions.

For large projects or with longer planning horizons, it is better to work with size. Iteration planning, with its short 1–4 week planning horizons, is often based on effort estimates. The discussion in this section is in terms of effort – the same estimation techniques work for both size and effort.

Estimating Effort from Size

Consider the problem of estimating development effort E from program size S. In other words, determine a function f such that

$$E = f(S)$$

If f is a linear function, then estimated effort E is proportional to size S: if size doubles, then effort doubles.

Effort does indeed increase with size, but not necessarily linearly. Does it grow faster than size, as in the upper curve in Fig. 4.12? Or does it grow slower than size, as in the lower curve? The dashed line corresponds to effort growing linearly with size.

The three curves in Fig. 4.12 were obtained by picking suitable values for the constants a and b in the equation

$$E = aS^b \qquad (4.1)$$

The curves in Fig. 4.12 correspond to the following cases:

- *Case b = 1* (dashed line). The function in Equation 4.1 is then linear.
- *Case b < 1* (lower curve). This case corresponds to there being economies of scale; for example, if the team becomes more productive as the project proceeds, or if code from a smaller project can be reused for a larger project. When writing drivers for devices, the first one is hard, the second one less so, and the third is easier.
- *Case b > 1* (upper curve). The more usual case is when $b > 1$ and larger projects become increasingly harder, either because of the increased need for team communication or because of increased interaction between modules as size increases. In other words, the rate of growth of effort accelerates with size.

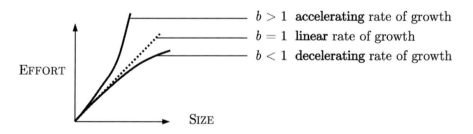

Figure 4.12 How does development effort E grow with program size S? The three curves are for different values of the constant b in the equation $E = aS^b$, where a is also a constant.

4.6.2 The Cocomo Family of Estimation Models

Equation 4.1, expressing effort as a function of size is from a model called Cocomo-81. The name Cocomo comes from Constructive Cost Model. The basic Cocomo model, introduced in 1981, is called Cocomo-81 to distinguish it from later models in the Cocomo suite.[21]

For a given project, the constants a and b in Equation 4.1 are estimated from historical data about similar projects. IBM data from waterfall projects in the 1970s fits the following (E is effort in staff-months and S is in thousands of lines of code):[22]

$$E = 5.2\, S^{0.91} \tag{4.2}$$

Meanwhile, TRW data from waterfall projects fits the following (the three equations are for three classes of systems):

$$
\begin{aligned}
E &= 2.4\, S^{1.05} \quad \text{Basic Systems} \\
E &= 3.0\, S^{1.12} \quad \text{Intermediate} \\
E &= 3.6\, S^{1.20} \quad \text{Embedded Systems}
\end{aligned}
\tag{4.3}
$$

The constants in (4.3) can be adjusted to account for factors such as task complexity and team productivity. For example, for a complex task, the estimated effort might be increased by 25 percent. (The actual percentage depends on historical data about similar projects by the same team.) Such adjustments can be handled by picking suitable values for the constants a and b in the general equation (4.1).

Cocomo II: A Major Redesign

Cocomo-81 was applied successfully to waterfall projects in the 1980s, but it lost its predictive value as software development processes changed. As processes changed, the data relating effort and size changed and the earlier statistical models no longer fit.

A major redesign in the late 1990s resulted in Cocomo II. The redesign accounted for various project parameters, such as the desired reliability and the use of tools and platforms. With Cocomo II and its many variants, the relationship between effort E and size S is given by the general formula

$$E = aS^b + c. \tag{4.4}$$

Constants a, b, and c are based on past data about similar projects. Factors like team productivity, problem complexity, desired reliability, and tool usage are built into the choice of constants a, b, and c.

New estimation models continue to be explored. As software engineering evolves, the existing models lose their predictive power.[23] Existing models are designed to fit historical data, and the purpose of advances in software development is to improve upon (disrupt) the historical relationship between development effort, program size, and required functionality.

4.7   Conclusion

Requirements analysis is at the interface between the requirements and the design steps of a project. It shapes user needs and goals into a consistent prioritized set of functional requirements and quality attributes for a product. Rough prioritization suffices with agile methods, since each iteration focuses on the highest-priority items for that iteration. Later iterations can take advantage of experience and information gained during earlier iterations. By comparison, plan-driven requirements analysis must plan down to every last detail, since planning is done once and for all, at a time when uncertainty is the greatest. The longer the planning horizon, the greater the uncertainty.

A logical progression of analysis activities appears in the following list. Some items in the progression may just be checklist items for smaller or simpler projects. For other projects, the items may be major activities, or even processes.

- Confirm the list of major stakeholders and their goals. Chapter 5 introduces use cases, which describe how a user interacts with the system to accomplish a goal.
- Identify the significant quality attributes (also known as nonfunctional requirements). Users tend to overlook quality attributes.
- Clarify and refine the top-level user goals. The questions and goal analysis techniques in Section 3.6 refine soft starting goals into specific SMART goals.
- Select prioritization criteria. Cost-benefit criteria suffice for most projects. Users estimate benefits, developers estimate costs. Additional criteria may be needed if users have conflicting priorities. For example, a project may focus first on primary stakeholders and then fold in the requirements for other stakeholders.
- Classify the requirements or work items into prioritized categories. TClassification involves trade-offs between properties such as value, cost, and risk. A complementary approach is to classify requirements based on what satisfies users and what dissatisfies them; see Section 4.5 for Kano analysis.
- As needed, apply formal statistical models distilled from past experience, to make estimates for the current project. Statistical estimation models are used primarily with plan-driven methods. Expert assessment can be more accurate, but it is expensive and does not scale well to large projects; see Section 4.3 for group consensus estimation techniques. Statistical models can provide quick estimates; for example, of work effort as a function of code size. The approaches can be used together, by relying on models broadly and expert assessment selectively.

Further Reading

- For agile estimation and iteration planning, see the book by Cohn [51].
- For Kano analysis, download the paper by Kano [108]; see also the Wikipedia article on Kano Analysis.
- Jørgensen [106] reviews the state of the art of estimation for development effort.

Exercises for Chapter 4

Exercise 4.1   Come up with your own examples of products that are

a) Useful, but neither usable nor desirable
b) Usable, but neither useful nor desirable
c) Desirable, but neither useful nor usable
d) Useful and usable, but not desirable
e) Useful and desirable, but not usable
f) Usable and desirable, but not useful
g) Useful, usable, and desirable

Your examples need not relate to software.

Exercise 4.2   Are the following statements generally true or generally false? Briefly explain your answers.

a) The expected overall planning effort is less with up-front planning than with agile planning.
b) The Iron Triangle illustrates connections between time, cost, and scope.
c) The Agile Iron Triangle fixes time and scope and lets costs vary.
d) Anchoring is the human tendency to stick to a position, once taken.
e) The shorter the planning horizon, the lower the uncertainty.
f) Anchoring reduces uncertainty during planning.
g) Planning Poker involves successive rounds of individual estimation and group discussion.
h) Wideband Delphi involves successive rounds of individual estimation and group discussion.
i) Three-point estimation takes the average of the best, the most likely, and the worst case estimates.
j) With traditional projects, development effort always grows exponentially as program size increases.

Exercise 4.3   Use the nine-box grid in Fig. 4.13 to classify features during Kano analysis. Give a one-line explanation for why a given class of features belongs in one of the boxes in the grid. (Note that the ordering of rows and columns in Fig. 4.13 is different from the ordering in Fig. 4.9.)

Exercise 4.4   For each of the following categories, give an example of a feature related to video conferencing. Be specific and provide realistic examples.

a) Key
b) Attractor
c) Expected
d) Indifferent
e) Reverse

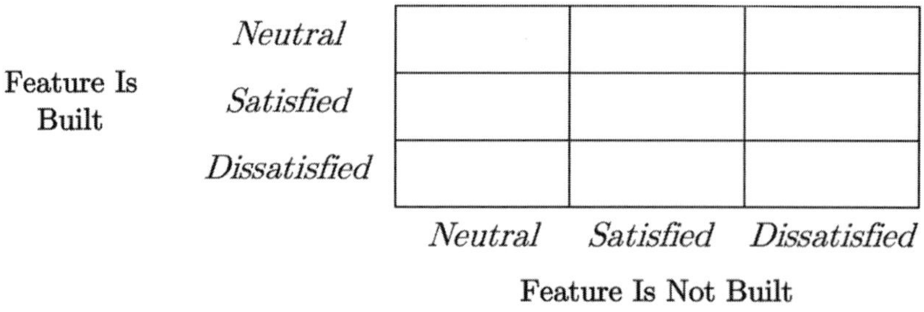

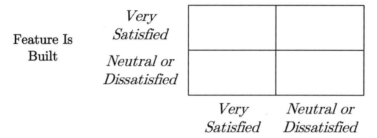

Figure 4.13 Classification of features during Kano analysis. The rows and columns have been scrambled, relative to Fig. 4.9.

Figure 4.14 Classification of features during Kano analysis.

Exercise 4.5   Consider Kano analysis using the four-box grid in Fig. 4.14, instead of the nine-box grid in Fig. 4.9.

a) How would you classify features using the four-box grid? Explain your answer.
b) For each of the four boxes, give an example of a specific feature that belongs in that box. Why does it belong in the box?

Exercise 4.6   Table 4.2 shows the change in customer satisfaction for Attractors and Expected features as the degree of sufficiency of a feature increases. Create the corresponding tables for Key, Reverse, and Indifferent features.

Exercise 4.7   Magne Jørgensen and Barry Boehm engaged in a friendly debate about the relative merits of expert judgment and formal models (e.g., Cocomo) for estimating development effort. Read their debate [107] and summarize their arguments pro and con for:

a) expert judgment.
b) formal models.

   Based on their arguments, when and under what conditions would you recommend estimation methods that rely on

c) expert judgment.
d) formal models.

5   Use Cases

A *use case* describes how a user interacts with a system to accomplish something of value to the user. Written in plain English, use cases are intended to be a single description that is suitable for all stakeholders. Their three main elements can be identified by asking:

a) Who is the use case for? Call that role the *primary actor* of the use case.
b) What does the primary actor want to accomplish with the system? Call that the *user goal* of the use case.
c) What is the simplest sequence of actions, from start to finish, by users and the system that successfully accomplishes the user goal? Call that sequence the *basic flow* of the use case.

As might be expected, the three main elements of a use case are the primary actor, the goal, and a basic flow.

This chapter will enable the reader to:

- Provide a system description, readable enough for users yet specific enough for developers, of the system's external behavior in pursuit of user goals.
- Develop a use case incrementally, starting by identifying users and their goals, then adding basic flow, outlining conditional and exceptional behavior, and finally filling out alternative behavior as needed.

5.1   Elements of a Use Case

A well-written collection of use cases characterizes a system's externally visible behavior. Actors represent the main users. Actors and goals provide an outline or overview of the system. Basic flows are helpful for an intuitive understanding of the system's responses to user actions.

5.1.1   Actors and Goals Outline a System

Use cases are typically developed during requirements analysis; see Fig. 5.1.

Since requirements can change, it is better to develop use cases incrementally, in the following order: the main users, their goals, basic flows. Start with goals, which

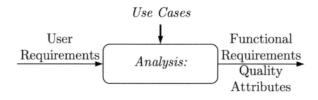

Figure 5.1 Use cases span user and functional requirements.

can be extracted from user requirements. Then, add basic flows and identify additional behaviors that are essential, but are not directly related to accomplishing the goals for the basic flows. Evolve the use cases by adding details as needed. With this incremental approach, the use cases grow from an outline (goals) into a description of the system's functionality (external behavior). Use cases do not address quality attributes, which are also known as nonfunctional requirements.

Thus, scale, performance, reliability, and other quality attributes all have to be specified separately.

Actors Represent Roles

In order to allow for multiple user roles and automated entities, discussions of use cases refer to "actor" rather than "user." An *actor* represents a role or an entity. For example, Alice can be both the manager of a team and an employee of a company. Alice would be represented by two actors: manager and employee. As another example, an actor might be an external map service or a stock-price service.

In most of the examples in this chapter, users have a single role. For convenience, we use the terms "actor" and "user" interchangeably, unless there is a need to distinguish between them. Hence, primary actor and primary user are equivalent, unless stated otherwise.

Note that a use case can have multiple actors. A use case for a phone call has two actors: the caller and the callee, with the caller being the initiator (the primary actor).

Identifying User Goals

A prioritized set of user goals provide a "big picture" overview of what users want from a system. Goal discovery begins during requirements elicitation and continues into analysis. Motivation questions were introduced in Section 3.6 to explore the context for a user want. Section 3.6 also discusses the refinement of soft high-level goals into SMART goals.

Stakeholder feedback on the user goals for a system can reveal missing goals. It can also expose conflicts between stakeholder goals. As a small example, the security team's demand for strong, frequently changed passwords can conflict with the users' preference for passwords they can remember. Goal analysis is discussed in Section 3.6.3.

More generally, in the process of writing use cases, any inadequacies in the user requirements have to be addressed, in consultation with users. Any inconsistencies have to be resolved. For example, consider the goal of booking a flight. Writing a basic flow from start to finish is akin to debugging the user requirements for booking a flight.

5.1.2   Flows and Basic Flows

Any linear sequence of actions by either an actor or the system is called a *flow*. A *basic flow* has two additional properties (in addition to being a flow):

- A basic flow extends from the start of a use case to the end of the use case.
- A basic flow tells a story in which the primary actor accomplishes the user goal without any complications, such as errors and exceptions.

When the primary actor and the user goal are clear from the context, a simple use case can be shown by writing just the basic flow.

Example 5.1   It is common practice to write a flow as a single numbered sequence that includes both actor actions and system responses. The following basic flow describes how a user (the primary actor) interacts with the system to resize a photo (the user goal):

1. The user opens a photo.
2. The system offers a photo-editing menu.
3. The user chooses to resize by dragging.
4. The user drags a corner of the photo.
5. The system displays the resized photo.
6. The user exports the resized photo.
7. The user quits the system.

          □

Here are some developing basic flows; see also Section 5.3 for tips on writing use cases.

- Write text in language that is meaningful for all stakeholders, including users, developers, and testers.
- Start each action in a flow with either "The actor . . ." or "The system . . ."; see Example 5.1.
- For each basic flow, choose the simplest way of reaching the goal, from start to successful finish.
- See Section 5.2 for alternative flows, which represent additional behavior, beyond the basic flow.

5.2   Alternative Flows: Conditional Behaviors

The description of most systems is complicated by the many options, special cases, exceptions, and error conditions that the systems must be prepared to handle. An

BASIC FLOW: MAKE A PHONE CALL
1. The caller provides the callee's phone number.
2. The system rings the callee's phone.
3. The callee answers.
4. The caller and callee talk.
5. The callee disconnects.
6. The caller disconnects.
7. The system logs the phone call.

Figure 5.2 A basic flow for a phone call.

alternative flow models conditional behavior that is a variant of the success scenario represented by a basic flow. It models behavior that is essential to a system but is not central to an intuitive understanding of how the system can meet the user goal of a use case.

Ivar Jacobson introduced use cases in the mid-1980s to model phone systems, which can be enormously complex. Meanwhile, the basic idea of a phone call is simple: in the next example, a caller connects with a callee in a few steps.[1]

Example 5.2   The flow in Fig. 5.2 achieves a caller's goal of connecting with a callee. The basic flow avoids the complexity of handling cases like the following. What if the callee does not answer? What if the destination phone is busy? What if the destination phone number is no longer in service? What if the callee has turned on a do-not-disturb feature? The simple idea of a caller connecting with a callee can get lost among the myriad special cases.   ☐

The next example explores the question: what behavior do we model with a basic flow and what do we model with alternative flows? The short answer is that the goal of a use case drives what we model with a basic flow.

Example 5.3   Alexandra wants to buy a scanner from a shopping site. The shopping site takes security very seriously. After three failed login attempts, it locks an account. Does a use case for purchasing an item need to model the fact that the account will be locked after three failed attempts? After all, authentication is an important part of the shopping experience.

The answer is no. The reason is that the user goal of the use case is to purchase an item. A success scenario for shopping focuses on the purchase of the item.

Relative to the purchasing experience, authentication is not central. Saying so does not diminish the importance of security. It simply means that security needs to be specified separately.   ☐

The conclusion from the preceding example is to keep basic flows focused on the goal of the use case, no matter how important the additional behaviors may be. Important behaviors, such as authentication, can stem from goals that deserve use cases of their own. Section 5.5 treats authentication as an example of a use case to be "included" in another, say, for shopping. Meanwhile, we treat authentication failures as additional behaviors, relative to other goals.

During discussions with stakeholders, alternative flows can be elicited by exploring alternatives to the actions in the basic flow. Such discussions can lead to clarifications and refinements of the basic flow itself.

This section considers two kinds of alternative flows: specific and bounded. Looking ahead, specific alternative flows replace specific actions in a basic flow; for example, replacing successful authentication and related actions by unsuccessful authentication and its related actions. Looking ahead again, bounded alternative flows can be triggered at unexpected points in a basic flow; for example, they can model the handling of exceptions such as network failure.

For convenience, the term alternative flow by itself refers to a specific alternative flow. The term bounded alternative flow will be spelled out in full; it will not be abbreviated.

5.2.1   Specific Alternative Flows

A *specific alternative flow* is formed by replacing a contiguous subsequence of actions in a basic flow. This definition allows a basic flow to have alternative flows; it does not allow alternative flows to have their own alternative flows.

Example 5.4   Consider the basic flow in Fig. 5.2, which connects a caller with a callee. The following specific alternative flow handles the case where the caller leaves a message because the callee does not answer in time. This alternative flow was formed by replacing actions 3–5 in the basic flow:

ALTERNATIVE FLOW *A*: LEAVE A MESSAGE

1.	The caller provides the callee's phone number.
2.	The system rings the callee's phone.
3.1a.	The system invites the caller to leave a message.
3.2a.	The caller records a message.
6.	The caller disconnects.
7.	The system logs the phone call.

□

While writing an alternative flow, we do not need to repeat the unchanged segments of the basic flow. It is enough to show how the new sequence of actions diverges from and reconnects with the basic flow. In the next example, only the replacement actions are shown, along with instructions for where they attach to the basic flow.

Example 5.5   As another variant of the basic flow in Fig. 5.2, consider the case where the caller provides an invalid phone number.

ALTERNATIVE FLOW *B*: INVALID PHONE NUMBER

After Action 1 in the basic flow, if the phone number is invalid,

2b. The system gives an error message.

Resume the basic flow at Action 6.

□

5.2.2   Extension Points

Instead of writing alternative flows by referring to numbered actions in a basic flow, we can give names to points in a basic flow. Named points decouple an alternative flow from sequence numbers in the basic flow, so the sequence numbers can be changed without touching the alternative flows.

Extension points are named points between actions in a flow. In addition, there can be extension points just before the first action and immediately after the last action of a flow. The term "extension points" is motivated by their use for attaching additional behavior that extends the system. We follow the convention of writing the names of extension points in boldface. Within basic flows, extension points will be enclosed between braces, { and }.

Example 5.6   Cash withdrawal from an automated teller machine (ATM) is a classic example of a use case.[2] The basic flow in Fig. 5.3 has four extension points. This example uses two of them, **Bank Services** and **Return Card**, to attach an alternative flow for authentication failures.

ALTERNATIVE FLOW *A*: FAIL AUTHENTICATION

At {**Bank Services**}, if authentication has failed,

Display "Authentication failed."

Resume the basic flow at {**Return Card**}.

□

BASIC FLOW: WITHDRAW CASH

1. The cardholder inserts a card.
   { **Read Card** }
2. The system prompts for a passcode.
3. The cardholder enters a passcode.
4. The system authenticates the cardholder.
   { **Bank Services** }
5. The system displays options for bank services.
6. The cardholder selects Withdraw Standard Amount.
7. The system checks the account for availability of funds.
   { **Dispense Cash** }
8. The system dispenses cash and updates the account balance.
   { **Return Card** }
9. The system returns the card.

Figure 5.3 A basic flow with extension points in boldface.

Example 5.7   The alternative flow for insufficient funds attaches between {**Dispense Cash**} and {**Return Card**}:

ALTERNATIVE FLOW *B*: INSUFFICIENT FUNDS

At {**Dispense Cash**}, if account has insufficient funds,

Display "Insufficient funds in account."

Resume the basic flow at {**Return Card**}.

□

A Graphical Aside

The graphical view in Fig. 5.4 is included solely to illustrate the relationship between a basic flow and its alternative flows. It is **not recommended** for writing use cases because the separation of basic from alternative flows is central to the simplicity of use cases. To combine them in one representation would be bad practice.

The graph in Fig. 5.4 uses arrows to show how specific alternative flows attach to the basic flow for cash withdrawals from an ATM. Flows correspond to paths through the graph. The basic flow goes sequentially through the numbered actions, from the start to the end of the use case. The two alternative flows in the figure are for handling authentication failure and insufficient funds.

5.2.3   Bounded Alternative Flows

Bounded alternative flows attach anywhere between two named extension points in a basic flow.

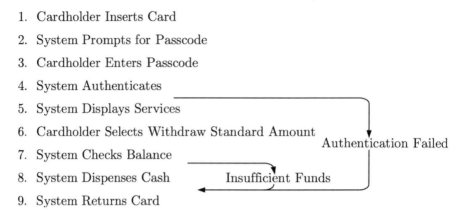

1. Cardholder Inserts Card

2. System Prompts for Passcode

3. Cardholder Enters Passcode

4. System Authenticates

5. System Displays Services

6. Cardholder Selects Withdraw Standard Amount

    Authentication Failed

7. System Checks Balance

8. System Dispenses Cash   Insufficient Funds

9. System Returns Card

Figure 5.4 Basic and specific alternative flows for cash withdrawals from an ATM. Such a graphical representation does not readily accommodate bounded alternative flows.

Example 5.8   What if the network connection between the ATM and the server is lost? Connection loss is an external event that can happen at any time; it is not tied to any specific point in the basic flow.

For simplicity, we assume that the actions in the basic flow are atomic; for example, power does not fail in the middle of an action. In particular, we assume that the action "Dispense cash and update account balance" is handled properly; that is, cash is dispensed if and only if the account is updated. A real system would use transaction processing techniques to ensure that the account balance reflects the cash dispensed.

With the basic flow and extension points in Fig. 5.3, the following bounded alternative flow returns the card if the network connection is lost before cash is dispensed:

> BOUNDED ALTERNATIVE FLOW: LOSE NETWORK CONNECTION
> _____
>
> At any point between {**Read Card**} and {**Dispense Cash**},
> if the network connection is lost,
>
>   Display "Sorry, out of service."
>
> Resume the basic flow at {**Return Card**}.
> _____

□

5.3   Writing Use Cases

Use cases are written so they can be read at multiple levels of detail. The actors and goals in a collection of use cases serve as an outline of a system. Basic flows,

Table 5.1 A representative template for writing use cases. The elements are listed in the order they can be added to a use case.

Name:	Active phrase for what will be achieved
Goal:	Brief description of the purpose of the use case
Actors:	Primary and other roles in the use case
Basic Flow:	Sequence of actions, readable by stakeholders
Alternative Flows:	List of variations on the basic flow
Extension Points:	Points in the basic flow for inserting behavior
Preconditions:	System state for the use case to operate correctly
Postconditions:	System state after the use case completes
Relationships:	Possible connections with other use cases

together with one-line descriptions of alternative flows, are helpful for an intuitive understanding of the system. Further information about system behavior can be provided by expanding the one-line descriptions of alternative flows. This ordering of the elements of uses cases allows them to be developed incrementally. The template in Table 5.1 can be filled in as information about a project becomes available. This section also distinguishes between the level of detail in (a) a use case that describes user intentions and (b) a use case that adds specifics about user–system interactions.

5.3.1   A Template for Use Cases

There is no standard format for writing the elements of a use case. The template in Table 5.1 is representative of templates that are used in practice. The elements are considered in this section in the order they can be added to a use case.

Name and Goal The first element in the template is a name for the use case. The name is preferably a short active phrase such as "Withdraw Cash" or "Place an Order." Next, if needed, is a brief description of the goal of the use case. If the name is descriptive enough, there may be no need to include a goal that says essentially the same thing.

The Basic Flow The basic flow is the heart of a use case. It is required. Begin a basic flow with an actor action. The first action typically triggers the use case; that is, it initiates the use case.

Alternative Flows Long use cases are hard to read, so the template asks only for a list of alternative flows. Identify an alternative flows by its name or its goal. Since requirements can change, alternative flows need not be fleshed out until the need arises.

Alternative flows must be about optional, exceptional, or truly alternative behavior. Otherwise, the relevant actions may belong in the basic flow. If the behavior is not conditional, it is not alternative behavior and may not belong in this use case; it may belong in some other use case.

Extension Points Use extension points in the basic flow only to indicate points for inserting additional behavior. Alternative flows, both specific and bounded, attach to a basic flow at named extension points; for examples, see Section 5.2.

Preconditions and Postconditions Preconditions are assertions that must be true for the use case to be initiated. For example, a Cancel Order use case may have a precondition that an order exists or is in progress. If there is no order, there is nothing to cancel. Similarly, postconditions are assertions that must be true when the use case ends. In simple examples, preconditions and postconditions are often omitted.

Relationships See Section 5.5 for relationships between use cases.

5.3.2   From Actor Intentions to System Interactions

Use cases can be written at multiple levels of detail. The terms actor intention, system interaction, and user interface represent increasing levels of detail. Let us define the intention, interaction, and interface levels as follows:

- The *intention* level is technology-free and implementation-free. This level is suitable during early stakeholder discussions, where the focus is on eliciting what users want.
- The *interaction* level is implementation-free, but may have technology dependencies. This level is suitable once user goals have settled and the focus shifts to the desired system response to a user action.
- The *interface* level can depend on design and implementation choices. Use cases need not go down to the interface level, where the focus is on layouts and messages at the user–system interface.[3]

Example 5.9   Consider authentication. The following intention-level flow is independent of any specific authentication technology:

    1a. The user initiates Login.
    2a. The system prompts for identification.
    3a. The user provides credentials.
    4a. The system authenticates the user.

At the intention level, it does not matter whether the technology relies on a fingerprint, a password, or a verification code sent to the user's device. The technology choice does matter at the interaction level. The following interaction-level flow relies on a verification code:

    1b. The user initiates login.
    2b. The system sends a verification code to the device on file.
    3b. The user supplies the verification code.
    4b. The system authenticates the user.

Compare actions 2a–3a with 2b–3b in the two flows. In general, an interaction-level flow may have more actions than an intention-level flow.   □

A single intention can be refined into multiple interactions. For the single intention to authenticate, the preceding example mentions three choices (fingerprints, passwords, verification code) for interactions. For a given interaction, there can be multiple possible interfaces. Interface and implementation details do not belong in use cases, although some design and implementation choices may creep in.

5.3.3   How to Build Use Cases

Use cases can be built incrementally. A full-blown use case can involve significant effort, some of which may be wasted if requirements change. The following is a suggested order for iteratively building use cases as a project proceeds:[4]

1. Begin with a list of actors and goals for the whole system. Such a list can be reviewed with users to (a) validate and prioritize the list of stakeholders and goals and (b) explore the boundaries of the proposed system.
2. Draft basic flows and acceptance tests for the prioritized goals. The draft can focus on user intentions, with system interactions included as needed. Acceptance tests are helpful for resolving ambiguities and for reconciling the basic flow and the goal of a use case.
3. Identify and list alternative flows; see Section 5.2. A list of alternative flows may be enough to guide design decisions and to create backlog items during development.
4. Finally, fill in alternative flows as needed during development.

Box 5.1 Use Cases and Iterative Development

Ivar Jacobson and his colleagues provide three guidelines for iterative software development based on use cases:[5]

- **Build the system in slices**. Instead of implementing an entire use case all at once, consider slicing it, where a "slice" is a subset of the flows in the use case, along with their test cases. In other words, a slice corresponds to a set of paths through a flow graph, such as the one in Fig. 5.4.
- **Deliver the system in increments**. Use an iterative process, based on delivering slices of use cases. Begin with the slice or slices that provide the most value.
- **Adapt to meet the team's needs**. Fit the development process to the project. A small cohesive team in a close collaboration with stakeholders might document just the bare essentials of use cases, relying on informal communication to address any questions along the way. A large team would likely require documented use cases with key details filled in.

5.4   Use-Case Diagrams

Use case diagrams are intended for an overall understanding of a system with multiple use cases. A *use-case diagram* summarizes the use cases for a system by showing the goals of the use cases and the actors who interact with the goals. As discussed in Section 5.3, actors and goals are a good starting point for developing a collection of use cases.

5.4.1   Diagrams Highlight Goals and Actors

In diagrams, a use case is represented by an ellipse labeled with its goal. Actors are represented by stick figures; see Fig. 5.5. An interaction between actor and a goal is represented by an arrow from the initiator of the interaction. Note that an interaction potentially involves an exchange of messages back and forth between the two parties.

Example 5.10   The diagram in Fig. 5.5 shows the actors and use cases for a salary system. The two primary actors are employee and manager. These actors are roles, since the same person can be a manager and an employee.

Employees can view their own salaries by initiating the View My Salary use case. They can also initiate View Salary Statistics for perspective on how their salaries compare with similar roles both within their company and within their industry. Information about salaries outside the company is provided by a benchmarking service, which is shown as a secondary actor (on the right).

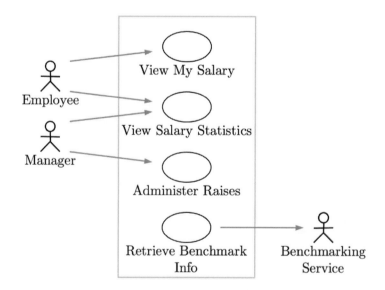

Figure 5.5   Use case diagram for a salary system. An individual can have two roles: employee and manager. Each role is represented by a different actor.

Managers can view salary statistics and can administer raises for the people they manage. The system can initiate the Retrieve Benchmark Info use case to get industry salary statistics from the benchmarking service actor.   □

Use Case Diagrams in Practice

Use-case diagrams are part of UML (Unified Modeling Language), a standard graphical language for modeling and designing software systems. (UML class diagrams are covered in Section 6.3.) Based on empirical surveys of UML usage by Marian Petre, the concepts of use cases are more popular than the diagrams themselves. The concepts may be combined with textual descriptions, as in the following comments by participants in a survey:

"It's hard to design without something that you could describe as a use case."
"Many described use cases informally, for example, as: 'Structure plus pithy bits of text to describe a functional requirement. Used to communicate with stakeholders.' "[6]

5.5   Relationships between Use Cases

Most systems can be described by collections of self-contained use cases. A self-contained use case may benefit from a private subflow that serves a well-defined purpose. Inclusion and extension relationships between use cases must be handled with care. As an influential book by Kurt Bittner and Ian Spence notes:

If there is one thing that sets teams down the wrong path, it is the misuse of the use-case relationships.[7]

5.5.1   Subflows

Even for simple systems, the readability of flows can be enhanced by defining subflows: a *subflow* is a self-contained subsequence with a well-defined purpose. The logic and alternatives remain tied to the basic flow if subflows are linear, where all the actions are performed or none of them are.

A subflow is *private* to a use case if it is invoked only within that use case.

5.5.2   Inclusion of Use Cases

An *inclusion* is a use case that is explicitly called as an action from a basic flow. The callee (the inclusion) is unaware of its caller. A possible application is to partition a use case by factoring out some well-defined behavior into an inclusion (a use case of its own). Alternatively, two or more use cases can share the common behavior provided by an inclusion.

Example 5.11   Authentication is a good candidate for an inclusion, since it is a well-defined, frequently occurring subgoal. Consider two use cases, *Withdraw Cash* and

Transfer Funds, which share an inclusion, *Authenticate Cardholder*. Action 3 in the following flow treats the inclusion as an action:

1. The actor inserts a card
2. The system reads the card
3. Include use case *Authenticate Cardholder*
   { **Bank Services** }
4. The system displays options for bank services

Upon successful authentication, the flow resumes at Action 4. See Example 5.6 for how to handle authentication failure by attaching an alternative flow at extension point **Bank Services**.   □

5.5.3   Extensions of Use Cases

An *extension* is a use case V that is invoked at a named extension point p in another use case U. The use case U is complete by itself and is unaware of the extension V. Extension is a form of inheritance. The purpose of an extension is to support an additional goal for an actor.

The distinction between inclusion and extension is as follows:

- *Inclusion* A use case knows about the inclusion that it calls. The inclusion use case is unaware of its caller.
- *Extension* An extension knows the underlying use case that it extends. The underlying use case provides extension points, but is unaware of the extension use case.

Example 5.12   Suppose that *Place Order* is a complete use case that allows shoppers to select a product and place an order. Its basic flow has an extension point **Display Products**:

BASIC FLOW: PLACE ORDER

1. The shopper enters a product category.
2. The system gets products.
   { **Display Products** }
3. The system displays products and prices.
4. The shopper places an order.

Now, suppose that the shopper has the additional goal of getting product recommendations. The extension use case *Get Recommendations* invokes itself at the extension point in *Place Order*:

EXTENSION: GET RECOMMENDATIONS

At {**Display Products**} in use case *Place Order*

⟨ system makes recommendations ⟩

With the extension, the shopper enters a product category, gets recommendations, then sees the products and prices, and places an order. The *Place Order* use case remains unchanged.   □

As another example, consider a surveillance system with a use case to monitor an area for intruders. Another use case notifies authorities. Surveillance and notification can be combined by making notification an extension of the surveillance use case.

At an extension point **Intruder Detected** in the surveillance flow, the notification use case can notify the authorities that an intruder has been detected.

5.6   Conclusion

Use cases model the externally visible behavior of a system. Functional requirements can therefore be described by writing a readable collection of use cases. The three required elements of a use case are a primary actor, the actor's goal with the system, and a basic flow.

The basic flow describes a complete user–system interaction that accomplishes the goal in the simplest possible way. Special cases, errors, exceptions, and any other conditional behaviors are handled separately by defining alternative flows.

The separation of alternative from basic flows is key to the readability of use cases. A list or diagram of actors and their goals provides an overview of a system. It can be used in stakeholder discussions to validate and prioritize the actors and goals. Basic flows provide the next level of detail; they are helpful for an intuitive understanding of system behavior. Alternative flows fill in additional behaviors that are required for the success of a system but are not essential to an intuitive understanding.

Implicit in the preceding discussion is a natural order for incrementally building a collection of use cases:

1. Identify actors and goals.
2. Write basic flows.
3. List the names or the goals of alternative flows. Add further information as needed.

Use Cases and User Stories   Use cases and user stories are complementary; they provide different perspectives on requirements and can be used together.[8]

Use Cases Provide Context   Whereas use cases describe end-to-end scenarios, user stories correspond to features or snippets of functionality. In introducing user stories along with Extreme Programming, Kent Beck noted, "you can think of [user stories] as the amount of a use case that will fit on an index card."[9] Use cases provide context because they illustrate how individual features fit together in a flow. Flows also help identify any gaps in the functionality needed to implement a system.

User Stories Are Lighter Weight User stories require less effort to create than use cases because a use is closer to a collection of related user stories than it is to an individual story.

   Note, however, that a use case need not be fully developed up front; it can be evolved as a project progresses. A project can opt for a combination of context and light weight by incrementally developing both use cases and user stories.

Further Reading

- Jacobson, Spence, and Kerr [98] introduce use cases, along with high-level guidelines for writing and using use cases. They offer use cases for broad use during software development, not just for requirements; see Box 5.1.
- Ivar Jacobson, who created use cases in the 1980s, highly recommends the book by Bittner and Spence [22].
- For how to develop a use case incrementally, see Cockburn [47, p. 17].

Exercises for Chapter 5

Exercise 5.1   What is the difference between

a) use cases based on intention and interaction?
b) user stories and use cases?
c) specific and bounded alternative flows?
d) inclusion and extension of use cases?

Common Instructions for Exercises 5.2–5.7

In each of the following exercises, write a use case that includes a descriptive name, a primary actor, the primary actor's goal, and the following:

a) A basic flow
b) A full specific alternative flow
c) A full bounded alternative flow
d) How the alternative flows attach to the basic flow using extension points
e) Inclusion of use cases

   For each alternative flow, show the full flow, not just the name of the flow. For inclusions, provide both a descriptive name and a brief comment about the role of the included use case.

Exercise 5.2   Write a use case for the software for the insurance company scenario from Exercise 3.9.

Exercise 5.3   Write a use case for the software to control a self-service gasoline pump, including the handling of payments, choice of grade of gas, and a receipt. In addition, when the screen is not being used otherwise, the system must permit targeted advertising on the screen. Targeted means that the ads are based on the customer's purchase history with the vendor.

Exercise 5.4   Prior to meeting with the customer, all you have is the following brief description of a proposed system:

The system will allow users to compare prices on health-insurance plans in their area; to begin enrollment in a chosen plan; and to simultaneously find out if they qualify for government health-care subsidies. Visitors will sign up and create their own specific user account first, listing some personal information, before receiving detailed information about the plans that are available in their area. [Description adapted from Wikipedia, CC-BY-SA 3.0 license.][10]

Write a use case based on this description.

Exercise 5.5   HomeAway allows a user to rent vacation properties across the world. Write a use case for a renter to select and reserve a vacation property for specific dates in a given city.

Exercise 5.6   Write a use case for an airline flight-reservations system. For cities in the United States, the airline either has nonstop flights or flights with one stop through its hubs in Chicago and Dallas. Your reservations system is responsible for offering flight options (there may be several options on a given day, at different prices), seat selection, and method of payment (choice of credit card or frequent flier miles). Another team is responsible for the pricing system, which determines the price of a round-trip ticket.

Exercise 5.7   Write a use case for the software to send a text message between two mobile phones, as described here. Each phone has its own Home server in the network, determined by the phone's number. The Home server keeps track of the phone's location, billing, and communication history. Assume that the source and destination phones have different Home servers. The destination Home server holds messages until they can be delivered. Also assume that the network does not fail; that is, the phones stay connected to the network.

6 Design and Architecture

For any software project, large or small, architecture is key to managing the intrinsic complexity of software. The design of a system includes its architecture, so, more broadly, design is key to managing software complexity. Informally, architecture partitions a system into parts that are easier to work with than the system as a whole. Let us refer to the parts as *architectural elements*, or simply *elements*. With a clean architecture, we can reason about the system in terms of the properties of its elements, without worrying about how the elements are implemented.

Like software, architecture is invisible. What we work with are descriptions or "views" of an architecture. Different views serve different purposes; for example, a source code view differs from a deployment view showing the geographic distribution of the servers.

This chapter provides guidelines for designing and describing system architecture. It progresses bottom-up from individual classes to whole systems. UML class diagrams are views of the classes in a system. It may take multiple views to describe a large system.

This chapter will enable the reader to:

- Design modular systems, where the elements have well defined responsibilities and interact only through their interfaces.
- Describe the architecture of a system by describing its elements and showing how the system interacts with its context.

6.1 The Role of Architecture

The terms "design" and "architecture" are often used loosely in practice.[1] This section clarifies how we will use the terms. In short, all architectural decisions are design decisions, but not all design decisions are architectural; see Fig. 6.1. Architecture is convenient for understanding and reasoning about a system and its properties. For an example of reasoning, consider the implications of a change to a line of code. Will the change break some other part of the system? Architecture can help us reason about the code to identify the parts that may be affected by the change.

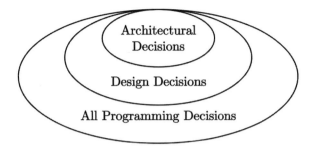

Figure 6.1 Architecture is used to reason about the overall properties of a system. Design is used to reason about both external and internal properties.

6.1.1 What Is Architecture?

For a simple system, a source code view of the class structure may be all we need. The following working definition applies to large and small systems. The *architecture* of a software system is characterized by a set of views needed to reason about how the system works. For example, in addition to a view of the classes and modules, we may need a run-time view of the objects that are created dynamically. A *view* identifies two things:

a) A set of architectural elements of the system.
b) The relationships between the elements; that is, how the elements work together to form the whole system.

Example 6.1   Suppose that a source-code view of a spelling checker has the following elements:

- *Spell-Check* is responsible for reading a stream of characters that may contain punctuation, numbers, and formatting commands. It produces a stream of words that are not in a dictionary. Here, a word is a contiguous sequence of letters.
- *Split* is responsible for removing unwanted characters, like punctuation and digits. It produces a stream of words.
- *Lookup* is responsible for answering true or false to whether a word is in the dictionary.

The only relationships between the elements are as follows:

> *Spell-Check*   *uses*   *Split*   to get words
> *Spell-Check*   *uses*   *Lookup*   to find words not in the dictionary

From these relationships we can conclude that *Split* and *Lookup* are independent of each other. Either can be changed without affecting the other.   □

Box 6.1 Conway's Sociological Observation

Sociological or organizational context can exert a powerful influence on software architecture. Melvin Conway observed:

Any organization that designs a system [defined broadly] will inevitably produce a design whose structure is a copy of the organization's communication structure.[2]

The premise for this sociological observation is that two software modules A and B cannot interface correctly with each other unless the designer of A communicates with the designer of B. Systems therefore reflect the social structure of the organizations that built them.

In general, each view of an architecture has a purpose. An effective view focuses on the aspects of the system that are relevant to the purpose and hides other aspects of the system. The purpose of the view of the spell checker in Example 6.1 is to highlight the responsibilities and relationships between the elements *Spell-Check*, *Split*, and *Lookup*, along with their relationships. The view hides or abstracts away the specifics of how these elements work. Such abstraction allows us to reason about how these elements work together, without having to dig through all the details of the implementation of the elements.

6.1.2   Design Includes Architecture

For our purposes, the distinction between architecture and design is that an architectural view abstracts away the internals of the elements in the view. Summarizing the above discussion, we have the following:

- Architecture is used to understand and reason about the external properties of a system and its parts. Such properties include the overall behavior, structure, quality attributes, and geographic deployment.
- Design is used to understand and reason about both the external and internal properties of the system and its parts.[3]

6.1.3   What Is a Good Software Architecture?

Asking what makes an architecture good is akin to asking what makes a piece of software good. There are no hard and fast rules; only guidelines. Here are some questions we might ask of any architecture:

- **Functional** Will the system meet its user requirements? Will it be fit for purpose? Will it be worth the cost? In short, will it do the job it is designed to do?
- **Quality Attributes** Will the architecture result in a system that has the desired quality attributes? Is the technology appropriate? In short, will the system do its job well?

- **Elegance** Is the architecture easy to understand and modify? Will it lead to a clean implementation? Can it be built iteratively and incrementally? Does the design have conceptual integrity; that is, is it consistent?

Incidentally, functionality, quality attributes, and elegance correspond to Vitruvius's three "virtues" for the architecture of buildings: utility, strength, and beauty. Vitruvius was a Roman architect in the first century BCE.[4]

6.2   Designing Modular Systems

The source code of a "modular" software system consists of a set of program elements that we call *modules*. A module can be as small as a class and as large as a subsystem. A system is *modular* if it has the following two desirable properties:

1. Each of its modules has a specific responsibility. In other words, each module provides a specific service to the rest of the system.
2. The modules interact only through the services that they provide each other.

For an everyday example of modularity, consider the Internet Protocols TCP and IP. The protocols correspond to modules. Section 7.1 outlines how TCP and IP work together, without going into how they are implemented. More generally, software layering leads to modular systems, with the layers as modules.

6.2.1   The Modularity Principle

Modularity, also known as *Implementation Hiding*, is the guiding principle behind modular systems.[5] The idea is that hidden implementations can be readily changed.
  Modular systems provide two related benefits:

- At the system level, we can reason about the system purely in terms of module responsibilities and relationships.
- At the module level, as long as a module continues to fulfill its responsibility, we can modify the module without affecting the rest of the system.

Modularity is more about conceiving and thinking of programs than it is about specific programming languages or constructs. Modules correspond to groupings of related program elements, such as values, operations, and classes. Modularity can be practiced by controlling the visibility of the program elements in a module. Private elements are hidden within the module. The public elements are part of the module's interface. In Java, modules correspond roughly to classes or packages.

A Small Modular System

The toy system in Fig. 6.2 is small enough to describe in detail, yet rich enough to prove the point that modular thinking is helpful at any level of granularity, from small to large. The problem is to encode plain text into what is called (encrypted) *cipher text*. Example 6.2 provides an overview of an encryption system in terms of the responsibilities of

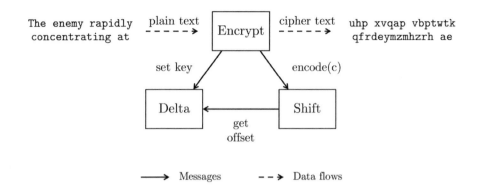

The enemy rapidly   plain text   cipher text   uhp xvqap vbptwtk
concentrating at   - - - - - →   Encrypt   - - - - - →   qfrdeymzmhzrh ae

                 set key   encode(c)

                 Delta   ←   Shift
                              get
                              offset

————→   Messages   - - →   Data flows

Figure 6.2 A modular encryption system with three modules: *Encrypt*, *Shift*, and *Delta*.

the three modules in Fig. 6.2. Without going into implementation details, Example 6.3 describes how the modules work together.

Example 6.2   The encryption system in Fig. 6.2 applies a substitution cipher, which encodes a document one letter at a time. Each letter is replaced by another in the alphabet. Case is ignored, so uppercase letters are treated as lowercase. Other characters (such as space and punctuation) are passed through unmodified. Consider the plain text

          The enemy rapidly concentrating
          at Louisville and Covington.

The following cipher text was formed by encoding the plain text, letter by letter:

          uhp xvqap vbptwtk qfrdeymzmhzrh
          ae ewgwjzjlwx izr tswiyzbab.

   This cipher text is from an 1862 message sent by General Kirby-Smith during the American Civil War. The message lay undeciphered for 137 years until the code was broken in 1999.[6]
   The responsibilities of the three modules in the system are as follows:

- *Encrypt*, the main module, is responsible for the user interface. Its primary job is to read plain text and write cipher text. It also gets an encryption key and initializes the *Delta* module with the key. It uses the *Shift* module.
- *Shift* is responsible for encoding a single letter. To do its job, it uses the *Delta* module.
- *Delta* is responsible for managing the encryption key. It tells *Shift* how much to "shift" a letter, as described in Example 6.3.

The modules have no other interactions.   □

The overview in Example 6.2 is intended for someone to decide if they want to learn more about the system. The next example describes how the modules interact to encrypt plain text.

Example 6.3   We begin with a description of the encryption method. Note that this description is part of the specification of what the system must do, not a description of an implementation. The method has been called the *Vigenère cipher* since the nineteenth century, although it was published in 1553 by Giovan Battista Bellaso.

The system in Fig. 6.2 encodes each letter in the alphabet by "shifting" it. Let the *position* of a letter be the number of letters before it in the alphabet: a is at position 0, b is at position 1, and so on, until z is at position 25.

To *shift* a letter at position i by k positions, replace it by the letter at position $(i + k)$ **mod** 26. Thus, to shift z by 1 position, replace it by a.

The cipher text in Fig. 6.2 was encrypted by shifting successive letters by a different amounts, where the shift amount was controlled by a key in Fig. 6.3. The key baltimore is in the top row of boxes. The key is repeated as needed so its letters line up above the plain text in the middle row of boxes. Recall that spaces are passed through, so they are skipped. Below each letter in the key is the position of the letter in the alphabet, starting with a at position 0. These positions are the shift amounts for the plain text below them. From the left, key letter b is at position 1, so the plain text T shifts by one position to cipher text u in the leftmost box in the bottom row of boxes. Key letter a is at position 0, so the plain text h is passed through as cipher text h. The third key letter l is at position 11, so plain text e shifts to cipher text p.

The modules in Fig. 6.2 work together as follows to encrypt the plain text in the figure:

1. The *Encrypt* module initializes the *Delta* module with the key baltimore.
2. *Encrypt* reads a character c of plain text and calls *Shift* to encode it.
3. If c is not a letter, *Shift* returns it unchanged. Otherwise, it calls *Delta* to get the next shift amount.
4. *Shift* shifts c by the shift amount and returns the shifted cipher text.
5. If there is more plain text, these steps repeat, starting at Step 2.

Key	b a l	t i m o r	e b a l t i m	o r e b a l t i
Shift by	1 0 11	19 8 12 14 17	4 1 0 11 19 8 12	14 17 4 1 0 11 19 8
Plaintext	T h e	e n e m y	r a p i d l y	c o n c e n t r
	↓ ↓ ↓	↓ ↓ ↓ ↓ ↓	↓ ↓ ↓ ↓ ↓ ↓ ↓	↓ ↓ ↓ ↓ ↓ ↓ ↓ ↓
Ciphertext	u h p	x v q a p	v b p t w t k	q f r d e y m z

Figure 6.3 Application of a Vigenère cipher, with key baltimore. The key is repeated in the top row of boxes. The positions of the letters in the key are the shift amounts for encrypting the plain text in the middle row of boxes. The cipher text is in the bottom row.

The above steps focus on the interactions between the modules. They do not go into the choice of programming language(s), data structures, and algorithms used for the modules.   □

The benefits of modularity become more evident with larger systems than in the small examples just presented. The modules in Fig. 6.2 are small-grained; that is, each can be implemented by a few lines of code. Thus, there are few implementation details to hide. For a larger example, see the description of the communications application in Section 6.5.

6.2.2   Coupling and Cohesion

Good modular systems have loose coupling between modules and high cohesion within modules. The terms coupling and cohesion are discussed in this section. See also the design guidelines at the end of this section.

Aim for Loose Coupling

In practice, systems can violate the modularity principle by having module dependencies or relationships that are not through well-defined interfaces. Coupling is an informal concept for talking about the extent to which a system is modular. Less coupling is better than more.[7]

Two modules are *loosely coupled* if they interact only through their interfaces. As an example, the modules in Fig. 6.2 are loosely coupled. Two modules are *tightly coupled* if the implementation of one module depends on the implementation of the other. The following list progresses from looser (better) coupling to tighter (worse) coupling:

- *Message Coupling* Modules pass messages through their interfaces.
- *Subclass Coupling* A subclass inherits methods and data from a superclass.
- *Global Coupling* Two modules share the same global data.
- *Content Coupling* One module relies on the implementation of another.

Depending on the language, there may be other possible forms of coupling. For example, in a language with pointers, module A can pass module B a pointer that allows B to change private data in A.

Aim for High Cohesion

Cohesion is an informal concept for talking about the design of a module. A module has *high cohesion* if the module has one responsibility and all its elements relate to that responsibility. A module has *low cohesion* if it has elements that are unrelated to its main responsibility. Higher cohesion is better: modules with higher cohesion are easier to understand and change. The following Unix maxim promotes high cohesion, if you apply it to modules as well as programs:

Make every program do one thing well.

The following forms of cohesion reflect different approaches to module design. The list progresses from higher (better) cohesion to lower (worse) cohesion:

- *Functional Cohesion* Design modules by grouping elements based on a single responsibility.
- *Sequential Cohesion* Group based on processing steps. For example, the following three steps count occurrences of words in a document: split the document into words; sort the words; count repeated words. Design different modules for different steps.
- *Data Cohesion* Group based on the data that is being manipulated. Such a module can potentially be split by grouping based on the purpose of the manipulations.
- *Temporal Cohesion* Group based on the order in which events occur; for example, grouping initializations or grouping housekeeping events that occur at the same time. Redesign modules based on object-oriented design principles.
- *Coincidental Cohesion* The elements of a module have little to do with each other. Redesign.

6.2.3   Design Guidelines for Modules

Summarizing the preceding discussion, the architecture of a modular system is characterized by the system's modules and their relationships. The following design guidelines are based on the modularity principle. They are due to David Parnas:[8]

- Begin with a list of significant design decisions or decisions that are likely to change. Then put each such design decision into a separate module so that it can be changed independently of the other decisions. Different design decisions belong in different modules.
- Keep each module simple enough to be understood fully by itself.
- Minimize the number of widely used modules. Design so that the more widely used a module, the more stable its interface.
- Hide implementations, so that the implementation of one module can be changed without affecting the behavior and implementation of the other modules.
- Plan for change, so that likely changes do not affect module interface, less likely changes do not affect the interfaces of widely used modules, and only very unlikely changes affect the modular structure of the system.
- Allow any combination of old and new implementations of modules to be tested, provided the interfaces stay the same.

Tony Savor and colleagues list modularity as one of three key requirements for introducing continuous deployment into an organization:

Secondly, highly cohesive, loosely coupled software makes small changes more likely to be better isolated.[9]

The other two requirements are (a) buy-in from senior management and the organization, and (b) support for tools and automation.

6.3   Class Diagrams

If we recursively partition a modular system into its subsystems, and the subsystems into their parts, we eventually get to units of implementation, such as classes and procedures. This section introduces UML class diagrams, a graphical notation for designing and describing classes and their relationships; that is, how the classes work together. Used properly, the notation enables the modularity concepts and guidelines in Section 6.2 to be applied at the class level. UML allows a class diagram to include as much or as little information about a class as desired. Thus, UML descriptions can contain implementation details, if a designer chooses to add them.

This section is a selective introduction to the syntax and semantics of class diagrams in UML (*Unified Modeling Language*). The language was formed by combining the object-oriented design methods of Grady Booch, James Rumbaugh, and Ivar Jacobson.[10] The full language is large and complex, with over twenty kinds of diagrams, each serving a specific purpose. The different kinds are typically used by themselves, independently of the others. For example, the use case diagrams of Section 5.4 are part of UML. Package diagrams are used to illustrate groupings of modules in Section 6.5.

6.3.1   Representing a Class

A UML class diagram is a developer's view of the significant classes in a system's design. UML enables us to highlight what we consider important about the classes and their relationships. Other information about the classes can be suppressed if it is not needed for understanding or documenting a design.

The simplest representation of an individual class is a box (rectangle) with just the name of the class. The general representation of a class contains its name, together with its significant attributes and operations. Informally, attributes correspond to fields for data. Operations correspond to methods or procedures/functions. Both attributes and operations are discussed in this section.

The class name is required. The attributes and operations are optional. When all three are present, the box for a class has lines to separate them, stacked with the name on top, the attributes in the middle, and the operations at the bottom.

Example 6.4   The class diagram in Fig. 6.4 is based on the modular design in Fig. 6.2 for an encryption system. The classes correspond to modules with the same name. The dashed arrows in the class diagram represent dependencies among classes; dependencies are discussed later in this section.

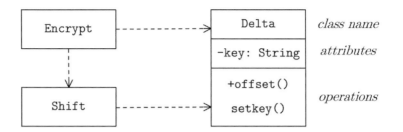

Figure 6.4 A class diagram with three classes. Classes Encrypt and Shift are represented by their names. The third class, Delta is represented by its name, attributes, and operations. The dashed arrows represent dependencies between classes.

In the class diagram, the two boxes to the left show classes Encrypt and Shift by their names alone. To the right, the box for class Delta is represented by its name, attribute key of type String, and operations offset() and setkey(). The visibility markers, + and −, stand for public and private, respectively. See also the discussion of visibility in what follows. □

Class Properties as Attributes

Technically, an *attribute* denotes a value associated with a class. In a class diagram, an attribute is written as a line of text in a box for a class. Class Delta in Fig. 6.4 has an attribute named key that denotes a string value. A class Shape that models geometric shapes potentially has attributes for the geometric center and the height of a shape.

From a design perspective, if a class models a real-world entity, then an attribute models some meaningful property of the entity. The class Delta models a key manager in an encryption system. The attribute key models an encryption key, such as the string

"baltimore"

The syntax for writing attributes has one required element: the name. All other elements in the following syntax are optional:

$$\langle visibility \rangle \; \langle name \rangle \; : \; \langle type \rangle \; \langle multiplicity \rangle = \langle default\text{-}value \rangle$$

Here, ⟨ and ⟩ enclose placeholders. The colon, :, goes with the type, and is dropped if the type is not provided. Similarly, the equal sign, =, is dropped if no default initial value is provided.

Example 6.5 The following are some of the ways of providing information about an attribute:

center	Only the name is required
center : Point	center has type Point
center : Point = origin	Default initial value is origin
+center	center is public

□

Visibility

The visibility markers are as follows:

+	public: visible to other classes
−	private: not visible outside the class
~	visible to classes within this package
#	"protected:" rules vary subtly across languages
⟨*empty*⟩	visibility unspecified

While the meanings of public and private visibility are essentially the same across languages, the interpretation of package and protected visibility can vary subtly. Java and C++ have different notions of protected. In Java, it means visible within the package and to subclasses, whereas in C++, it means visible only to subclasses.

Multiplicity

Just as a course can have multiple students, some properties may represent multiple objects. *Multiplicity* specifies a range for the number of objects represented by an attribute. A range is written as

*	One or more
$m..n$	Range, where $m \geq 0$ and $n \geq m$
n	Abbreviation for the range $1..n$

The symbol * represents some unlimited nonnegative number. Note that 1 is an abbreviation for $1..1$ and 5 for $1..5$.

When an attribute specification includes a multiplicity, the range is enclosed between [and], as in

$$\text{center : Point [1] = origin}$$

Here, [1] is redundant because 1 is the default, if multiplicity is not specified.

Operations

The simplest way to write an operation is to write the name, followed by a pair of parentheses, (). As previously noted, operations correspond to methods in a class. The syntax for operations is as follows:

$$⟨visibility⟩ \ ⟨name⟩ \ (\ ⟨parameters⟩ \ ) : ⟨return\text{-}type⟩$$

The name and the parentheses are required. The other elements of the syntax are optional. If present, the parameters are specified by writing a name followed by a colon and a type. If the return type is not specified, then the colon, :, is dropped.

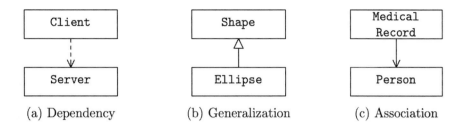

(a) Dependency   (b) Generalization   (c) Association

Figure 6.5 Simple examples of relationships between classes. (a) A client depends on a server, but the server does not depend on a client. (b) A generalization is a subclass-superclass relationship. A shape is more general than an ellipse, since a shape can also be a rectangle. (b) Associated with each medical record is a person (the patient).

Example 6.6   The following are some of the ways of describing the same operation:

`setkey()`	Just name and parentheses
`setlength(k : String)`	Show parameter k and its type
`setkey() : void`	Show return type
`setkey(k : String) : void`	Parameters and return type
`+setkey()`	Operation is public

□

6.3.2   Relationships between Classes

We turn now from individual classes to how classes work together. Class diagrams support three kinds of relationships between classes: dependencies, generalizations, and associations. Examples of these relationships appear in Fig. 6.5.

Dependencies A dependency is represented by a dashed arrow from the dependent class; see Fig. 6.5(a). The most common form of dependency is a caller-callee relationship, where the caller depends on the callee. In Fig. 6.4, an operation in class `Shift` calls operation `offset()` in class `Delta`, so `Shift` depends on `Delta`.

Dependence goes beyond a caller-callee relationship. For example, a producer can put data into a buffer for a consumer to pick up. The consumer depends on the producer, but the producer need not depend on the consumer – the producer may not even know the identity of the consumer. Dependence can also occur through event notifications; see, for example, the observer pattern in Section 7.2.

The preceding observations prompt the following definition: class *A depends* on class *B* if *A* cannot work correctly unless *B* works correctly.

Generalizations A generalization is a subclass-superclass relationship. It is represented by an arrow ending in an unfilled triangle touching the superclass. In Fig. 6.5(b), the arrow is from class `Ellipse` to the more general class `Shape`.

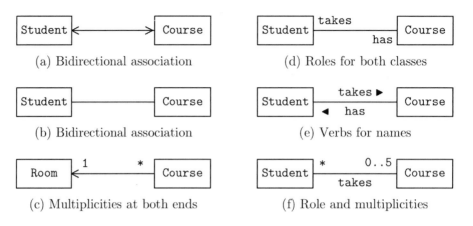

Figure 6.6 Examples of associations.

Class Properties as Associations

UML provides two ways of modeling the properties of a class: as attributes and as associations. With two different notations for properties, when do we use attributes and when do we use associations? Use attributes for properties that have relevance primarily to the given class. Recall that an attribute is written as a line of text within the box for a class. In Fig. 6.4, key is an appropriate attribute of class Delta because the other two classes do not need to know the encryption key.

Use an association when the property is a significant class in its own right. Associations are drawn as links between classes. The simplest form of an association is an arrow from a class to its property. The arrow from class Student to class Course in Fig. 6.6(a) represents an association. It means that a course object is a property of a student object.

Bidirectional Associations A *bidirectional association* represents a pair of complementary properties, depicted by a line between two classes. The line either has no arrowheads or has arrowheads at both ends.

Example 6.7   The real-world situation is that a student has a name and takes courses. Meanwhile, a course has a title, a list of students taking the course, and a meeting room if it meets in person.

Let us model the situation by two classes, Student and Course. These classes have the following complementary properties:

$$\begin{array}{ccc} \text{Student} & \textit{takes} & \text{Course} \\ \text{Course} & \textit{has} & \text{Student} \end{array}$$

Both classes seem equally important, so let us use a bidirectional association to model their complementary relationships; see the line connecting the boxes for the classes in Fig. 6.6(b).   □

Multiplicity In the preceding example, multiple students take multiple courses. Multiplicity is specified by placing a range next to a class at either the source or the target of an association. At the source, the range means that multiple objects of the class have the property. At the target, a range means that an object of the class has multiples of the property.

Example 6.8 Figure 6.6(c) shows a unidirectional association between `Course` and `Room`. The association has multiplicity * next to `Course` and 1 next to `Room`. These multiplicities mean that for an unlimited number of courses, each course has one room. □

Names: Roles and Verbs Associations can be named either after the underlying property or by the role played by a class. For example, given that students take courses, the role of a student is to take a course. So, `takes` is a suitable name for the association between class `Student` and class `Course`. Similarly, courses have students, so `has` is a suitable name for the association between `Course` and `Student`.

In a diagram, a role is shown next to the box for a class. For example, in Fig. 6.6(d), see the roles next to `Student` and `Course`.

Example 6.9 Let us relate names for attributes with roles in associations. As an attribute, the geometric center of a shape is written as a line of text within the box for `Shape`; for example,

center : Point

This property can alternatively be drawn as an association between classes `Shape` and `Point`; see Fig. 6.7. From a design perspective, attribute form seems more appropriate for the geometric center of a shape. □

If a name is a verb, it can be used in a sentence of the form

⟨*source class*⟩ ⟨*verb*⟩ ⟨*target class*⟩

Verbs are directional. The direction of a verb is indicated by a solid triangle. Verbs with directional triangles can be placed by the middle of the arrow for an association; see the example of verbs for students and courses in Fig. 6.6(e).

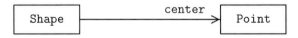

Figure 6.7 The geometric center as an association between classes `Shape` and `Point`.

Box 6.2 Parable: The Philosophers and the Elephant

Architecture is like the elephant in the proverbial tale of the blind philosophers who come upon an elephant for the first time. Each touches a different part of the elephant and comes up with a different view of the animal.

"It's like a thick snake," said the first philosopher, touching the trunk and feeling it moving about. "It's like a fan," argued the second, touching a large ear. "No, it's like a spear," observed the third, feeling the hard smooth tusk. "It's like a tree," said the fourth, touching the elephant's leg.

They were all right, and none of them described the elephant as a whole.[11]

Roles, direction, and multiplicity can be combined, as in "A student takes up to five courses"; see Fig. 6.6(f).

6.4　Architectural Views

The "right" view of an architecture depends on the audience and the architectural message to be conveyed by the view. For user discussions, a logical view shows how the elements in the view will provide the desired functionality and quality attributes. For developer work assignments, a decomposition view partitions the source code into modules that can be developed relatively independently. For system updates, a deployment view shows the distribution of the software onto physical servers. All of these are valid and useful views. By themselves, none of them is a complete characterization of the software architecture of the system. In fact, all of them together may not characterize a system fully.

This section offers four kinds of views for an architect to consider while describing a system: logical, development, dynamic, and deployment.

Views are at the heart of the guidelines in Section 6.5 for describing an architecture. The definition of software architecture in this section focuses on the views that are needed to reason about a system. The concept of views has been incorporated into international standards for architectural descriptions.[12]

Typically, a view outlines a solution to some architectural problem. Other aspects of the system that are not relevant to the solution are suppressed. It is better to keep a view focused and simple than it is to attempt to capture everything about an architecture in a single view.

6.4.1　The 4+1 Grouping of Views

The *4+1 grouping* of views has four kinds of views for a software architecture (see Fig. 6.8):

- *Logical views* describe the handling of functional requirements.
- *Development views* show the modular decomposition of the source text.

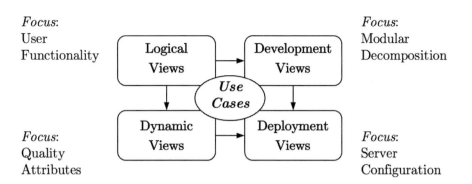

Focus:
User
Functionality

Focus:
Quality
Attributes

Focus:
Modular
Decomposition

Focus:
Server
Configuration

Figure 6.8 The 4+1 grouping of architectural views.

- *Dynamic views* present the run-time components and quality attributes.
- *Deployment views* display the mapping of the software onto servers.[13]

The 4+1 grouping is a helpful starting point for picking views for a project. The "+1" refers to selected scenarios or use cases that span the four kinds of views: see Fig. 6.8.

Logical Views
Logical views focus on end-user functionality. Developers can validate the architecture by tracing how the elements in the view will support a scenario or use case. Logical views facilitate early stakeholder feedback on questions like the following: Will the proposed solution meet user needs and goals? Will it satisfy all stakeholders? Are there any major missing gaps? The views are also useful for probing for potential requirements changes. Section 6.2 has design guidelines for modules that isolate anticipated changes.

Example 6.10   This example is motivated by technicians who provide on-site services; for example, the technicians in Example 1.7 who service swimming pools at customer homes. The logical view in Fig. 6.9 shows two user interfaces: a mobile interface for technicians and a browser interface for managers. The system relies on two external services: a map service that is used for routes to customer sites and a data store that holds customer information and service history.

The system itself is modular, with a layer that handles the user interfaces, an application-logic layer, and a layer that manages the external services.   □

Development Views
Development views guide the development and evolution of the source code for a system. The elements in these views are typically modules. Modules with clear interfaces allow developers of different modules to work independently and in parallel.

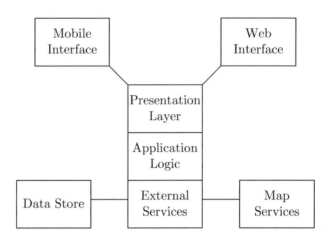

Figure 6.9 A logical view of a system that supports a mobile user interface for technicians and a web user interface for managers. The system uses an external map service and an external data store.

A *decomposition view* of the source code is a development view that shows the decomposition of modules into submodules. Documentation and training materials based on decomposition views can help maintainers, testers, and new team members narrow their searches for the parts of the system that are relevant to their needs; see the approach to architecture description in Section 6.5. Project managers can use decomposition views to estimate development effort, identify needed skills, and make work assignments.

Example 6.11   The diagram in Fig. 6.10 shows a decomposition view of a compiler. A compiler translates source text in a programming language into target code for a machine. The compiler has two modules: a front end that analyzes the source text and a back end that generates the target code. Dependencies on the programming language are confined to the front end and dependencies on the target machine are confined to the back end.

The front end itself is made up of two modules: a lexical analyzer and a syntax analyzer. The back end also has two modules: an optimizer and a code generator. By itself, the hierarchy in Fig. 6.10 does not provide any further information about the elements in the view.   □

Example 6.12   Companies that practice continuous deployment make numerous small changes a day to their production software. These changes have implications for development as well as deployment. The production software must be designed to accommodate code changes gracefully. Both development and deployment views are needed to implement the software updates.   □

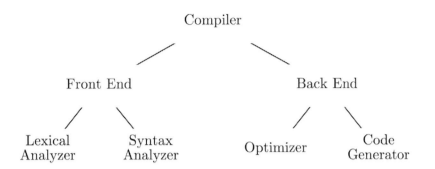

Figure 6.10 A development view of the architecture of a compiler that shows module-submodule relationships.

Dynamic Views

Dynamic views model the components, messages, and data flows that arise at run time. Examples of components include objects and processes. The views can handle distributed or concurrent systems.

Models based on dynamic views are useful for studying quality attributes such as performance, reliability, and security. Models are particularly useful for reasoning about the synchronization of concurrent processes.

Example 6.13   The dynamic view in Fig. 6.11 complements the development view in Fig. 6.10. Both views are of the same compiler. More to the point, both views are of the same architecture. The dynamic view deals with the flow of data at run time.

The compiler translates input text, a character at a time, and translates it in stages into target code for a machine. Each element in the dynamic view handles one stage of the translation. The output of one stage becomes the input to the next stage.   □

There is a sometimes subtle distinction between the architectural elements in development and dynamic views of the same architecture. An element in a development view is like a class and the elements in a dynamic view are like objects of that class. The next example uses a small mathematical problem to illustrate the dynamic creation of architectural elements. The problem arises in practice; for example, some websites spawn a virtual server to handle each request.

Example 6.14   The *sieve method* for finding prime numbers is based on the idea that n is a prime if it is not a multiple of any prime smaller than n.[14] Thus, 3 is a prime because it is not a multiple of 2. And, 5 is a prime because it is not any multiple of either 2 or 3.

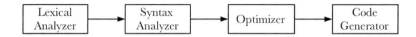

Figure 6.11 A dynamic view of the elements of a compiler at run time. A development view of the same underlying architecture appears in Fig. 6.10.

- The *count* element enumerates the integers, $2, 3, \ldots$.
- The elements called *filter*(p), for $p = 2, 3, 5, \ldots$, where *filter*(p) removes multiples of p.
- The *spawn* element reconfigures itself by creating *filter*(p) whenever an integer p reaches it.

The architecture for generating prime numbers in Fig. 6.12 has three kinds of elements:

The architecture starts out with two elements, *count* and *spawn*; see the snapshot at the top of Fig. 6.12. When 2 reaches *spawn*, it creates *filter*(2) and inserts it to its left, as in the second snapshot from the top. Since 3 is not a multiple of 2, it passes through *filter*(2) and reaches *spawn*, which creates and inserts *filter*(3), as shown in the third snapshot from the top of the figure.

The next integer from *count* is 4. It is a multiple of 2, so it is removed by *filter*(2). But 5 is neither a multiple of 2 nor of 3, so it reaches *spawn*, which inserts *filter*(5).

Since any integer p reaching *spawn* is not a multiple of any integer smaller than p, it must be a prime.

The sieve method is attributed to the Greek philosopher Eratosthenes. The version in this example is due to Doug McIlroy.   □

Deployment Views (Physical Views)

Deployment views are also known as physical views because they deal with the actual servers that the software runs on. The applications of deployment views include depictions of the geographic distribution of servers and replication of servers for scale, performance, and availability.

6.4.2   Structures and Views

In design discussions, it is convenient to use the term "structure" for a specific relationship between architectural elements. For example, Fig. 6.10 shows a "hierarchical module-submodule structure" of a compiler, and Fig. 6.11 shows a "data flow structure" of the same compiler. Here, we have two different structures for the same underlying architecture.

The intuitive notion of structure can be made precise by defining an *architectural structure* to be a binary relation on the elements in a view. Precision is needed when we reason about a system in terms of the elements in a view.

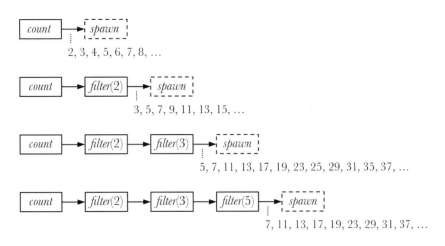

Figure 6.12 A dynamic view of a reconfigurable architecture for generating prime numbers.

Example 6.15   With the encryption system in Fig. 6.2, the *uses* structure of the system
is as follows:

$$\textit{Encrypt} \quad \textit{uses} \quad \textit{Delta}$$
$$\textit{Encrypt} \quad \textit{uses} \quad \textit{Shift}$$
$$\textit{Shift} \quad \textit{uses} \quad \textit{Delta}$$

Module *Encrypt* uses *Delta* to manage the key, and it uses *Shift* to encrypt the plain text,
one letter at a time. Module *Shift* uses *Delta* to help decide how to encrypt individual
letters.   ☐

In general, a view can have multiple structures. For example, views of a model-
view-controller architecture use different kinds of arrows to distinguish between
caller-callee message flows and event notifications, as we shall see in Section 7.3.
The different arrows represent the calling structure and the notification structure.

Definition of Software Architecture

Software architecture has proven hard to pin down and define. The Software Engineering Institute (SEI) has compiled a list of a dozen definitions from "some of the more
prominent or influential books and papers on architecture."[15] Previously, SEI collected
over 200 definitions from visitors to its website.

The working definition of architecture in Section 6.1 is a variant of the following
definition due to Leonard Bass, Paul Clements, and Rick Kazman, all formerly from
SEI:[16]

The *software architecture* of a system is the set of structures and views needed to reason about
the system. The structures comprise software elements, relations among them, and properties of
both.

Note that this definition does not mention any specific structures or views. An architect has the flexibility to choose the most appropriate views for a given purpose.

6.5   Describing System Architecture

Sooner or later, an architect will be called upon to present the architecture of a system to stakeholders or managers. What should the architect present?

An effective approach is to provide two things: (a) an overview of the system, (b) the main views. Include the rationale for the design in the system overview. This approach is also suitable for lightweight documentation. The documentation need not be elaborate and it need not be completed up front. All projects need some documentation, because products can have a long life, extending long past the initial delivery date.[17]

6.5.1   Outline for an Architecture Description

The following outline is suitable for presentations to a broad range of stakeholders. It can also be used for documentation. It addresses some of the top concerns about software development that emerged from a survey of architects, developers, and testers at Microsoft. The list of concerns is topped by the following:

"Understanding the rationale behind a piece of code"

In the survey, 66 percent agreed that this statement represents a "serious problem for me." The list includes the following:

"Understanding code that someone else wrote."	56 percent
"Understanding the impact of changes I make on code elsewhere."	55 percent

Again, the percentages refer to those agreeing that the statement is a serious problem.[18]

Part I: System Overview

Start with the motivation and context for the architecture. Architecture reviews begin with the problem to be solved, as we shall see in Section 8.1. Reviewers probe for whether the architecture adequately addresses the problem. What is the external environment that this system live within?

Such questions motivate the following outline for a system overview. For readability, use plain language, without jargon.

1. **Introduction**

   1 Introduce the problem.
   2 Identify the challenges.
   3 Summarize the rationale for the design, including what not to change with the design.

2. **Context Diagram(s)** A context diagram shows interactions between the current system – the one that is being described – and its environment.

   (a) Clearly mark the boundaries of the current system.
   (b) Show message and data flows across the boundary between the current system and external platforms, databases, and services; for example, for locations and maps.
   (c) If the current system is part of a larger system, highlight interactions across the boundary with the rest of the larger system.
   (d) Keep the context diagram simple. Use views to describe the current system itself.

3. **Views** The views are the heart of the description of a software architecture. In this overview, mention the main views and their purpose. See Part II (following) for how to prepare guides for the views.

Part II: Guides for the Views

The purpose of view guides is to show how the system works. Guides serve as aids during discussions with stakeholders. Developers who want to dig deeper can use view guides to search for the parts of the system that are relevant to their work. In other words, the guides help narrow their search for specific information about an implementation.

Here is an outline for preparing a view guide. Note: Avoid unnecessary duplication. Put information where it fits, between the system overview and a view guide.

1. **Primary Diagram**

   (a) Show the architectural elements in the view and their relationships.
   (b) In a caption or a legend within the diagram, define what the symbols, lines, and boxes represent.
   (c) Briefly describe the view in plain language.

2. **Element Catalog** An element catalog can begin simply with the name and purpose of an element. Further information can be added as needed.

   (a) Name of the element.
   (b) Briefly describe the purpose of the element and the services it provides.
   (c) Include the element's relationships with other elements.
   (d) Add notes on key design decisions for the element, including what not to change.

3. Optional: add any other view-specific information.

6.5.2   System Overview of a Communications App

Example 6.16 This example provides a system overview for a communications app for a tablet or smartphone. Let us call it CommApp.[19]

Introduction to CommApp

Problem Statement CommApp enables a user to communicate via any combination of audio, video, and text with others, who may or may not be using CommApp. A user can be in multiple communication sessions at the same time. Users can split and merge sessions for sidebar conversations. Convenience and usability are prime concerns.

Challenges The biggest challenge is the effective use of the screen space, especially on a smartphone. The user interface could change, perhaps drastically, based on feedback from user trials.

Design Rationale Since the user interface is subject to change, the design uses a model-view-controller architecture, which isolates the look-and-feel of the interface in the View module. The Model module manages the data and logic for CommApp. The Controller module sets up and tears down audio/video/text connections with the help of the media-handling facilities of the tablet or smartphone. (See Section 7.3 for model-view-controller architectures.)

Context Diagram
The context diagram for CommApp in Fig. 6.13 shows two external services: Data Store and Media. The Model uses persistent Data Store to hold data about current sessions, and communication history. The Controller works with the Media module, which represents the audio/video/text services of the underlying tablet or smartphone.

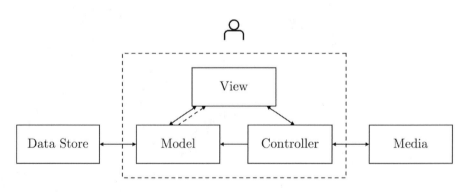

Figure 6.13 Context diagram for the communications application CommApp. The dashed box marks the boundary of the system. Arrows represent message flows; the dashed arrow represents notifications. The external elements are Data Store and Media (for access to media services for audio, video, and text).

Views

This architecture description for CommApp has two main views:

- **Message View**. Shows the division of work between Model, View, and Controller. The view also shows the flow of messages between them.
- **Decomposition or Module Hierarchy View**. Shows the next level of detail for Model and View. The view shows the module-submodule relationships in the source code.

(The hierarchy view is described in the following section.)   □

6.5.3   A Development View: Module Hierarchies

Beyond a dozen or so modules, it becomes increasingly difficult to find the modules that are relevant to some specific aspect of a system. A *module hierarchy* is a decomposition view. It groups modules based on their module-submodule relationships. A hierarchy is an aid for navigating through the modules in a large system.

Primary Diagram for a Module Hierarchy

The primary diagram of a module hierarchy view is a tree with modules at the nodes. The parent-child relationship in the tree represents the module-submodule relationship in the source code.

Example 6.17   The partial module hierarchy in Fig. 6.14 is for the communications app in Example 6.16. The root of the tree is for the entire app. The children of the root represent the three main modules: Model, View, and Controller. The hierarchy also shows submodules for Model and View.   □

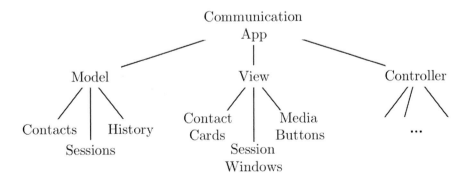

Figure 6.14 A partial module hierarchy for CommApp in Example 6.16.

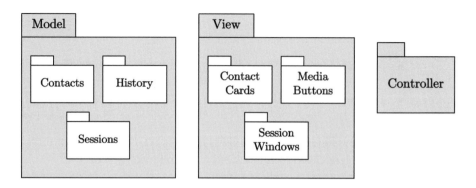

Figure 6.15 UML packages corresponding to the module hierarchy in Fig. 6.14.

UML Package Diagrams

Modules correspond roughly to packages in UML, and module hierarchies correspond to package diagrams. A **UML package** is a grouping of UML elements. Packages can be nested; that is, a package can have sub-packages.

The package diagram in Fig. 6.15 corresponds to the module hierarchy in Fig. 6.14. In UML package diagrams, packages are represented by tabbed boxes. The simplest representation of a package is a box with the name of the package in the box; for example, see the box for the Controller on the right. The contents of a package can be shown within the box for the package. When the contents are shown, the name of the package belongs in the tab; for example, see the representation of the View in the middle of Fig. 6.15.

Example: An Element in the Catalog

Example 6.18   The elements in the hierarchy in Fig. 6.14 are the modules at the nodes in the tree. This example illustrates the description of an element.

Element View

Purpose The View handles the presentation of the current communications sessions, contacts, and history. Each session is represented by a window; each contact is represented by a small card. A user may add and remove contacts from sessions by dragging their cards in and out of the relevant session windows. The user can split and merge sessions for sidebar conversations.

Rationale The look and feel of the app are subject to change, so the look-and-feel decisions are isolated within the View module. For example, session windows need not be rectangles with hard edges.

The approach of managing sessions by moving contact cards is not subject to change.

Relationships The View relies on the Model to manage the data and the Controller to manage the connections for the audio, video, and text streams.   □

6.6   Conclusion

Design and architecture enable stakeholders to understand and reason about the behavior of a system. Architecture is used to describe how the parts of a system support its external behavior and attributes. Design includes architecture. It is used to describe both the internal and external properties of the system. Descriptions of design and architecture focus on the aspects of a system that are relevant for a given purpose. They simplify the description by suppressing or hiding the all other aspects.

An architectural view highlights a set of the system into parts – the parts are called architectural elements, or simply elements. In a modular system, the elements interact with each other only through their interfaces. Different views highlight potentially different elements and their relationships.

There are no hard-and-fast rules for how to pick elements for a view. The 4+1 grouping of views identifies four kinds of views that occur frequently in practice:

- Logical views focus on end-user functionality. They are useful for confirming that a proposed solution will meet user needs.
- Development views focus on program structure and the source text. They are useful for assembling the required skills and for assigning work to developers.
- Dynamic views focus on run-time components and their behavior; for example, on objects and processes. They are useful for modeling system properties, such as quality attributes (scale, performance, availability, and so on).
- Deployment views focus on system configurations and distribution of software onto servers. They are useful for system installation, operation, and maintenance.

These views are accompanied by scenarios or use cases that can touch multiple views. Scenarios account for the +1 in the name 4+1.

Classes and modules are typical architectural elements in development views. "Module" is a general term that applies not only to classes, but to any grouping of related data, operations, and other constructs. Modules have well-defined interfaces. Implementation hiding is a key principle for the design of modules. The idea is to give each module a specific responsibility and then hide the implementation of the responsibility from the other modules. This hiding is achieved by having modules interact only through their interfaces.

Systems that embody implementation hiding are called modular. Modularity makes systems easier to work with, since we can reason about their properties in terms of module responsibilities; that is, the services that the modules provide each other. Modularity also makes systems easier to modify. As long as the interface to a module remains intact, we can change the module's implementation without touching the rest of the system. Thus, we can plan for change by isolating likely changes within modules.

See Section 6.2 for guidelines for designing modules. The guidelines also apply to classes.

A presentation or lightweight documentation about a system architecture can be created by using the following outline:

System Overview

1. **Introduction** Introduce the problem and the challenges. Summarize the rationale for the solution.
2. **Context Diagram** Show the system and its environment; for example, with external services.
3. **Views** List the main views and their purposes.

Guide for a View

1. **Primary Diagram** Show the view's architectural elements and their relationships.
2. **Element Catalog** List each element's name and purpose. As needed, briefly describe the rationale for its design and its relationships with other elements.

Further Reading

- Fowler [70] provides an introduction to UML.
- For more on describing a system architecture, see Clements et al. [46].
- Bass, Clements, and Kazman [14] is a general reference for software architecture.

Exercises for Chapter 6

Exercise 6.1   Modules are a key concept in software architecture and design.

- What is Information Hiding? Define it in a sentence, explain it in at most three sentences, and give an example in at most a paragraph.
- What is a Module Guide? List its main elements and their purpose or roles.

Exercise 6.2   Are the following statements generally true or generally false? Briefly explain your answers.

a) The Information Hiding Principle refers to hiding the design decisions in a module.
b) A Module Guide describes the implementation of each module.
c) A module with a secret cannot be changed.
d) A Module Interface Specification specifies the services provided and the services needed by modules.
e) With the XP focus on the simplest thing that could possibly work and on refactoring to clean up the design as new code is added, there is no need for architecture.

f) A system that obeys the Information Hiding principle is secure.

g) If module A uses module B, then A and B must have an ancestor-descendant relation in the module hierarchy.

h) If module A uses module B, then B must be present and satisfy its specification for A to satisfy its specification.

i) A Development View of an architecture specifies the internal structure of modules.

j) Conway's "Law" implies that the architecture of a system reflects the social structure of the producing organization.

Exercise 6.3   A video-streaming service wants to track the most frequently requested videos. They have asked your company to bid on a system that will accept a stream of video orders and incrementally maintain the top ten most popular videos so far. Requests contain other information besides the item name; for example, the video's price, its category (for example, Historical, Comedy, Action).

a) Using Information Hiding, give a high-level design. Include each module's secret.

b) Change your design to track both the top ten videos and the top ten categories; for example, to settle whether Comedy videos are more popular than Action videos.

Exercise 6.4   Coupling is the degree to which modules are interrelated. Forms of coupling include the following:

a) *Message*: pass messages through their interfaces.

b) *Subclass*: inherit methods and data from a superclass.

c) *Global*: two or more modules share the same global data.

d) *Content*: one module relies on the implementation of another.

For each of the preceding cases, suppose modules A and B have that kind of coupling. How would you refactor A and B into modules $M_1, M_2, \cdots$ that comply with Information Hiding and provide the same services as A and B? That is, for each public function $A.f()$ or $B.f()$ in the interfaces of A and B, there is an equivalent function $M_i.f()$ for some refactored module M_i.

Exercise 6.5   For the system in Exercise 6.3, you decide to treat the system as a product family because you recognize that the same approach can be applied to track top-selling items for a retailer or the most emailed items for a news company.

a) What do product family members have in common?

b) What are the variabilities; that is, how do product family members differ?

Exercise 6.6   KWIC is an acronym for Key Word in Context. A KWIC index is formed by sorting and aligning all the "significant" words in a title. For simplicity, assume that capitalized words are the only significant words. As an example, the title `Wikipedia the Free Encyclopedia` has three significant words, `Wikipedia`, `Free`, and `Encyclopedia`. For the two titles

```
KWIC is an  Acronym for Keyword in Context
Wikipedia the Free Encyclopedia
```

the KWIC index is as follows:

```
              KWIC is an    Acronym for Keyword in Conte
    is an Acronym for Keyword in    Context
           Wikipedia the Free    Encyclopedia
               Wikipedia the    Free Encyclopedia
        KWIC is an Acronym for    Keyword in Context
                                 KWIC is an Acronym for Keywo
                                 Wikipedia the Free Encyclope
```

Design an architecture for KWIC indexes that hides the representation of titles in a module.

a) Give brief descriptions of the modules in your architecture.
b) For each module, list the messages to the module and the corresponding responses from the module.
c) Give a module hierarchy.
d) Describe the secret of each module.

Exercise 6.7   Given a month and a year, the Unix `cal` command produces a calendar for that month; for example, cal 10 1752 produces

```
       October 1752
    Su Mo Tu We Th Fr Sa
     1  2  3  4  5  6  7
     8  9 10 11 12 13 14
    15 16 17 18 19 20 21
    22 23 24 25 26 27 28
    29 30 31
```

Given a year, as in `cal 2000`, the output is a calendar for that year.

Your task is to design a modular architecture for a proposed implementation of the `cal` command. (See instructions below.)

a) List the modules in your architecture. Design each module so it has a coherent responsibility and so it can be modified independently of the others. Use descriptive names for the modules.
b) Provide a brief overview of how the modules interact to produce the calendar for a month.
c) Provide a view guide that consists of a module hierarchy and an element catalog.

Here are some instructions:

• Allow for your version of `cal` to be modified, if needed, to produce dates in the European style, with Monday as the first day of the week in the calendar for a month. Note that the preceding example is in the US style, with Sunday as the first day of the week.
The format for a yearly calendar has yet to be determined.

- As a simplification, your design must work for months starting October 1752 and full years starting 1753. Thus, the start date for your calendar is Sunday, October 1, 1752. (The US calendar changed in September 1752: the month had only 19 days instead of the usual 30.)
- Note that this exercise is about a modular software architecture, not its implementation.

7   Architectural Patterns

Rather than start each design from scratch, software architects tend to adapt earlier successful designs for similar problems. Even if they do not reuse any code, the solution approach gives them a head start with the current problem. Problems like fault tolerance have been addressed over and over again. (The idea for a solution is to have a live backup system that takes over if the primary system fails due to a hardware or software fault.)

An *architectural pattern* outlines properties that are common to all solutions of a design problem that occurs over and over again. A pattern provides the *core of a solution*, in the form of guidelines for designing a specific solution.

This chapter introduces some frequently occurring architectural patterns. A partial list appears in Fig. 7.1. To aid the selection of a pattern in a given situation, the figure mentions what each pattern is good for. Additional patterns related to clients and servers are covered in Section 7.5. Section 7.6 deals with product families and product lines, where products share a "core" of common properties.

> This chapter will enable the reader to:
>
> - Explain, with examples, the concept of architectural patterns.
> - Design software systems using patterns such as layering, model-view-controller, dataflow, and client-server.
> - Describe the creation of a product line by identifying product commonalities (common properties) and variabilities (properties specific to a member of the product line).

7.1   Software Layering

The selection of patterns for a project is often based on the desired functionality and quality attributes. The Layered pattern is popular because it is useful for building software that is reusable and/or portable. A module is said to be *ported* when it is moved from one system to another. The pattern can be used on both a small scale for individual modules and a large scale for entire subsystems.

Model-View-Controller

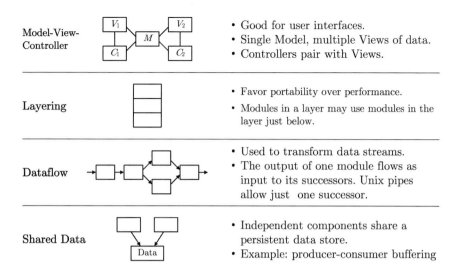

- Good for user interfaces.
- Single Model, multiple Views of data.
- Controllers pair with Views.

Layering

- Favor portability over performance.
- Modules in a layer may use modules in the layer just below.

Dataflow

- Used to transform data streams.
- The output of one module flows as input to its successors. Unix pipes allow just one successor.

Shared Data

- Independent components share a persistent data store.
- Example: producer-consumer buffering

Figure 7.1 Some frequently occurring patterns.

Box 7.1 Alexander's Patterns

Patterns for software design and architecture were modeled on the work of the building architect and urban planner Christopher Alexander and his colleagues.[1] Alexander's patterns have three sections: context, problem, and the core of a solution. Each problem is some fundamental aspect of a design. The context ranges from designs for an entire community to designs for the interior spaces of a single building.

   For example, pattern 116 of 253, Cascade of Roofs, is for roofs for a building cluster. The core of a solution for this pattern includes the design guidance: place "the largest, highest, and widest roofs" in the middle, "over those parts of the building which are the most significant." The Hagia Sophia in Istanbul has such a cascade of roofs; see Fig. 7.2.[2]

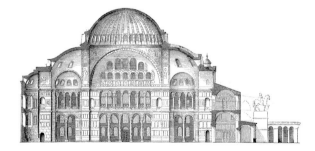

Figure 7.2 Cross section of the Hagia Sophia. Public domain image, by Wikimedia Commons.

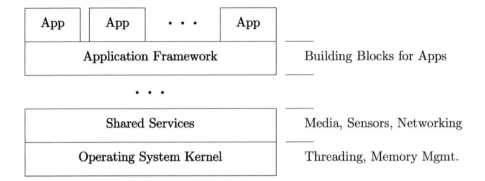

Figure 7.3 A layered architecture for implementing apps.

The layered pattern was used in Example 1.7 for an app for mobile technicians. The examples in this section illustrate the use of the pattern for smartphone operating systems and Internet communication protocols. A *protocol* is a set of rules for exchanging data between devices and applications. The section also examines design trade-offs associated with layering. Trade-offs occur when there are competing design goals, such as reusability and efficiency, or portability and performance.

7.1.1   The Layered Pattern

Problem Design and build reusable and portable software.

Core of a Solution Partition the system into groups of related modules called *layers*, where each layer has a specific responsibility. Organize the layers so they can be stacked vertically, one layer above another, as in Fig. 7.3. The modules in a layer A may use the modules in layer A and in layer B immediately below A, but they may not use any modules in any layer above A.

Example 7.1   The diagram in Fig. 7.3 is motivated by apps running on a smartphone. The top layer is for apps available to the user. The layer just below it is for a framework that provides building blocks for assembling apps.

The bottom layer is for the operating system, which hides the hardware. Immediately above the operating system is a layer that supports services that are shared by the apps, such as services for audio, video, sensors, and network connections.

In between the top two and the bottom two layers there may be one or more other layers. For example, the Android architecture has a "runtime" layer that insulates the apps: each app has its own virtual machine.   □

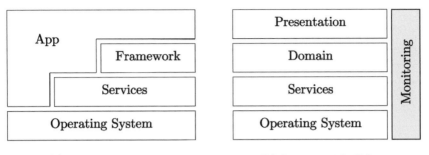

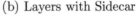

    (a) Layer Bridging   (b) Layers with Sidecar

Figure 7.4 Variants of the layered pattern.

Reusability and Portability These two attributes are related, but they are distinct. For a shining example of reusability, the existing Internet infrastructure was reused for a new purpose when web browsing was layered above it, without any change to the infrastructure. Specifically, HTTP was layered above the Internet protocols, TCP and IP. For an example of portability, the Unix operating system is ported whenever it is moved from one machine to another kind of machine.

In short, an upper layer is ported when we move it from atop one lower layer to another. Meanwhile, a lower layer is reused when we add a new upper layer above it.

Variants of the Layered Pattern
The layered pattern has spawned a number of variants. Two of them are layer bridging and layers with sidecar; see Fig. 7.4.

Layer Bridging With *layer bridging*, a layer may have more than one layer directly below it. In Fig. 7.4(a), the App layer is drawn so it touches each of the other layers below it. Thus, modules in the App layer may use modules in any of the other layers: Framework, Services, and Operating System.

Layers with Sidecar The *layers with sidecar* pattern differs from the layered pattern by having one layer – called the *sidecar* – that vertically spans all the other horizontal layers; for example, see Fig. 7.4(b). A vertical cross-cutting sidecar layer may be used for debugging, auditing, security, or operations management. In Fig. 7.4(b), the sidecar layer is a monitoring layer.

Care is needed with a sidecar to ensure that layering is preserved; that is, lower layers cannot access upper layers indirectly through the sidecar. Layering can be preserved if communications with the sidecar are one-way, either to or from the sidecar, but not in both directions. In a debugging or audit setting, modules in the sidecar may reach into the other layers and use modules in the horizontal layers. On the other hand, in a logging or monitoring setting, modules in the horizontal layers may use the sidecar to deposit event logs.

7.1.2   Design Trade-offs

The layered pattern results in *strict layering*, where each layer knows only about itself and the interface of the layer directly below. Layer boundaries are hard and layer implementations are hidden. New layers can be added without touching the layers below.

In practice, designers face trade-offs between strictness of layering and other goals. The designers of the Internet protocols chose strictness and reusability, accepting some loss of efficiency in data transmission. By contrast, when Unix was ported from one machine to another, the designers sacrificed some portability (strictness) for performance. They favored performance at the expense of some added effort because an operating system is ported once to a new machine, and then used over and over again on the new machine.

Internet Protocols: Prioritize Reusability over Efficiency
Strict layering has proven to be enormously successful for the Internet. The *Internet Protocol Suite* has four layers of protocols: Application, Transport, Internet, and Link. The layers are referred to collectively as the IP stack.

Each endpoint attached to the Internet runs a copy of the IP stack, which it uses to exchange data with other endpoints. Data goes from a source to a destination in chunks called *packets*. Logically, a packet goes from a given layer of the IP stack at the source to the corresponding layer of the IP stack at the destination. The dashed arrows in Fig. 7.5 represent the flow of packets between corresponding layers at two endpoints. In fact, data packets follow the path of the solid arrows: they go do down the IP stack at the source, across links in the network to the destination, and then up the IP stack to the matching layer. The responsibilities of the layers are outlined in Box 7.2.

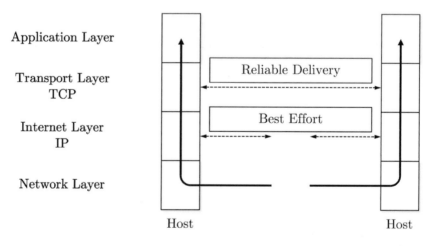

Application Layer

Transport Layer
TCP

Reliable Delivery

Internet Layer
IP

Best Effort

Network Layer

Host   Host

Figure 7.5 Each endpoint (host) attached to the Internet runs a copy of the IP stack of protocols. The dashed arrows represent the logical flow of data between corresponding layers at the endpoints. The solid arrows represent the actual path between applications at the endpoints.

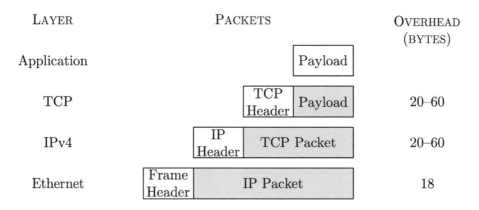

Figure 7.6 Packet headers represent overhead during data communication. The size of an application packet (payload)) is 64–1518 bytes. Each layer adds its own headers.

Example 7.2   Strict layering of Internet protocols results in some data transmission overhead. The lower layers of the IP stack are unaware of the layers above them, so each layer adds its own identifying information to a packet, in the form of a *header*; see Fig. 7.6. The actual data that the endpoints want to exchange, called the *payload*, must carry the packet headers with it as overhead.

Starting at the top of Fig. 7.6, a TCP header is added when a payload of between 64 and 1518 bytes goes down the IP stack to the TCP layer. The payload is shaded at the TCP level, since TCP does not look inside the packet at the payload. An IP header is added as the now TCP packet goes to the IP layer. At the IP level, the TCP packet is shaded since IP does not look inside it. Another header is added at the Link layer. At the destination, the headers are stripped as a packet goes up the IP stack to deliver the payload to the application there.

The header sizes in Fig. 7.6 are based on the assumption that IPv4 (IP version 4) is the Internet Layer protocol and that Ethernet is the Link Layer protocol. For simplicity, we abbreviate IPv4 to IP.   □

Unix Design Trade-offs: Performance and Portability

Different projects make different trade-offs between strictness of layering and performance. In the next example, some one-time portability effort was sacrificed for continuing performance for users. Measured in lines of code, the first version of Unix in C was 95 percent portable. By contrast, IP protocols are 100 percent reusable (strict).

Example 7.3   The Unix operating system and its derivatives, including Linux, run on a wide range of machines, from small smartphones to huge server farms in data centers. For each machine class, the operating system is ported once to that class of machines. Users, perhaps millions of them, then run copies of the operating system on their individual machines of that class.

When Unix was first ported from one machine to another, the designers wanted both performance for users and portability for designers. Efficient performance was a higher priority. Some portability was sacrificed: the resulting C code for the core operating system was 95 percent the same across machines.

One of the design goals was "identifying and isolating machine dependencies." The 5 percent of the code that was machine dependent was there for efficiency: it took advantage of the special features of the underlying machine.[3]   □

7.2   Three Building Blocks

The three patterns in this section are useful in their own right. They are also useful building blocks for other more complex patterns. The three patterns are shared-data, observer, and publish-subscribe. The shared-data and observer patterns will be used in Section 7.3 for the model-view-controller pattern. Observers and subscribers have enough similarities that we discuss them both in this section.

Box 7.2 Layers of the IP Stack

The following is a brief overview of the layers of the IP stack:

a) **Application Layer**. HTTP, *Hypertext Transfer Protocol*, is an Application Layer protocol. A browser sends an HTTP packet to a web server to retrieve a web page. The data transfers occur through the Transport layer.

b) **Transport Layer**. TCP, *Transmission Control Protocol*, is the main Transport Layer protocol. TCP at a source and TCP at its destination cooperate to ensure reliable delivery of data packets. Packets go through the Internet Layer. If a packet gets lost en route, the destination TCP asks the source TCP to retransmit the packet. Retransmission can result in delivery delays.

c) **Internet Layer**. IP stands for *Internet Protocol*. The Internet layer is responsible for routing packets through a network of router devices connected by links. A route is a path of links from a source to a destination. One packet from a source in San Francisco to a destination in New Delhi might go through a router in London, while another goes through Tokyo. IP aims for timely delivery, but packets may be dropped or delivered out of order due to delays along a route.

d) **Link Layer**. The links between routers in the network use various wired and wireless technologies. Link Layer protocols are responsible for carrying packets along a link.

In short, TCP provides reliable delivery, but packets may be delayed. IP provides timely "best effort" delivery, where packets may be lost.

7.2.1   The Shared-Data Pattern

The need for a shared data repository arises whenever two or more independent components want to access common data, but none of them wants to own and manage all the data. That is, managing the data does not logically fit with the responsibilities of any of the components. The shared data could be anything from a data structure shared by two components to a very large distributed data store that holds a company's business transactions.

Example 7.4   As a small example, consider two components, a producer and a consumer. The producer sends objects at its own pace, and the consumer accepts the objects at its own pace. At times, the producer sends objects faster than the consumer can accept them. At other times, it runs slower.

A shared data buffer allows the producer and the consumer to run at different rates. If the producer runs ahead, the buffer holds objects until the consumer is ready for them. If the buffer fills up, the producer waits until space frees up. At other times, the consumer might work down some of the objects held in the buffer. If the buffer is empty, the consumer waits until the producer adds another object to the buffer.

The use of a separate shared buffer simplifies the design of both the producer and the consumer. The design also allows the implementation of the buffer to be changed without affecting the producer and the consumer.   □

Name The Shared-Data Pattern.

Problem Allow multiple independent components to access and manipulate persistent data that does not logically belong with any of them.

Core of a Solution For convenience, call the multiple independent components *accessors*. Simplify the design of the accessors by adding a new component to hold and manage the persistent data that does not logically belong with any of the accessors. Call the new component a *shared data store*. The data store provides an interface through which the accessors access and manipulate the data. The accessors interact with each other only through the data they put into and get from the data store.

The accessors use the data store, but the data store is not aware of them – it responds to requests through its interface.

Building on the Shared-Data Pattern

Since the shared data store isolates and hides its implementation behind an interface, the implementation can be enhanced without affecting the accessors. Large critical data stores often have enhancements like the following:

- **Reliability** With multiple accessors depending on it, a single shared data store is potentially a single point of failure. The data store can be made fault tolerant by adding a backup copy of the data. If the primary fails, the backup takes over. If the backup is at a different geographic site, a disaster at one site need not bring down the data store.

- **Performance** A shared data store is also a potential performance bottleneck. Performance can be improved by caching, locally or within a network. If a local cached copy of the data is available, then network delays can be avoided.
- **Scalability** Copies of the data can improve scalability, but they bring with them the problem of keeping the copies consistent with each other.

7.2.2   Observers and Subscribers

The observer and the publish-subscribe patterns are closely related. In both patterns, a *publisher* component raises (publishes) an event, unaware of who is interested in being notified about the event. The two patterns differ in whether the interested component knows the publisher. An interested component is called an *observer* if it knows the identity of the publisher. It is called a *subscriber* if it does not know the publisher.

Shared Context for Observers and Subscribers The term component refers to processes and objects that are created and garbage collected dynamically at run time. Independent components may need to communicate during a computation, but may not know one another's identity. The reasons are twofold. The first is that components can come and go dynamically at any time. The second is that identities may be hidden by design.

The Observer Pattern

Problem How can observers be notified about events raised by publishers? An observer knows the identity of a publisher, but a publisher is unaware of the identities – or even the existence – of its observers.

Core of a Solution For simplicity, assume that each publisher raises just one class of events. Associated with each publisher is a set S of registered observers. The publisher knows its set S, but it does not see the contents of S, so it is unaware of its observers.

1. A component C registers for S, the set of observers for a publisher. It registers to get notifications whenever the publisher raises an event. Recall that the publisher's identity is known, so component C knows how to find the set S for the publisher.
2. When a publisher has something to communicate (publish), it raises an event.
3. The publisher's set S delivers notifications of the event to all registered observers in set S.

Example 7.5   Observer registration and notification are often handled by maintaining a list of registered observers. One option is to have a list manager module as part of the publisher. The list manager isolates the list of observers from the rest of the code for the publisher. This isolation supports the claim that the publisher does not know its observers.

A component registers by accessing the list manager through the publisher's interface. When it registers, the component is added to the list of observers. When a publisher raises an event, it tells the list manager of the event. The list manager then notifies all registered observers of the event.   □

The Publish-Subscribe Pattern

Problem How can subscribers be notified about events raised by publishers, when neither publishers nor subscribers are aware of each others' identity? A component can be both a publisher and a subscriber (of different classes of events).

Core of a Solution Add a third party to provide a level of indirection. Both publishers and subscribers know about the third party, but they do not know about each other. The third party takes the form of *middleware*, which sits in a layer between the operating system and an application. The publishers and subscribers are part of the application.

Communication between publishers and subscribers is through the middleware:

1. Each publisher of events registers with the middleware.
2. A subscriber registers with the middleware to be notified about a specific class of events.
3. A publisher raises an event through the middleware.
4. The middleware broadcasts the event to all subscribers.
5. Subscribers are notified of all events. They pick out the events that are of interest to them.

Notes The overhead of scanning for events of interest increases as the ratio of uninteresting events increases. The routing of events through the middleware also adds latency to event delivery. In other words, the use of the middleware adds a delay between the time a publisher raises an event and the time the event is delivered to a subscriber.

7.3   User Interfaces: Model-View-Controller

Interactive user interfaces are routinely based on a model-view-controller (MVC) architecture, which takes its name from the three main components in the architecture. In Trygve Reenskaug's original 1979 design for Smalltalk, the model consisted of run-time objects, a view was a representation of the model on a screen, and a controller mediated between a user and a view.[4] This section explores the design decisions behind MVC variants.[5]

7.3.1   Design Decisions

The central idea behind MVC architectures is *separated presentation*: separate the application domain objects from their presentation through a user interface. This design decision enables multiple presentations of the same objects. In an MVC architecture, the model is responsible for the domain objects and logic. Together, a view and its controller are responsible for a presentation of data from the model. Each view-controller pair has its own way of presenting the same data. MVC architectures differ in the division of work between views and controllers.

When it is clear from the context, we use the terms "presentation" and "view" interchangeably. Both terms refer to the display of information to a user.

Separated Presentation

The popular saying "The map is not the territory" illustrates the distinction between views and models: a model corresponds to the territory and a view corresponds to a map. There can be many maps of the same territory; for example, a satellite map, a street map, or a topographical map. The following example illustrates the separation between models and views.

Example 7.6   In a photo-editing application, the photo objects belong in the model. Each photo object has attributes such as the photo's height, width, resolution, and the pixels that make up its image. The model also includes the logic for operations on the photo; for example, for resizing it or cropping it.

Two presentations of a photo object appear in Fig. 7.7. Both presentations get their information from the model, but they display different attributes. The image view on the left displays a picture of the Mona Lisa; that is, it displays the pixels in the photo object. The dialog view on the right displays numeric values for the photo's height, width, and resolution in pixels per inch. The height and width are given in both inches and in pixels.   □

Observing the Model for Changes

By design, all views present the same data from the model. So, when the user makes a change through one view, the change must be propagated not only to the model, but to all the other views as well. In short, the views and the model need to remain synchronized.

Example 7.7   Consider again the photo-editing application in Example 7.6 and the two presentations of a photo in Fig. 7.7. For this example, suppose that the proportions of the photo are fixed. In other words, the ratio of height to width is fixed: if the height changes, the width changes accordingly, and vice versa.

inches   pixels

Width: 1.00   300

Height: 1.50   450

Resolution: 300

Cancel   OK

Figure 7.7 Two views of a photo object. Public domain image of the Mona Lisa, by Wikimedia Commons.

Now, suppose that the user doubles the numeric value of the height from 450 to 900 pixels in the dialog view. The model is unaware of the presentations, but in the other direction, the presentations know about the model. Between them, the view and the controller for the dialog presentation can therefore send a message to the model that the height has doubled. The model can then update the other photo attributes: the width must double and the pixels from the original image have to be mapped onto the pixels for the doubled image. (Both the height and width double, so the number of pixels quadruples.)

When the model changes, both presentations must synchronize with the model to ensure that they display the current state of the photo object.   □

To synchronize a presentation with the model, MVC architectures use the observer pattern introduced in Section 7.2. Between them, either a view or its controller observe the model. When they are notified of a change, they retrieve the current information from the model.

Is it the view or is it the controller that observes the model? The answer depends on the specific MVC architecture.

7.3.2 The Basic Model-View-Controller Pattern

The basic MVC pattern builds on the preceding discussion of separated presentation and observer synchronization.

Problem Design a graphical user interface for an application. Allow the same information to be presented in multiple ways.

Core of a Solution The key design decision is to use separated presentation: separate the user input/output (the presentation) from the application-domain logic and objects. The solution approach has three kinds of components (see Fig. 7.8):

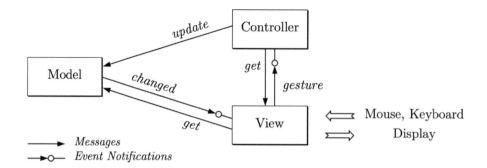

Figure 7.8 A classic model-view-controller architecture. The view interacts with the user and notifies the controller of user activity. The controller gets and interprets the activity. It informs the model about updates. When the model changes, it raises an event. The view observes the model for changes and retrieves any updates so it can stay synchronized with the model.

- **Model** The *model* is responsible for the domain logic and objects. There is one model per application domain.
- **View** A *view* is responsible for (a) displaying information from the model and (b) detecting user activity through mouse clicks, keystrokes, and touch gestures. Each view is paired with a controller. When a view detects user activity, it passes the activity to its paired controller.
- **Controller** A *controller* is responsible for (a) interpreting user activity detected by the view, and (b) informing the model about the activity, so the model can update domain objects, as appropriate.

While a user interface always has just one model, it can have multiple view-controller pairs. Between them, a paired view and controller are responsible for observing the model. If they are notified of a change to the model, they retrieve the relevant updated information to synchronize the view with the model. In practice, MVC architectures vary in exactly how they observe the model and retrieve updates. In the architecture in Fig. 7.8, the view does the observing and retrieving.

Example 7.8   With the MVC architecture in Fig. 7.8, this example traces how a user change made through one view is reflected in all views. The dialog view of a photo object in Fig. 7.7 has several fields that are linked. The height appears in both pixels and inches. Furthermore, we continue to assume that the proportions of the photo are maintained, so if the height doubles, the width must double too.

When the user types 9, then 0, then 0 in the field for the height in pixels, the view raises an event to notify its controller. The controller gets the digits and passes the new height 900 to the model. The model resizes the photo object, which doubles the height to 900 and the width to 600.

The model then raises an event about the change in the photo object. All views are observers of the model, so they are notified of the changes. They retrieve the latest information about the photo object and synchronize their displays with the model. Thus, the user activity in the pixel-height field in the dialog view is propagated not only to the photo view, but also to other fields in the dialog view, with the MVC architecture in Fig. 7.8.   □

7.3.3   Keep Views Simple

Views are harder to test than the other components in an MVC architecture because they involve user interaction. Hence the guidance to keep views simple while dividing work between views and their controllers. Controllers and models communicate via messages and notification, which are more readily tested using automated frameworks than user activity; see Chapter 9 for unit test frameworks.

Humble Views

The *humble* approach is to minimize the behavior of any object that is hard to test.[6] A *humble view* is limited to detecting user activity and rendering information on a display. Its controller observes the model and tells the view what to display. It is easier to intercept and automate testing of messages from a controller to a view than it is to test what is actually displayed on a screen.

Example 7.9   Let us revisit Example 7.8, this time with a humble view. When the user enters 900 for the height of the photo in pixels, the humble view notifies its controller. The controller tells the model of the change. The model resizes the photo object and raises an event about the update to the photo.

    The controller is the observer, so it retrieves the new height and the width. The controller then tells the humble view exactly what to display in each field in the dialog view.   □

Complex Presentations: Rely on the Controller

A complex user interface can involve more than a passive display of information from the model. It can involve some decisions and computations that are specific to a presentation. Such logic is specific to the given view and has no relevance to the other views. It therefore does not belong with the model. It belongs in the controller, since we want to keep views humble.[7]

Example 7.10   Large companies maintain communication networks with links between sites across the world. Engineers monitor the links to ensure that the data traffic through them is flowing smoothly. If a link is overloaded, the engineers take appropriate actions.

    The engineers at one company want two views of traffic across the company network:

- A list view of links that have loads above a threshold. The threshold is set by a slider. The list changes as the user moves the slider.
- A map view of overloaded links across the entire network. A link is overloaded if its traffic load is above a threshold.

Both views involve view-specific logic. In each case, the threshold is specific to that view. It the list view the list-specific threshold determines the list of links that are displayed. In the map view, the map-specific threshold determines the links that are highlighted.

If the model is to be truly unaware of its presentations, it cannot be told about the list-specific and map-specific thresholds. These thresholds and associated logic belong in the relevant controller.   □

7.4   Dataflow Architectures

With a *dataflow pipeline*, a stream of data is transformed as it flows from one software component to the next. Each component does a well-defined, perhaps simple, job; for example, time stamp a music request from a user device, or reformat a data item. The components in a pipeline have a single input and a single output stream. More generally, in a *dataflow network*, an output data stream from one component becomes an input stream for another component. That is, a network allows a component to have multiple inputs and output streams.

The appeal of the dataflow approach is that a set of reusable focused components, called *software tools* can be combined to perform a wide range of software tasks. The tools are designed so they can be used with each other. The power of the tools lies in their combinations, not in the individual tools.

In the early 1960s, Doug McIlroy envisioned a catalog of standard components that could be coupled "like garden hose – screw in another segment when it becomes necessary to massage data in another way."[8] Tools that transform data are called *filters*, a reference to optical filters that transform light as it passes through them. Like optical filters, software filters can be mixed and matched.

This section begins with pipelines in which the output of one component becoming the input to the next in line. The concept of pipelines comes from Unix. The concept of filtering extends to global-scale dataflow networks that analyze massive data streams from business transactions and streaming services.

7.4.1   Dataflow Pipelines

Unix pipelines are a popular form of dataflow pipelines. We can create our own pipelines by breaking a task into subtasks and then implementing the subtasks by a pipeline. The following two examples illustrate common uses of pipelines.

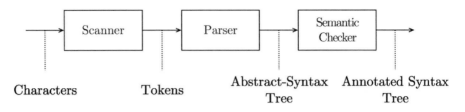

Figure 7.9 A partial pipeline for a compiler.

Example 7.11 The extract-transform-load (ETL) pattern addresses the problem of transferring data between databases. The issue is that the source and target databases may have different formats and data representations. The core of a solution is to set up a pipeline:

> Extract the desired data from the source database;
> Reshape and reformat it;
> Load it into the target database;

Such "glue" code is useful for data transfers between components in any software system. The benefit of the glue code is that neither the source nor the target need to be touched.   □

Example 7.12 Compilers for programming languages such as C and Java are typically structured as pipelines that transform a stream of characters (source text) into a stream of instructions for an actual or virtual machine. The first three components of such a pipeline appear in Fig. 7.9. The scanner groups characters into tokens. Characters correspond to letters and tokens to words in English text. The characters < followed by = are grouped into the token for the operator ≤. The parser produces a representation of the source progrm called an abstract-syntax tree. The semantic checker performs consistency checks and annotates the syntax tree with type information.

How are the connections in the pipeline implemented? A main procedure (not shown) calls the parser, which builds the entire syntax tree and returns. While building the tree, the parser gets tokens as it needs them from the scanner.   □

Unix Pipelines

Unix pipelines are composed by using the *pipe* operator |. A pipeline with the three tools p, q, and r is written as

$$p \mid q \mid r$$

The Unix operating system takes care of connecting the output of p to the input of q and the output of q to the input of r.

The operating system comes with a set of useful tools that are designed to work together in pipelines. The tools work with streams of characters. The following tools are used in Examples 7.13 and 7.14. For more information about them, use the Unix man command with the name of the tool.

- sort alphabetically sorts lines of text. Use the −n option to sort numerically and the −r option to reverse the direction of the sort.
- uniq removes consecutive repeated lines. Use the −c option to prefix each line with a count of the number of repetitions of the line.
- tr A−Z a−z translates uppercase letters to lower case. All other characters are copied as is to the output. Use the −C option to translate the complement of a set of characters. In particular, use

$$\texttt{tr -C a-zA-Z '\textbackslash n'}$$

to translate all nonalphabetic characters to the newline character.

Example 7.13   This example and the next are motivated by the Unix tools and pipelines that were used to manage the TEXsource for this book. The following pipeline transforms lines of text into a sorted list of words, one per line (see Fig. 7.10):

$$\texttt{tr -C a-zA-Z '\textbackslash n' | tr A-Z a-z | sort | uniq}$$

Suppose that the input to this pipeline consists of the two lines of text:

```
Avoid fancy words!
Avoid fancy fonts!
```

The leftmost component of the pipeline transforms the two lines of text into a list of word occurrences, with each occurrence on a separate line. Thus, Avoid occurs as

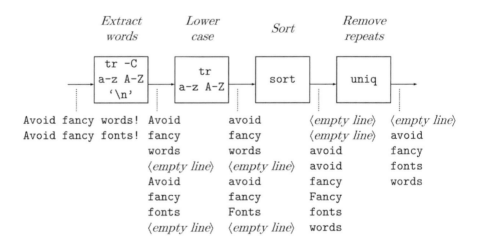

Figure 7.10 Pipeline for making a list of words in a document.

twice on the list, as does `fancy`. The second component lowers any uppercase letters, so `Avoid` is transformed to `avoid`. The third component sorts the lines of word occurrences. The fourth component removes repeated lines, thereby producing the desired sorted list of words.

In more detail, the first component

```
tr -C a-zA-Z '\n'
```

translates all nonalphabetic characters into newline characters. While this translation puts each word occurrence on a line by itself, it also introduces unwanted newline characters, but these unwanted newline characters. In Fig. 7.10 the positions of these newlines are highlighted by the placeholders ⟨*empty-line*⟩. All but one of these newlines is later removed by `uniq`.   □

Example 7.14   Suppose we want to count the frequency with which words occur in a text file. The following variant of the pipeline in Fig. 7.10 will do the job:

```
tr -C a-zA-Z '\n' | tr A-Z a-z |  sort | uniq -c | sort -n
```

As in Example 7.13, the first three components of the pipeline produce an alphabetical list of word occurrences. Then, `uniq -c` counts repetitions of a line. The final numeric sort puts the list of words in order of increasing frequency. Given the input

```
She sells sea shells by the sea shore
But the sea shells
```

the output, in two columns, is

```
1 but       1 shore
1 by        2 shells
1 sells     2 the
1 she       3 sea
```

□

7.4.2   Dataflow Networks

We get dataflow networks instead of pipelines if we lift the restriction that each component must have a single input stream and a single output stream.

Pattern Name Dataflow.

Problem Easily create custom software applications that transform data streams.

Core of a Solution Define and assemble independent filters into acyclic networks, where an output from a filter becomes either (a) an input stream for another filter, or

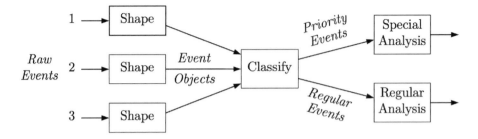

Figure 7.11 Streams of raw events are shaped into time-stamped event objects. The object streams are merged and then classified into high-priority and regular events for data analysis.

(b) an output stream for the network. If every filter has at most one input stream and at most one output stream, the network is called a *pipeline*.

Note On Windows, dataflow networks of components with multiple inputs or outputs can be implemented by using named pipes: "*Named pipes* are used to transfer data between processes that are not related processes and between processes on different computers."[9] Windows pipes can also be used to set up two-way communication between processes.

Example 7.15   The dataflow network in Fig. 7.11 is inspired by a music streaming service that has users across the world. The app for the service generates an event each time a user searches for a song, requests a song, or takes some other action. The app sends a raw text description of the event to one of the service's gateways, which time-stamps and shapes the event into an object. The gateways send event objects to a classifier, which separates priority events from regular events. (Priority events include billing events.) Priority events are sent, reliable delivery, for special analysis. Regular events are sent, best effort, for regular analysis.

   Analysis is used not only to respond to requests, but to make recommendations and maintain lists of popular songs.[10]   □

7.4.3   Unbounded Streams

For all practical purposes, the massive global streams of financial, entertainment, and scientific data are unbounded. An *unbounded* stream has no end. A stream is *bounded* if it has a beginning and an end. When a compiler is applied to a source program or when a Unix pipeline is applied to a file, the input and output data streams are almost always bounded. With bounded data streams, it is feasible for a filter to see the entire data stream before producing any output.

   Unbounded streams have no end, so it does not make sense to sort an entire stream. Nor is it meaningful to count the number of occurrences of an item, such as a song title. The solution is to work with finite segments of an unbounded stream.

Example 7.16   Several billion videos are viewed on YouTube every single day. The stream of usage data from these videos is unbounded. From such streams, advertisers want usage counts. Writing about streaming services in general, authors from Google observe:

Advertisers/content providers want to know how often and for how long their videos are being watched, with which content/ads, and by which demographic groups. . . . They want all of this information as quickly as possible, so that they can adjust . . . in as close to real time as possible.[11]

□

Mapping and Reducing Transformations   Let us apply the term *mapping* to element-by-element transformations on data streams. Let us apply the term *reducing* to transformations that potentially depend on the entire data stream. The terms are motivated by the *map* and *reduce* functions in Lisp.

Example 7.17   The first two components in the pipeline in Fig. 7.10 perform mapping transformations. Translation of nonalphabetic characters to newlines and the translation of uppercase to lowercase can both be done a character at a time. Sorting is a prime example of a reducing function. Note that fonts moves up from the last position after the sort. The fourth component, uniq, is closer to a mapping than a reducing transformation. It compares consecutive lines and drops repetitions, so its decisions are based on local context. In the extreme case, if all the lines in a stream are the same, it reduces the stream to a single line. In practice, uniq behaves like a mapping.   □

Mapping transformations carry over from bounded to unbounded streams. Reducing transformations, however, can only be applied to finite segments of an unbounded stream.

Windowing   Slicing a data stream into finite segments is called *windowing*; the segments are called *windows*. Spotify, the music service, has been using hourly windows for usage events. Each window is finite, so it can be treated as a bounded stream. In general, windows can be of any size. Furthermore, for different kinds of analysis, the same data stream can be sliced in different ways.

7.4.4   Big Dataflows

Scale and geographic distribution introduce engineering issues with managing data streams.

Parallelism   Mapping transformations can be applied in parallel to the elements of a data stream. The popular MapReduce programming model divides an application into two stages: a map stage for element-wise filtering and a reduce stage for aggregation. The experience with MapReduce is summarized as follows:

A large class of massive-scale "computations are conceptually straightforward. However, the input data is usually large enough that the computations have to be distributed across hundreds or thousands of machines in order to finish in a reasonable amount of time."[12]

Apache Hadoop is a reverse-engineered version of MapReduce.

Reliability If the processes in a pipeline are physically running entirely within the same data center, then their designers can ignore the possibility of data loss between processes in the pipeline. Data transfers within a data center can be safely assumed to be reliable. (This observation applies to any dataflow network, not just pipelines. We talk of pipelines to avoid any confusion between network as in "dataflow network" and network as in "data communications network" like the Internet.)

   With geographically distributed pipelines, we need to look more closely at the producer-consumer relationship between components of the pipeline. Who ensures the reliability of queues between a producer and a consumer? Do the queues **have** to be reliable? Reliability across a network comes with delays. Lost data must be retransmitted, as we saw in the discussion of reliable (TCP) and best effort (IP) in Section 7.1.2. Reliable delivery is needed for applications such as billing. Best-effort deliver or even data sampling may, however, suffice for a poll of customer preferences.

Example 7.18 Spotify switched from best-effort to reliable queues for their Event Delivery pipeline. The earlier design assumed that the elements of the data stream could be lost in transit. The producer processes were responsible for queuing their output until the consumers acknowledged receipt of transmitted elements. This design worked, but it complicated design of the producers.

   The later design is based on reliable queues, which simplifies the role of the producers. The processes in the pipeline can therefore concentrate on transforming inputs to outputs, without worrying about buffers and queues.[13]   ☐

Network Bandwidth With massive data streams, do the pipes in a pipeline have the carrying capacity to handle the volume of data between processes? Volume becomes an issue when the processes are in separate data centers, connected by a network. Pipelines need to be designed to conserve data transfers across a network. Is a large stream of raw data being transferred across a continent, only to be reduced to a count or an average on the other side? If so, consider reducing the large-scale raw stream at the source and transferring the much smaller-scale reduced stream to the destination.

7.5   Connecting Clients with Servers

Conceptually, a client sends a request to a server, and the server responds with the result of processing the client request. For example, a web server responds with a web page,

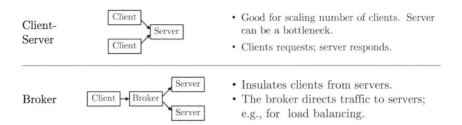

Figure 7.12 Ways of connecting clients and servers.

a map server with a map, a music server with an audio stream, an academic server with courses that match given criteria, and so on. Clients and servers typically connect over a network.

Here, clients and servers are logical (software) components. If the need arises, we can use the terms "physical client" and "physical server" for the related pieces of hardware.

This section begins with the client-server pattern: clients connect directly with a known server. In practice, there are too many clients for a single server to handle. The client load is distributed across multiple servers. Instead of connecting directly, a client is dynamically matched with a server. Dynamic matching is done by adding components like name servers and load balancers. The broker pattern provides a component that provides the functionality needed to dynamically match clients with servers. See Fig. 7.12 for brief notes on the client-server and broker patterns.

Dynamic matching of clients and servers is also useful for continuous deployment, where new or updated software components can be added to a running production system.

7.5.1   The Client-Server Pattern

Context The sequence of patterns in this section builds up to the general problem of matching clients with servers.

Problem Connect multiple clients directly with a specific server.

Core of a Solution The connection in this pattern is many-to-one: many clients connect with one server. The clients request services; the server replies with a response.

The clients know the server's identity, so they know how to send a direct request. The request contains information about the client, so the server knows where to send a reply. With the reply, the connection between client and server is closed. A new request opens a new connection. The server does not initiate a connection with the client.

Typically, the request-reply interaction is synchronous. That is, upon sending a request, the client waits until a reply arrives. Alternatively, the interaction between client and server can be asynchronous. In the asynchronous case,

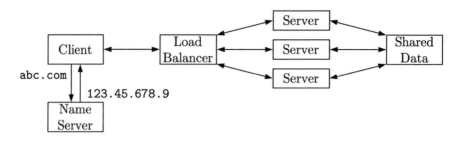

Figure 7.13 A dynamic variant of a client-server architecture.

The client sends a request.
The server acknowledges the request.
The server works on a response.
The server replies with a response.

After sending an asynchronous request, the client can continue to work as it waits for a response.

A Dynamic Variant of Client-Server
The architecture in Fig. 7.13 goes beyond the client-server pattern in three ways:

- Clients use a name as keys to look up the location(s) of the servers.
- At the location, a *load balancer* assigns a server to handle the client request. (Large systems need multiple servers to handle the load from large numbers of clients.)
- All client-related data is held in a persistent data store shared by the servers.

With the architecture in Fig. 7.13, a request-reply interaction goes as follows. The client queries a *name server*, using a name (e.g., abc.com) to look up an address (e.g., 123.45.678.9) for the location of the servers. The client then sends a request to the address it looked up. At that location, the request goes to a load balancer. The load balancer picks an available server and forwards the client request to that server. The server processes the request and replies to the client.

A key point to note is that servers need to be stateless. That is, the servers must not keep any client-related information. The reason is that the next client request could be assigned to a different server.

So, any client information is kept in a persistent shared data store, accessible by all the servers. Client-related information includes any preferences, any history of past interactions, any data from the current interaction that might be helpful for future interactions – all such information belongs in the shared data store.

7.5.2   Deploying Test Servers

The architecture with the name server (Fig. 7.13) scales readily to multiple locations. Suppose that for abc.com there are two locations, with addresses 123.45.678.9 and 135.79.246.8. (The approach works for more locations as well.) For key abc.com, the name server returns a list with both these addresses. The client can then go down the list, one by one. If one address times out, the client tries the next one on the list.

The architecture with the name server also allows new or updated software to be eased into production. Suppose that the servers are running version n and we have just created a new version $n + 1$ of the software. Version $n + 1$ has been fully tested in development and it is time to deploy it in a production environment. Caution demands that the new version $n + 1$ be deployed in stages, leaving open the option of rolling back to the previous version n, if there is a hitch with the new version n at any stage. Here are some possible stages:

1. **Test Environment** Run the new version on a copy of the incoming stream of client requests. In Fig. 7.14, the production load balancer passes a copy of each client request to the load balancer in the test environment. The test environment mirrors the production environment, except that it runs the new version $n + 1$.
2. **Partial Production** If the new version performs well in a test environment, it can be put into production, but the new version runs in a separate location, with its own address. The name server directs a small percentage of the client traffic to the new version. The flow of traffic is still to the location with the old version n. If requests for the same client can be directed to either version n or version $n + 1$ of the software, then both versions n and $n + 1$ must share the persistent data store.
3. **Trial Period** After successfully handling some of the real client load, the new version $n + 1$ is ready for full production; that is, ready to handle all client requests. During a trial period, the earlier version n remains on standby.

The time frames for the preceding stages are measured in hours or days.

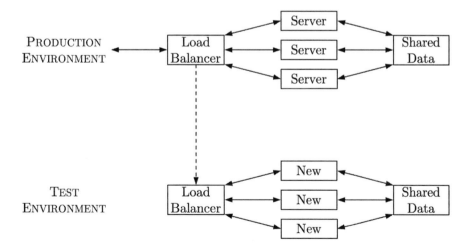

Figure 7.14 Deploying a new server software in a test environment. The dashed arrow indicates that the production load balancer sends copies of all client requests to the test environment. The boxes labeled "New" represent the new version of the server software.

7.5.3   The Broker Pattern

We continue with the theme of large numbers of clients seeking services that are provided by servers. The goal is to connect clients with servers, dynamically. The architecture in Fig. 7.13 provides a solution using building blocks: name servers and load balancers. The broker pattern uses these same building blocks in a way that is not visible to clients.

Problem   Ensure that clients get the services they want through a service interface, without needing to know about the infrastructure (including servers) that is used to provide the services.

Core of a Solution   Introduce an intermediary called a *broker* that clients deal with. Clients send the broker a service request, and the broker does the rest.

The broker uses a name server and balancer to select a server to process the client request. Once the server prepares a response, the broker forwards the response to the client.

(The following observation is about servers, not about brokers. It is included because it applies to an overall solution that includes brokers. If servers are drawn from a pool, the servers need to be stateless. As in the architecture in Fig. 7.13, all client-related information belongs in a shared persistent data store.)

In this description, name service and load balancing are logical functions. They can be part of the broker.

The broker may also include a client proxy. A *proxy*, P, acts on behalf of another component, A. All communication intended for component A goes through the proxy P. In a broker, the role of a client proxy is to manage the communication protocol for receiving and sending messages to the client.

Cautions with Brokers   All communication between clients and servers flows through the broker, which brings up some concerns:

- **Performance Bottleneck** The broker needs to have enough capacity to handle the expected client load. The silver lining is that load balancing can aid performance because it can direct client requests to the least busy server.
- **Latency** The forwarding of communications between clients and servers adds latency (delay) compared to direct communication between clients and servers. The benefit of dynamically matching clients and servers outweighs the cost of latency.
- **Single Point of Failure** The broker needs to be designed for fault tolerance, with respect to both hardware and software faults. Fault tolerance is a topic in its own right. The basic idea is to have a primary and a backup for each critical component. Normally, the primary does the work. The backup takes over if it detects that the primary has failed.
- **Security Vulnerability** Since all client-server communications flow through the broker, it represents a security vulnerability. The broker therefore needs to be

designed to resist a security attack. It also needs to be protected by network security measures.

7.6 Families and Product Lines

When there are several versions of a product, the versions surely share some common properties. The ways in which they vary from each other must also be bounded. This idea extends to a set of products. A *software product family* is a set of products where it is worth doing the following:

- First, study the common properties of the set.
- Then, determine the special properties of the individual family members.[14]

A *software product line* is a set of products that are specifically designed and implemented as a family. The annual Software Product Lines Conference has a Hall of Fame that honors organizations with commercially successful product lines. The application domains for the honorees include software for automotive systems, avionics, financial services, firmware, medical systems, property rentals, telecommunications, television sets, and training.[15]

7.6.1 Commonalities and Variabilities

The common properties of a family are called *commonalities* and the special properties of the individual family members are called *variabilities*. Using the terminology of patterns, the family follows a pattern; the family's commonalities and variabilities are part of the pattern's core of a solution.

Product lines arise because products come in different shapes, sizes, performance levels, and price points, all available at the same time. Consider iOS and Android versions of an app that runs on smartphones, tablets, and desktops, not to mention languages from different regions. Without a family approach, each version would need to be developed and maintained separately. A family approach can lead to an order of magnitude reduction in the cost of fielding the members of the family.

Example 7.19 HomeAway, a startup in the web-based vacation home rental market, grew quickly through acquisitions. Each acquired company retained the look and feel of its website.[16]

HomeAway's first implementation approach was to lump the systems for the various websites together, with conditionals to guide the flow of control. This umbrella approach proved unwieldy and unworkable due to the various websites having different content management, layouts, databases, and data formats.

The second approach was to merge the various systems onto a common platform, while still retaining the distinct look and feel of the different websites. This approach had its limits:

"A thorough code inspection eventually revealed that over time 29 separate mechanisms had been introduced for managing variation among the different sites."

"Testing ... impoverished though it was, discovered 30 new defects every week – week after week – with no guarantee that fixing one defect did not introduce new ones."

The company then turned to a software product-line approach. Within weeks, the product-line approach paid for itself. The quality sent up and the software footprint and deployment times went down. Modularity meant that changes to one site no longer affected all the other sites. □

7.6.2　Software Architecture and Product Lines

Software architecture plays a key role in product-line engineering. To the guidelines for defining modules in Section 6.2 we can add:

- Address commonalities before variabilities, when designing modules.
- Hide each implementation decision about variabilities in a separate module. Related decisions can be grouped in a module hierarchy.

One of HomeAway's goals for a product line approach (see Example 7.19) was to make the cost of implementing a variation proportional to that variation, as opposed to the previous approaches, where the cost was proportional to the number of variations.

Support for the significance of architecture in product-line engineering comes from SEI's experience with helping companies implement product lines:

The lack of either an architecture focus or architecture talent can kill an otherwise promising product line effort.[17]

7.6.3　Economics of Product-Line Engineering

Product-line engineering requires an initial investment, which pays off as the number of products increases; see Fig. 7.15. Here are some areas for investment: identify commonalities and variabilities; build a business case that encompasses multiple products; design a modular architecture that hides variabilities; create test plans that span products; and train developers and managers. One of the keys to the success of

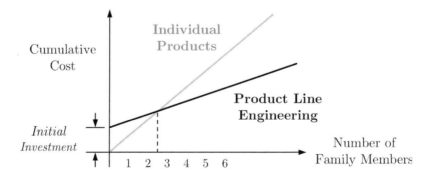

Figure 7.15 Schematic of the economics of software product lines.

Table 7.1 Quality attributes influence the choice of patterns for a software problem.

PATTERN	GOODFOR
Layering	Portability and reuse
Shared Data	Persistent data
Observer	Event notifications
Publish-Subscribe	Broadcast events
Model-View-Controller	User interfaces
Dataflow	Operations on data streams
Services	Interoperability
Client-Server	Scalability of services

product-line engineering at Bell Labs was a small, dedicated group that worked with development groups on their projects.

Management support is essential. Product-line engineering projects that have lacked management support or initial investment have failed to deliver the promised improvements in productivity, quality, cost, and time to market. The schematic in Fig. 7.15 illustrates the economic trade-offs.[18] With the traditional approach, each family member is built separately, so costs rise in proportion to the number and complexity of the family members. For simplicity, the schematic shows costs rising linearly with the number of family members.

With product-line engineering, there is an initial investment, which adds to the cost of the first product. The payoff begins as more products are delivered, since the incremental cost of adding a product is lower. Based on the Bell Labs experience, the crossover point is between two and three family members. The greater the number of family members, the greater the savings, past the crossover point.

7.7   Conclusion

An architectural pattern provides design guidelines for solving a recurring problem. It outlines lessons from experience that apply to all possible solutions to the problem. Patterns are therefore a good starting point for a new design. For brief notes on the patterns in this chapter, see Fig. 7.1 and Fig. 7.12.

The choice of patterns for a project is strongly influenced by the goals and quality attributes for a project. Table 7.1 shows some of the goals and attributes supported by various patterns. A design may use multiple patterns; for example, an application may be structured as a dataflow pipeline, be layered above a virtual machine, and be a client of an external service

Further Reading

- The book by Alexander, Ishikawa, and Silverstein [5] is the definitive source for Alexander's patterns for communities and buildings.

- The design patterns in the Gang-of-Four book by Gamma et al. [74] complement the architectural patterns in this chapter.
- Fowler [71] traces the evolution of the Model-View-Controller pattern.

Exercises for Chapter 7

Exercise 7.1   Relate the following dialogue from Plato's *The Republic* to architectural patterns:

a) What is the recurring problem in the dialogue?
b) What is the core of a solution?

There "are beds and tables in the world – plenty of them, are there not?"
"Yes."
"But there are only two ideas or forms of them – one the idea of a bed, the other of a table."
"True."
"And the maker of either of them makes a bed or he makes a table for our use, in accordance with the idea."

The Republic dates back to circa 380 BCE.[19]

Exercise 7.2   For each of the following statements, answer whether it is generally true or generally false. Briefly explain your answer.

a) Patterns are used to create cookie-cutter complete solutions for recurring problems.
b) With strict layering, a module in layer L may only use modules in layer L or the layer directly below L.
c) A module in any layer may communicate freely with modules in a sidecar.
d) In a publish-subscribe pattern, subscribers know the identity of their publishers, but observers in an observer pattern do not know their publishers.
e) A model-view-controller architecture can be implemented by layering a view above its controller and then the controller above the model.
f) The recommended approach is to put view-specific logic in the view. itself.
g) Just as all pipes in a Unix pipeline carry character streams, all links in a dataflow pipeline carry streams of the same data type.
h) Information hiding is not applicable with a dataflow network.
i) The links in a dataflow network correspond to shared data stores.
j) IP links can lose packets between geographically distributed data centers, so dataflow networks are confined within individual data centers.

Exercise 7.3   The basic model-view-controller pattern relies on separated presentation and observer synchronization, and leaves open the choice between the following options:

a) The view observes the model.
b) The controller observes the model.

For each of these options, answer the following questions.

- What specifically are the roles of the view and its controller? Clearly list any assumptions.
- In an implementation with two views, what is the sequence of messages and/or notifications when the user updates one of the views. Number the elements of the sequence.
- Between the model, view, and controller, where would you put view-specific logic, while maintaining the spirit of the pattern? Briefly provide the reasons for your choice.

Exercise 7.4   Use Unix tools to create pipelines for the following problems. In addition to the tools `sort`, `uniq`, and `tr` introduced in Section 7.4, the suggested tools are the stream editor `sed` and the programming language `awk`. Both `sed` and `awk` work a line at a time, where a line is a sequence of characters ending in the newline character 'n'.

a) Split an input file into a list of words, one per line, where a word is a sequence of uppercase and lowercase letters. Preserve word order. Remove all other characters, except for the newline characters following each word.
b) Modify the preceding pipeline to identify repeated words; that is, successive occurrences of the same word. As output, produce the repeated word and the next five words.
c) Count the number of lines and words in a file.
d) Count the number of figures in a TEXfile. Assume that all figures begin with \begin{figure}.
e) Extract an outline from a TEXfile. Extract chapter titles and section and subsection headings from lines of the form:

```
\chapter{Architectural Patterns]
\section{Software Layering}
\subsection{Design Tradeoffs}
```

Exercise 7.5   Parnas [147] uses KWIC indices to illustrate the modularity principle; for a quick introduction to KWIC indices, see Exercise 6.6. For the problem of creating a KWIC index, design separate modular solutions using each of the following approaches:

a) Use the shared-data pattern. Hide the representation of the index in the shared repository.
b) Use a dataflow pipeline. Unix tools enable quick solutions using pipelines.

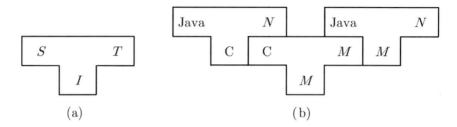

Figure 7.16 T diagram for a compiler from source language S to target language T, written in implementation language I. (b) Translation of the source code in C for a compiler from C to N, the language of a new machine, by a C compiler on an existing machine M.

The following example of a KWIC index is from Exercise 6.6:

```
              KWIC is an    Acronym for Keyword in Conte
 is an Acronym for Keyword in    Context
          Wikipedia the Free    Encyclopedia
             Wikipedia the    Free Encyclopedia
       KWIC is an Acronym for    Keyword in Context
                             KWIC is an Acronym for Keywo
                             Wikipedia the Free Encyclope
```

Exercise 7.6   This exercise explores the use of T diagrams to describe a boot-strapping process for creating a compiler for a new class of machines N, which has no software to begin with. The basic *T diagram* in Fig. 7.16(a) shows the three languages that characterize a compiler: the source language S to be translated, the target language T produced as output, and the implementation language I that the compiler is written in. The diagram in Fig. 7.16(b) shows the translation of a compiler. The base of the diagram is a C compiler on an existing machine M; that is, a compiler from C to M, written in M, the language of the existing machine. Its input is the source code in C for a compiler from C to N, the new machine. This C source code is translated into target code in M: the target is a compiler from C to N that runs on the existing machine M.

   Use T diagrams to illustrate the creation of compilers in both of the following cases.

a) On the existing machine M, write a compiler from C to N in C. Derive from it a compiler from C to N in N, with the help of the existing C compiler on M.

b) As in the preceding case, create a C compiler for the new machine N; that is, a compiler from C to N in N. Then, use it to create a Java to N in Java compiler as well as a Java to N in N compiler.[20]

8   Static Checking

The combination of reviews, static analysis, and testing is highly effective at detecting defects during software development. By themselves, the individual techniques are much less effective; see Section 10.4. Testing is covered in Chapter 9; the other techniques are covered in this chapter.

A *software review* (or simply *review*) is a process for getting feedback or approval for a project or artifact from one or more carefully selected peers or experts. This chapter begins with *architecture reviews*, which examine the clarity of the user goals for a project and the adequacy of a proposed architecture for addressing those goals. The chapter then introduces code reviews and static analysis. *Static analysis* applies automated tools to identify potential defects and anomalies in code. The tools are called *checkers* because they check for compliance with predefined rules and programming-style guidelines.

The checking techniques in this chapter appear in the upper half of Fig. 8.1. Reviews and static analysis check code statically, without running it. Reviews can also handle artifacts that cannot be run, such as designs and documents. Testing checks code dynamically, by running it. From Section 2.5, to validate is to check that an artifact will do what users want. To verify is to check that an artifact is implemented correctly.

This chapter will enable the reader to:

- Explain the role and benefits of architecture reviews, code reviews, and static analysis.
- Describe how to conduct architecture and code reviews.

8.1   Architecture Reviews

Requirements can be a problem area for software projects, so it is not surprising that, often, design issues can be traced to one of two related causes: either (a) the goals for a project are not completely or clearly defined, or (b) the architecture does not adequately address the goals. These observations are supported by over 700 architecture reviews conducted through Bell Labs and successor organizations between 1988 and 2005.[1] In

	VALIDATION	VERIFICATION
STATIC	Architecture Reviews	Code Reviews Static Analysis
DYNAMIC	Testing	Testing

Figure 8.1 Selected techniques for validation and verification.

addition a review can uncover other issues related to the project, such as the lack of management support or the inadequacy of the team's tools and domain knowledge.

8.1.1   Guiding Principles for Architecture Reviews

This section explores the guiding principles in Fig. 8.2.[2] See Section 8.2 for how to conduct a review. The full benefits of reviews are realized when they follow a formal process. The guiding principles are also helpful for informal peer reviews, where developers go over each other's work.

The Review Is for the Project Team's Benefit The purpose of a review is to provide a project team with objective feedback. It is then up to the project team and its management to decide what to do with the feedback. The decision may be to continue the project with minor changes, to change the project's direction, or even to cancel the project.

Reviews have been found to be cost effective for both projects that are doing well and for projects that need help. Reviews are not meant to be an audit on behalf of the project's management. They are not for finding fault or assigning blame.

Since the project team will be the one to act on reviewer feedback, members of the development team have to participate in the review. The team's participation also helps to build trust between the team and the reviewers, which increases the likelihood that the team will act on the feedback from the review.

The Expert Reviewers Are Independent For the review to be objective, the reviewers need to be independent of the project and its immediate management. For the review to be credible, the reviewers need to include respected subject-matter experts.

The independent experts may be either from outside the company or from other parts of the company. Side benefits of drawing reviewers from other parts of the company is that (a) they spread best practices to other projects and (b) the company builds up a stable of experienced reviewers.

Figure 8.2 Guiding principles for architecture reviews.

The Project Has a Clear Problem Definition During requirements development, user needs are identified and analyzed, with the intent of defining the problem to be solved. Revisiting an example from Section 3.6, consider the following need and some options for a problem definition:

Customer Need:	Listen to music
Option 1:	Offer songs for purchase and download
Option 2:	Offer a free streaming service with ads

During an architecture review, the independent experts respectfully provide feedback on the clarity and completeness of the problem definition.

Issues can arise with the problem definition if there are multiple stakeholders with conflicting needs or goals. For example, one stakeholder may be fanatical about keeping costs low, while another is equally passionate about maximizing performance. As another example, conflicts can arise when balancing convenience and security.

The Architecture Fits the Problem

The reviewers confirm that the architecture will provide a reasonable solution to the problem. Developers often focus on what the system is supposed to do; that is, they focus on the functional requirements for the system. They tend to pay less attention to quality attributes, such as performance, security, and reliability. Reviewers therefore pay particular attention to quality attributes. Early reviews help because quality attributes need to be planned in from the start. Otherwise, they can lead to redesign and rework later in the project.

For example, with iterative and agile processes, early iterations focus on a minimal viable system, in order to get early customer feedback on the basic functionality. Special cases, alternative flows, and error handling get lower priority and are slated for later iterations. Concerns about quality attributes may not surface until late in the project. An early architecture review can prevent later rework.

The Project Has a System Architect Any project that is important enough to merit a formal architecture review is important enough to have a dedicated system architect. The "architect" may be a person or a small team. The reviewers rely on the architect to describe the architecture and provide the rationale for the design decisions.

The reviewers also assess the team's skills. Does anyone on the team have prior experience with such a system? Are the tools new or known to the team?

8.1.2   Discovery, Deep-Dive, and Retrospective Reviews

The focus of a review varies from project to project and, for a given project, from stage to stage in the life of a project. The following three kinds of reviews are appropriate during the early, middle, and late stages of a project, respectively:

- A discovery review for early feedback.
- A deep dive for an evaluation of a specific aspect of the architecture.
- A retrospective for lessons learned.

An *architectural discovery review* assesses whether an architectural approach promises a suitable solution. A discovery review can begin as soon as preliminary design decisions are made, while the architecture is at an early stage. The reviewers focus on the problem definition, the feasibility of the emerging design, and the estimated costs and schedule. A short checklist of questions for a discovery review appears in Table 8.1.

The benefit to the project team of an early discovery review is that design issues are uncovered before the architecture is fully developed.

Table 8.1 A short checklist for an architecture discovery review.

Problem Definition	Team
• How will the customer benefit? • What is the rationale for choosing this opportunity?	• Has the team built something like this before? • Is the team colocated or distributed?
System Architecture	**Constraints and Risks**
• What are the prioritized requirements? • What are the main components of the system? How do they support the basic scenario? • What is the desired performance? Scale? Availability?	• Are there any business constraints? Time to market? • Are there any ethical, social, or legal constraints? • What are the risks associated with the external technology and services?

An *architectural deep dive* examines the requirements, the architecture, and high-level design of either the entire project or some aspect of the project. The project team may identify specific areas for feedback. The following is a small sample of focus areas from several architecture reviews:

user experience	performance	interoperability
user interface	security	software upgrades
disability access	reliability	deployment

Deep dives are conducted during the planning phase, before implementation begins.

An *architectural retrospective* is a debriefing to identify lessons learned that could help other projects. The reviewers ask what went especially well and what did not. Retrospectives are useful for sharing best practices and recommendations for problems that other projects might encounter.

8.2   Conducting Software Inspections

Roughly speaking, an inspection is a formal review by a group of experts who provide feedback on a project or an artifact. From reviewer selection to reviewer feedback, traditional inspections can take days or weeks. By contrast, the code reviews discussed in Section 8.3 are applied to relatively short segments of code and are completed within hours. The two approaches complement each other and can be used either separately or together.

When inspections were introduced at IBM in the 1970s, the company reported "substantial" improvements in software quality and productivity.[3] Since then, inspections have become a standard quality improvement technique. For a dramatic example of their use, see the box on the software for a Mars mission.

This section introduces traditional inspections and some key questions to be addressed in organizing one. The questions relate to the number of reviewers, how reviewers prepare, and whether it is necessary for the reviewers to meet face-to-face.

8.2.1   The Phases of a Traditional Inspection

The main phases of an inspection are represented by boxes in Fig. 8.3.

a) Planning, including reviewer selection.
b) Individual preparation by reviewers.
c) Group examination of materials.
d) Follow-up and rework by the project team to address reviewer feedback.

The questions on the right represent decisions to be made in organizing an inspection. To the left in the figure are the goals of the phases in a traditional inspection. Traditional inspections are also known as *Fagan inspections*, after Michael E. Fagan of IBM. The basic flow of a traditional inspection appears in Table 8.2.

Table 8.2 The basic flow of a traditional software inspection.

Planning
 A project team requests an inspection.
 The moderator assembles a team of independent reviewers.
 The moderator confirms that the materials meet entry criteria.

Overview and Preparation
 The moderator spells out the objectives.
 The author provides an overview of the materials.
 The reviewers study the intent and logic individually.

Group Meeting
 The moderator facilitates and sets the pace.
 The reviewers examine the materials for defects.
 The reviewers conclude with preliminary findings.

Rework and Follow Up
 The reviewers compile a report with significant findings.
 The author reworks the materials to fix defects.
 The moderator verifies that issues are addressed.

The main event of a traditional Fagan inspection is a moderated face-to-face group meeting, where the reviewers examine the materials, line by line. The underlying assumption is that the group dynamics promote defect detection. Group meetings often cause delays, as schedules have to be coordinated. This assumption has been questioned, as we shall see.

Screening Projects for Inspection Since the purpose of an inspection is to provide a project team with objective feedback, the request for an inspection must come from the project team. They are the ones to benefit from and act on the findings. As part of the request, the project team may indicate specific areas of focus for the inspection; for example, usability, accessibility, security, and reliability.

Inspections are not for assessing a team's performance or for assigning blame. If the project team is pressured into having an inspection or is resistant to acting on the findings, the inspection could turn out to be a waste of everyone's time.

Companies typically have a screening process to prioritize requests for inspections. Inspections have a cost: they require a time commitment by both the reviewers and the project team. Screening is based on the perceived cost effectiveness of an inspection.

Roles in a Traditional Inspection The main roles associated with an inspection are as follows:

- **Moderator** The moderator organizes the inspection and facilitates group interactions to maximize effectiveness. Moderators need special training; they need to be objective. Hence they must be independent of the project and its immediate management.

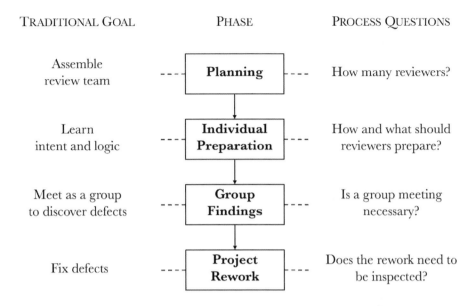

TRADITIONAL GOAL	PHASE	PROCESS QUESTIONS
Assemble review team	Planning	How many reviewers?
Learn intent and logic	Individual Preparation	How and what should reviewers prepare?
Meet as a group to discover defects	Group Findings	Is a group meeting necessary?
Fix defects	Project Rework	Does the rework need to be inspected?

Figure 8.3 Phases of a software inspection. Goals from a traditional inspection are on the left. The questions on the right are based on empirical studies.

- **Author** The author may be a person or a small team. The author prepares the materials for review and answers questions about the project.
- **Reviewer** Reviewers need to be independent, so they can be objective. They are often drawn from other projects within the same company. See also the comments about reviewers in Section 8.1.1.

The moderator role can be split into two: organizer of the inspection and moderator of the group interactions. Similarly, the author role can be split into two: author of the artifact, and reader who paraphrases the content to be reviewed.

8.2.2 Case Study: Using Data to Ensure Effectiveness

At one level, the next example describes how one company uses data to ensure the effectiveness of its inspections. At another level, the example illustrates the increasing role of data collection and process improvement in software engineering. See Chapter 10 for more on metrics and measurement.

Example 8.1 The data in Table 8.3 shows just a few of the internal benchmarks for inspections at Infosys, around 2002. For requirements documents, preparation by individual reviewers was at the rate of 5–7 pages per hour. During the group review meeting, the progress rate was about the same. The group found 0.5–1.5 minor and 0.1–0.3 major defects per page. For code inspections, the individual preparation rate

Table 8.3 Selected benchmark data from inspections at Infosys. From the left, the columns are for the artifact under review, the preparation rate for individual reviewers, the progress rate during a group meeting, and minor and major defects found by the inspection.

ARTIFACT	PREPARATION per hour	MEETING per hour	DEFECTS minor	DEFECTS major
Requirements	5–7 pages	5–7 pages	0.5–1.5 per page	0.1–0.3 per page
Code	100–200 lines	110–150 lines per line	0.01–0.06 per line	0.01–0.06

was 100–200 lines per hour and the progress rate during the group meeting was 110–150 lines per hour. The review found about equal numbers of minor and major defects: 0.01–0.06 per line.

Infosys began with code inspections and extended the reviews to all other development activities.[4]

Benchmark data was used to assess the effectiveness of an inspection/review, to plan follow-ups, and to make process improvements. For example, if an inspection found fewer defects than the benchmark, what were the possible causes and next steps?

- Was the reviewed artifact too simple? If so, use one-person reviews for later phases of this project. Alternatively, combine its review with that of other simple projects.
- Was the inspection thorough enough? Confirm by checking other metrics, such as the progress rate during the meeting. If the review was not thorough, reinspect with different reviewers. Also check if the current reviewers need training.
- Is the artifact of very good quality? Confirm using another metric; for example, the progress rate, the reviewers' experience, and the author's track record. if it is confirmed, check whether the quality can be duplicated elsewhere. Also revise the downstream estimates for this project.

There is a corresponding set of questions and next steps for an inspection that found more defects than the benchmark:

- Was the artifact too complex? Consider breaking it down into simpler parts. Revise downstream estimates for this project and for system testing.
- Did the inspection find too many minor defects and too few major ones? Check whether the reviewers understood the artifact well enough. Also check whether the reference document was precise enough. Was this the first review for an artifact from this project?
- Was the artifact of low quality? If so, does the author need training or a simpler work assignment? Rework the artifact.

While the data in this example is dated, it continues to be relevant. Technology has changed in the interim, but preparation, progress, and defect-discovery rates today are very likely to be similar to those in Table 8.3. □

8.2.3   Organizing an Inspection

The moderator assembles a team of independent reviewers. The moderator also ensures that the project team provides clear objectives and adequate materials for inspection. For example, for an architecture review, the project must provide a suitable architectural description. For a code inspection, the code must compiled and tested.

How Many Reviewers? The cost of an inspection rises with the number of reviewers: how many are enough? The number of reviewers depends on the nature of the inspection: with too few, the review team may not have the required breadth of expertise; with too many, the inspection becomes inefficient. The fewer reviewers, the better, not only for the cost of the reviewers' time, but because it takes longer to coordinate schedules and collect comments from the reviewers.

A typical inspection has three to six reviewers. For code inspections, there is evidence that two reviewers find as many defects as four.[5]

Overview and Individual Preparation Individual preparation by the reviewers may optionally be preceded by a briefing session to orient the reviewers. During the briefing, the project team provides an overview of the project, drawing attention to the areas of focus for the inspection.

The reviewers then work on their own to prepare. What kind of preparation?

- In a traditional review, the goal of preparation is to understand the review materials. The "real work" of finding defects occurs in a moderated group meeting.
- An alternative approach is to change the goal of preparation, so reviewers focus on finding defects before providing collective feedback.

How Should Reviewers Prepare? Reviewers are often given checklists or scenarios to guide their individual preparation. Such guidance is to avoid two problems: duplication of effort and gaps in coverage. Duplication of effort occurs when multiple reviewers find the same defects. Gaps in coverage occur if defects remain undiscovered: no reviewer finds them.

In one study, reviewers who used scenarios or use cases were more effective at finding defects than reviewers who used checklists.[6]

Moderated Group Findings In a traditional Fagan inspection, the reviewers meet face-to-face to find defects. Reviewers are expected to have studied the materials prior to the meeting. The meeting is where defect detection is expected to take place.

The moderator sets the pace and keeps the meeting on track. The entire review team goes over the materials line-by-line to find defects. The detected defects are recorded: the meeting is for finding defects, not for fixing them. At the end of the meeting, the reviewers may confer privately and provide preliminary feedback to the project team.

Inspection meetings are taxing, so the recommended length of a meeting is two hours. Meetings for complex projects may take multiple days.

Is a Group Meeting Really Necessary? The group meeting is the main event of a traditional inspection. Is a group meeting necessary?

In a Bell Labs study, 90 percent of the defects were found during individual preparation; the remaining 10 percent were found during the group meeting.[7] This data argues against group meetings, which are expensive. Schedule coordination alone can take up a third of the time interval for an inspection.[8]

Rework and Follow Up After reviewer feedback is collected, the reviewers provide a report with significant findings. The report classifies issues by severity: major issues must be addressed for the project to be successful; minor issues are for consideration by the project team. Finally, the moderator follows up to verify that the reported issues get addressed. The issues identified by the reviewers may include false positives – a false positive is a reported defect that turns out not to be a defect on further examination. The author must respond to all issues, even if it is to note that no rework is needed.

8.3   Code Reviews: Check Intent and Trust

Review-then-Commit is the best practice of reviewing all code before it becomes part of the main code repository. The purpose of a code review is to check that the code is readable and that it can be trusted to do what it is intended to do. Any code to be reviewed is assumed to be working code that the author has tested and is ready to commit. In short, people check code for intent and trust, automated tools check for consistency and rule violations. People are better than tools at getting to the root cause of a problem and in making judgments about design and style. Meanwhile, static analysis tools (Section 8.4) and type checkers are better than people at applying rules to check for defects and guideline violations.

This section describes how code reviews are conducted. Some properties of code reviews appear in Table 8.4. For concreteness, the properties are from open-source code reviews. Similar comments apply to technology companies like Google.[9]

8.3.1   Invested Expert Reviewers

Open-source projects often have hundreds of contributors, who are geographically dispersed.[10] A trusted group of core developers is responsible for the integrity of the code base.

Contributions are broadcast to a developer mailing list for review. Reviewers self-select, based on their expertise and interests. They respond with comments and suggested fixes. While the number of reviewers for each contribution is small, between one and three, a larger community of developers is aware of the review.[11]

At Google, the main code repository is organized into subtrees with owners for each subtree.

Table 8.4 Properties of Open-Source Code Reviews. Note that there may be exceptions to these general observations.

OPEN-SOURCE REVIEWS	
Frequency	per Commit
Code Size	Tens of lines
Reviewers	Invested (1–3)
Goal of the Review	Detect and Fix defects
Interactions	By messages
Elapsed Time	Hours

All changes to the main source code repository MUST be reviewed by at least one other engineer.[12]

The author of a change chooses reviewers; however, anyone on the relevant mailing is free to respond to any change. All changes to a subtree must be approved by the owner of the subtree.

In general, self-selected reviewers have considerable expertise.

8.3.2   Reviewing Is Done within Hours

It is a good practice to review all code before it is committed; that is, before it goes live in a production setting. Major companies, like Google, require a review before a commit. Open-source software projects require code from new contributors to be reviewed before it is committed.

Projects that review all code have frequent reviews of small pieces of code: tens of lines, say 30–50, instead of the hundreds of lines in a traditional inspection. Code for review is self-contained, so reviewers see not only the change, but the context for the change.

The *Review-then-Commit* process is illustrated in Fig. 8.4(a). A contributor submits code for review. The reviewers examine the code for defects and suggest fixes. The contributor reworks the code and resubmits. Once the reviewers have no further comments, the code is committed and becomes part of the production code base. The dashed line indicates that rework is conditional on reviewers having comments that need to be addressed.

An alternative review process is followed if a change is urgent or if the contributor is known and trusted. The *Commit-then-Review* process is illustrated in Fig. 8.4(b). A contributor commits the code and notifies potential reviewers, who examine the change. Based on their comments, the commit either holds or the change is rolled back and reworked. The dashed line represents the case in which the change is reworked until it is approved by the reviewers.

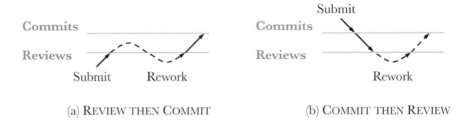

(a) REVIEW THEN COMMIT   (b) COMMIT THEN REVIEW

Figure 8.4 The Review-then-Commit and Commit-then-Review processes.

Asynchronous Rapid Responses

With self-selected geographically distributed reviewers, code reviews are *asynchronous*: there is no group meeting. Reviewer comments are collected by email or though an online tool. Reviewers typically respond within hours.

8.4   Automated Static Analysis

Static analyzers perform optional compliance checks on source code, checks that are in addition to the ones that are built into compilers. For example, compilers do type checking. They also check that variables are declared before they are used, and warn about unreachable code. Static analyzers complement compilers. Lint, an early static analyzer, was separated out of a C compiler and packaged as an optional independent tool.[13] They warn about many questionable program constructions; that is, program fragments that reflect poor development practices or are highly likely to be problematic. In practice, the checkers are effective enough that static analysis has become an essential verification technique, along with reviews and testing. Here, effectiveness refers to the proportion of warnings that turn out to be real issues.

Static checkers are good at performing automated checks across the code, even across millions of lines of code. The checks do not guarantee program correctness, good design, or product quality. The checkers are only as good as the rules and guidelines they apply. Human reviewers are better at making judgment calls about design and development practices. The combination of automated checks and expert reviews is therefore much more effective than either checks or reviews by themselves.

A drawback of static analysis is that it can raise false alarms, along with flagging critical defects. In the past, the volume of false alarms was a barrier to adoption. Now, static analyzers use heuristics and deeper analysis to hold down the number of false alarms. They also prioritize their warnings: the higher the priority, the more critical the defect.

Box 8.1 Verifying Code for a Mars Mission

After traveling 350 million miles in 274 days, the Mars rover, Curiosity, landed flawlessly on the planet's surface on August 5, 2012. The crucial sequence from entry into the thin Mars atmosphere to the landing was called "seven minutes of terror" by the engineers who designed it. So many things had to go right to slow the spacecraft from 11,200 miles an hour to 0 and land the rover without crashing on top of it.

Software controlled all functions on the rover and its spacecraft. The landing sequence was choreographed by 500,000 of the 3 million lines of code, written mostly in C by a team of 35 people. Verification was deeply entwined with the other development activities.[14]

- Designs and code were inspected line-by-line by peers. All 10,000 comments gathered during 145 peer code reviews were individually tracked and addressed.
- All code was automatically checked nightly for consistency and compliance with the team's coding standards. The team used four different commercial static analysis tools, since each tool picked up issues that the others did not. They used Coverity, Codesonar, Semmle, and Uno.
- The code for the mission was highly parallel, with 120 tasks. Parallel programs are notoriously hard to verify. The team used a powerful technique called logic model checking.

Overall, every precaution was taken to ensure the success of the mission. What distinguishes the project is not the novelty of the verification techniques, but the rigor with which the techniques were applied.

8.4.1 A Variety of Static Checkers

Automated static analysis tools consist of a set of *checkers* or *detectors*, where each checker looks for specific questionable constructions in the source code. Questionable constructions include the following:

- A variable is used before it is defined.
- A piece of code is unreachable (such code is also known as *dead code*).
- A resource *leaks*; that is, the resource is allocated but not released.
- A loop never terminates; for example, its control variable is never updated.

This list of constructions is far from complete. New checkers continue to be defined, inspired by real problems in real code. The examples in this section are drawn from real problems in production code.

Static analyzers rely on compiler techniques to trace control and data flows through a program. (Control flow graphs are discussed in Section 9.3.1.) *Control-flow analysis* traces execution paths through a program. *Data-flow analysis* traces the connections between the points in a program where the value of a variable is defined and where that value could potentially be used. The two are related, since data-flow analysis can help with control-flow analysis and vice versa.

Checking for Infinite Loops

The general problem of detecting infinite loops is undecidable, as noted earlier in this section. Many loops have a simple structure, however, where the value of a variable, called a *control variable*, determines when control exits the loop. Simple deductions may suffice for deciding whether such a loop is infinite.

Example 8.2   The following code fragment is adapted from a commercial product:

```
for ( j = 0; j < length; j-- ) {
    ...  // j is not touched in the body of the loop
}
```

If the value of length is positive, j < length will remain true as j takes on successively larger negative values.

An infinite loop is probably not what the programmer intended.   □

Checking for Unreachable Code

Control-flow analysis is needed for detecting unreachable code. Such code is typically a sign of a bug in the program.

Example 8.3   For 17 months, between September 2012 and February 2014, a security vulnerability lay undetected in code running on hundreds of millions of devices. The code had been open sourced, available for all to see.

The vulnerability was in the Secure Sockets Layer (SSL) code for the operating systems for iPhones and iPads (iOS), and Macs (OS X).[15] The vulnerability was significant, since it left the door open for an attacker to intercept communication with websites for applications such as secure browsing and credit card transactions.

The vulnerability was due to a bug, in the form of an extra unwanted goto; see Fig. 8.5. The indentation of the second circled goto on line 9 is deceptive. Lines 7–11 have the following form:

```
7)   if( condition₁ )
8)       goto fail;
9)   goto fail;          // bug: unwanted goto
10)  if( condition₂ )
11)      goto fail;
```

Note that the unwanted goto on line 9 prevents control from reaching the conditional on line 10.

A static analyzer would have detected the unreachable code on lines 10–11.   □

```
1)  if ((err = ReadyHash(&SSLHashSHA1, &hashCtx)) != 0)
2)          goto fail;
3)  if ((err = SSLHashSHA1.update(&hashCtx, &clientRandom)) != 0)
4)          goto fail;
5)  if ((err = SSLHashSHA1.update(&hashCtx, &serverRandom)) != 0)
6)          goto fail;
7)  if ((err = SSLHashSHA1.update(&hashCtx, &signedParams)) != 0)
8)          goto fail;
9)          goto fail;
10) if ((err = SSLHashSHA1.final(&hashCtx, &hashOut)) != 0)
11)         goto fail;
```

Figure 8.5 A bug in the form of an extra "goto fail;" introduced a vulnerability into an implementation of SSL.

```
1)   Logger logger = null;
2)   if (container != null)
3)       logger = container.getLogger();
4)   if (logger != null)
5)       logger.log(... + container.getName() + ...);
6)   else
7)       System.out.println(... + container.getName() + ...);
```

Figure 8.6 A program fragment from the open-source Apache Tomcat Server with a null-dereference bug.

Checking for Null-Dereference Failures

Null is a special value, reserved for denoting the absence of an object. A *null-dereference failure* occurs at run time when there is an attempt to use a null value. Static analysis can detect potential null references.

The following Java program fragment assigns the value null to variable logger of class Logger and then promptly proceeds to use null value:

```
Logger logger = null;
...            // code that does not change the value of logger
logger.log(message);
```

Using data-flow analysis, we can deduce that the value of logger will be null when control reaches the last line of the preceding program fragment. At that point, a failure will occur: there will be no object for logger to point to, so the method call log(message) will fail.

Before reading the next example, can you find the potential null dereferences in Fig. 8.6?

Example 8.4   The real code fragment in Fig. 8.6 avoids a null dereference for `logger`, but it introduces a null dereference for `container`.

Data-flow analysis would discover that `logger` in Fig. 8.6 is defined in two places and used in two places. The two definitions are on lines 1 and 3. The two uses are on lines 4 and 5. As for `container`, there are no definitions; there are four uses, on lines 2, 3, 5, and 7.

A null-dereference failure will occur if `container` is `null` when line 1 is reached. Control then flows from the decision on line 2 to line 4, leaving `logger` unchanged at `null`. From the decision on line 4, control therefore flows to line 7, which has a use of `container`. But `container` is `null`, so we have a null-dereference failure.

There is no null dereference if `container` is non-null when line 1 is reached, even if `container.getLogger()` returns `null`.   □

The open-source static analyzer FindBugs would warn about two potential null dereferences for the uses of `container` on lines 5 and 7.[16] From Example 8.4 only the null dereference on line 7 is possible. The FindBugs warning about the use of `container` on line 5 is therefore a false alarm. Such false alarms are called false positives.

8.4.2   False Positives and False Negatives

A warning from a static analyzer about a piece of code is called a *false positive* if the code does not in fact have a defect. False positives arise when a static analyzer errs on the side of safety and flags a piece of code that *might* harbor a defect. If further analysis reveals that the piece of code does not in fact have a defect, then the warning is a false positive.

A *false negative* is a defect that is not detected by static analysis.

Static analysis tools choose to hold down the number of false positives at the expense of introducing some false negatives. The designers of a commercial static analyzer, Coverity, observe:

In our experience, more than 30% [false positives] easily cause problems. People ignore the tool. . . . We aim for below 20% for "stable" checkers. When forced to choose between more bugs or fewer false positives we typically choose the latter.[17]

From the preceding quote, the designers of Coverity traded some false positives for some false negatives. They chose fewer false positives at the expense of some additional false negatives. More false negatives means more bugs missed. Other static analysis tools make the same choice.

8.5   Conclusion

The quality improvement techniques in this chapter complement each other. They apply at different levels of granularity, from the whole system down to a code fragment.Each technique has its own purpose, and its own cost, in terms of time and effort. Architecture inspections are done at the system level by groups of independent experts. The inspections take days to organize, but can steer a project in the right direction. Code reviews are done on tens of lines of working code by between one and three reviewers, who have an interest in the code. The reviews take just hours, and elicit defect findings and suggested fixes. Static analysis is done on code fragments by automated tools that perform rule-based consistency check. The analysis is essentially instantaneous and produces warnings of rule violations and deviations from programming-style guidelines. All of the above techniques perform static checking; that is, for checking software artifacts without running them.

A *review* is the process of getting comments, defect reports, or approval from one or more people. Reviews include inspections. An *inspection* is a formal review by a group of expects who provide their collective findings.

Architecture Reviews (Inspections) Architecture reviews are inspections, but are often referred to as architecture reviews or design reviews. The five guiding principles for architecture reviews are as follows:

- The review is for the project team's benefit.
- The expert reviewers are independent.
- The project has a clear problem definition.
- The architecture fits the problem.
- The project has a system architect.

An *architectural discovery review* is conducted in the early stages of a project to clarify the goals of a project and to assess whether an architectural approach promises a suitable solution. An *architectural deep-dive* is conducted during planning, before implementation begins, to get feedback on the whole system design or on some aspect of the design. An *architectural retrospective* is a debriefing to identify lessons learned that could help other projects.

Conducting Software Inspections In a *traditional* or *Fagan inspection*, a group of three to six independent experts prepares in advance for a group meeting to detect and collect defects in a software artifact. Subsequent studies have shown that two committed expert reviewers may be enough and that a face-to-face group meeting is not necessary. Instead, reviewer comments can be collected asynchronously by email or through an online tool.

Code Reviews The primary purpose of *code reviews* is to check whether the code does what it is intended to do and whether it can be trusted. It is a good practice to review all code before it is committed; that is, before it goes live in a production setting. *Asynchronous code reviews* are conducted using email and online tools. Small contributions, say 30–50 lines, are examined by either named reviewers or by self-selected reviewers, based on their expertise and interests.

- With a *Review-then-Commit* process, a contribution must be approved before it is committed.

- If a change is urgent or if a reviewer is trusted, the *Commit-then-Review* process allows a contribution to be committed first and then reworked, if needed.

Static Analysis   *Static analysis* examines a program for defects without running the program. Automated static analysis tools consist of a set of *checkers* or *detectors*, where each checker looks for specific questionable constructions in the source code. For example, there are checkers for undefined variables, unreachable code, null-dereferences, and infinite loops.

A warning from a static analyzer about a piece of code is a *false positive* if that code does not in fact have a defect. A *false negative* is a defect that is not detected by static analysis. Developers ignore static analyzers that produce too many false positives, so static analyzers hold down false positives at the risk of missing some defects; that is, at the risk of having some false negatives.

Further Reading

- Maranzano et al. [129] provide guiding principles for architecture reviews.
- For code reviews, see the review of six major open-source projects by Rigby et al. [157].
- Although Bessey et al. [21] focus on the commercial tool Coverity, their description brings out the issues and trade-offs faced by designers of static analysis tools.

Exercises for Chapter 8

Exercise 8.1   The following checks are from an early checklist for a software inspection.[18] Between software inspections, code reviews, and static analysis, which technique, if any, would you use to perform each check? Justify your answer.

a) "Have all variables been explicitly declared?"
b) "Are there any comparisons between variables having inconsistent data types (e.g., comparing a character string to an address)?"
c) "Is a variable referenced whose value is unset or uninitialized?"
d) "When indexing into a string, are the limits of the string exceeded?"
e) "Will every loop eventually terminate?"

Exercise 8.2   The following questions have been proposed for an architecture discovery review. Rank order the questions, from most to least important, in your opinion. Explain your reasons for the ordering. There is no single right or wrong answer.

a) Is there a primary customer?
b) Do the goals for the system capture the customer's desired user experience?
c) Is there a stakeholder for each use case?

d) For each use case, is there a set of modules that implements the use case?
e) Is there any functionality that is not needed for the use cases?
f) Is the architecture clean?
g) Have the quality attributes been defined?
h) Are the quality attributes supported by the architecture?
i) Does the team have the expertise for implementing the system?
j) Does the project have management support?

Exercise 8.3   Suppose that it is two years from now. Your current project has turned into a successful company. For a deep-dive architecture review, come up with 10 independent security-related questions. Ensure that there are no redundant questions.

Exercise 8.4   For a deep-dive architecture review, come up with 10 independent performance-related questions.

9   Testing

Software testing is the process of running a program in a controlled environment to check whether it behaves as expected. The purpose of testing is to improve software quality. If a test fails – that is, the program does not behave as expected – there must be a fault, either in the program or in the specification of expected behavior. Either way, the test has uncovered a problem that should be resolved.

The recurring theme of this chapter is the selection of a "good enough" set or suite of tests. Test selection is geared to the level of the software under test. White-box testing uses knowledge of the code and is suitable for smaller pieces of software that are called units of implementation. A suite of white-box tests is good enough if its execution exercises (covers) a specified fraction of the code. For code coverage, this chapter considers statement, branch, and MC/DC coverage. Black-box testing focuses on inputs and outputs, treating the code as if it was hidden. A suite of black-box tests is good enough if it adequately samples (covers) the input domain, the set of possible inputs. The black-box techniques in this chapter are equivalence partitioning and combinatorial testing.

This chapter will enable the reader to:

- Describe the main issues during testing: when to use white-box and/or black-box testing, setting up a test environment, test selection, and evaluation of test outputs.
- Select and design tests to achieve the desired levels of code coverage for white-box testing, and input domain coverage for black-box testing.

9.1   Overview of Testing

The code in Fig. 9.1 is from the clock driver of a processor used in digital media players produced by Microsoft and Toshiba. On December 31, 2008, owners of the player awoke to find that it froze on startup. On the last day of a leap year, the code loops forever.[1]

What went wrong?

```
 1)   year = ORIGINYEAR; /* = 1980 */
 2)   while (days > 365)
 3)   {
 4)       if (IsLeapYear(year))
 5)       {
 6)           if (days > 366)
 7)           {
 8)               days -= 366;
 9)               year += 1;
10)           }
11)       }
12)       else
13)       {
14)           days -= 365;
15)           year += 1;
16)       }
17)   }
```

Figure 9.1 On the last day of a leap year, this code fails. Where is the fault?

Example 9.1   Suppose that the code in Fig. 9.1 is reached with variable days representing the current date as an integer. January 1, 1980 is represented by the integer 1; December 31, 1980 by 366 since 1980 was a leap year; and so on.

Variable year is initialized to 1980 on line 1. On exit from the while loop on lines 2–17, variable year represents the current year. The body of the loop computes the current year by repeatedly subtracting 366 for a leap year (line 8) or 365 for a non-leap year (line 14). Each subtraction is followed by a line that increments year (lines 9 and 15). In other words, the body of the loop counts down the days and counts up the years.

On the 366th day of 2008, a leap year, line 6 is eventually reached with value 366 for days. Control therefore loops back from line 6 to line 2 with days unchanged. Ad infinitum.   □

How is it that "simple" bugs escape detection until there is an embarrassing product failure? The rest of this section explores the process of testing and its strengths and limitations.

9.1.1   Issues during Testing

The issues that arise during testing relate to the four main elements in Fig. 9.2:

- **Software under Test** The software under test can be a code fragment, a component, a subsystem, a self-contained program, or a complete hardware-software system.

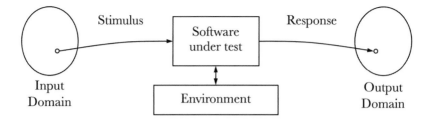

Figure 9.2 Software can be tested by applying an input stimulus and evaluating the output response.

- **Input Domain** A tester selects an element of some input domain and uses it as test input.
- **Output Domain** The output domain is the set of possible output responses or observable behaviors by the software under test. Examples of behaviors include producing integer outputs, as in Example 9.1, and retrieving a web page.
- **Environment** Typically, the software under test is not self-contained, so an environment is needed to provide the context for running the software.

If the software under test is a program fragment, the environment handles dependencies on the rest of the program. The environment also includes the operating system, libraries, and external services that may be running either locally or in the cloud. In the early stages of development, external services can be simulated by dummy or mock modules with controllable behavior. For example, an external database can be simulated by a module that uses a local table seeded with a few known values.

Example 9.2   Suppose that the software under test is the code on lines 1–17 in Fig. 9.1. The input domain is the set of possible initial integer values for the variable days. The output domain is the set of possible final integer values for the variables year and days.

The code in Fig. 9.1 cannot be run as is, because it needs a definition for ORIGINYEAR and an implementation for function IsLeapYear(). These things must be provided by the environment. (We are treating the initial value of variable days as an input, so the environment does not need to provide a value for days.)   □

The following questions capture the main issues that arise during testing:

- How to stabilize the environment to make tests repeatable?
- How to select test inputs?
- How to evaluate the response to a test input?
- How to decide whether to continue testing?

9.1.2   Test Selection

The judicious selection of test inputs is a key problem during testing. Fortunately, reliable software can be developed without exhaustive testing on all possible inputs – exhaustive testing is infeasible.

The Input Domain

The term *test input* is interpreted broadly to include any form of input; for example, a value such as an integer; a gesture; a combination of values and gestures; or an input sequence, such as a sequence of mouse clicks. In short, a test input can be any stimulus that produces a response from the software under test.

A set of tests is also known as a *test suite*.

The *input domain* is the set of all possible test inputs. For all practical purposes, the input domain is typically infinite. Variable days in Fig. 9.1 can be initialized to any integer value and, machine limitations aside, there is an infinite supply of integers.

Some faults are triggered by a mistimed sequence of input events. Therac-25 delivered a radiation overdose only when the technician entered patient-treatment data fast enough to trigger a fault; see Section 1.6.3. Other faults are triggered by an unfortunate combination of values. Avionics software is tested for interactions between multiple inputs; for example, a decision may be based on data from a variety of sensors and a failure occurs only when the pressure crosses a threshold and the temperature is in a certain range.

It is important to test on both valid and invalid inputs, for the software must work as expected or valid inputs and do something sensible on invalid inputs. Crashing on invalid input is not sensible behavior.

Input domains can therefore consist of single values, (b) combinations of values, or (c) scenarios consisting of sequences of values.

Black-Box and White-Box Testing

During test selection, we can either treat the software under test as a black box or we can look inside the box at the source code. Testing that depends only on the software's interface is called *black-box* or *functional testing*. Testing that is based on knowledge of the source code is called *white-box* or *structural testing*. As we shall see in Section 9.2, white-box testing is used for smaller units of software and black-box testing is used for larger subsystems that are built up from the units.

Test design and selection is a theme that runs through this chapter.

9.1.3   Test Adequacy: Deciding When to Stop

Ideally, testing would continue until the desired level of product quality is reached. Unfortunately, there is no way of knowing when the desired quality is reached because, at any time during testing, there is no way of knowing how many more defects remain undetected. If a test fails – that is, if the output does not match the expected response – then the tester knows with certainty that there is a defect to be explained. But, if the test passes, all the tester has learned is that the software works as expected on that particular test input. The software could potentially fail on some other input. As Edsger Dijkstra put it,

Testing shows the presence, not the absence of bugs.[2]

So, how many successful tests should the software pass before its quality is deemed "high enough"? In what follows, we consider answers to this question.

Stopping or Test-Adequacy Criteria

A *test-adequacy* criterion is a measure of progress during testing. Adequacy criteria support statements of the form, "Testing is x percent complete." Test-adequacy criteria are typically based on three kinds of metrics: code-coverage, input-coverage, and defect-discovery.

- *Code coverage* is the degree to which a construct in the source code is touched during testing. For example, statement coverage is the proportion of statements that are executed at least once during a set of tests. Code coverage is discussed in Section 9.3 on white-box testing.
- *Input coverage* is the degree to which a set of test inputs is representative of the whole input domain. For example, in Section 9.4 on black-box testing, the input domain will be partitioned into equivalence classes. Equivalence-class coverage is the proportion of equivalence classes that are represented in a test set.
- The *defect-discovery rate* is the number and severity of the defects discovered in a given time interval. When combined with historical data from similar projects, the discovery rate is sometimes used to predict product quality. See Section 10.4 for more about product-quality metrics.

Adequacy criteria based on coverage and defect discovery are much better than arbitrary criteria, such as stopping when time runs out or when a certain number of defects have been found. They cannot, however, guarantee the absence of bugs.

While testing alone is not enough, it can be a key component of an overall quality-improvement plan based on reviews, static analysis, and testing; see Section 10.4.

9.1.4   Test Oracles: Evaluating the Response to a Test

Implicit in the preceding discussion is the assumption that we can readily tell whether an output is "correct"; that is, we can readily decide whether the output response to an input stimulus matches the expected output. This assumption is called the oracle assumption.

The *oracle assumption* has two parts:

1. There is a specification that defines the correct response to a test input.
2. There is a mechanism to decide whether or not a response is correct. Such a mechanism is called an *oracle*.

Most of the time, there is an oracle, human or automated. For values such as integers and characters, all an oracle may need to do is to compare the output with the expected value. An oracle based on a known comparison can be easily automated.

Graphical and audio/video interfaces may require a human oracle. For example, how do you evaluate a text-to-speech system? It may require a human to decide whether the spoken output sounds natural to a native speaker.

Questioning the Oracle Assumption

The oracle assumption does not always hold. A test oracle may not be readily available, or may be nontrivial to construct.

Example 9.3   Elaine Weyuker gives the example of a major oil company's accounting software, which "had been running without apparent error for years."[3] One month, it reported $300 for the company's assets, an obviously incorrect output response, since assets were expected to be in the billions of dollars. This is an example of knowing that a response is incorrect, without an oracle that provides the right response.

There was no test oracle for the accounting software. Even an expert could not tell whether "$1,134,906.43 is correct and $1,135,627.85 is incorrect."   □

Example 9.4   Consider a program that takes as input an integer n and produces as output the nth prime number. On input 1 the program produces 2, the first prime number; on 2 it produces 3; on 3 it produces 5; and so on. On input 1000, it produces 7919 as output.

Is 7919 the 1000th prime? (Yes, it is.)

It is nontrivial to create an oracle to decide if a number p is the nth prime number.[4]   □

9.2   Levels of Testing

Testing becomes more manageable if the problem is partitioned: bugs are easier to find and fix if modules are debugged before they are assembled into a larger system. A modules-before-systems approach motivates the levels of testing in Fig. 9.3. Testing proceeds from bottom to top; the size of the software under test increases from bottom to top.

Each level of testing plays a different role. From Section 2.5, to validate is to check whether the product will do what users want, and to verify is to check whether it is being implemented correctly, according to its specification. The top two levels in Fig. 9.3 validate that the right product is being built. The lower levels verify the product is being built right (correctly).

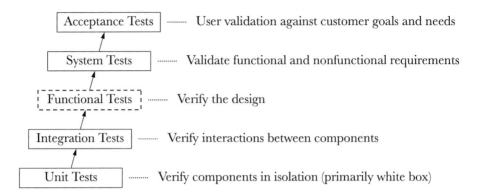

Figure 9.3 Levels of testing. Functional tests may be merged into system tests; hence the dashed box.

System and functional testing may be combined into a single level that tests the behavior of the system; hence the dashed box for functional tests. The number of levels varies from project to project, depending on the complexity of the software and the importance of the application.[5]

Based on data from hundreds of companies, a rough estimate is that each level catches about one in three defects.[6]

9.2.1   Unit Testing

A *unit* of software is a logically separate piece of code that can be tested by itself. It may be a module or part of a module. *Unit testing* verifies a unit in isolation from the rest of the system. With respect to the overview of testing in Fig. 9.2, the environment simulates just enough of the rest of the system to allow the unit to be run and tested.

Unit testing is primarily white-box testing, where test selection is informed by the source code of the unit. White-box testing is discussed in Section 9.3.

xUnit: Automated Unit Testing

Convenient automated unit testing profoundly changes software development. A full suite of tests can be run automatically at any time to verify the code. Changes can be made with reasonable assurance that the changes will not break any existing functionality. Code and tests can be developed together; new tests can be added as development proceeds. In fact, automated tests enable test-first or test-driven development, where tests are written first and then code is written to pass the tests.

Convenience was the number one goal for *JUnit*, a framework for automated testing of Java programs. Kent Beck and Erich Gamma wanted to make it so convenient that "we have some glimmer of hope that developers will actually write tests."[7]

JUnit quickly spread. It inspired unit testing frameworks for other languages, including CUnit for C, CPPUnit for C++, PyUnit for Python, JSUnit for JavaScript, and so on. This family of testing frameworks is called *xUnit*.

An xUnit test proceeds as follows:

set up the environment;

run test;

tear down the environment;

From Section 9.1, the environment includes the context that is needed to run the software under test. For a Java program, the context includes values of variables and simulations of any constructs that the software relies on.

Example 9.5 The pseudo-code in Fig. 9.4(a) shows a class Date with a method getYear(). The body of getYear() is not shown – think of it as implementing the year calculation in Fig. 9.1.

The code in Fig. 9.4(b) sets up a single JUnit test for getYear(). The annotation @Test marks the beginning of a test. The name of the test is test365. A descriptive name is recommended, for readability of messages about failed tests. Simple tests are recommended to make it easier to identify faults.

The test creates object date and calls getYear(365), where 365 represents December 31, 1980. JUnit supports a range of assert methods; assertEquals() is an example. If the computed value year does not equal 1980, the test fails, and JUnit will issue a descriptive message.

For more information about JUnit, visit junit.org.   □

9.2.2 Integration Testing

Integration testing verifies interactions between the parts of a subsystem. If previous unit testing has been effective, then it is likely that a failure during integration testing is due to interactions between modules, instead of being due to a fault within some module. Hence, integration testing is typically black-box testing.

This section considers *incremental* integration testing, which verifies interactions between modules by adding them one or more at a time. An incremental approach is much better than *big bang* integration testing, where the whole system is assembled all at once from individually unit tested modules. Big-bang approaches often end badly; for example, see the teething pains of healthcare.gov, described in Example 2.12.

```
public class Date {
    ...
    public int getYear(...) {
        ...
    }
    ...
}
```

```
public class DateTest {
    @Test
    public void test365() {
        Date date = new Date();
        int year = date.getYear(365);
        assertEquals(year, 1980);
    }
}
```

(a) Software under Test   (a) A JUnit 4 Test

Figure 9.4 A JUnit test.

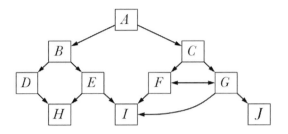

Figure 9.5 Modules to be integrated. The horizontal line between F and G means that they use each other.

Dependencies between Modules

Incremental integration testing must deal with dependencies between modules.

Example 9.6   In a model-view-controller architecture, the view displays information that it gets from the model. The view depends on the model, but not the other way around.

The model in Example 7.6 held information about a picture of the Mona Lisa, including a digital photo and the height, width, and resolution of the photo. There were two views: one displayed the digital photo; the other displayed the height, width, and resolution of the photo.

Both views got their information from the model, so they depended on the model. The model, however, was not dependent on the views.   □

Dependencies between modules can be defined in terms of a uses relationship: module M *uses* module N, if N must be present and satisfy its specification for M to satisfy its specification.[8] Note that the used module need not be a submodule of the using module. In Example 9.6, the views used the model, but the model was not a submodule of either view.

During incremental integration, suppose module M uses module N. Then, either M must be added after N or there must be a "stub" that can be used instead of N for testing purposes. More precisely, module N' is a *stub* for N if N' has the same interface and enough of the functionality of N to allow testing of modules that use N.

Example 9.7   The edges and paths in Fig. 9.5 represent the uses relation between the modules in a system. Module A uses all the modules below it. A uses B and C directly; it uses the other modules indirectly.

A uses B, so B must be present and work for A to work. But, B uses D and E, so D and E must also be present and work for A to work.   □

Bottom-Up Integration Testing

With bottom-up integration testing, a module is integrated before any using module needs it; that is, if *M* uses *N*, then *M* is integrated after *N*. If two modules use each other, then they are added together. Bottom-up integration testing requires drivers: a *driver* module sets up the environment for the software under test. Drivers and stubs are two different types of scaffolding. Automated testing tools like the xUnit family set up the environment, so there is no need for separate drivers.

Example 9.8 Consider the modules in Fig. 9.5. Any ordering that adds a child node before a parent node can serve for incremental integration testing, except for modules *F* and *G*, which use each other. They must be added together.

Here are two possible orderings for bottom-up testing:

$$H, D, I, E, B, J, F \text{ and } G, C, A$$
$$J, I, F \text{ and } G, C, H, E, D, B, A$$

□

Top-Down Integration Testing

With stubs, integration testing can proceed top-down. Testing of module *A* in Fig. 9.5 can begin with stubs for *B* and *C*. Then, testing of *A* and *B* together can begin with stubs for *C*, *D*, and *E*. Alternatively, testing *A* and *C* together can begin with stubs for *B*, *F*, and *G*.

A disadvantage with top-down integration testing is that stubs need to provide enough functionality for the using modules to be tested. Glenford J. Myers cautions that

Stub modules are often more complicated than they first appear to be.[9]

9.2.3 Functional, System, and Acceptance Testing

Functional testing verifies that the overall system meets its design specifications. *System testing* validates the system as a whole with respect to customer requirements, both functional and nonfunctional. The overall system may include hardware and third-party software components.

Functional testing may be merged into system testing. If the two are merged, then system testing performs a combination of verification and validation.

System testing is a major activity. Nonfunctional requirements include performance, security, usability, reliability, scalability, serviceability, documentation, among others. These are end-to-end properties that can be tested only after the overall system is available.

Testing for properties like security, usability, and performance are important enough that they may be split off from system testing and conducted by dedicated specialized teams.

Acceptance Testing

Acceptance testing differs from the other levels of testing since it is performed by the customer organization. Mission-critical systems are usually installed in a lab at a customer site and subjected to rigorous acceptance testing before they are put into production. Acceptance tests based on usage scenarios ensure that the system will support the customer organization's business goals.

9.2.4   Case Study: Test Early and Often

Testing was a top priority during the development of a highly reliable communications product at Avaya. Tests were a deliverable, along with the code they tested. The development process called for extensive unit, functional, integration, system, interoperability, regression, and performance testing. *Interoperability testing* verifies that a given product will work together with other products, including products from other vendors. Regression testing reruns all tests after a change to verify that the change did not break any existing functionality. Performance testing is one of many kinds of testing for quality attributes.

The relative ordering of tests in the Avaya project is reflected in Fig. 9.6. Otherwise, the figure is a simplified variant of the Avaya process. The figure has phases, whereas the Avaya process staggered coding and testing across time-boxed sprints.

Example 9.9   This example describes a generic development process that emphasizes testing. The diagram in Fig. 9.6 focuses on the coding and testing phases of a product development. The phases in the diagram correspond to levels of testing, starting with unit testing, represented by the box at top-left. The horizontal bars represent ongoing tests.

During the first (unit) phase, multiple subteams work in parallel: each subteam writes and delivers code and unit tests for a set of features. The code must pass additional sanity tests upon delivery. Together, the subteams deliver a comprehensive set of unit tests, perhaps thousands of them. The unit tests are to be run many (perhaps hundreds) of times a day in this and later phases.

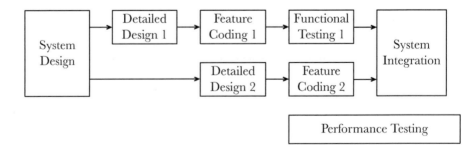

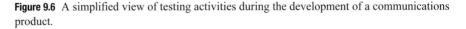

Figure 9.6 A simplified view of testing activities during the development of a communications product.

The purpose of the next (functional) phase is to ready the unit-tested features for integration. The deliverables from this phase are more code and automated functional tests, perhaps hundreds of them. The unit and functional tests are to be run automatically during nightly builds (integrations).

Integration testing both validates the design and verifies the implementation of the functionality. It prepares the code base for the system verification (SV) team. The tests cut across features. The SV team conducts its own system tests for functionality, behavior under heavy load, and handling of failure scenarios. The SV team must approve the system before it gets to alpha testing with friendly users. Alpha testing is typically within a company. Beta testing is with friendly outside users.

In Fig. 9.6, the horizontal bars below the phases are for ongoing tests that begin as early as possible. Interoperability testing begins along with functional testing. Formal regression testing for the project is in addition to the developers' own regression tests during coding. Formal regression testing begins with the integration phase. Beginning with the integration phase, formal regression testing runs all automated tests. Bug fixes prompt new unit and functional tests. Performance testing begins with the system testing phase. □

9.3   Code Coverage I: White-Box Testing

Since program testing cannot prove the absence of bugs, it is unrealistic to expect that testing must continue until all defects have been found. The test-adequacy criteria in this section are based on code coverage, which is the degree to which a construct in the source code is executed during testing. In practice, the adequacy of test sets is measured relative to coverage targets. Code coverage is closely, but not exclusively, associated with white-box testing, where test selection is based on knowledge of the source code.

9.3.1   Control-Flow Graphs

A *control-flow graph*, or simply *flow graph*, represents the flow of control between the statements in a program. Flow graphs have two kinds of nodes:

- *Basic nodes* have one incoming and one outgoing edge.
- *Decision nodes* have one incoming and two or more outgoing edges.
  Basic nodes represent assignments and procedure calls. Decision nodes result from Boolean expressions, such as those in conditional and while statements. The two outgoing edges from a decision node are called *branches* and labeled *T* for *true* and *F* for *false*. If the Boolean expression in the decision node evaluates to *true* control flows through the *T* branch. Otherwise, control flows through the *F* branch.

For convenience, a sequence of one or more basic nodes may be merged to form a node called a *basic block*. As a further convenience, assume that a flow graph has

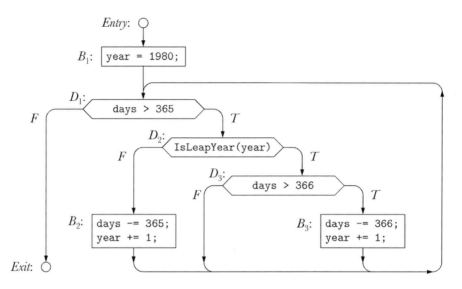

Figure 9.7 Control-flow graph for the code fragment in Fig. 9.1.

a single *entry* node with no incoming edges and a single *exit* node with no outgoing edges.

Example 9.10   The flow graph in Fig. 9.7 represents the flow of control between the statements in Fig. 9.1. The flow graph has three basic blocks, B_1–B_3, and three decision nodes, D_1–D_3. Basic block B_1 has one assignment, which initializes year. (We take the liberty of initializing year to 1980, instead of ORIGINYEAR.) B_2 has two assignments:

```
days -= 365;
year += 1;
```

Decision node D_1 corresponds to the decision in the while statement

```
while (days > 365) { ... }
```

D_2 corresponds to the decision in the conditional statement

```
if (IsLeapYear(year)) { ... } else { ... }
```

□

The flow graph for a program can be constructed by applying rules like the ones in Fig. 9.8. The rules are for a simple language that supports assignments, conditionals, while loops, and sequences of statements. Variables E and S represent expressions and statements, respectively. The rules can be applied recursively to construct the flow graph for a statement. It is left to the reader to extend the rules to handle conditionals with both then and else parts.

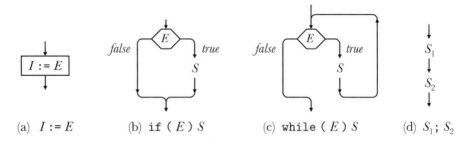

Figure 9.8 Rules for constructing a control-flow graph.

Paths through a Flow Graph

A test corresponds to a path through a flow graph. Intuitively, the path is the sequence of statements that are reached when the test is run. More precisely, a *path* through a flow graph is a sequence of contiguous edges from the entry node to the exit node. Two edges are *contiguous* if the end node of the first edge is the start node of the second edge. A path can be written as a sequence of nodes $n_1, n_2, \ldots$, where there is an edge from node n_i to node n_{i+1}, for all i.

A *simple path* is a path with no repeated edges. A simple path through a loop corresponds to a single execution of the loop. If there were a second execution, one or more of the edges in the loop would repeat.

Example 9.11   This example relates tests of the code in Fig. 9.1 with paths through the flow graph in Fig. 9.7. A test of the code consists of an execution, where the test input is an initial value for the variable days.

Consider the test 365; that is, the initial value of days is 365. The Boolean expression days > 365 evaluates to false, so control skips the body of the while-loop. This execution corresponds to the simple path

$$Entry, B_1, D_1, Exit$$

With test 367, control goes through the body of the while loop exactly once before exiting. Variable year is initialized to 1980, a leap year, so this test traces the simple path

$$Entry, B_1, D_1, D_2, D_3, B_3, D_1, Exit$$

Although node D_1 appears twice, this path is simple because no edge is repeated.   □

9.3.2   Control-Flow Coverage Criteria

In defining code-coverage criteria, let us treat dead code as an exception – and ignore it. Any coverage criteria we define will err on the safe (strict) side because they will apply to all of the code, including the dead code. By definition, dead code is unreachable, so it cannot be covered (reached) by any test. For example, in programs with dead statements, 100 percent statement coverage is unattainable. The no-dead-code assumption applies to conditions and decisions as well; that is, neither is always true or always false.

If there is no dead code, the correspondence between tests and paths is one-to-one. Each test of a program traces to a path through the program's flow graph, and vice versa. Code-coverage criteria can therefore be expressed either in terms of program constructs like statements, decisions, and executions of the program or in terms of nodes, edges, and paths, respectively.

Coverage tracking is a job best done by automated tools that build flow graphs and keep track of coverage information as tests are run. Given the close correspondence between flow graphs and the source code, the tools display coverage information by annotating the source code. For example, statement coverage is typically displayed by showing the number of times each line of code is executed by a test set. The tools also produce reports that summarize the coverage achieved by a test set.

All-Paths Coverage: Strong but Unrealistic

With *all-paths coverage*, each path is traced at least once.

The set of all paths through a flow graph corresponds to the set of all possible executions of the program. All paths coverage therefore corresponds to exhaustive testing. Exhaustive testing is the strongest possible test-adequacy criterion: if a program passes exhaustive testing, then we know that the program will work for all inputs.

Exhaustive testing is also impossible. A flow graph with loops has an infinite number of paths: given any path that goes through a loop, we can construct another longer path by going one more time through the loop.

Since all-paths coverage is an unattainable ideal, many more or less restrictive coverage criteria have been proposed. The rest of the this section considers some widely used code coverage criteria.

Node or Statement Coverage

Node coverage, also known as *statement coverage*, requires a set of paths (tests) that touch each node at least once. Node coverage is the weakest of the commonly used coverage criteria.

Example 9.12 For the flow graph in Fig. 9.7, 100 percent node coverage can be achieved without triggering the known leap-year bug: on the last day of a leap year the code loops forever.

From Example 9.11, the paths traced by the test inputs 365 and 367 are as follows (for readability, the entry and exit nodes are omitted):

Test Input	Path
365	B_1, D_1
367	$B_1, D_1, D_2, D_3, B_3, D_1$

The test set $\{365, 367\}$ covers the nodes

$$B_1, B_3, D_1, D_2, D_3$$

Note that node B_2 is not yet covered. For B_2 to be covered, control must take the F branch of decision node D_2 in Fig. 9.7. The first time through D_2, control will take the T branch, since the initial value of year is 1980, a leap year.

The path for test 732 takes the F branch to B_2 the second time the path reaches D_2. The path is

$$B_1, D_1, D_2, D_3, B_3, D_1, D_2, B_2, D_1$$

The singleton test set $\{732\}$ happens to cover all nodes in Fig. 9.7. Multiple tests are usually needed to achieve the desired level of node coverage.   □

While 100 percent node coverage is a desirable goal, it may not be achievable. If the software under test has dead code, by definition, the dead code cannot be reached during any execution. No test can therefore reach it. While dead code can be removed by refactoring, legacy systems are touched only as needed.

In practice, companies set stricter node coverage thresholds for new than for legacy code.

Branch Coverage Is Stronger Than Node Coverage
Branch coverage, also known as *decision coverage*, requires a set of paths (tests) that touch both the true and false branches out of each decision node. Branch coverage is a stronger criterion than node coverage. (As we shall see, branch coverage does uncover the leap-year bug in Fig. 9.7.)

Specifically, branch coverage *subsumes* node coverage, which means that any test set that achieves 100 percent branch coverage also achieves 100 percent node coverage. The converse is false, as the next example demonstrates.

Example 9.13   From Example 9.12, the tests 365, 367, and 732 correspond to the following paths

TEST INPUT	PATH
365	B_1, D_1
367	$B_1, D_1, D_2, D_3, B_3, D_1$
732	$B_1, D_1, D_2, D_3, B_3, D_1, D_2, B_2, D_1$

The branch coverage of these tests is as follows:

TEST INPUT	D_1	D_2	D_3
365	F		
367	T, F	T	T
732	T, F	T, F	T

These tests achieve 100 percent node coverage, but they do not achieve 100 percent branch coverage because they do not cover the F branch from D_3 to D_1. (In fact, test 732 alone covers all branches covered by the other tests.)

This F branch out of D_3 is covered only when the code is in an infinite loop. Here's why. For the branch (D_3, D_1) to be taken, the following must hold:

$$
\begin{array}{lll}
\texttt{days > 365} & \textit{true} & \text{at node } D_1 \\
\texttt{IsLeapYear(year)} & \textit{true} & \text{at node } D_2 \\
\texttt{days > 366} & \textit{false} & \text{at node } D_3
\end{array}
$$

Together, these observations imply that, when the branch (D_3, D_1) is taken, days must have value 366 and year must represent a leap year. With these values for days and year, the program loops forever.

Thus, a test suite designed to achieve 100 percent branch coverage would uncover the leap-year bug.

The smallest test input that triggers the infinite loop is the value 366 for days – the corresponding date is December 31, 1980.   □

Other Control-Flow Coverage Criteria

In practice, node and branch coverage are the most popular control-flow-based adequacy criteria. Branch coverage subsumes node coverage: any test set that achieves 100 percent branch coverage also achieves 100 percent node coverage. A number of other control-flow-based criteria have been proposed; for example,[10]

- *Loop count coverage*: exercise each loop up to k times, where k is a parameter.
- *Length-n path coverage*: cover all subpaths of length n.

9.4   Input Coverage I: Black-Box Testing

From the overview of testing in Section 9.1, testing proceeds roughly as follows:

- Select a test input for the software under test.
- Evaluate the software's response to the input.
- Decide whether to continue testing.

Test inputs are drawn from a set called the input domain. The input domain can be infinite. If not infinite, it is typically so large that exhaustive testing of all possible inputs is impossible. Test selection is therefore based on some criterion for sampling the input domain.

The selection criteria in this section are closely, but not exclusively, associated with black-box testing, which treats the source code as if it were hidden. Test selection is based on the software's specification.

9.4.1   Equivalence-Class Coverage

Equivalence partitioning is a heuristic technique for partitioning the input domain into subdomains with inputs that are equivalent for testing purposes. The subdomains are called equivalence classes. If two test inputs are in the same equivalence class, we expect them to provide the same information about a program's behavior: they either both catch a particular fault or they both miss that fault.

A test suite provides *equivalence-class coverage* if the set includes a test from each equivalence class.

There are no hard-and-fast rules for defining equivalence classes – just guidelines. The following example sets the stage for considering some guidelines.

Example 9.14   Consider a program that determines whether a year between 1800 and 2100 represents a leap year. Strictly speaking, the input domain of this program is the range 1800–2100, but let us take the input domain to be the integers, since the program might be called with any integer. Integers between 1800 and 2100 will be referred to as valid inputs; all other integers will be referred to as invalid inputs.

As a first approximation, we might partition the input domain into two equivalence classes, corresponding to valid and invalid integer inputs. For testing, however, it is convenient to start with three equivalence classes: integers up to 1799; 1800 through 2100; and 2101 and higher.

These equivalence classes can be refined, however, since some years are leap years and some years are not. The specification of leap years is as follows:

Every year that is exactly divisible by four is a leap year, except for years that are exactly divisible by 100, but these centurial years are leap years if they are exactly divisible by 400.[11]

This specification distinguishes between years divisible by 4, 100, 400, and all other years. These distinctions motivate the following equivalence classes (see Fig. 9.9):

- Integers less than or equal to 1799.
- Integers between 1800 and 2100 that are not divisible by 4.
- Integers between 1800 and 2100 that are divisible by 4, but not by 100.
- The integers 1800, 1900, and 2100, which are divisible by 100, but not by 400.
- The integer 2000, which is divisible by 400.
- Integers that are greater than or equal to 2101.

The leap-year program can now be tested by selecting representatives from each equivalence class.   □

Guidelines for Designing Equivalence Classes

The choice of equivalence classes is up to the designer. Two testers, working from the same specification, could potentially come up with different designs. The following are some guidelines for getting started with equivalence partitioning:[12]

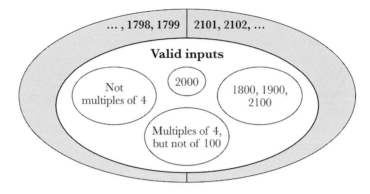

Figure 9.9 Equivalence classes for a leap-year program. The two shaded regions are for invalid test inputs.

- If the inputs to a program are from a range of integers m–n, then start with three equivalence classes. The first class contains invalid inputs that are less then or equal to $m - 1$; the second contains the valid inputs $m, m - 1, \ldots, n$; the third contains the invalid inputs greater than or equal to $m + 1$. This guideline can be generalized from integers to other data types.
- If an equivalence class has two or more inputs that produce different outputs, then split the equivalence class into subclasses, where all of the inputs in a subclass produce the same output.
- If the specification singles out one or more test inputs for similar treatment, then put all inputs that get the "same" treatment into an equivalence class.
- For each class of valid inputs, define corresponding classes of invalid inputs.

Once equivalence classes are designed, tests can be selected to cover them; that is, select a test input from each equivalence class.

9.4.2   Boundary-Value Coverage

Suppose that the input domain is ordered; that is, for two inputs i and j, it makes sense to talk of i being less than or before j, written $i < j$. Then, a value is a *boundary value* if it is either the first or the last – alternatively, the least or the greatest – with respect to the ordering.

Based on experience, errors are often found at boundary values. For example, the date-calculation code in Fig. 9.1 fails on December 31st of a leap year, a boundary value.

Boundary-value testing leverages the equivalence classes defined during equivalence partitioning.

Example 9.15   In Fig. 9.9, consider the equivalence classes for valid and invalid inputs. The valid inputs are the years between 1800 and 2100. The boundaries of this equivalence class are 1800 and 2100. There are two classes for invalid inputs: the smaller class of years less than 1800 and the bigger class of years greater than 2100. The upper boundary for the smaller class is 1799, but there is no lower boundary, since there is an infinite number of integers smaller than 1800. Similarly, the lower boundary for the bigger class is 2101 and there is no upper boundary.

For the equivalence class of years between 1800 and 2100 that are not multiples of 4, the lower boundary is 1801 and the upper boundary is 2099.   □

A test suite provides *boundary value coverage* if it includes the upper and lower boundaries of each of the equivalence classes. For an equivalence class with one element, the lower and upper boundaries are the same. In Fig. 9.9, the year 2000 is in a class by itself.

9.5 Code Coverage II: MC/DC

Branch coverage, also known as *decision coverage*, is adequate for the vast majority of applications. MC/DC, short for Modified Condition/Decision Coverage, is a stronger form of white-box testing that is required for some critical applications. MC/DC applies to decisions involving complex Boolean expressions containing operators such as & (logical and) and | (logical or) For example, suppose the value of the following decision is *false*:

```
(pressure > 32) & (temperature <= LIMIT)
```

Is it *false* because pressure is less than or equal to 32 or is it *false* because temperature is greater than LIMIT?

In discussing Boolean expressions, it is helpful to distinguish between atomic expressions, which do not contain Boolean operators, and general expressions, which could. A *condition* is an atomic Boolean expression; for example, days >365 or IsLeapYear(year). A *decision* is a Boolean expression formed by applying Boolean operators to one or more conditions.

Branch coverage is adequate for decisions involving a single condition, as in

```
while (days > 365) {...}
```

A study by Chilenski and Miller found that almost 85 percent of the decisions in a collection of software tools were based on just one condition

For system safety and security, however, it is not enough for a coverage criterion to be adequate 85 percent of the time. A hacker can use a single security vulnerability to gain access to a system, so a single flaw could jeopardize a mission-critical system. Avionics software can have complex Boolean expressions with multiple conditions. The same study found that 17 percent of the decisions in a flight-instrumentation system had two or more conditions, and over 5 percent had three or more conditions.

For avionics software, the US Federal Aviation Administration recognizes MC/DC. An ISO standard requires MC/DC for automotive software.[13] MC/DC has also been suggested for detecting security back-doors.[14]

9.5.1   Condition and Decision Coverage Are Independent

Let T and F denote the Boolean truth values, *true* and *false*, respectively. Let the lowercase letters $a, b, c, \ldots$ denote conditions; for example,

Condition a: `pressure > 32`
Condition b: `temperature <= LIMIT`

The expression $a \& b$ is a decision, representing

`(pressure > 32) & (temperature <= LIMIT)`

Condition coverage requires that each condition in a decision take on both truth values, T and F. *Decision coverage* requires each decision to take on both truth values. As we shall see, condition coverage does not ensure decision coverage, and vice versa.

While discussing condition and decision coverage, it is convenient to summarize tests by writing tables like the following for decision $a \mid b$:

TEST	a	b	$a \mid b$
1	T	T	T
2	T	F	T
3	F	T	T
4	F	F	F

Each row of this table represents a test. The columns represent the values of the conditions a and b and the decision $a \mid b$. In test 2, a is T and b is F, so $a \mid b$ is T.

Example 9.16   Tests 2 and 3 provide condition coverage, but not decision coverage. Condition coverage follows from the observation that in tests 2 and 3, a is T and F, respectively; b is F and T, respectively. But, the two tests do not provide decision coverage, since $a \mid b$ is T in both tests.

Tests 2 and 4 provide decision coverage, but not condition coverage. While the value of $a \mid b$ flips from T to F in these tests, b is not covered, since b is F in tests 2 and 4.   □

9.5.2   MC/DC Pairs of Tests

MC/DC is a stronger criterion than either condition or decision coverage. *Modified Condition/Decision Coverage (MC/DC)* requires each condition to independently affect the outcome of the decision. Independently means that, for each condition x, there is a pair of tests such that all three of the following hold:

1. From one test to the next, the outcome (truth value) of the decision flips from T to F, or vice versa.
2. The value of condition x also flips.
3. The values of the remaining conditions stay the same across the tests.

Such a pair of tests is called an *MC/DC pair* of tests for x.

This section provides a heuristic for defining MC/DC tests for a decision. The idea is to identify the MC/DC pairs for each condition in the decision. As we shall see, with three conditions, there are at most four pairs for each condition. The next step is to pick a pair of tests for each condition. Since pairs can overlap, we will likely end up with fewer than $2n$ tests for a decision with n conditions. It is not unusual to have four tests with three conditions.

Example 9.17   The following two tests provide both condition and decision coverage, but not MC/DC coverage:

TEST	a	b	$a\,|\,b$
1	T	T	T
4	F	F	F

Each of the conditions takes on both truth values, so these tests provide condition coverage. The decision flips, so it is covered. But, the tests are not an MC/DC pair for a, since they meet only the first two of the three requirements for an MC/DC pair: the value of b does not stay the same across the tests. (In this example, b does not have an MC/DC pair either.) □

Example 9.18   The following three tests provide MC/DC coverage for the decision $a\,|\,b$:

TEST	a	b	$a\,|\,b$
2	T	F	T
3	F	T	T
4	F	F	F

Tests 2 and 4 are an MC/DC pair for a: the outcome changes from T to F, the value of a flips, and the value of b stays the same. Similarly, tests 3 and 4 are an MC/DC pair for b. Thus, we have verified that the test set provides MC/DC coverage for the decision. Note that test 4 in both MC/DC pairs, so it is reused. Therefore, with $n = 2$ conditions we have $3 < 2n$ tests. □

Pairs Tables

A *pairs table* succinctly identifies the MC/DC pairs for the conditions in a decision.[15] The pairs tables for $a\,|\,b$ and $a\,\&\,b$ appear in Table 9.1. A pairs table is an extension

Table 9.1 Pairs tables for decisions $a \mid b$ and $a \mathbin{\&} b$ on the right.

TEST	a	b	$a \mid b$	a	b		TEST	a	b	$a \mathbin{\&} b$	a	b
1	T	T	T				1	T	T	T	3	2
2	T	F	T	4			2	T	F	F		1
3	F	T	T		4		3	F	T	F	1	
4	F	F	F	2	3		4	F	F	F		

of a truth table for the decision. A truth table has a column for each condition and a column for the decision. It has a row for each combination of values for the conditions. A pairs table adds a column for each condition x. If (i, j) is an MC/DC pair for x, then the added column for x has j in row i and i in row j.

Example 9.19   The pairs table for the decision $(a \mathbin{\&} b) \mid c$ appears in Table 9.2. The columns in the table are in three sections, separated by vertical lines. From the left, the first section has a column for each condition. The second section is for the decision. The third section has added columns to keep track of the MC/DC pairs for each condition.

There is only one MC/DC pair for a: it is $(2, 6)$. In the added column for a, the pairs table therefore has 6 in row 2 and 2 in row 6. None of the other pairs of tests qualifies as an MC/DC pair for a, since the outcome is not flip. The outcome of the decision remains T for the pairs $(1, 5)$ and $(3, 7)$, and it remains F for the pair $(4, 8)$.

The only pair for b is $(2, 4)$. There are three pairs for c: they are $(3, 4)$, $(5, 6)$, and $(7, 8)$.   □

Selecting MC/DC Tests

The MC/DC tests for a decision can be deduced from its pairs table. The fewer the tests, the better.

In the following heuristic approach to test selection, "pair" is short for "MC/DC pair."

> **for** each condition with only one pair,
>   pick that pair of tests;
> **for** the next conditions x with the fewest pairs,
>   pick the pair that adds the fewest tests;

Example 9.20   For the decision $(a \mathbin{\&} b) \mid c$ in Table 9.2, $(2, 6)$ is the only pair for a and $(2, 4)$ is the only pair for b, so these pairs must be picked. In other words, tests 2, 4, and 6 must be selected.

Condition c has three pairs. Either $(3, 4)$ or $(5, 6)$ would add just one more test, since 4 and 6 have already been selected. The pair $(7, 8)$ would add two tests, since neither 7 nor 8 has been selected. Choosing the pair $(3, 4)$ for c, we get four tests:

Table 9.2 Pairs tables for the decision $(a \& b) \mid c$.

TEST	a	b	c	$(a \& b) \mid c$	a	b	c
1	T	T	T	T			
2	T	T	F	T	6	4	
3	T	F	T	T			4
4	T	F	F	F		2	3
5	F	T	T	T			6
6	F	T	F	F	2		5
7	F	F	T	T			8
8	F	F	F	F			7

TEST	a	b	c	$(a \& b) \mid c$
2	T	T	F	T
3	T	F	T	T
4	T	F	F	F
6	F	T	F	F

☐

Recall that a conditions represent true/false expressions without Boolean operators. Suppose a is the expression

$$\texttt{pressure > 32}$$

A test that requires a to be *true* can be implemented by picking a test value for `pressure` that is greater than 32.

9.6   Input Coverage II: Combinatorial Testing

Combinatorial testing is a form of black-box testing for detecting interaction failures, which result from a combination of factors. A *factor* is a quantity that can be controlled during testing. The challenge with combinatorial testing is that the number of possible tests grows exponentially with the number of factors. In practice, combinatorial testing focuses on interactions between a small number of factors at a time.

This section introduces covering arrays, which lead to efficient (smaller) test sets. Fortunately, tools are available for finding covering arrays. For example, the US National Institute of Standards and Technology (NIST) provides a tool called ACTS for finding good-enough covering arrays.[16] The problem of finding optimal covering arrays is reported to be NP-hard.

Combinatorial testing is often used for highly parameterized or configurable systems. The following example considers a product that must work with multiple combinations of elements.

Example 9.21   Consider the problem of testing a software product that must support multiple browsers (Chrome, Explorer, Firefox, Safari), run on multiple platforms (Linux, Mac OS, Windows), and interface with multiple databases (MongoDB, Oracle, MySQL).

With four browsers, three platforms, and three databases, the number of combinations is $4 \times 3 \times 3 = 36$. That's 36 test sets, not tests, since the full test set must be run for each combination. The problem gets worse if the product must support not only the current version of a browser, but previous versions as well.   □

A software failure that results from a specific combination of factors is called an *interaction failure*. A two-way interaction involves two factors, a three-way interaction involves three factors, and so on. An empirical study found that roughly 60 percent of web-server failures involved two or more factors. A NIST study found that failures for web servers and browsers had more complex interactions than failures for either medical devices or a NASA application.[17]

Combinatorial testing is based on the following empirical observation from a 2014 keynote on the subject by Richard Kuhn:

most failures are triggered by one or two factors, and progressively fewer by three, four, or more factors, and the maximum interaction degree is small.

Pairwise Interactions

Pairwise testing addresses two-way interactions. The idea is to test all combinations of values for each pair of factors. For the system in Example 9.21 the pairs of factors are

(browser, platform), (browser, database), (platform, database)

Some conventions will be helpful in organizing sets of tests. Let the letters $A, B, C, \ldots$ represent factors; for example, A represents browser, B represents platform, and C represents database. Let the integers $0, 1, 2, \ldots$ represent factor values; for example, for factor B (platform), 0 represents Linux, 1 represents Windows, and 2 represents Mac OS. Let two-letter combinations $AB, AC, BC, \ldots$ represent the pairs of factors $(A, B), (A, C), (B, C), \ldots$, respectively.

Consider tests involving two factors A and B, each of which can take on the two values 0 and 1. With two factors and two values, there are four possible combinations of values for the two factors. A test consists of a specific combination of values. The following table represents an exhaustive set of tests involving the two factors:

TEST	A	B
1	0	0
2	0	1
3	1	0
4	1	1

Table 9.3 Tables for three factors, each of which can have two possible values. See Example 9.22.

TEST	A	B	C
1	0	0	0
2	0	0	1
3	0	1	0
4	0	1	1
5	1	0	0
6	1	0	1
7	1	1	0
8	1	1	1

(a) All combinations

TEST	A	B	C
2	0	0	1
3	0	1	0
5	1	0	0
8	1	1	1

(b) A 2-way covering array

In such tables, columns represent factors, rows represent tests, and table entries represent values for the factors.

A set of tests is a *t-way covering array* if the tests include all possible combinations for each subset of *t* factors. The next two examples illustrate two-way covering arrays.

Example 9.22   Consider a simplified version of Example 9.21, where each factor can have one of two values. Factor *A* (browser) can take on the two values 0 and 1 (Chrome and Safari); factor *B* (platform) the values 0 and 1 (Linux and Windows); and factor *C* (database) the values 0 and 1 (MongoDB and Oracle).

Table 9.3(a) shows all possible combinations for three factors, where each factor can have one of two values. Tests 1–8 therefore constitute an exhaustive test set for three factors.

The four tests in Table 9.3(b) constitute a covering array for pairwise testing of three factors. The three pairs of factors are *AB*, *AC*, and *BC*.

Let us verify that the four tests cover all combinations of values for each of these pairs. Consider the pair *AC*. All possible combinations of values for *AC* are 00, 01, 10, and 11. These combinations are covered by tests 3, 2, 5, and 8, respectively. Test 3 has the form 0x0, where both *A* and *C* have value 0. The value of *B* is ignored for now, since we are focusing on the pair *AC*. Tests 2, 5, and 8 have the form 0x1, 1x0, and 1x1, respectively.

The combinations of values for the pair *AB* are covered by the tests 2, 3, 5, and 8. For the pair *BC*, consider the tests 5, 2, 3, and 8.   □

Example 9.23   Now, suppose that factor *B* can take on three values 0, 1, and 2 (for Linux, Windows, and Mac OS) and that factors *A* and *C* can have two values, as in Example 9.22. The total number of combinations for the three factors are $2 \times 3 \times 2 = 12$.

For pairwise testing, 6 tests are enough. All combinations for the pairs *AB*, *AC*, and *BC* appear in Table 9.4, along with a covering array with 6 tests. For pair *AB*, tests 1–6, in that order, correspond to the rows in the combinations-table for *AB*. For pair *AC*, see

Table 9.4 All combinations for pairs AB, AC, and BC, and a covering array. See Example 9.23.

A	B		A	C		B	C		TEST	A	B	C
0	0		0	0		0	0		1	0	0	1
0	1		0	1		0	1		2	0	1	0
0	2		1	0		1	0		3	0	2	1
1	0		1	1		1	1		4	1	0	0
1	1					2	0		5	1	1	1
1	2					2	1		6	1	2	0

tests 2–5, in that order. For pair BC, tests 4, 1, 2, 5, 6, and 3, correspond to the rows in the combinations-table for BC.   □

Multi-Way Covering Arrays

The discussion of two-way interactions generalizes directly to the interaction of three or more factors. More factors need to be considered since two-way testing finds between 50 percent and 90 percent of faults, depending on the application. For critical applications, 90 percent is not good enough. Three-way testing raises the lower bound from 50 percent to over 85 percent.

The benefits of combinatorial testing become more dramatic as the size of the testing problem increases. The number of possible combinations grows exponentially with the number of factors. By contrast, for fixed t, the size of a t-way covering array grows logarithmically with the number of factors. For example, there are $2^{10} = 1024$ combinations of 10 factors, with each factor having two values. There is a three-way covering array, however, that has only 13 tests; see Table 9.5.[18]

Algorithms and tools are available for finding covering arrays. The general problem of finding covering arrays is believed to be a hard problem. A naive heuristic approach is to build up a covering array by adding columns for the factors, one at a time. Entries in the new column can be filled in by extending an existing test, or by adding a row for a new test.

```
start with an empty array;
for each factor F:
    add a column for F;
    mark F;
    for each three-way interaction XYF, where X and Y are marked:
        for each combination in the combinations table for XYF:
            if possible:
                fill in a blank in an existing row to cover the combination.
            else:
                add a row with entries in the columns for X, Y, and F;
                comment: leave all other entries in the row blank
```

Table 9.5 Three-way covering array for 10 factors.

TEST	A	B	C	D	E	F	G	H	I	J
1	0	0	0	0	0	0	0	0	0	0
2	1	1	1	1	1	1	1	1	1	1
3	1	1	1	0	1	0	0	0	0	1
4	1	0	1	1	0	1	0	1	0	0
5	1	0	0	0	1	1	1	0	0	0
6	0	1	1	0	0	1	0	0	1	0
7	0	0	1	0	1	0	1	1	1	0
8	1	1	0	1	0	0	1	0	1	0
9	0	0	0	1	1	1	0	0	1	1
10	0	0	1	1	0	0	1	0	0	1
11	0	1	0	1	1	0	0	1	0	0
12	1	0	0	0	0	0	0	1	1	1
13	0	1	0	0	0	1	1	1	0	1

9.7 Conclusion

Since exhaustive testing of software is generally impossible or impractical, defects are detected by running the software on selected test inputs. The recommended approach is to start testing early, while code is being written or modified. In other words, start with (low level) units of implementation and then test larger (higher level) pieces of software. This approach gives us multiple levels of testing: unit, functional, integration, system, and acceptance testing, from low to high.

With smaller pieces of software, we can use white-box testing, where tests are selected to cover or exercise constructs in the code. Black-box testing, based on inputs and outputs, is used for larger, more complex pieces of software. Black-box tests are selected to be a representative sample of the set of all possible inputs.

The idea is to select a good enough set of tests so we can be confident that the software will behave as expected when it is used. "Good enough" is quantified by defining two kinds of coverage criteria: code coverage for white-box, and input-domain coverage for black-box testing.

Code coverage is the degree to which a set of tests exercises specific programming constructs such as statements and decisions. Of the two, decision coverage is stronger: it detects more defects. MC/DC (Modified Condition/Decision Coverage) is an even criterion that is required for aviation and automotive software. For complex decisions with multiple conditions, MC/DC requires each condition to independently affect the outcome of the decision.

Input-domain coverage is the degree to which a test set is a representative sample of all possible inputs. Equivalence partitioning is a technique that partitions a potentially infinite input domain into a finite number of equivalence classes, where all tests in the same equivalence class either all pass together or all fail together. Testing of highly configurable systems must contend with a combinatorial explosion of configurations; for example, choose one from the column for factor A, one from the column for factor B, and so on. Combinatorial testing avoids the explosion by considering all combinations of a few, say $k = 3$, of the factors instead of all possible factors.

Further Reading

- The overview of testing in Section 9.1 is motivated by Whittaker's [190] "practical" tutorial.
- Whittaker, Arbon, and Carollo [191] describe how Google tests software.
- The classic 1979 book by Myers [140] on the art of testing has a third 2011 edition coauthored by Badgett and Sandler [141].
- For more on test-driven development, see the special May–June 2007 issue of *IEEE Software* (Vol. 24, No. 3).
- Kuhn's [115] keynote at an IEEE testing conference is on the rationale and impact of combinatorial testing.

Exercises for Chapter 9

Exercise 9.1   For each of the following pairs of terms, what is the distinction between the terms? Be specific. Give examples where possible.

a) fault and failure
b) validation and verification
c) code and input coverage
d) branch and decision coverage
e) condition and decision coverage
f) all-paths coverage and coverage from exhaustive testing
g) integration and system testing

Exercise 9.2   How would you select "good" tests for test-driven development?

Exercise 9.3   What is the best match between the testing phases of the development process in Fig. 9.10 and unit, functional, integration, system, and acceptance testing? Explain your answer.
   Here are brief descriptions of the testing phases:

- *Parameter Testing.* Test each component by itself, guided by the coding specification.
- *Assembly Testing.* As parameter testing completes, the system is gradually assembled and tested using first simulated inputs and then live data.
- *Shakedown.* The completed system is tested in its operational environment.
- *System Evaluation.* After assembly, the system is ready for operation and evaluation.[19]

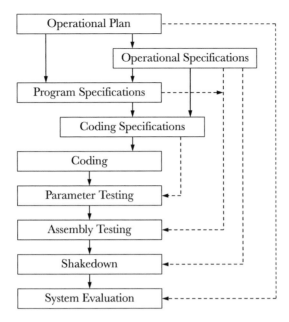

Figure 9.10 The development process for the SAGE air-defense system.

Exercise 9.4   Consider white-box testing of the code in Fig. 9.11.

a) Draw a control-flow graph for the code.
b) Define a test set that maximizes coverage of the nodes in the flowgraph. For each test, identify the nodes that the test covers.
c) Define a test set that maximizes coverage of the edges in the flowgraph. For each test, identify the edges that the test covers.

Exercise 9.5   Consider black-box testing of a stack data structure, where the input domain consists of sequences of *push* and *pop* operations. The stack is initially empty. The software under test produces error messages if a *pop* is applied to an empty stack or if a *push* is applied to a stack that is full. The stack can hold at most *max* elements, where *max* is a parameter that the tester can set.

The testing strategy is to partition the valid input sequences into three equivalence classes, representing states of the stack; *empty, partially full*, and *full*.

a) Draw a directed graph with three nodes representing the equivalence classes for valid sequences. Add edges labeled either *push* or *pop* to represent changes in the state of the stack under the operations.
b) Define a test set that covers all edges in the graph.
c) How does your test set handle invalid inputs?

Exercise 9.6   For each of the following decisions, define a minimal set of MC/DC tests. Briefly explain why the set is minimal. The symbol ! denotes logical negation.

```
1)    while (x > y) {
2)         if (x > z) {
3)              if (y > z) {
4)                   x = x-1;
5)              }
6)         }
7)         else {
8)              if (y > z) {
9)                   z = z-1;
10)             }
11)        }
12)        y =y+1
13)   }
```

Figure 9.11 Code for white-box testing in Exercise 9.4.

---

a) $a | (b \& c)$
b) $(!a) \& (b|c)$

Exercise 9.7 Suppose that a system can be configured by setting four binary-valued factors, and that you want to test all two-way interactions between factors.

a) Create no more than six tests to test all two-way interactions. Explain why your solution works.
b) Find a solution that requires no more than five tests.

10   Quality Metrics

For metrics to be useful, they must be consistent with our intuitions about the real world. As an example, defects can be a useful metric for product quality – the fewer severe defects, the better. This chapter recommends the following four-step approach to designing and using meaningful metrics:

a) Begin with the purpose or motivating goal. What do we hope to learn through metrics and data collection?
b) Select metrics that assess progress towards achieving the goal.
c) Validate the metrics through measurements and analysis of the measured data.
d) Finally, analyze the data for insights to guide decisions and predictions related to the goal.

   The goal in this chapter is to assess and improve software quality, especially product quality, operations quality, and customer satisfaction. For data analysis, the chapter introduces techniques from descriptive statistics to display and summarize data.

This chapter will enable the reader to:

- Design and use meaningful metrics for assessing and improving software quality.
- Display data graphically, using bar charts, Gantt charts, box plots, and histograms.
- Analyze data using variance, confidence intervals, and simple linear regression.

10.1   Meaningful Metrics

Metrics are designed to quantify attributes (properties) of real-world entities, such as artifacts, activities, and events. When developers assign two story points to a user story, we have the following:

entity	the user story
attribute	estimated complexity
metric	number of story points
data	the measured value

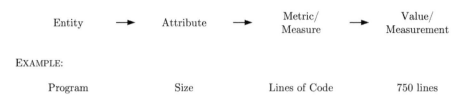

Figure 10.1 An overview of the measurement process.

This section introduces the measurement process in Fig. 10.1, which relates entities, attributes, metrics, and measured data values: measurement simply provides data. As the Microsoft Access case study in this section illustrates, any conclusions we draw from measured data need to be validated.

10.1.1 Metrics Quantify Attributes

Let us define a *measurement process* by choosing entities, attributes, and metrics as follows:

1. Given a goal, identify a set of *entities* of interest.
2. Define *attributes* for each entity, representing properties to be measured.
3. Select one or more *metrics* that associate numbers or symbols with an attribute.
4. Associate *data values* with the metrics.

This approach to measurement dates back at least to Lord Kelvin; see Box 10.1.

Example 10.1   In the example in Fig. 10.1, a program entity has a size attribute that is measured in lines of code. The specific program has 750 lines, so 750 lines is a data point.   □

Example 10.2   This example shows that an attribute can have more than one metric. Again, let the entity of interest be a program and the attribute be program size. Consider two metrics *loc* and *ncsl*, for lines of source code with and without comments, respectively. The names of the metrics are acronyms for "lines of code" and "non-comment source lines."

As a variant, suppose that the program includes some open-source code. We may want two separate metrics for the number of lines with and without the open-source code.   □

Measure Has Two Meanings   The term *measure* has two meanings. As a noun, it is a synonym for metric; for example, lines of code is a measure of size. As a verb, "to measure" is to associate a value with a metric.

The term "measurement" is also overloaded. As a process, *measurement* defines metrics, so values or symbols can be assigned to attributes. As a value, a *measurement* is a specific data value for a metric. For example, 500 lines and 750 lines are measurements.

Direct, Derived, and Proxy Metrics

For some attributes, we can define a metric that reflects our intuitive understanding of the attribute; for example, the number of severe defects is a reasonable metric for product quality (attribute quality of entity product). For other attributes, it may be impractical to measure or impossible to find a metric that is closely related to the specific attribute. Customer satisfaction is an attribute that is hard to quantify with a metric. Customers may not tell us whether they are satisfied.

The following are three forms of association between metrics and attributes:

- The value of a *direct metric* for an attribute is independent of the value of any other metrics.
- The value of a *derived metric* for an attribute is calculated from the values of one or more other attributes.
- A proxy metric is used as an indicator for attributes that cannot be easily measured, or perhaps measured at all. The value of a *proxy metric* for an attribute is calculated independently of that attribute.

10.1.2   Selecting Useful Metrics

For a metric to be useful, the data it provides must help us make decisions and achieve goals in the real world. The number of critical defects is useful for deciding whether a product is ready for delivery to customers. (A product with a critical defect is not ready!) In the case study that follows, the team discovered that the number of downloads is not useful for the goal of assessing and improving customer satisfaction. The downloads metric has other uses, so a metric that is useful for one purpose may not be useful for another. As we shall see with lines of code, a metric does not have to be accurate to be useful.

Box 10.1 Lord Kelvin on Measurement

Lord Kelvin began a lecture on May 3, 1883 by observing that a first step in learning any scientific subject is to find principles for quantifying and measuring some "quality connected with it."[1] (Note the use of the term "qualities" for the properties of entities.)

His lecture began as follows: "I often say that when you can measure what you are speaking about, and express it in numbers, you know something about it; but when you cannot express it in numbers, your knowledge is of a meagre and unsatisfactory kind: it may be the beginning of knowledge, but you have scarcely, in your thoughts, advanced to the stage of science, whatever the matter may be."

A measurement process simply provides data. The validation of whether a metric is useful or not is an interpretation of the measured data, and not part of the measurement process for the metric. Suppose a measurement process tells us how much water there is in a glass. One interpretation is that the glass is half full. Another interpretation is that the glass is half empty. Neither interpretation is part of the measurement process. Thus, data is like form or syntax, and its significance is like meaning or semantics.

Measuring Customer Satisfaction

Customer satisfaction with a product is known to be good for business, but it is something that cannot be measured objectively. Instead, a proxy is used to approximate customer satisfaction. The proxy, *Net Promoter Score (NPS)*, is a measure of the willingness of customers to recommend a product, on a scale of 0 to 100. Higher scores are better. NPS can be measured through surveys and interviews. Example 10.3 illustrates the use of NPS.

Case Study: Microsoft Access Product

Example 10.3   The Microsoft Access team was delighted that total downloads of their new database product had jumped from 1.1 million to 8 million over 18 months. Then, they observed that customers were not using the product. The team followed up with phone interviews and found that the Net Promoter Score was "terrible." The verbatim customer comments were "brutal."

The team fixed the product, including 3–4 design flaws and some pain points. They also made some training videos. The videos turned out to be most popular. The Net Promoter Score jumped an impressive 35 points.[2]   □

Data about product downloads is easy to collect automatically. The number of downloads is not, however, a useful metric for customer satisfaction, as the team discovered in the preceding example. See what follows for more on customer satisfaction.

Lines of Code: Flawed But Useful

Metrics do not have to be perfect to be useful. Depending on the situation, a roughly right metric may be good enough. Lines of code is a prime example. Despite its limitations, it continues to be widely used to measure program size.

The main issue with lines of code as a metric is its dependence on the programming language. The "same" task can take more lines if it is written in C than it does in an object-oriented language like Java. Furthermore, line counts penalize code that is elegant and short, compared to code that is sloppy and verbose. There are also lesser issues about differences in programming style. Comments are sometimes handled by counting only non-comment lines.

The limitations of lines of code are well understood. Teams that use the same programming language and have similar style guidelines can use lines of code for meaningful comparisons. More technically, attribute program-size changes value if there are changes to other attributes, such as language and style. Language and style are examples of hidden variables. Teams that use lines of code control these hidden variables; for example, by using the same language. Even so, there can be size variations in code written by different programmers. Lines of code, therefore, continues to be a popular metric.

10.1.3   Goal-Directed Measurement

Metrics are a means to an end, so before choosing metrics, we need to ask: What is the motivating goal? What do we hope to quantify and measure? Without goals, there is no guarantee that the metrics we define are the right ones for the job. Nor can we be certain that the data we collect for metrics is relevant and complete.[3]

Examples of motivating goals include the following:

- Increase customer satisfaction.
- Deliver a product by a deadline.
- Reduce the number of customer-found defects.

Such motivating or starting goals typically need to be refined by defining specific measurable subgoals, such as

- Reduce product failures by improving testing.
- Further, strengthen the test coverage criterion from statement to branch coverage.

See Section 3.6.3 for how to refine high-level goals into SMART subgoals, where SMART stands for specific, measurable, achievable, relevant, and time-bound. Since SMART goals are measurable, metrics can be defined for them.

With software projects, goals can be grouped as follows:

a) *Business goals* are tied to organizational objectives, such as "Reduce costs" and "Increase revenues." Business goals are independent of specific strategies for achieving them.
b) *Software goals* are tied to the product to be developed. Software goals can be obtained from business goals by asking *How* questions. For example, "Increase revenues" can be refined into a software goal: "Deliver a cloud service to do *x*," where *x* relates to the organization's business.
c) *Project goals* are tied to the implementation of a particular product. They can be refined from software goals by asking *How* and *How-Much* questions. For example, project goals can be tied to project deliverables or team training.

10.2   Software Quality

Software quality is a fertile setting for illustrating the use of metrics. There is much more to quality than the number of defects in the source code. *Software quality* is a general term for the six forms of quality shown in Fig. 10.2: functional, process, product, operations (ops), aesthetic, and customer satisfaction.[4] This section introduces

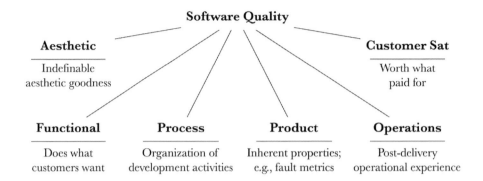

Figure 10.2 A model of software quality.

the forms of quality. The examples in this chapter focus on product quality, ops quality, and customer satisfaction.

10.2.1   The Many Forms of Software Quality

Software development is driven by the goal of satisfying customers with a product that does what they want and works reliably for them when they operate it. In other words, customer satisfaction depends on product functionality and reliable operations. Thus, there are dependencies between the various forms of quality.

Functional Quality The definition of *functional quality* is the degree to which a software product does what users want. One measure of functional quality is how well the product supports the use cases or scenarios for the product.

Process Quality Process effectiveness and process compliance are two possible interpretations of *process quality*. In the first sense, process quality is the degree to which it is effective in organizing development teams and their activities. In the second sense, process quality is the degree to which the team follows the prescribed process.

Example 10.4   As an example of effectiveness, iterative processes tend to be more effective than waterfall processes at delivering the right product on time and within budget. As another example, strengthening the code-coverage criterion from statement to branch coverage is a process-quality improvement. It strengthens testing, so it potentially improves the overall effectiveness of the development process.   □

Example 10.5   As an example of compliance, regulatory agencies mandate certain process activities for safety-critical software. Aviation software is subject to MC/DC

testing. Process compliance requires that code be subjected to the level of testing specified by the documented process. If not, the team's activities are not in compliance.   □

Process quality is relatively independent of the product being developed. Consider
the process decision that all code must be reviewed before it becomes part of the code
base. This decision is independent of the product.

Product Quality The distinguishing feature of a *product quality* is that it relates to
inherent properties of a product that cannot be altered without altering the product
itself.[5] For example, the number of known defects is a measure of product quality. See
Section 10.4 for product-quality metrics.

Ops Quality *Ops quality* refers to a customer's experience with operating a product
after it is delivered. The average time between failures is one measure of ops quality.
Other ops-quality metrics are based on the idea of counting the number of customer
sites that report a severe defect within the first three months. One such metric is defined
in Section 10.5.

Example 10.6 This example illustrates the distinction between product and ops quality. A team at Nortel spent almost six months carefully testing the new features in a
communications product. But once the product was released, customer reports about
its quality were negative: customers felt it was a bad release. The product was bundled
with a code coverage tool, so the Nortel team analyzed coverage data for how customers used the product. The team learned that their six months of careful testing had
focused on one-tenth of one percent of what customers use.

In other words, the Nortel team spent six months improving product quality as measured by the number of defects in the source code in the release. The defects they fixed
through testing were, however, largely in parts of the code that were not reached during customer use. The ops quality of the release did not improve because testing barely
touched the parts that customers did use. Defects remained in the used parts of the code.

For the next release the team focused on improving ops quality. They retargeted their
testing efforts onto the 1% of the code that was used in practice. The result? Customers
said the next release was fantastic. Customers hardly ever used the new features.[6]

One lesson here is that while developers tend to focus on new features and product
quality, customers tend to care the features they rely on and ops quality. The defects that
matter to customers are the defects that they encounter when they use a product.   □

Aesthetics *Aesthetic quality* refers to the indefinable "I'll know it when I see it" goodness of a product. It is about perceptions and taste and cannot be measured directly.

For example, Google has maintained the aesthetic of a simple uncluttered home page through continuing refinements of its search capabilities. Apple is known for the look and feel (aesthetics) of its products.

Customer Satisfaction This form of software quality goes by names such as *worth what paid for* and *value* as well as *customer satisfaction*. Net Promoter Score is a proxy metric for this form of quality. Companies care a great deal about the extent to which their customers are satisfied. The case study in Section 10.2.2 illustrates the challenges of measuring customer satisfaction.

10.2.2   Measuring Customer Support

Customer support can be as, if not more, important than ops quality to customer satisfaction. So, how do we measure it? Within IBM, you were "likely to get two conflicting answers" if you asked which of the following metrics had a greater impact on customer satisfaction:[7]

- The number of problems on a product.
- Service call response time.

An IBM study set out to address the larger question of which of the many metrics in use within the company had the greatest impact on customer satisfaction.

Example 10.7   The IBM study was based on three years of actual data from service centers that handled customer calls. It examined 15 different metrics for an operating systems product. The metrics related to customer-found defects and to customer service requests; see Table 10.1.

The study examined the correlation between the 15 metrics and customer satisfaction surveys. It found the greatest correlation between the following two factors and satisfaction surveys:

1. Number of defects found in previous "fixes" to code or documentation.
2. Total number of customer service requests that were closed.

The next two metrics were much less significant than the first two:

3. Total number of fixed customer-found defects in code or documentation.
4. Number of days to resolution for requests handled by Level 2.

□

Defective fixes during corrective maintenance are also referred to as *breakage*. Breakage is a significant dissatisfier. Customers do not like it when something stops working.

Table 10.1 Which of these customer-service metrics has the most effect on customer satisfaction? All 15 were managed and tracked.

- Total number of fixed customer-found defects in code or documentation
- Number that were dubbed "genuine" and reported for the first time
- Number that were rejected by the Level 3 support personnel
- Number of pointers to components touched by a first-time genuine defect
- Number of defects found in previous "fixes"
- Number of defects in code or documentation that were received
- Backlog of defects in code or documentation
- Total number of customer service requests that were closed
- Number that were for preventive service
- Number that were for installation planning
- Number that were for code or documentation; for example, 2nd+ defect reports
- Number that were not related to IBM code or documentation
- Number of customer service requests handled by Level 2 support
- Number of days to resolution for requests handled by Level 2
- Number of users, a measure of the size of the installed base

10.3   Graphical Displays of Data Sets

Since the value of a metric can be a symbol or a number, values can be of many kinds; for example, product names, user story points, release dates, code coverage ratios, and days to resolution for a customer problem. Each of these metrics has a different kinds of value. Both "release date" and "days to resolution" involve schedules, but the value of the former is a date and the value of the latter is a number. We can subtract two dates to get a number (of days between them), but is it meaningful to add two dates? No, it is not.

This section introduces scales of measurement, which spell out the operations that are meaningful for a set of values. We then consider simple graphical displays for entire data sets. The simple displays are bar charts for data points grouped by category and Gantt charts for dates and schedules. For histograms and box plots, see Section 10.6.

10.3.1   Data Sets

A *data set* is a sequence of data points (values), where data points may be repeated – a later measurement can yield a data point that has been seen before. When we need to distinguish between the known subset and an entire data set, the known subset is called a *sample* and the entire data set is called the *population*. The data points in a sample are also known as *observations*.

Two Data Sets

Most of the examples in this section are based on one or the other of two data sets. The first data set deals with installations of a product at customer sites – *installs* for short. The data points represent defects per 100 installs for a sequence of releases of a product:

$$3.8, \ 2.1, \ 1.6, \ 5.0, \ 1.7, \ 1.9, \ 2.1, \ 2.0, \ 2.2 \tag{10.1}$$

The second data set represents contractor bids for building a system to the same requirements. The bids are in thousands of euros, rounded to the nearest integer):

$$
\begin{aligned}
&3, 4, 5, 5, 9, \\
&10, 12, 12, 12, 17, 18, 19, \\
&20, 20, 21, 25, 26, 26, 26, 27, 29, 29, 29, \\
&33, 34, 34, 34, 35, 38, \\
&45, \\
&52, 57, \\
&61, 69, \\
&70
\end{aligned}
\tag{10.2}
$$

Median, Mean, Mode

The median is a widely used summary statistic. The *median* is the middle element of a linearly ordered data set with an odd number of data points, say $2n + 1$. Not counting the median, which is the $n + 1$st element, n data points are in the lower half and n data points are in the upper half of the data set. (The halves are with respect to the linear ordering.) This definition will be refined in Section 10.6 to handle data sets with an even number of data points.

The mean and the mode complement the median. They provide different summary information and serve different purposes. The *arithmetic mean* or simply *mean* of a data set is the average of the values in the data set. A *mode* is a most frequently occurring value. A data set can have more than one mode. A *bimodal* data set has two modes.

Example 10.8   Data set 10.1 has nine data points, so its median is 2.1, the fifth data point in the following linear ordering:

$$1.6, \ 1.7, \ 1,9, \ 2.0, \ 2.1, \ 2.1, \ 2.2, \ 3.8, \ 5.0$$

The mean is the average, 2.49. The mode is the most frequently occurring data point, 2.1.   □

10.3.2   Scales of Measurement

A *scale of measurement* consists of a set of values and a set of operations on the values. With the Stevens system, product names, story points, release dates, and coverage ratios are on different scales. Numbers are on an absolute scale that is not part of the Stevens system.

The Stevens System

The *Stevens system* has four scales or levels of scales. In order, they are called nominal, ordinal, interval, and ratio. The nominal scale supports the fewest operations on its values.

Nominal Scales Values on a nominal scale are unordered. The only operation is comparison for equality of nominal values. The set of contractor names is an example of a nominal scale. Such scales are also known as *categorical scales* because nominal values are typically used to group entities into categories; for example, product names can be used to group support requests.

  Caution. Sometimes, numbers are used for nominal values; for example, for anonymity, contractors may be assigned numbers. In this case, the numbers are being treated as symbols, with comparison for equality being the only operation.

Ordinal Scales Values on an ordinal scale are linearly ordered. The only operation is comparison with respect to the ordering. These comparisons allow ordinal values to be sorted. As an example, the priority values *high*, *medium*, and *low* form an ordinal scale. Like nominal values, ordinal values are used as categories; for example, we can group requirements by priority.

  Caution. Sometimes, ordinal values are numbered; for example, a user story may be assigned one, two, or three story points. In this case, the numbers are simply symbols and the "distances" between them are not defined. All we can say is that a one-point story is relatively simple, that a three-point story is complex, and that a two-point story is somewhere in between. Where it falls in between is not defined.

Interval Scales Dates are a prime example of interval values. There is a fixed "distance" of one unit between successive dates. Each value represents a distance from a chosen origin or value zero. Values on an interval scale are linearly ordered by their distance from the origin, positive or negative.

  For example, on both the Celsius and Fahrenheit scales, a temperature reading represents an interval from a chosen zero. On Unix, the internal date zero is January 1, 1970. Microsoft Excel has used two date scales, one with its origin in 1900 and one with its origin in 1904.

  An *interval* is defined by two values: a start value and an end value, with the end value greater than the start value. The *length* of the interval is a number obtained by subtracting the start value from the end value. It is meaningful to subtract one value from another and obtain a number (of units), but it does not make sense to add, multiply, or divide two intervals.

  Operations involving a number and an interval are different from operations involving two intervals. A number can be added or subtracted from an interval to yield an interval. We can also multiply and divide intervals by nonnegative numbers and get intervals.

Ratio Scales Values on a ratio scale have the form m/n, where both m and n are on a scale that supports arithmetic operations. Typically, both m and n are numbers. See Section 10.4 for the use of ratios for measuring product quality.

Note While the Stevens system has been challenged, it continues to be widely used.[8]

Absolute Scale
The Stevens scales that we have just discussed are in addition to the *absolute scale*, where values correspond to integers. Counts are on the absolute scale; for example, the count of the number of lines of code in a program. The term "absolute" comes from the scale having an absolute zero value. It makes sense to talk of zero defects in a program that has no defects. An absolute scale may or may not support negative values; for example, it does not make sense for a program to have a negative number of defects.

10.3.3   Bar Charts Display Data by Category

Graphical displays of data are routinely used to present and summarize data about the status of a software projects. Charts and plots readily convey information that could otherwise get lost in a sea of numbers. With displays, we can spot trends and formulate hypotheses that can then be tested through data analysis. Here are a couple of typical questions about trends:

- Is the rate of defect discovery going down?
- Are project milestones slipping?

    Bar charts show numeric values by bars that are either drawn vertically or horizontally; see Fig. 10.3. The height or length of a bar is determined by the value it represents.

Applications Bar charts are used to display values by category. In Fig. 10.3, the categories are contractors and the values are their bids. The categories in a bar chart can be on either a nominal or an ordinal scale; for example, products are on a nominal scale, months are on an ordinal scale.

Example 10.9   For a study of reproducibility in software development, the Simula Research Lab sought bids for developing the "same" system. Specifically, all potential bidders were given the same requirements. Thirty-five companies submitted bids. The median bid was 25,940 euros.[9]

    Data set 10.2 consists of the bids, in thousands of euros (rounded to the nearest integer. (The original data appears as a bar chart in Fig. 10.3.) The median of the data

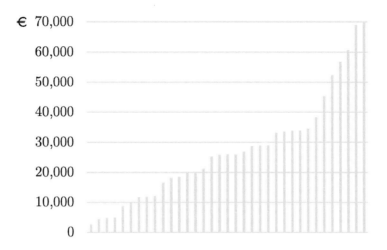

Figure 10.3 Firm-price independent bids for developing a system to meet the same requirements. Data set 10.2 is derived from these bids.

set, 26, tells only part of the story. The bids are spread across a wide range, from 3 to 70.   □

Bar Charts for Nominal Values Categories on a nominal scale (for example, contractors) are unordered. Therefore, in a bar chart, the horizontal position of a nominal category can be changed without losing information. In Fig. 10.3, contractors are sorted by the values of their bids. Another option is to sort them by contractor name.

Bar Charts for Ordinal Values Categories on an ordinal scale (for example, calendar months) are linearly ordered. Therefore, in a bar chart, the horizontal position of ordinal categories is significant. For example, project managers use bar charts to show trends over time. Trends related to the rate of discovery of new defects are of particular interest. A bar chart shows at a glance whether this rate is going down, month after month.

Single-Variable (Univariate) Data Bar charts display data points for a single metric; for example, the number of known defects in a product. Single-metric data is called *univariate* data, or data for a single variable. Univariate data is conveniently represented by a bar chart.

For two-variable data, we can use an *x-y* plot, also known as a scatter plot. With two related variables, such as program size and defects, data points are pairs of the form (x_i, y_i), where x_i is a value for the independent variable (for example, size) and y_i is a value for the dependent variable (for example, defects). The plot measures x_i along the horizontal axis and y_i along the vertical axis.

10.3.4   Gantt Charts Display Schedules

Gantt charts are a form of horizontal bar chart, in which the bars represent time intervals. The horizontal axis represents time, increasing from left to right. An interval is represented by a bar or a line between the start and end times of the interval. Given a set of intervals, the chart has a row for each interval.[10]

Gantt charts can be augmented to indicate dependencies between rows; for example, by drawing lines between rows.

Applications   The main use of Gantt charts is for planning and tracking schedules. Here are two examples:

- The work breakdown schedule for a project shows the order and time intervals in which tasks must be completed. Otherwise, the project will overrun its schedule. The tasks are represented by rows in a Gantt chart.
- A product-portfolio roadmap shows the projected schedule for the products in the portfolio. When two companies merge, they can use a roadmap to show the plan for merging overlapping products from the companies. Products are represented by rows in a Gantt chart.

The next example uses a Gantt chart to track a project's history of schedule changes. Each row in the Gantt chart represents a snapshot of the schedule; see Fig. 10.4.

Example 10.10   The table and the Gantt chart in Fig. 10.4 provide two views of a project's changing schedule. Each row/line in the Gantt chart represents a snapshot of the schedule. The heavy dots represent project milestones. The dotted lines show schedule slips for the milestones.

The first (top) horizontal bar in the Gantt chart is a snapshot on 7/23, the start date of a brief planning period. The only milestone in this snapshot is a plan review on 8/13 to decide whether to commit to the project or to drop it.

The review slips by a week to 8/20. The project is committed, with a planned release date of 11/26. The team plans to finish coding by 9/10.

Coding takes seven weeks, not three. The third row is for the snapshot on 10/08, the actual finish date for coding. The team is now four weeks behind their original plan, but they decide to compress the schedule and keep the release date of 11/26.

The compressed schedule should have been a warning sign. The fourth row is the snapshot on 10/29, the actual finish date for testing. This time, the release date slips from late November to early January, the next year.

The table view has a column for each milestone. The table rows represent snapshots of the schedule on the actual date that a milestone is reached. The rows get shorter as milestones are met. The left cell of row *i* lines up under milestone *i*. Thus, milestone 1 is met on 7/23, milestone 2 on 8/20, and so on. The last two rows of the table are empty because the corresponding milestones have not yet been reached.   □

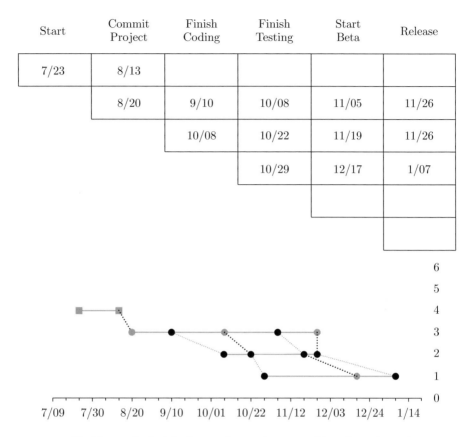

Start	Commit Project	Finish Coding	Finish Testing	Start Beta	Release
7/23	8/13				
	8/20	9/10	10/08	11/05	11/26
		10/08	10/22	11/19	11/26
			10/29	12/17	1/07

Figure 10.4 The history of schedule changes for a project, as a table and as a Gantt chart.

10.4 Product Quality: Measuring Defects

Metrics for defects merit special attention because defect detection and removal are such an integral part of software development and maintenance. This section addresses three questions related to defects:

- How effective are techniques such as testing at detecting defects?
  Answer: Data based on a metric called "defect-removal efficiency" suggests that the combination of reviews, static analysis, and testing can be up to 97 percent effective.
- What exactly is a customer-found defect? When two customers find the same defect, does that count as one defect or two?
  Answer: One.
- If product A has fewer defects than product B, does A have better product quality than B?
  Answer: Not necessarily. We need to adjust defect counts for product size, complexity, and volume (number of installs). Appropriate ratios are a better indicator of quality than numbers of defects.

Recall that a *defect* is a fault: it is a flaw or omission in source code, a design, a test suite, or some other artifact.

10.4.1   Severity of Defects

All defects are not equal: some are critical, some are harmless. Defects are typically classified into four levels of decreasing *severity*. The following levels form an ordinal scale:

1. *Critical* Total stoppage. Customers cannot get any work done.
2. *Major* Some required functionality is unavailable and there is no workaround.
3. *Minor* There is a problem, but there is a workaround, so the problem is an inconvenience rather than a roadblock.
4. *Cosmetic* All functionality is available.

The severity levels may be identified either by number or by name. The lower the number, the more severe the defect. The levels are sometimes referred to as critical, high, medium, and low. Companies tend not to ship a product with known critical or major defects.

Convention When it is used by itself in this chapter, the term *defect* refers to a critical or major defect.

10.4.2   Defect-Removal Efficiency

Defect-removal efficiency is based on the intuitive idea of comparing the number of defects removed *before* delivery with the total number that are detected before and after delivery. The efficiency level is then the percentage of total defects that are removed before delivery.

Such percentages (or ratios) would allow fair comparisons across products. A larger, more complex product is likely to have many more defects than a smaller, simpler one. The effect of size and complexity cancels out, however, because it applies equally to both the numerator and denominator in the ratio

(defects removed during development) / (total defects)

A problem with the intuitive idea is that the total number before and after delivery cannot be measured. "After" is an infinite interval that starts with delivery and does not end. In accumulating the total, we could wait forever for another defect to be found and removed.

The solution to this problem is to approximate the total by putting a time limit on the interval after product delivery. In practice, there is an initial flurry of customer-found defects, as customers exercise the product in ways that the developers may not have fully tested. This flurry dies down in the first few months after delivery.

The 90-day interval in Fig. 10.5 strikes a balance between (a) getting early feedback about the product and (b) waiting long enough for customer trouble reports to die down.

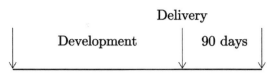

Figure 10.5 Defect-removal efficiency is the percentage of total defects removed during development, where total defects is the total number removed during development and detected within 90 days after delivery.

Defect-removal efficiency (DRE) is defined by:

$$DRE = before/total_{90}$$

where

$$before = \text{numbers removed before delivery}$$
$$total_{90} = \text{detected before and within 90 days after}$$

(10.3)

Example 10.11 Suppose that a product is delivered with 91 defects removed and 2 known defects remaining. After delivery, 7 additional defects are detected within the first 90 days. The defect-removal efficiency is 91 percent

$$DRE = 91/(91 + 2 + 7) = 91/100 = 91 \text{percent}$$

□

Measuring Defect-Removal Techniques

Defect-removal efficiency provides insights into the effectiveness of techniques for finding defects during development. Based on the data in Table 10.2, the individual techniques by themselves are no more than 65 percent efficient. Together, reviews, static analysis, and testing are 97 percent efficient. The natural conclusion is that we need to use a combination of techniques for defect removal.

Table 10.2 Defect-removal efficiency (DRE) data for reviews, static analysis, and testing. Source: Capers Jones.[11]

TECHNIQUES	MEDIAN DRE
Reviews alone	65%
Static Analysis alone	65%
Testing alone	53%
Reviews, Static Analysis, and Testing	97%

10.4.3   Customer-Found Defects (CFDs)

When two customers find the same defect, the product has one fault and two failures. One fault, because there is one defect/fault for developers to fix. Two failures, because two customer installations of the product were affected by failures – presumably, the customers found the defect because they had a failure of some sort.

Both defects and affected installations are carefully tracked by major companies. A defect is an inherent property of a product: it cannot be removed without changing the product. Defect counts are therefore metrics for product quality. Counts of affected installations are metrics for ops quality: they reflect the customer experience with operating the product. This section deals with metrics for defects. Section 10.5 is a case study of an ops quality metric derived from counts of affected systems.

Example 10.12   Typically, only the first report of a fault is counted as a customer-found defect. Subsequent reports about the same defect are counted separately. The following IBM metrics distinguish between the first and subsequent reports of a defect:

- Numbers that were dubbed "genuine" and reported for the first time
- Numbers that were for code or documentation; for example, 2nd+ defect reports

Note the phrase "dubbed 'genuine' " in the first of these three metrics. Many trouble reports from customers are handled by support personnel, so relatively few reach the development team as reports about product faults.   □

Definition of Customer-Found Defects
Prompted by the observations, a *customer-found defect (CFD)* satisfies the following:

1. **Product Defect** It is a product defect. Customer trouble reports about functionality, improper installation, or misconfiguration are taken seriously and are handled separately from product defects.
2. *It is the first report of this product defect.* Even if there are multiple reports, they are about the same defect in the product. A fix to the defect will handle all of the trouble reports. It therefore makes sense to classify only the first report as a CFD. (Meanwhile, the number of reports about a defect is a measure of operations quality, since it reflects the customer experience with the product.)
3. *It is either a critical or a major defect.*

10.4.4   CFDs Measure Installs, Not Quality

Products with more customer installations (installs) tend to have more trouble reports and more CFDs than products with fewer installs. Thus, the ratio of CFDs to installs is a better metric than CFDs alone for comparisons across different products. The ratio can also be used for comparing releases of the same product.

Example 10.13   Release R4 of a product had too many customer-found defects: 449. So, for R5, the next release, the team made a real effort. They added more code reviews, more tests, and otherwise improved its development practices. The result for R5: 1,037 CFDs.

What happened?

For an answer, consider another metric: the number of installs. Release R4 had 9,025 installs; R5 had 62,713! Thus R4 had 5.0 defects per 100 installs, whereas R5 had only 1.7.   □

The following ratio is a better indicator of product quality than the number of CFDs:

$$defects \ / \ installs$$

where *defects* is the number of CFDs and *installs* is the number of installs.

Here, *installs* is an independent variable and *defects* is a dependent variable. As *installs* grows, so does *defects*. By using the preceding ratio, we factor out the effect of installs on defects.

In practice, products with similar quality have similar defects/installs ratios. Products with better quality have lower ratios than products with worse quality. We can therefore use the ratios for quality comparisons. (See also simple linear regression in Section 10.9, for approximating the relationship between two variables by a linear function.)

Example 10.14   Continuing Example 10.13, the bar charts in Fig. 10.6 show data for nine releases of a product. The data is for two metrics: (a) installs and (b) defects.

The ratios of defects per 100 installs for the releases are as follows:

$$3.8, \ 2.1, \ 1.6, \ 5.0, \ 1.7, \ 1.9, \ 2.1, \ 2.0, \ 2.2$$

The ratios cluster around the median, 2.1 defects per 100 installs. In other words, the function

$$defects \ = \ 2.1 \, installs/100$$

approximates the relationship between defects and installs. Releases with ratios below the median have better quality than the releases with ratios above the median.

These conclusions are consistent with customer feedback about the releases. Releases 1 (ratio 3.8) and 4 (ratio 5.0) were exceptions to an otherwise consistent track record of high product quality.

Since the data in this example is for releases of the same product, it allows us to focus on the relationship between installs and defects. Other factors, such as product size, complexity, and developer expertise were relatively constant across the releases. The number of installs was the dominant independent variable.   □

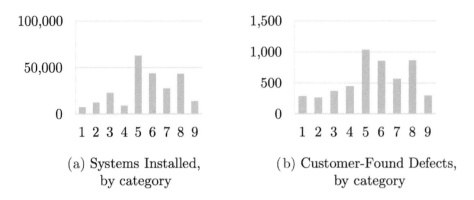

(a) Systems Installed, by category

(b) Customer-Found Defects, by category

Figure 10.6 Numbers of (a) installs and (b) customer-found defects for a sequence of releases. Both bar charts are for the same releases of a product.

10.5   Ops Quality Improvement: A Case Study

The case study in this section describes a company-wide software quality improvement effort at Avaya. The effort was driven by an ops-quality metric derived from the number of customer installations that reported a defect (CFD). To allow meaningful quality comparisons across products, the metric adjusted for the size of a product's installed base and the product's maturity. Ops quality improves as a product matures; for example, early problems get fixed. The metric was named customer quality metric (CQM) to emphasize its role as a proxy for the customer experience with a product. CQM-improvement targets were met by making product and process improvements.[12]

10.5.1   How to Improve Software Quality

Quality improvement metrics are typically validated through user feedback and proxies for customer satisfaction. The Microsoft Access, IBM, and Nortel teams in Examples 10.3, 10.7, and 10.6, respectively, all used combinations of feedback and Net Promoter Score. Customer satisfaction is therefore the overall or top-level goal in the hierarchy of improvement goals in Fig. 10.7. As we shall see, the hierarchy shows how process and product improvements contribute to ops quality, which directly reflects the customer experience with a product.

From Section 3.6.3, a goal hierarchy refines a high-level goal into specific measurable goals. Each node in the hierarchy represents a goal. The children of a node represent subgoals. In this hierarchy, all parent nodes are *and* nodes, which means that the subgoals at all of the children must be met for the goal at the parent node to be met.

This discussion focuses on how developers can contribute to improving the customer experience. Let us assume that the product does what customers want; that is, it provides the desired functionality. Functional quality is therefore not part of the discussion.

Figure 10.7 A partial hierarchy that refines the top-level goal of improving customer satisfaction with current and future products. The "leaf" goals can be refined further to get specific measurable goals. The hierarchy includes some customer-support subgoals that must be met for customer satisfaction to improve.

Starting at the top of Fig. 10.7, customer satisfaction depends on more than reliable operation (ops quality). Another key factor is product support in the event of a failure. All products have defects, so the question is when, not if, a product fails during operations. In words, the root of the hierarchy represents the following: for customer satisfaction to improve, both ops quality and the support experience must improve.

The support experience is included as a subgoal because it is part of the context for ops quality. Developers are not responsible for installing, configuring, and maintaining a product at a customer site. Developers are responsible, however, for fixing customer found defects.

The hierarchy shows two subgoals for improving ops quality:

- Fix the current product by performing corrective and preventive maintenance. Preventive maintenance refactors and improves risky code.
- Improve the quality of future products so they will have better ops quality after they are delivered and operated.

The subgoals for improving future product quality are to (a) identify and (b) make process improvements. Development practices are the main lever for improving the quality of future products, including products that are still in development. In short, better processes today will develop better products for tomorrow – better products that are expected to fail less often. If they fail less often, they will have better ops quality. The goal hierarchy therefore shows:

process improvement contributes to better
product quality, which contributes to
ops quality improvement

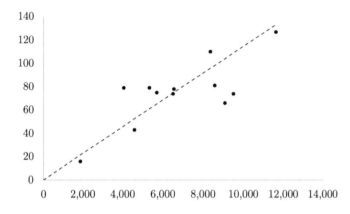

Figure 10.8 Data showing the growth of affected installs (vertical axis) with total installs (horizontal axis). An install is *affected* if it reports a customer-found defect. The data points are for a sequence of releases.

Specific process improvements are discussed later in this section.

10.5.2   The Customer Quality Metric

How might we measure ops quality? Failures and defects during operations are bad, so CQM begins with counts of *affected* installs, short for installs that are affected by customer-found defects. The metric adjusts the counts to normalize for three factors: the size of the installed base, product maturity, and reporting interval.

Installed Base The size of the installed base is the total number of installs of a product. Based on empirical evidence, affected installs grow linearly with total installs; see Fig. 10.8 for supporting data. CQM therefore takes the ratio of affected to total installs. This ratio represents the likelihood (probability) that an install will be affected.

Product Maturity Quality improves as a product matures. Defects get reported and fixed. Later installs go more smoothly. Most issues are resolved in the first few months. Let a *maturity period* be the m-month time interval that starts with the release of a product. The maturity period m is a parameter in the definition of CQM. The use of the same maturity period enables comparisons between products at different maturity levels. A typical value for m is 6–7 months. By then, most defects have been fixed and there is likely to be a new release.

Reporting Interval CQM is derived from a count of installs that are affected within a fixed time period after their date of installation. That time period is called the *reporting interval*. The length of the reporting interval is a parameter, say n-months. Typical values of n are 1, 3, and 6 months.

For CQM, the installation date must be within the product maturity period for the install to be included in the counts of affected and total installs; see Fig. 10.9. The

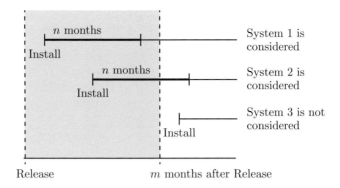

Figure 10.9 To be considered for the n-month CQM ops-quality metric for a product, an installation date must be within the product maturity period, which is the first m months after product release. The thick lines indicate the reporting interval, which is the first n months after the installation date.

dashed vertical line represents the end of the maturity period. Installation dates past the maturity period are not included in the counts. Reporting intervals are shown as solid lines. As long as a reporting interval begins within the maturity period, it can extend past the maturity period. All reporting intervals have the same length: n months.

Definition of CQM The preceding discussion of product-maturity period and reporting interval sets the stage for the definition of CQM. The *n-month CQM* metric for a product is the ratio of installs within the first m months after release that report a defect within the first n months after installation.

10.5.3 Subgoals: Product and Process Improvement

CQM treats code as a black box. It can flag products that need to improve, but it cannot tell us how to achieve product and process improvements. At Avaya, two additional metrics guided improvements:

- For product improvement, a risky-file indicator focused attention on 1 percent of the files; for example, on 200 files in a system with 20,000 files.
- For process improvement, a metric called Implementation Quality Index (IQI) assessed a team's practices.

An Ops Quality Target
Development teams at Avaya were challenged to achieve a CQM level of 2 percent or better; see the top-level goal in Fig. 10.10. The 2 percent CQM target was based on data from highly reliable past products. Phrased differently, the goal was to have at least 98 percent of the installs operate smoothly, without reporting a defect in the first six months.

The CQM parameters were as follows. The product maturity period was $m = 7$ months. There were three intervals for reporting defects from an install: $n = 1$ month

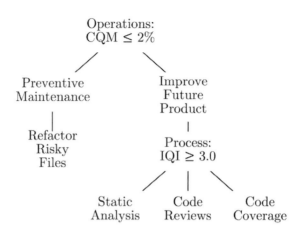

Figure 10.10 Quality-improvement goals driven by two metrics: CQM for ops quality, and IQI for process quality.

for an early measure, $n = 6$ months for a relatively stable measure, and $n = 3$ months for an intermediate value.

In Fig. 10.10, the top-level CQM goal has two subgoals:

- **Current Products** Perform preventive maintenance to fix trouble spots in the code, before they fail under use.
- **Future Products** Improve the effectiveness of development practices so they produce better products. Effectiveness of practices was measured by IQI, a process quality metric.

A Risky File Indicator

Development teams need help with identifying the parts of the code that need improvement. Imagine the plight of a team with 25 million lines of code. Where do they start? At Avaya, a metric based on the following factors was used to identify so-called *risky files*. Across multiple products, two-thirds or more of all customer-found defects could be traced to the top 1 percent of files flagged as risky. The risk predictor for a file was derived from the following metrics:

- Number of past customer found defects that were fixed.
- Number of authors who had left the project.
- Number of product-related service requests.
- Number of unique versions of the file.

The risk posed by a file needs to be confirmed by an expert; for example, some related files, such as header files, also get flagged as potentially risky.

10.5.4   Measuring Process Improvements

The goals in Fig. 10.10 include three development practices: static analysis, code reviews, and code coverage. Process quality depends not only on the use of specific practices, but on how effectively these practices are used. For example, 90 percent is a more effective level of code coverage than 70 percent. The *Implementation Quality Index (IQI)* is a rough measure of the effectiveness of a team's practices. On a scale of 0 (worst) to 4 (best), IQI is the average of the scores for the individual practices. Teams self-assessed their scores, which were then peer-reviewed for consistency across teams. For self-assessment, teams were provided with guidelines; for example, the level of coverage corresponding to a given score.

On a scale of 0–4, an IQI level of 3.0 was set as a target because diminishing returns set in above it. Through data analysis, an IQI level of 3.0 during development was shown to be a reliable predictor of an ops quality CQM score of 2.0 or better (less), after the product was completed and delivered to customers.

The quality-improvement program in this case study began with one product and spread, until it was adopted company wide. Over the three-year period covered by the study (2010–2013) the program led to 30 percent year-over-year improvements in ops quality, as measured by CQM.

10.6 Data Dispersion: Boxplots and Histograms

Boxplots and histograms are graphical summaries of the dispersion of data values in a data set. They display the number of values that fall within a given interval. Boxplots show display counts by quartile. Histograms show counts by (typically) fixed-size intervals. Visually, boxplots and histograms look quite different.

10.6.1 Medians and Quartiles

The median and the mean represent complementary approaches to summarizing the dispersion of data points in a data set: by position and by value, respectively. The median is based on the relative positions of the data points in a linear ordering, whereas the mean is based on the values of the data points. The median of the data set

$$2, \ 2, \ 8, \ 32, \ 56$$

is the middle data point 8. The mean is

$$(2 + 2 + 8 + 32 + 56)/5 \ 100/5 \ = \ 20$$

Both are useful summary statistics. The difference between the median 8 and the mean 20 is a reflection of the dispersion of the data points.

In practice, the median can be a more realistic statistic about a "typical" data point because the median is not skewed by a few unusually large or unusually small values. The mean averages values, so it is affected by extreme data points. When a billionaire walks into a room full of regular people, the median net worth of the people in the room may shift by one, but the mean net worth goes through the roof.

Definition of Median

The following definition generalizes the earlier view of a median as the middle data point. In particular, the median is a value; it does not have to be a member of the data set.

A *median* of a data set is any value such that the values in the data set satisfy both of the following conditions:

- At most half of the values are less than the median.
- At most half of the values are greater than the median.

For a data set with an even number of data points, we follow the convention of picking the median to be the average of the middle two values. With the data set

$$1, 1, 2, 3, 5, 8$$

the two middle values are 2 and 3. By convention, we choose $(2 + 3)/2 = 2.5$ as the median. (Note that the definition allows either of the two middle data points to be chosen as the median.)

Note The definition of median applies to any scale that allows values to be linearly ordered. The values do not need to be evenly spaced. In particular, the definition applies to ordinal scales.

The Five Quartiles

The median partitions a data set into two halves – with an odd number of data points, the median is in neither half. Quartiles partition a data set into four quarters. The *lower quartile* is the median value of the lower half; the *upper quartile* is the median of the upper half of the data set.

Example 10.15   Let us identify the upper and lower quartiles for data set 10.1. Sorted by value, the data points are

$$1.6, \ 1.7, \ 1,9, \ 2.0, \ 2.1, \ 2.1, \ 2.2, \ 3.8, \ 5.0$$

The median, 2.1, partitions this data set into two halves, each with 4 data points. The lower quartile is the median, 1.8, of

$$1.6, \ 1.7, \ 1,9, \ 2.0$$

The upper quartile is the median, 3.0, of

$$2.1, \ 2.2, \ 3.8, \ 5.0$$

□

Intuitively, quartiles are values that mark the boundaries of the four quarters of a data set. Quartiles will be used in the following in box plots, which show the range of values between quartiles. As we shall see, box plots visually summarize the dispersion of data points. The following definitions are convenient for working with box plots.

A data set is characterized by the five *quartiles*, Q_0-Q_4:

Q_0 the minimum value
Q_1 the lower quartile
Q_2 the median value   (10.4)
Q_3 the upper quartile
Q_4 the maximum value

The *interquartile range (IQR)* is the length of the interval between the lower and upper quartiles:

$$IQR = Q_3 - Q_1 \qquad (10.5)$$

10.6.2 Box Plots Summarize Data by Quartile

Box plots or *boxplots*, also known as *box and whiskers plots*, summarize the dispersion of data points by showing the intervals between quartiles. Boxplots can be drawn horizontally or vertically. In horizontal boxplots, the minimum value is at the left; see Fig. 10.11. In vertical boxplots, the minimum value is at the bottom.

The middle half of the data set is identified by a box in the middle of a boxplot. Specifically, the box identifies the interquartile range between the lower and upper quartiles. The median is drawn as a line across the box.

The lines that extend from the box toward the left and right ends of a boxplot are called *whiskers*. Whiskers can be drawn all the way to the minimum and maximum values, as in Fig. 10.11(a), or can stop short to show outliers, as in Fig. 10.11(b). The latter boxplot, in Fig. 10.11(b), has two outliers at the high end, and no outliers at the low end. See Example 10.17 for how to draw whiskers.

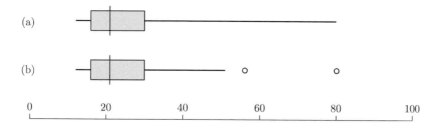

Figure 10.11 Two boxplots for the same data set. (a) The whiskers in the upper boxplot extend all the way to the minimum value at the left end and to the maximum value at the right end. (b) The lower boxplot shows outliers as dots.

Example 10.16 The boxplots in Fig. 10.11 are for the data set

$$12, \ 12, \ 16, \ 19, \ 20, \ 21, \ 22, \ 24, \ 30, \ 56, \ 80$$

The lower half of this data set is $12, 12, 16, 19, 20$, so the lower quartile is 16. The upper half is $22, 24, 30, 56, 80$, so the upper quartile is 30.

Both boxplots in Fig. 10.11 extend from the minimum 12 to the maximum 80. In both, the box lies between the lower quartile 16 and the upper quartile 30. The median, 21, is shown as a vertical line across the box.   □

Outliers

Outliers are defined in terms of the interquartile range, IQR, between the upper and lower quartiles. A data point is an *outlier* if it is more than $1.5 \times IQR$ past the lower or the upper quartile.

Example 10.17 For the data set in Example 10.16, the lower quartile is 16 and the upper quartile is 30, so

$$1.5 \times IQR \ = \ 1.5 \times (30 - 16) \ = \ 1.5 \times 14 \ = \ 21$$

The data set has two outliers: 56 and 80. They are both greater than $51 = 30 + 21$. There are no outliers at the low end of this data set.   □

In a boxplot showing outliers, the whiskers extend as follows:

- The whisker from the lower quartile extends to the minimum, Q_0, or to $Q_1 - 1.5 \times IQR$, whichever is greater.
- The whisker from the upper quartile extends to the maximum, Q_4, or to $Q_3 + 1.5 \times IQR$, whichever is lesser.

10.6.3   Histograms of Data Spread

A *histogram* is a graphical display of the number of data points that fall within a given interval; that is, within a given range of values. Informally, a histogram approximates the dispersion or spread of data points in a data set. Two examples of histograms appear in Fig. 10.12.

In a vertical histogram, the vertical axis represents the number of data points that fall within an interval. Meanwhile, the horizontal axis is partitioned into adjacent intervals, called *bins*. Typically the bins are of equal *width*, where the width is the difference between the high and low values of the bin.

The data points in a bin are represented by a vertical bar associated with the bin. The height of a vertical bar is proportional to the number of data points in the bin. The

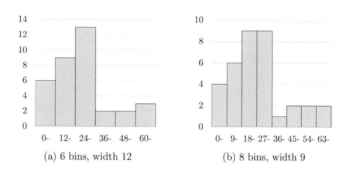

(a) 6 bins, width 12   (b) 8 bins, width 9

Figure 10.12 Two histograms for the contractor bids data set 10.2.

width of a bar is proportional to the width of a bin, and there are no spaces between the bars; see Fig. 10.12.

Histograms are drawn without spaces between bars to distinguish them from bar charts, which do have spaces between the bars. The difference between the two is that the horizontal axis of a bar chart is for categories, whereas the horizontal axis of a histogram is for intervals of values.

Example 10.18 Compare the histograms in Fig. 10.12 with the bar chart in Fig. 10.3. They are all based on the same data about contractor bids. Entity contractor has two metrics: *name* and *bid*. In the bar chart, the horizontal axis has a category for each contractor name. The height of each bar represents the value of that contractor's bid. Thus, there is a bar for each data point (bid).

In the histograms, the horizontal axis represents the values of the bids. The vertical bars count the number of bids that fall within a bin/interval.   □

Example 10.19 Both of the histograms in Fig. 10.12 are for the contractor bids data set 10.2. The histogram on the left has 6 bins; the bin width is 12. Here is how we get the bin width. The 6 bins must cover data points ranging from 3 to 70, so the width must be at least

$$(70 - 3 + 1)/6 = 68/6 = 11.33$$

Since we are working with integers, we need width 12. Specifically, the 6 bins in Fig. 10.12(a) are

$$0–11, 12–23, 24–35, 36–47, 48–59, 60–71$$

Similarly, on the right, with 8 bins, the histogram in Fig. 10.12(b) has bin width 9. Its bins are

$$0\text{-}8, 9\text{-}17, \ldots, 63–71$$

The histograms in Fig. 10.12(a–b) are for the same data set, but their visual appearance is different. Changing the number of bins can change the shape of a histogram. Shifting the bins can also perturb the shape.

Consider the effect of shifting the bins in the left histogram by 1. The contents of the first bin change as follows:

$$\text{bin } 0\text{–}11: 3, 4, 5, 5, 9, 10$$
$$\text{bin } 1\text{–}12: 3, 4, 5, 5, 9, 10, 12, 12, 12$$

For any given data set, it is worth experimenting with the bin parameters to get a feel for the distribution of the data points.   □

How Many Bins?

The *square-root rule* is a simple rule for choosing the number of bins: use the square root of the size of the data set. If N is the number of data points, then

$$\text{number of bins} = \lceil \sqrt{N} \rceil \qquad (10.6)$$

In words, the number of bins is the smallest integer that is greater than or equal to the square root of the number of data points. This rule yields 6 bins for the 35 contractor bids; see the histogram in Fig. 10.12(a).

10.7   Data Dispersion: Statistics

This section introduces variance, a key summary statistic for the dispersion of data points in a data set. The *standard deviation* of a data set is the positive square root of its variance. The section then briefly introduces distributions. A discrete probability distribution describes the relative frequency with which observed data points will have a given sample value. A continuous probability distribution describes the likelihood (probability) that a randomly chosen data point will have a specific value.

10.7.1   Variance from the Mean

Variance measure of the spread or deviation of data points from the mean.

Example 10.20   The data points in Fig. 10.13 represent the ops quality of a sequence of releases of a product. The releases are identified by the numbers along the horizontal axis. The vertical axis represents the percentage of installs that were affected by severe defects.

The mean 2.49 of the data set is one summary statistic for the quality of the releases; see the horizontal line. Variance quantifies how clustered or how dispersed the data points are from the mean. The vertical lines show the deviations or distances of the data points from the mean.   □

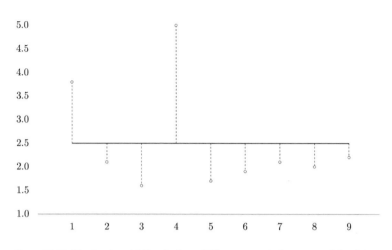

Figure 10.13 The horizontal line in the middle represents the mean of the data set. The dashed vertical lines show the deviations of the data points from the mean.

Definition: Variance of a Finite Data Set

The *variance* of a finite data set is defined as the average of the squares of the distances between the data points and the mean. (This definition is restated in what follows in mathematical notation.) Variance is written as σ^2 or $Var(X)$, for data set X. The *standard deviation* of a data set is σ, the square root of the variance.

Example 10.21   Consider the data set

$$1, 2, 3, 4, 5$$

The mean of this data is

$$(1 + 2 + 3 + 4 + 5)/5 \;=\; 15/5 \;=\; 3$$

The variance is the average of the squares of the deviations from the mean:

$$
\begin{aligned}
\sigma_2 &= ((1-3)^2 + (2-3)^2 + (3-3)^2 + (4-3)^2 + (5-3)^2)/5 \\
&= ((-2)^2 + (-1)^2 + 0^2 + 1^2 + 2^2)/5 \\
&= (4 + 1 + 1 + 4)/5 = 10/5 \\
&= 2
\end{aligned}
$$

□

With small data sets, summary statistics can be swayed by a few extreme data points.

Example 10.22 The extreme data point 5.0 has an outsize influence on the variance of data set 10.1, repeated here for convenience:

$$3.8, \ 2.1, \ 1.6, \ 5.0, \ 1.7, \ 1.9, \ 2.1, \ 2.0, \ 2.2$$

Let us round the mean 2.49 to 2.5, to keep the numbers simple. The variance is the average of the squares of the deviations from the mean:

$$
\begin{aligned}
sigma^2 &= (1.3^2 + 0.4^2 + 0.8^2 + 2.5^2 + 0.8^2 + 0.6^2 + 0.4^2 + 0.5^2 + 0.3^2)/9 \\
&= (1.69 + 0.16 + 0.81 + 6.25 + 0.64 + 0.36 + 0.16 + 0.25 + 0.09)/9 \\
&= (4.16 + 6.25)/9
\end{aligned}
$$

The following table summarizes the influence of data point 5.0 on key statistics:

	POINTS	MEDIAN	MEAN	VARIANCE	STD DEV σ
with 5.0	9	2.10	2.49	1.157	1.075
drop 5.0	8	2.05	2.18	0.414	0.644

While the median is relatively unchanged, the standard deviation drops from 1.075 to 0.644.

Data point 5.0 was indeed for a troubled release. The development team investigated and took actions to ensure that future releases would have higher quality. □

Definition of Variance, Revisited

In mathematical notation, the variance of a finite data set X is defined by summing the squares of the deviations of the data points x_i from the mean μ, and the dividing the sum by the number of data points N. The arithmetic mean μ is the average of the values of the data points:

$$\mu = \frac{1}{N} \sum_{i=1}^{N} x_i \tag{10.7}$$

The deviations $(x_i - \mu)$ in the following equation correspond to the vertical distances from the data points to the mean in Fig. 10.13:

$$\sigma^2 = \frac{1}{N} \sum_{i=1}^{N} (x_i - \mu)^2 \tag{10.8}$$

The variance of a finite data set is a special case of the concept of variance in probability and statistics.

10.7.2   Discrete Probability Distribution

A distribution describes the relative frequency or likelihood that a random data point will have a given sample value. For clarity, we refer to the values of data points as *sample values*, to distinguish them from the values "returned" by functions. Sample values can be discrete or continuous. A discrete probability distribution is defined over discrete sample values.

Example 10.23   Severity levels are discrete. Consider a data set with 100 defects (data points): 5 critical, 10 major, 60 minor, and 25 cosmetic. From these sample values, we can estimate the probability with which a randomly selected defect will have a given severity. The following table shows the frequency of sample values in the data set and the probability estimates:

SEVERITY	FREQUENCY	PROBABILITY ESTIMATE
Critical	5	0.05
Major	10	0.10
Minor	60	0.60
Cosmetic	25	0.25
Total	100	1.00

□

A *probability mass function* maps a sample value x to a probability, a real number between 0 and 1. Let us use the Greek letter ϕ ("phi") for a probability mass function. In Example 10.23,

$$\phi(\text{critical}) = 0.05$$

We can use ϕ to determine the probability of a subset of sample values. For example, the following is the probability that a random defect in Example 10.23 is either critical or major:

$$\phi(\text{critical}) + \phi(\text{major}) = 0.05 + 0.10 = 0.15$$

With integers, an interval defines a contiguous subset of integers. A probability mass function over integers can therefore be used to determine the probability that a random data point falls within the interval. For example, if ϕ is a function over integer contractor bids, then the probability that a bid will be in the interval $(25, 29)$ is given by

$$\phi(25) + \phi(26) + \phi(27) + \phi(28) + \phi(29)$$

A distribution can be specified either by a probability mass function or by a cumulative function. For a linearly ordered set of sample values, a *cumulative distribution function* maps a sample value x to the sum of the probabilities of sample values that are less than or equal to x. Let us use the capital Greek letter Φ for a cumulative distribution function. For nonnegative integer sample values, $\Phi(x)$ is the probability that a random data point lies in the interval $(0, x)$:

$$\Phi(x) = \phi(0) + \phi(1) + \cdots + \phi(x) \tag{10.9}$$

For integer sample values, the interval for $\Phi(x)$ is $(-\infty, x)$.

10.7.3 Continuous Distributions

Continuous distributions are useful for data analysis even for data sets of discrete sample values. The counterpart of a probability mass function for discrete sample values is a *probability density function*, which maps a real sample value x to a relative likelihood that a random data point will have that sample value. Again, we use ϕ to denote a probability density function. Examples of probability density functions appear in Fig. 10.14.

Note that for any real number x, the probability $\phi(x)$ is 0. Why? Consider a uniform distribution, where all real sample values between 0 and 1 are equally likely. There are an infinite number of reals (not floating-point numbers!) between 0 and 1, so the probability is 0 that a random sample will **exactly** equal 0.5 or 0.1415926535 or any other of the infinite number of possible sample values.

More generally, think of approximating a continuous density function over the reals by a discrete mass function over the integers. In the approximation, a real number is rounded to an integer. In the discrete approximation, the mass function applied to an integer n represents the probability that a random data point is in the interval $(n - 0.5, n + 0.5)$ in the continuous distribution. As we expand this interval, the probability of a random data point falling in the expanded interval increases. As we shrink the interval, the probability decreases. In the limit, as we continue to shrink, the probability of a random data point falling within the approximation interval goes to zero.

With continuous distributions, we work with probabilities in intervals. The area under the curve of a probability density function is 1. In other words, the area under the curve of a probability density function between $-\infty$ and $+\infty$ is 1. With the distributions in Fig. 10.14, the density function drops off sharply as the distance from the mean increases.

10.7.4 Introduction to Normal Distributions

The four probability density curves in Fig. 10.14(a) are all for a family of distributions called *normal* distributions. "Normal" is their name, as opposed to a characterization,

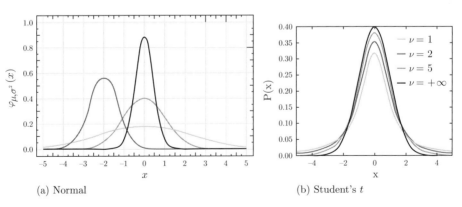

(a) Normal   (b) Student's t

Figure 10.14 (a) Normal distributions: three with mean 0 and variance 0.2, 1.0, and 5.0; and one with mean -2 and variance 0.5. Source: public domain image by Wikimedia Commons. (b) Student's t-Distribution. Source: Skbkekas, CC3.0 BY license.[13]

as in, "it is normal for the sun to rise in the east." The shape of the curves has led to the popular name "bell curve" for normal distributions, although other distributions also have bell-shaped curves; for example, see the Student's t-distribution in Fig. 10.14(b). Normal distributions are widely used because they fit many natural phenomena. They also readily support mathematical analysis.

A normal distribution is characterized by two parameters: its mean μ and its standard deviation σ (or variance σ^2). A *standard normal distribution* has mean $\mu = 0$ and equal variance and standard deviation, $\sigma^2 = \sigma = 1$. The larger the standard deviation, the wider and flatter the curve. The tall, narrow curve in Fig. 10.14(a) with a peak at value 0 has mean $\mu = 0$ and variance $\sigma^2 = 0.2$. The wider curves with mean $\mu = 0$ have variance 1.0 and 5.0. The fourth curve has $\mu = -2.0$ and $\sigma^2 = 0.5$.

A normal distribution is symmetric around the mean. The probability density function falls off rapidly as we move away from the mean. The following table shows the percentage of data points that are within $n\sigma$ of the mean; that is, within the interval $(\mu - n\sigma, \mu + n\sigma)$.

$$1\sigma \quad 68.27\%$$
$$2\sigma \quad 95.40\%$$
$$3\sigma \quad 99.73\%$$

10.7.5 Introduction to Student's t-Distributions

Normal distributions work well with large sizes, but not with small. Student's t-distributions were motivated by the problem of small sample sizes, perhaps as small as 3 data points. The distributions arise when small numbers of data points are drawn from a population with a normal distribution. The name comes from the pseudonym "Student" used by William Sealy Gosset when he published the distributions in 1908. The distributions are also referred to simply as *t-distributions*.[14]

Members of the family of Student's t-distributions are characterized by a parameter called the *degrees of freedom*, commonly denoted by the Greek letter ν ("nu"). For a sample size N, the relevant t-distribution has $\nu = N - 1$; see Fig. 10.14(b) for probability density functions for $\nu = 1, 2, 5, \infty$. The density curve for a t-distribution resembles the curve for a normal distribution with mean 0 and standard deviation 1, except that t-distributions have more probability mass further away from the mean. As the number of degrees of freedom increases, the curve for a t-distribution approaches a normal distribution with $\mu = 0$ and $\sigma = 1$. In other words, the curve for a t-distribution is bell shaped and symmetric. It becomes narrower and taller as the number of degrees of freedom increases; in the limit it equals a normal distribution.

10.8 Confidence Intervals

Intuitively, the reliability of a prediction (or estimate) increases with the number of data points on which the prediction is based. In other words, as the size of a random sample grows, we can be increasingly confident that the sample faithfully reflects the population from which the sample is drawn. We can then use the sample to predict some property of the population, such as the population's mean.

Confidence intervals quantify the informal notion of confidence in a prediction about a largely unknown population. We have a known sample, but the rest of the population is unknown. Instead of predicting a single point value, the idea is to predict an interval, a range of values. We want the prediction to be right with a specified probability, say 95 percent. Here, "right" means that the predicted interval contains the population's property of interest. This probability is called the confidence level. The higher the desired confidence level, the wider the interval. Conversely, the narrower the confidence interval, the lower the confidence level.

10.8.1   Definition of Confidence Interval

For concreteness, let the property of interest be the mean μ of the population and let the desired confidence level be 95 percent. We refer to the population mean μ as the *true mean*.

A *95 percent confidence interval* is an interval

$$(predicted\text{-}low, predicted\text{-}high)$$

such that, with a 95 percent confidence level (probability), the predicted interval contains the true mean.

Confidence intervals are calculated relative to an estimated value. The predicted low and high are expressed as offsets from the estimate. The offsets are called *error bounds*. For simplicity, we assume that the error bounds are equal on both the low and high sides of the estimate. The interval is therefore expressed as

$$(estimate - error\text{-}bound, estimate + error\text{-}bound)$$

With the true population mean as the property of interest, the estimate is the sample mean.

More precisely, consider a sample data set X with N data points x_i. Let $\bar{x}$ be the average of the N data points. This average $\bar{x}$ is the *sample mean*

$$\bar{x} = \frac{1}{N} \sum_{i=1}^{N} x_i \tag{10.10}$$

The 95 percent confidence interval for the true mean μ is an interval

$$(\bar{x} - error\text{-}bound, \bar{x} + error\text{-}bound) \tag{10.11}$$

where *error-bound* is such that, with a 95 percent confidence level, the preceding interval contains the true mean μ.

The calculation of the error bound depends on four factors:

- **Confidence Level** We have assumed that the level is 95 percent. The approach carries over to other levels; for example, 90 percent or 98 percent.
- **Sample Size** It is N.
- **Population Distribution** Assume that the population has a normal distribution. It is beyond the scope of this book to consider other distributions.

- **Population Standard Deviation, σ** Typically, the population's standard deviation σ is unknown. The two cases, known and unknown σ, are considered separately in Sections 10.8.2 and 10.8.3.

10.8.2 If the Population Standard Deviation Is Known

For completeness, the property of interest is the true mean μ of a normally distributed population with a known standard deviation σ. The error bound for a confidence interval centered at the sample mean $\bar{x}$ is given by

$$\text{error-bound} = c\sigma/\sqrt{N} \qquad (10.12)$$

where c is a *coverage factor* that depends on the confidence level. For a 95.4 percent level, the factor $c = 2$. The numbers 95.4 percent and 2 come from the fact that a randomly chosen data point has a 95.4 percent probability of being within 2σ of the mean; see what follows for the justification. Here are some pairs of confidence levels and coverage factors:

LEVEL	FACTOR
90%	1.645
95%	1.96
98%	2.326
99%	2.576

Sample Size N The term $\sqrt{N}$ in Equation 10.12 adjusts for the convergence of samples mean $\bar{x}$ on the true population mean μ for increasing values of N. In the limit, the sample equals the population and $\bar{x} = \mu$.

Consider the simple case of samples drawn from a population with a standard normal distribution; that is, $\mu = 0$ and $\sigma = 1$. Each random sample will have its own sample mean $\bar{x}$. For example, the sample $1.1, -0.3, 0.7$ has $N = 3$ and

$$\bar{x} = (1.1 - 0.3 + 0.7)/3 = 1.5/3 = 0.5$$

and the sample $-0.5, 0, 1.2, -0.3$ has $N = 4$ and

$$\bar{x} = (-0.5 + 0 + 1.2 - 0.3)/4 = 0.4/4 = 0.1$$

In such instances, $\bar{x}$ acts as a random variable. We can form a data set of $\bar{x}$ values by drawing random sample sets. A data set of $\bar{x}$ values will have its own distribution. We can also form a data set of $\bar{x}\sqrt{N}$ values.

Standard normal distributions have the property that $\bar{x}\sqrt{N}$ has a standard normally distribution.

An intuitive interpretation of this property is that the multiplier $\sqrt{N}$ in $\bar{x}\sqrt{N}$ adjusts for the following: as the sample size N grows, the sample mean $\bar{x}$ converges on the true mean $\mu = 0$ at a rate of $1/\sqrt{N}$. Hence the denominator $\sqrt{N}$ in the equation for the error bound.

Population Standard Deviation σ The term σ in Equation 10.12 is needed because the population has a general (not a standard) normal distribution. To generalize from $\mu = 0$ and σ, let us rewrite $\bar{x}\sqrt{N}$ as

$$(\bar{x} - 0)\sqrt{N}/1$$

For a general normal distribution

$$(\bar{x} - \mu)\sqrt{N}/\sigma \tag{10.13}$$

is a random variable with a standard normal distribution that has mean 0 and standard deviation 1.

Note that $(\bar{x} - \mu)$ represents the deviation of the sample mean from the true population mean.

Coverage Factor c For any normal distribution, with 95 percent probability, a random data point is within 1.96σ of the mean. Since the term (10.13) has $\mu = 0$ and $\sigma = 1$, with a 95 percent confidence level, its absolute value is less than or equal to $c = 1.96$:

$$|(\bar{x} - \mu)\sqrt{N}/\sigma| \leq c = 1.96$$

Since both σ and $\sqrt{N}$ are nonnegative,

$$|(\bar{x} - \mu)| \leq \frac{c\sigma}{\sqrt{N}} = error\text{-}bound.$$

Thus, with a 95 percent confidence level, the true mean μ is in the confidence interval centered at the sample mean $\bar{x}$, with the preceding error bound.

10.8.3   If the Population Standard Deviation Is Unknown

Often, the population's σ is unknown. The approach to determining the error bound in a confidence interval remains the same as in the known σ case, with two exceptions. First, an adjusted version of the sample's standard deviation is used instead of the population's σ. Call this adjusted version S, where

$$S^2 = \frac{1}{N-1} \sum_{i=1}^{N} (x_i - \bar{x})^2 \tag{10.14}$$

Second, the counterpart of the random variable (10.13), with the sample's S instead of the population's σ

$$(\bar{x} - \mu)\sqrt{N}/S$$

has a t-distribution with $N - 1$ degrees of freedom.

The error bound is given by

$$error\text{-}bound = tS/\sqrt{N}, \tag{10.15}$$

where the value of t can be found in the Student's t-distribution tables. For convenience, selected table entries are shown in Table 10.3. The rows in the table are for degrees of

Table 10.3 Partial table of $t_{\alpha,\nu}$ values for Student's t-distribution. Here, ν is the degrees of freedom; CL is short for Confidence Level; and $\alpha = (1-CL)/2$. For $\nu = \infty$, the t-distribution equals a standard normal distribution.

	$\alpha = 0.05$ $CL = 90\%$	$\alpha = 0.025$ $CL = 95\%$	$\alpha = 0.01$ $CL = 98\%$
6	1.943	2.447	3.143
7	1.895	2.365	2.998
8	1.860	2.306	2.896
9	1.833	2.262	2.821
10	1.812	2.228	2.764
15	1.753	2.131	2.602
20	1.725	2.086	2.528
30	1.697	2.042	2.457
∞	1.645	1.960	2.326

freedom, ν. With N data points, $\nu = N - 1$. CL stands for Confidence Level. For large values of ν, a t-distribution approaches a standard normal distribution; for $\nu = \infty$, it is a normal distribution.

Table entries for a t-distribution are sometimes denoted by $t_{\alpha,\nu}$, where $\alpha = 1 - CL/2$.

Example 10.24 The data set 10.2 of $N = 35$ contractor bids is a sample from an unknown population. Let us assume that the population is normally distributed and that the confidence level is 95 percent. The calculation of the error bound is summarized by the following:

$$
\begin{aligned}
\bar{x} &= 27.6 && \text{sample mean} \\
S &= 17.767 && S^2 = \sum_{i=1}^{N}(x_i - \bar{x})^2/(N-1) \\
t &= 2.032 && \text{from t-distribution table, } \nu = N = 34 \\
EB &= 6.1 && \text{error bound } tS/\sqrt{N}
\end{aligned}
$$

The estimate for the true population mean is the sample mean, 27.6. The 95 percent confidence interval is

$$(27.6 - 6.1, 27.6 + 6.1) = (21.5, 33.7).$$

This interval is an approximation because we have assumed that the population is normally distributed. If our assumptions hold, then the confidence interval can be interpreted as follows. If we ran this experiment 100 times, we would expect to observe a mean bid between 21.5 and 33.7 about 95 out of those 100 times. Conversely, only rarely (about 5 times) would we observe a mean outside that range. □

A Common Misconception about Confidence Intervals

The "confidence" in confidence levels and intervals refers to the reliability of the estimation process based on a sample, not to guarantees about the properties of the population. The true population mean need not lie within the calculated confidence interval. Furthermore, if the sample is biased, the prediction will be off the mark. We can have faith in the prediction/estimation process, even if the prediction itself turns out to be inaccurate. In other words, we can have 95 percent confidence in the estimation process and have an inaccurate prediction.

It is tempting but incorrect to interpret a 95 percent confidence interval as a statement about the population. It is a statement about the prediction.

10.9 Simple Linear Regression

Statements of the form

Defects grow with program size.

express a (typically linear) relationship between a dependent variable (defects) and an independent variable (size). Simple linear regression approximates the dependence between variables by a linear function. On an x-y plot, the function is represented by a straight line. The plot has the independent variable x along the horizontal axis and the dependent variable y along the vertical axis.

Example 10.25   The plot in Fig. 10.15 shows two regression lines for a data set, one solid, the other dashed. The methods and criteria for fiting these lines to the data points are explored in this section.

The data points (dots) in the plot represent releases of a product. The x-axis shows the number of installs at customer sites in the first three months after the release date; the y-axis shows the number of installs affected by a customer-found defect. The data points are (x, y) pairs:

$$
\begin{array}{llll}
(1867, 16) & (5310, 79) & (6529, 78) & (9070, 66) \\
(4042, 79) & (5680, 75) & (8342, 110) & (9495, 74) \\
(4582, 43) & (6486, 74) & (8558, 81) & (11604, 127)
\end{array}
\qquad (10.16)
$$

This data set comes with a real-world constraint: a product with zero customer installs has zero installs affected by defects. In other words, a regression line must pass through the origin $(0, 0)$.   □

Simple linear regression is closely associated with a "goodness of fit" criterion called ordinary least squares. Given a set of N two-dimensional data points (x_i, y_i), *simple linear regression* fits a line defined by the equation

$$ f(x) = ax + b, \qquad (10.17) $$

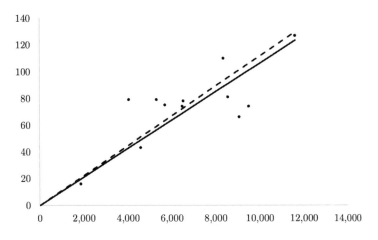

Figure 10.15 Two regression lines for a data set. The solid line is based on the ordinary least-squares criterion. The dashed line has half the data points above it, half below.

where a and b are constants. The *ordinary least-squares* criterion minimizes a measure of the vertical distance (deviation) between the data points and the regression line. The vertical deviation between the data point (x_i, y_i) and the regression line is $y_i - f(x_i)$. The measure is the sum of the squares of the deviations:

$$\sum_{i=1}^{N}(y_i - f(x_i))^2. \tag{10.18}$$

The solid regression line in Fig. 10.15 satisfies the least-squares criterion.

10.9.1   The Simpler Case: Line through the Origin

Ratios like defect-removal efficiency (Section 10.4) and customer-quality metric (Section 10.5) correspond to a special case where the regression line must pass through the origin; see Fig. 10.15. Regression lines through the origin are motivated by practical examples; for example, a program with 0 lines of code has 0 defects; see also Example 10.25.

We have $f(0) = 0$ when the regression line passes through the origin, so Equation 10.17 reduces to

$$f(x) = ax + 0 = ax. \tag{10.19}$$

The linear regression problem therefore reduces to the problem of choosing a suitable value for the parameter a.

Working with Ratios

Given $b = 0$, the parameter $a = f(x)/x$. As a candidate for a, consider the median of the ratios y_i/x_i, which we will call a'. The median a' has the desirable property that with $a = a'$, half the data points will be above the regression line and half will be below it. Why? Since the median is the middle value, at most half the ratios will be above a' and at most half will be below. With $y_i/x_i \geq a'$, we get $y_i \geq a'x$, so data point (x_i, y_i) is above the line

$$y = f(x) = a'x.$$

Similar reasoning applies to $y_i/x_i \leq a'$.

Example 10.26   The dashed regression line in Fig. 10.15 is defined by the median of the ratios y_i/x_i for the data set 10.16. The median of the ratios is 1.19 percent, so the dashed line is for the function

$$y = 0.0119x.$$

□

With the mean of the ratios as a candidate for the parameter a, we need to know if the outliers are exceptions to be ignored, or if they provide meaningful information. This knowledge requires insights from the real-world application represented by the data points. If the outliers are exceptions, then they unduly sway the mean.

10.9.2   Ordinary Least-Squares Fit

We begin with an ordinary least-squares fit through the origin. The solution for the slope a in $f(x) = a$ will then be adapted for the case where $f(x) = ax + b$.

Ordinary Least Squares: Line through the Origin

For an ordinary least-squares regression line through the origin, the intuitive idea is to use a weighted average of the y_i values for the parameter a in $f(x) = ax$. With one data point, $N = 1$, the regression line passes through the origin and the lone data point, (x_1, y_1). Thus,

$$f(x_1) = ax_1 = y_1.$$

So, $a = y_1/x_1$. Let us rewrite this equality as

$$a = \frac{1}{x_1}y_1 = \frac{x_1}{x_1^2}y_1$$

and treat x_1/x_1^2 as a weight applied to y_1, for the case $N = 1$.

For the general case, $N \geq 1$, let $\overline{x^2}$ be the average of the squares x_i^2 for the N data points. Then, the weight for y_i is $x_i/\overline{x^2}$. The regression function $f(x) = ax$ is defined by

$$a = \frac{1}{N}\left(\frac{x_1}{\overline{x^2}}y_1 + \frac{x_2}{\overline{x^2}}y_2 + \cdots + \frac{x_N}{\overline{x^2}}y_N\right). \tag{10.20}$$

This equation can be simplified and stated informally as

$$a = \frac{\text{average of } x_i y_i}{\text{average of } x_i^2}. \tag{10.21}$$

Example 10.27   With data set 10.16, the ordinary least-squares regression line is

$$f(x) = 0.0106x.$$

This function is represented by the solid line in Fig. 10.15.   □

Regression Line with Slope and Intercept
The linear regression function

$$f(x) = ax + b$$

has two parameters: a for the slope of the line, and b for where the line intercepts the y-axis. The intercept is the point $(0, f(0))$. In this case, the ordinary least-squares regression line passes through what we might call the intercept point and the center of mass of the data points, $(\bar{x}, \bar{y})$. Here $\bar{x}$ is the average of the x_i values and $\bar{y}$ is the average of the y_i values.

To get the slope a of the regression line $f(x) = ax + b$, let us rewrite the slope of a regression line through the origin:

$$\frac{\text{average of } x_i y_i}{\text{average of } x_i^2} = \frac{\text{average of } (x_i - 0)(y_i - 0)}{\text{average of } (x_i - 0)^2}.$$

The 0 terms in the preceding equation make explicit the fact that the line passes through the origin, $(0, 0)$. For a regression line that passes through the center of mass $(\bar{x}, \bar{y})$, we substitute $\bar{x}$ and $\bar{y}$ for the 0 terms. The slope a for $f(x) = ax + b$ through the center of mass is

$$a = \frac{\text{average of } (x_i - \bar{x})(y_i - \bar{y})}{\text{average of } (x_i - \bar{x})^2}. \tag{10.22}$$

The intercept b is given by

$$b = \bar{y} - (a\bar{x}). \tag{10.23}$$

More formally, the slope of an ordinary least-squares regression line is

$$a = \frac{\sum_{i=1}^{N}(x_i - \bar{x})(y_i - \bar{y})}{\sum_{i=1}^{N}(x_i - \bar{x})^2}. \tag{10.24}$$

To force a regression line through some other point (u, v) instead of the center of mass, substitute u and v for $\bar{x}$ and $\bar{y}$, respectively.

Table 10.4 The top five of 145 data-related questions from a survey of Microsoft engineers. Begel and Zimmerman presented the results in 2014.

1. "How do users typically use my application?"
2. "What parts of a software product are most used and/or loved by customers?"
3. "How effective are the quality gates we run at checkin?"
4. "How can we improve collaboration and sharing between teams?"
5. "What are the best key performance indicators (KPIs) for monitoring services?"

10.10   Conclusion

A metric quantifies an attribute (property) of an entity in the real world, such as source code, a development activity, a delivery event, or a team. A measurement process quantifies an attribute by associating a data value with a metric; for example, associating the symbol "critical" as the value of attribute severity of an entity product defect.

This chapter introduces data measurement, description, and analysis techniques by applying them to the goal of software quality assessment and improvement. While software quality is important in its own right, the applications of metrics extend beyond quality to all areas of software engineering. For example, a 2014 survey collected 145 questions about software engineering that Microsoft engineers would like data scientists to address. The questions were grouped into 12 categories such as customers and requirements, development practices, and teams and collaboration. The top five questions appear in Table 10.4.[15]

Software quality takes six forms:

- *Functional*: the degree to which a product does what users want.
- *Process*: the degree to which a process is (a) effective or (b) compliant with the prescribed process.
- *Product*: the degree to which a product has a property that cannot be changed without changing the product; for example, the property of being free of defects.
- *Operations (ops)*: refers to a customer's experience with using the product; for example, the degree to which a product runs reliably.
- *Aesthetics*: refers to a customer's perception of the goodness or desirability of the product.
- *Customer satisfaction*: refers to a customer's sense of satisfaction with a product, or the sense that the product is worth what they paid for it.

Quality improvement often begins either with the goal of improving customer satisfaction, or with reducing dissatisfaction. Let us take as a given that the product must provide the desired functionality. As we shall see, the path to reducing dissatisfaction due to failures goes through ops, product, and process quality. A failure under use is a dissatisfier, so dissatisfaction can be reduced by improving ops quality. Fewer failures are expected from products with fewer defects in the parts that customers actually use. So, better ops quality can be achieved through selective improvements in product quality. Finally, the development team can deliver higher product quality by using better practices and processes. Thus, process improvements ripple through the product and its operation, resulting eventually in reduced customer dissatisfaction due to failures.

The recommended approach to designing metrics is to start with a goal and then select metrics to measure progress toward meeting the goal. The goal may be left unstated if it is clear from the context; for example, with metric delivery date, the unstated goal is completion and delivery of a product. The "right" metric for a job often follows directly from the goal, especially if the goal is specific and measurable. Metric selection can, however, be a challenge. For example, consider the following two goals extracted from Question 2 in Table 10.4:

- Identify the parts of a product that are most used by customers.
- Identify the parts that are most loved by customers.

We can instrument a product to measure the number of times the parts are reached when the product is used, but it is hard to measure what customers love.

For an attribute (property) that is hard or impossible to measure directly, we can select derived metrics, which depend on one or more other attributes. Defect density, the ratio of ratio of program defects to program size, is a derived metric for attribute program quality: it depends on two attributes, defects and size. A proxy metric is a substitute that is expected to provide insights into the property of interest. As a prime example, Net Promoter Score (NPS) is typically used as a proxy for customer satisfaction. NPS is a measure of the willingness of customers to recommend a product.

Once metrics and data collection (measurement) are defined, we can describe and analyze the collected data. Bar charts, Gantt charts, and scatter plots graphically display entire data sets. The bars in a bar chart show counts or values by category, the lines in a a Gantt chart show time intervals, and the points in a scatter plot show the positions of (x, y) pairs in two dimensions. Boxplots and histograms graphically summarize the dispersion of data values in data sets. A boxplot identifies quartiles, and a histogram shows the number of data values that fall within a given interval.

The summary statistics in the chapter are the mean, mode, median, quartiles, variance, and standard deviation of a finite data set. The mean is the average of the values. A mode is a most frequently occurring value. A median is a value such that at most half the data values are greater than the median and at most half are less than it. The five quartile values partition the data set into four quarters: the five quartiles are the maximum, the minimum, the median, and the medians of the upper and lower halves, above and below the median, respectively. The variance is a measure of the distances between the data points and the mean. The standard deviation is the square root of the variance.

The chapter also introduces probability distributions, confidence intervals, and simple linear regression.

Further Reading

- Kitchenham and Pfleeger [111] pinned down the elusive concept of software quality by adapting a model of quality for physical products. The six forms of quality in this chapter are derived from their model.
- Jones [104] summarizes quality data from "600" client companies. The data includes the median defect-removal efficiencies of various combinations of reviews, static analysis, and testing.
- See Fenton and Bieman [68] for data description and analysis techniques.

Exercises for Chapter 10

Exercise 10.1   In each of the following cases, what are the issues, if any, with the use of the metric for the intended purpose?

a) cost per fix (of a defect) for programmer productivity
b) defect removal efficiency for product quality
c) lines of code per month for comparing productivity across countries
d) cost per line of code for programmer productivity

Exercise 10.2   Classify the metrics in Table 10.1 according to the six approaches to software quality in Section 10.2.

Exercise 10.3   For the contractor bids data set 10.2 in Section 10.6, determine
a) the mean   d) the five quartiles
b) the mode(s)   e) the variance
c) the median   f) the standard deviation

Exercise 10.4   Follow the instructions in Exercise 10.3 with the data set

$$16, 79, 78, 66, 79, 75, 110, 74, 43, 74, 81, 127$$

Exercise 10.5   Given the data set

$$1.6, 1.6, 1.7, 1.9, 2.0, 2.1, 2.1, 2.2, 3.8, 5.0, 7.0, 7.4$$

a) Determine the five quartiles
b) Check for outliers
c) Create a boxplot

Exercise 10.6   Determine the following confidence intervals for the true mean, given the contractor bids data set 10.2:

a) 90%
b) 95%
c) 98%

Exercise 10.7   For the following data set, what is the slope a of a regression line through the origin, where the line $f(x) = ax$ is determined using the following approaches:

a) the median of the y/x ratios
b) the mean of the y/x ratios
c) the ordinary least squares criterion

The data set is

$$
\begin{array}{llll}
(43, 319) & (90, 449) & (169, 277) & (435, 865) \\
(59, 223) & (125, 265) & (229, 369) & (441, 860) \\
(77, 288) & (138, 299) & (276, 572) & (627, 1037)
\end{array}
$$

Appendix: A Team Project

ACM-IEEE curriculum guidelines stress that "the best way to learn to apply software engineering theory and knowledge is in the practical environment of a [significant] project."[1] This appendix offers suggestions for organizing a course with a semester-long team project. The suggestions include a timeline and templates for a project proposal and status reports. The templates contain questions similar to those for an architecture discovery review.

The suggestions are based on several years of experience at the University of Arizona. Students are encouraged to have a real customer (outside the team) for their project ideas. To a large extent, the team experience, deliverables, and demos are more important than what they choose to build. Here are three examples of student project: provide online routes and customer information for on-site pool-service technicians, remotely monitor the climate in a lunar greenhouse, and offer reliable medical information for seriously ill children and their parents. These projects motivated Examples 1.7, 3.9, and 3.16, respectively.

This appendix will enable the reader to:

- Organize an iterative team project to elicit customer needs, write user requirements, define a product, design a solution, and build a system to meet the needs.
- Write a project proposal and status reports, leading up to a final report on the project's customer benefits, system architecture, technical accomplishments, and project management. The reports conclude with reflections on what went well, and what didn't.
- Summarize and present the work of the team to peers.

A.1   Overview

The timeline, templates, and tips in this appendix are offered as a starting point for customization to suit the context and objectives of an introductory course with a project. This overview sketches the rationale for the suggestions.

Looking ahead, the concepts and project tracks are aligned while processes and requirements are introduced in, say, the first third of the course. Once projects are launched, the concepts track has more flexibility with the selection and pacing of topics. The proposal and status reports serve as touch points between the tracks: they ask students to apply specific concepts to their projects. The two tracks are unlikely to be a perfect match because the concepts typically apply to software projects in general, not just to the student projects in the course.

This section outlines ways of coupling the concepts and project tracks. The comments in this section are for a semester-long project for students with some programming maturity. Say, they know how to build a user interface. Coupling is easier if the start of the project is delayed by an iteration to allow more of the concepts to be covered in class before they are needed for the student projects. A 9–10-week project is long enough to provide students with a team experience.

A.1.1   Goals for a Project

Software is built by teams, so software engineers need both technical and people skills. Roughly speaking, the lectures take the listener to the familiarity level in the following *learning hierarchy*, whereas a project can aim for the competence level.[2]

1. *Familiarity*. Can remember and understand.
2. *Guided Usage*. Can use, given direction and examples.
3. *Competence*. Can use and apply to new situations.
4. *Mastery*. Can evaluate, create, and assess relative to alternative approaches.

The proposed goals for the project are:

- Foster competence in the technical concepts that are applied in the project.
- Develop teamwork skills to the guided usage level.

For the goal of developing teamwork skills, familiarity is not enough. A team may have to experience the need for a best practice before they appreciate its value and are motivated to use it and really learn it.

Example A.1   Teams start out knowing that it is important for them to communicate, to meet regularly, to have an agenda, to prepare ahead of time, and to take notes during the meetings. If nothing else, they can ask each other variants of the three Scrum questions:

1   What did I do yesterday?
2   What do I plan to do today?
3   Are there any obstacles?

Yet, the need for better communication appears regularly in the reflections sections of status reports. Familiarity with a practice is not the same as experiencing the consequences of inadequate usage of the practice.

Communication typically improves as a project progresses!   □

A.1.2   The Team Experience

The preferred team size is four. Three works, but five has not worked as well for the projects that students tend to pick at Arizona.

Scrum Roles and Events   Scrum is strongly recommended for a team project. Teams benefit from Scrum's structured roles and events. Within that structure, they have the flexibility to choose their projects and development practices. The next example illustrates the value of structure. It illustrates how one team learned that the team experience is not the same as a social experience.

Example A.2   One student team decided that Scrum was not for them. They began with:

"We're good friends. We see each other every day. We're all equals. We don't need roles and a [development] process."

At the end of the first status review they assigned roles: product owner, scrum master, developers. Why? Because they were well behind not only the other teams, they were behind their own plans.   □

Iterations and Reviews   The proposed timeline in Fig. A.1 defines three-week iterations that end with review events. The content of the iterations is outlined by the proposal and status templates. The reviews consist of presentations and demos in class. Having something to show in class can be a powerful motivator.

Students often report that the project and the team experiences were the best part of the course. One team showed up for the final demo in matching T-shirts: light blue with the team team name on the back. Appreciations for the course content have tended to come later, after they get to the workplace.

A.1.3   Coupling the Classroom and Project Experiences

The suggested approach is to first lay out a project timeline as in Fig. A.1, and then set the concepts timeline. The duration of the project depends on the programming maturity of the incoming students.

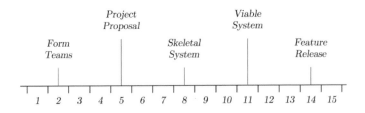

Figure A.1   Suggested timeline for a semester-long team project.

A shorter project allows more time for concepts to be covered in class before they are needed for the project. A longer project is suitable for students who have had the experience of writing a program with a few modules and a user interface. Presumably, they were given a specification and perhaps implementation tips.

The rest of this section explores the linkages between the project and concepts tracks.

Initial Alignment

Processes and requirements are appropriate topics to cover early. Incoming students are not expected to have worked on a team. They may or may not have been exposed to development processes. They are not expected to have had to write requirements. Processes and requirements are also needed early for the projects. With respect to the timeline in Fig. A.1, alignment between the concepts and project tracks comes naturally for the first third of the course.

Cover Scrum in the first two weeks to allow students to choose roles as they form teams. Then, introduce requirements and user stories, so teams can elicit customer needs and write user requirements for their project proposals.

Most teams begin with the needs articulated by users. Requirements changes, if any, are part of the learning experience.

Architecture Student projects frequently have variants of the following architecture: a user interface or two, some application logic, a database, and (potentially) access to external services, such as a map service. This architecture is similar to the one in Example 1.7 about pool-service technicians. (At Arizona, some projects have only a web interface, some only a mobile interface, and some have both.)

A predictable architecture allows projects to be launched before design and architecture are fully covered in the classroom. For a semester-long project, we have assumed that students have had the experience of building a user interface. They can therefore start development once their project proposals are done.

Testing Given the importance of testing, an overview appears in Section 1.4, test-driven development is discussed with XP in Section 2.3, and levels of testing (unit, functional, integration, system, acceptance) are introduced with V processes in Section 2.5. Thus, testing can be introduced early in a course. Testing after every change increases confidence in the code during coding and can save debugging time.

Test adequacy criteria based on code and input coverage appear in Chapter 9.

Proposal and Status Reports These reports serve two purposes. First, they ask leading questions to guide project activities; for example, the proposal asks about the customer, their needs within the context of an end-to-end experience, and the proposed benefit to be provided by the project.

Second, the reports serve as touch points between the concepts and project tracks. They ask students to apply specific concepts to their projects:

Proidal   Write user stories for customer wants

Proposal	Write user stories for customer wants
Status Report 1	Write a use case for each main user goal
Status Report 2	Present a system architecture; see Section 6.5

If desired, the questions in the templates can be replaced by questions for other forms of user requirements, functional requirements, and system description, respectively. With the timeline in Fig. A.1, the reports are due in weeks 5, 8, and 11, respectively. The reports place a hopefully weak constraint on the concepts track.

A.2   Project Proposal

Between weeks 2 and 5 on the timeline in Fig. A.1, the teams propose a project, preferably one with a real customer (outside the team). They elicit requirements, set project goals, outline an implementation, and come up to speed on the tools and platforms that they will use. Meanwhile, the lectures cover user needs and requirements. The detailed questions in the proposal template enable the teams to work in parallel with the lectures.

During week 5, the teams present their proposals to the whole class. The feedback helps students tune their project goals. The goals have to be challenging enough, yet doable.

The proposal and the status reports build up to a comprehensive final report. All of the reports therefore have essentially the same sections. The proposal emphasizes the Customer Needs and Project Goals sections. Material from these sections can be reused in later reports.

Proposal Template

Note In this proposal and the reports, put information where it fits best. Avoid repeating the same information in a later section.

Descriptive Title Focused on the User Benefits

Team Name: Team Members

1. **Introduction**

   Opening Paragraph

   - What is the project?
   - What is the motivation for this project?
   - What is novel about it?
   - Anything else to orient the reader?

   Challenges

   - Briefly describe the main challenges for the team.
   - Briefly, how will you address them?
   - Is the technology known or new to the team?

2. **Customer Need**

    - Who is the primary customer, outside the team?
    - Who are the secondary stakeholders?
    - What do the stakeholders want? Why?
    - What is their desired overall experience?

    User Requirements

    - Write SMART user stories based on the stakeholder needs and wants. Use the "As a ... I want ... so that ..." template.
    - Write acceptance tests for the user stories, using the "Given ... when .... then ..." template.

3. **Project Goals**

    - What customer problem have you chosen to address?
    - In implementation-free terms, what user benefit will the system provide?
    - How will the benefit support the customer's desired overall experience?

    Measures of Success

    - Who outside the team have you tested the idea on?
    - Describe the real outside customer, if any.
    - How will you know whether the customer got their desired benefits?
    - What are your customer-centric measures of success?

4. **System Description**

    For this proposal, a rough draft of this section is enough.

    - Draw a block diagram to show how the proposed system will interact with external services, databases, and so on. Clearly mark the boundaries of the system.
    - Use the preceding diagram to introduce the system.
    - What are the main elements of the proposed system?

5. **Solution Approach**

    A brief rough draft of this section is enough for this proposal.

    - Briefly describe how the system will work.
    - What platforms, tools, libraries, and the like will you use?
    - How will you test it?
    - How will you evaluate the adequacy of your test strategy?

6. **Project Management**

Start a Change Log to track any changes to the project as described in this Proposal. For each entry in the Log, include four things: the date, description, motivation, and implications of the change.

- What development process will you use?
- What is a minimal working system that you plan to build in the upcoming iteration?
- What is your wish list of features for the proposed system?

Team Coordination

- How will you distribute and coordinate the work?
- How will you meet as a team? How often?
- What do you plan to accomplish during the meetings?

7. **Team**

Backgrounds

- What are the backgrounds of the team members?
- Any prior internships or work experience related to software development?
- Has anyone on the team built something like this before?
- Are the tools known or new to the team?

Roles

- What are the planned roles for the team members during this project?

8. **Constraints and Risks**

- Are there any social, ethical, policy, or legal constraints?
- Will you have access to the data, services, and resources you need?
- Is there anything else you might need?

A.3   Skeletal System: Status Report 1

The purpose of Status Report 1 is twofold: maintain momentum on the project, and provide functional requirements in the form of use cases. As described in Chapter 5, a well-written collection of use cases provides an overview of a system. More precisely, the user goals provide an overview, and the basic flows describe the desired functionality.

Status Report 1 introduces a Reflection section for teams to look back over what went well and what didn't. Teams often get better at following processes and at communicating as the semester progresses.

Status Report 1 Template

Note Again, avoid duplication of information.
  Project Title

Team Name: Team Members

1. **Introduction**

   Highlights

      – What was the plan for this iteration?
      – Highlight what the team accomplished.

   Changes

      – Summarize any major changes since the Proposal.
      – Include the date, motivation, description, and implications of each change.
      – If there were none, simply note that there were no changes.

2. **Customer Need**

      – Briefly describe the customer's desired overall experience.

3. **Project Goals**

      – Summarize the customer problem addressed by the project.
      – What benefits will the project provide?

   Use Cases

      – Write a use case for each main user goal for a primary or secondary
        customer.
      – Show the title, user goal, and full basic flow for each use case. Choose
        meaningful titles.
      – For alternative flows on your wish list for implementation, give only the
        title, a one-line description, and how the alternative flow connects with its
        basic flow.

4. **System Description**

      – Introduce the system and the main challenges.

5. **Current Status**

      – Any goals for this iteration, beyond what is in the Introduction?
      – What's working? Include screenshots.

    — Any challenges?
    — Use a block diagram to explain the current state of the system.
    — What tests have you run?
    — How many lines of code have you written, collectively?

6. **Project Management**

Continue to maintain the Change Log. Add any new changes to the project, tracking the date, motivation, description, and implications of each change.

    — Show the Change Log to date.
    — What are the goals for the next iteration?
    — What is the plan for the rest of the semester?

7. **Team**

    — What were the team roles for this iteration?
    — What did each team member contribute?
    — Give rough estimates of the percentage contributions to the project by each team member.

8. **Reflection**

    — What went well?
    — What didn't go well?
    — For the goals that were not met, what were the issues?
    — How do you plan to overcome the issues?
    — What do you plan to do differently in the next iteration?

A.4   Viable System: Status Report 2

By week 11, the basic functionality is expected to be implemented and available for a demo. The focus of Status Report 2 is on the System Description and Current Status sections. For the system description, the report follows the approach of Section 6.5.

Avoid unnecessary duplication while describing the system. Put information where it fits best, between the Introduction and the parts of the System Description.

Status Report 2 Template

Project Title

Team Name: Team Members

1. **Introduction**

   Highlights

   - What was the plan for this iteration?
   - Highlight what the team accomplished.

   Changes

   - Summarize any major changes since the Proposal.
   - Include the date, motivation, description, and implications of each change.
   - If there were none, simply note that there were no changes.

2. **Customer Need**

   - Briefly describe the customer's desired overall experience.

3. **Project Goals**

   - Summarize the customer problem addressed by the project.
   - What benefits will the project provide?

4. **System Description**

   System Overview

   - Introduce the system and the main challenges.
   - Summarize the rationale for the design.
   - Draw a Context Diagram showing how the system interacts with external services, databases, and so on. Clearly mark the boundaries of the system.
   - Briefly explain the system's external interactions.

   Guides to the Main Architectural Views

   - For each view, provide a Primary Diagram.
   - For the architectural elements in a Primary Diagram, provide an Element Catalog with the name and purpose of each element.
   - For each element, identify a single owner on the team, even if multiple team members are contributing to the element.

5. **Current Status**

   - Any goals for this iteration, beyond what is in the Introduction?
   - What's working? Include screenshots.
   - Any challenges?
   - Use a block diagram to explain the current state of the system.
   - What tests have you run?
   - How many lines of code have you written, collectively?

6. **Project Management**

Continue to maintain the Change Log. Add any new changes to the project, tracking the date, motivation, description, and implications of each change.

- Show the Change Log to date.
- What are the goals for the next iteration?
- What is the plan for the rest of the semester?

7. **Team**

- What were the team roles for this iteration?
- What did each team member contribute?
- Give rough estimates of the percentage contributions to the project by each team member.

8. **Reflection**

- What went well?
- What didn't go well?
- For the goals that were not met, what were the issues?
- How do you plan to overcome the issues?
- What do you plan to do differently in the next iteration?

A.5   Comprehensive Final Report

The Final Report is intended to be the one source to consult for an overview of any aspect of the project. It is expected to include updated information about the customer value from the Proposal, about the problem definition from Status Report 1, and about the system description from Status Report 2. The Reflection section is for a retrospective look at the entire project. Feel free to reuse content from the previous reports, including the user stories, use cases, the Context Diagram, and the Guides for the architectural views.

Final Report Template

Descriptive Title Focused on the User Benefits

Team Name: Team Members

1. **Introduction**

Opening Paragraph

- What is the project?
- What was the motivation for the project?

- What is novel about it?
- Anything else to orient the reader?

Challenges

- Briefly describe the main challenges for the team.
- How did you address them?
- Was the technology known or new to the team?

Highlights

- Highlight what was accomplished.

Changes

- Summarize any major changes to any aspect of the project during the semester.
- Include the date, motivation, description, and implications of each change.

2. **Customer Need**

- Who is the primary customer, outside the team?
- Describe the real customer, if there is one.
- Who are the secondary stakeholders?
- What are the stakeholder wants? Why?
- What is their desired overall experience?

User Requirements

- Include SMART user stories, written using the "As a . . . I want . . . so that . . ." template.
- Include acceptance tests for the user stories, using the "Given . . . when . . . . then . . ." template.

3. **Project Goals**

- What customer problem did you choose to address?
- In implementation-free terms, what user benefits does your system provide?
- How does the benefit support the customer's desired overall experience?
- Who did you validate the idea with?

Use Cases

- Include a use case for each main user goal for a primary or secondary customer.
- Show the title, user goal, and full basic flow for each use case. Choose meaningful titles.

- For alternative flows that have been implemented, give only the title, a one-line description, and how the alternative flow connects with its basic flow.

Measures of Success

- How do you know whether the customer got their desired benefits?
- What are your customer-centric measures of success?

4. System Description

System Overview

- Introduce the system and the main challenges.
- Summarize the rationale for the design.
- Include a Context Diagram showing how the system interacts with external services, databases, and so on. Clearly mark the boundaries of the system.
- Briefly explain the system's external interactions.

Guides to the Main Architectural Views

- For each view, provide a Primary Diagram.
- For the architectural elements in a Primary Diagram, provide an Element Catalog with the name and purpose of each element.
- For each element, identify the single owner in the team, even if multiple team members contributed to the element.

5. Final Status

- What works? Include screen shots.
- What tests have you run?
- Estimate the adequacy of your tests.
- How many lines of code has the team written altogether?

6. Project Management

- Describe your actual development process.
- What were the major events during the project? Include dates.
- Anything else?

Team Coordination

- When and how often did the team meet?
- How else did you communicate?
- What did you accomplish during the meetings?
- How else did you communicate?

7. **Team**

   Backgrounds

   - What were the backgrounds of the team members?
   - Did anyone have prior internships or work experience related to software?
   - Had anyone on the team built something like this before?
   - Were the tools known or new to the team?

   Roles

   - What were the roles of the team members during this project?
   - What did each team member contribute?
   - Use the Element Catalogs to identify individual contributions.
   - Give rough estimates of percentage contributions by each team member.

8. **Constraints and Risks**

   - Were there any social, ethical, policy, or legal constraints?
   - Did you have access to the data, services, and resources you needed?
   - Was there anything else you needed?

9. **Reflection**

   - What were the lessons learned from doing this project?
   - What went well?
   - Which of your practices would you consider to be best practices?
   - What didn't go well?
   - What isn't working and how did you work around it?
   - For the features that were not implemented, what were the issues?

   Recommendations

   - What would you do differently?
   - What advice do you have for other teams?

Notes

Notes for the Preface

1 Guideline 9 in the 2014 IEEE-ACM software engineering curriculum guidelines [93, p. 43] stresses the importance of continual learning.

Notes for Chapter 1: Introduction

1 The definition of software engineering is adapted from the IEEE definition by adding customers and constraints. From SWEBOK 3.0 [36, p. 29], the IEEE definition is: software engineering is the "application of a systematic, disciplined, quantifiable approach to the development, operation, and maintenance of software; that is, the application of engineering to software."

2 Boehm [30] writes, "On my first day on the job [around 1955], my supervisor showed me the GD ERA 1103 computer, which filled a large room. He said, 'Now listen. We are paying $600 an hour for this and $2 an hour for you, and I want you to act accordingly.'"

3 The focus of the 1968 NATO conference was on the "many current problems in software engineering." See [143, p. 13–14].

4 Dean's advice on scaling of software systems is from his talk to a Stanford class [59].

5 Example 1.3, with the speech-therapy program, is from an article in an 1843 magazine [124].

6 Gomez and Hunt [80] describe the algorithms behind Netflix's recommender system.

7 In a classic paper, Brooks [38] argues that software is intrinsically complex.

8 Example 1.7 is motivated by a student project by Michael Carolin, Jacob Groh, Dan Decina, and Austin George [refpool-2017].

9 Miller [136] notes that "the accuracy with which we can identify absolutely the magnitude of a unidimensional stimulus variable . . . is usually somewhere in the neighborhood of seven." Unidimensional refers to like chunks of information, such as bits, words, colors, and tones. Faces and objects differ from one another along multiple dimensions, hence we can accurately distinguish hundreds of faces and thousands of objects.

10 Example 1.8 is based on a congressional hearing into the loss of Mariner 1 [180, pp. 100–101].

11 For more on the issues that arise during testing, see the "practice tutorial" by Whittaker [190].

12 Martin Barnes is credited with creating the Iron Triangle for a 1969 course [187]. Trilemmas have been discussed in philosophy for centuries.

13 Software project management builds on project management in general. The Project Management Institute publishes PMBOK, a guide to the project management body of knowledge [154].

14 Wikipedia has a comprehensive article entitled "Volkswagen emissions scandal."

15 The Therac-25 accidents were never officially investigated. Leveson and Turner [126] relied on court documents, correspondence, and information from regulatory agencies to

infer information about the manufacturer's software development, management, and quality control practices. See also [125].

16 The Bauer definition of software engineering is by Fritz Bauer [15], one of the organizers of the 1968 NATO workshop [143]. The SEI definition was created by the Software Engineering Institute for planning and explaining their own activities [69]. The IEEE definition is from [36, p. 29].

17 Parnas [150, p. 415] credits Brian Randell with the characterization of software engineering as "multi-person development of multi-version programs."

18 The list of forces in Exercise 1.3 is from an ACM SIGSOFT webinar by Booch.

19 The code in Exercise 1.5 is based on an example in [123] of function self-application. Apologies to Henry Ledgard for taking his code out of context.

Notes for Chapter 2: Software Development Processes

1 "Who will do what by when and why" is a variant of Boehm's [28, p. 76] "Why, What, When, Who, Where, How, How Much."

2 Madden and Rone [128] describe the iterative process used for the parallel development of the hardware, software, and simulators for the Space Shuttle.

3 Larman and Basili [121] trace the roots of iterative and agile methods to the "plan-do-study-act" quality improvement cycles proposed by Walter Shewhart at Bell Labs in the 1930s.

4 The Unix practices in Section 2.1.3 are from McIlroy, Pinson, and Tague's foreword to a 1978 collection of papers on Unix [135].

5 Agile Manifesto: ©2001 by Kent Beck, Mike Beedle, Arie van Bennekum, Alistair Cockburn, Ward Cunningham, Martin Fowler, James Grenning, Jim Highsmith, Andrew Hunt, Ron Jeffries, Jon Kern, Brian Marick, Robert C. Martin, Steve Mellor, Ken Schwaber, Jeff Sutherland, and Dave Thomas. The Agile Manifesto may be freely copied in any form, but only in its entirety through this notice. http://agilemanifesto.org/

6 Fowler [73].

7 The Agile Alliance provides a short history of "Agile" [2].

8 The definition of agile method follows the Agile Alliance's description of agile software development [2].

9 The 2019 State of Agile Survey [52] found that 58% of agile projects used Scrum by itself; 85% used Scrum or a hybrid.

10 The "Definitive Guide" by Scrum's creators, Schwaber and Sutherland [167] is the primary reference for Section 2.2.

11 Beck 16] is an early paper on XP. It includes a brief description of the roots of XP. The quote about taking practices to the extreme is from [17].

12 The 3C acronym for Card, Conversation, Confirmation is due to Jeffries [100].

13 In an early study with undergraduates, Cockburn and Williams [49] found that pair programming added 15% to the cost of programming. A decade later, a review by Wray [194] concluded: "We are no longer in the first flush of pair programming, yet the gulf between enthusiasts and critics seems as wide as ever."

14 Fowler [72] attributes the acronym *yagni* to a conversation between Kent Beck and Chet Hendrickson, in which Hendrickson proposed a series of features to each of which Beck replied, "you aren't going to need it."

15 In the second edition of *Extreme Programming Explained* [17, ch. 7], Beck notes that some of the teams misinterpreted the first edition as recommending deferring design until the last moment – they created brittle, poorly designed systems.

16 Beck and Andres [17] open with, "Extreme Programming (XP) is about social change." The premise of XP is from [17, ch. 17].

17 Benington [20] is the earliest known published account of a waterfall process. The diagram in Fig. 2.9 is based on an influential 1970 paper by Royce [159]. Royce did not use the term

"waterfall." It came later. While Royce is often credited as the source for waterfall processes, the paper includes, "In my experience, however, the simpler [waterfall] method has never worked on large software development efforts."

18 The committee chairman's opening remarks are from [181, p. 2]. For the extent of system and end-to-end testing, see [181, p. 57]. The cost of the website is from [182, p. 19].

19 The chart on the cost of fixing a defect is due to Boehm [30, 24].

20 During a 2002 workshop [169], projects from IBM Rochester reported a 13:1 in the cost of a fix between coding and testing, and then a further 9:1 between testing and operation. Toshiba's software factory with 2,600 workers reported a 137:1 ratio for the time needed to fix a severe defect before and after shipment.

21 US government contracts promoted the use of waterfall processes through standards such as MIL-STD-1521B, dated June 4, 1985 [179].

22 Figure 2.11 is from Siy and Perry [170].

23 The V-shaped process diagram for SAGE in Fig. 2.12 is a redrawing of the original diagram. Paraphrasing Benington [20], a programmer must prove that the program satisfies the specifications, not that the program will perform as coded. Furthermore, "test specifications . . . can be prepared in parallel with coding."

24 The right-product/product-right characterization of validation and verification is due to Boehm [25].

25 The Internet Tidal Wave reference is from the title of an internal Microsoft memo by Gates [77]. The sleeping giant allusion is from Gates's opening comments at Microsoft's December 1995 analysts conference [55, p. 109]

26 Cusumano and Yoffie [55, p. 251] relate how the initial requirements for Netscape 3.0 were set. They quote Bill Turpin, "The original way we came up with the product ideas was that Marc Andreessen was sort of our product marketing guy. He went out and met with lots of customers. He would meet with analysts. He would see what other new companies were doing."

27 Iansiti and MacCormack [91] note that by the late 1990s, companies in a wide range of industries "from computer workstations to banking" had adopted iterative product development to deal with uncertain and unexpected requirements changes.

28 For the challenges faced by the Netscape Communicator 4.0 project, see the remarks by Rick Schell, senior engineering executive [55, p. 187].

29 See Boehm [29] for more on the Spiral Framework. An early version of the framework appears in [27]. The treatment in Section 2.7 follows [29], where Boehm emphasizes that the framework is not a process model. He describes it as a "risk-driven process model generator."

30 Benington described the experimental prototype in a fresh Foreword when his 1956 paper on SAGE was reprinted in 1983 [20]. He also noted, "I do not mention it in the [1956] paper, but we undertook the programming only after we had assembled an experimental prototype."

31 Example 2.19 is due to Boehm [31].

32 2019 State of Agile Report [52].

33 Jalote [99, p. 37] describes the Infosys development process. Infosys is known for its highly mature processes.

Notes for Chapter 3: User Requirements

1 The definition of the term requirement is adapted from Zave's description of requirements engineering [195].

2 Example 3.1 on the failed BBC Digital Media Initiative is based on a report by the UK National Audit Office [142] and a news report [79].

3 The Fast Feedback process in Fig. 3.4 is adapted from the Fast Feedback Cycle in De Bonte and Fletcher [58].

4 IEEE Standard 830-1998 includes the characteristics of a good SRS [92, pp. 4–8] and several templates for writing an SRS [92, pp. 21–26].

5 The classification of needs in Section 3.3.1 is adapted from Sanders [162, 163]. She writes about a "shift in attitude from designing **for** users to one of designing **with** users" [163].

6 The Scott Cook quote about basing future products on customer actions, not words, is from [175, p. 221].

7 Example 3.9 is motivated by a student project by Yikai Cao, Marcos Gomez, Hui Du, Martina Mitchell, and Anh Nam Tran [42]. The prototype Lunar Greenhouse at the University of Arizona has a hydroponic plant-growth chamber. It is intended as a bio-regenerative life support system. https://cals.arizona.edu/lunargreenhouse/.

8 Rogers's classic 1952 paper [158] on listening was reprinted by *Harvard Business Review* in 1991.

9 Griffin and Hauser [82] refer to Voice of the Customer as an industry practice.

10 For Intuit's Design for Delight: see, for example, Ruberto [160].

11 Rabinowitz [155] outlines the development of Intuit's QuickBooks app for the iPad.

12 The INVEST checklist for user stories is attributed to William Wake.
https://xp123.com/articles/invest-in-good-stories-and-smart-tasks.

13 Dan North [145] created the template for acceptance tests with Chris Matts. "We started describing the acceptance criteria in terms of scenarios, which took the 'Given-when-then' form."

14 The stylized English syntax for features in Table 3.2 is adapted from Mavin and Wilkinson [131].

15 For an in-depth treatment of user-experience (UX) scenarios, see the book on Scenario-Focused Engineering by De Bonte and Fletcher [58]. The book uses the term "scenario" by itself.

16 Example 3.16 is motivated by a student project by Kristoffer Cabulong and Trevor Scott Fasulo [41].

17 SMART criteria originated in a business setting. They are attributed to Peter Drucker's management by objectives. The acronym SMART is attributed to Doran [62].

18 The temporal classification of goals is from Dardenne, Lamsweerde, and Fickas [57]. See Lamsweerde [119] for a retrospective account.

19 Lamsweerde, Darimont, and Massonet [120] write, "*why* questions allow higher-level goals to be acquired from goals that contribute positively to them. . . . *how* questions allow lower level goals to be acquired as subgoals that contribute positively to the goal considered."

20 Goal analysis appears to have been independently reinvented in multiple contexts. Lamsweerde [118] provides a guided tour of research on goal-oriented requirements engineering. Basili and Weiss [13] advocate the use of goals to drive data collection and measurement. Schneier [165] introduces attack trees for identifying potential security attacks.

21 Lamsweerde [117] notes, "This [BART] case study is appealing for a number of reasons: it is a real system; it is a complex real-time safety-critical system; the initial document was provided by an independent source involved in the development."

Notes for Chapter 4: Requirements Analysis

1 The useful, usable, and desirable views of products build on Sanders [162].

2 A review in the New York Times, June 3, 2017, p. B1 found recent smartphones to be innovative but uninviting.

3 The terms cognitive bias and anchoring are due to Tversky and Kahneman [178].

4 Example 4.2 is based on a case study by Aranda and Easterbrook [8].

5 From Aristotle [9, Book 3, Part 11], "the many, of whom each individual is an ordinary person, when they meet together may very likely be better than the few . . . for some understand one part, and some another, and among them they understand the whole."

6 Example 4.5 is based on Smith and Sidky [171, ch. 14].

7 Dalkey and Helmer [56] describe the original Delphi method. They observe that a roundtable "induces the hasty formulation of preconceived notions, an inclination to close one's mind to novel ideas, a tendency to defend a stand once taken or, alternatively and sometimes alternately, a predisposition to be swayed by persuasively stated opinions of others." See Helmer [85] for a retrospective on the Delphi method.

8 Boehm [26, p. 335] is credited with the Wideband Delphi method.

9 See Cohn [51, ch. 6] for Planning Poker.

10 Three-point estimation is based on a statistical model developed for time estimates in conjunction with an operations research technique called PERT. Moder, Phillips, and Davis [139, ch. 9] discuss the statistical underpinnings of the weighted-average formula for Three-Point Estimation. PERT (Program Evaluation and Review Technique) is a project-management tool that was developed for the US Navy in the 1950s.

11 Clegg, Barker, and Barker [45, p. 27] describe MoSCoW prioritization.

12 Cohn [51, ch. 9] is the source for the two-step method in Section 4.4.3 for prioritization based on value, cost, and risk.

13 Kano [108] is the source for the treatment of Kano analysis in Section 4.5. The oft-cited paper by Kano et al. [109] is in Japanese.

14 Kano analysis is included in De Bonte and Fletcher's [58] description of Scenario Focused Engineering at Microsoft.

15 Herzberg [87, ch. 6] et al. interviewed 200 engineers and accountants to test the hypothesis that people have two sets of needs: "the need as an animal to avoid pain" and "the need as a human to grow psychologically." They asked about times when the interviewees felt especially good about their jobs and probed for the reasons behind the good feelings. In separate interviews, they asked about negative feelings about the job. The results from the study were that satisfiers were entirely different from dissatisfiers. Herzberg et al. used the term "motivators" for job satisfiers and the term "hygiene" for job dissatisfiers. The corresponding terms in this chapter are *attractors* and *expected* features.

16 Clippy was included in Microsoft Office for Windows versions 97 through 2003, according to the Wikipedia article entitled, "Office Assistant." A USA Today article dated February 6, 2002 noted, "The anti-Clippy site has gotten 22 million hits since launching April 11." [184].

17 See the TeXShop Change History [176].

18 Jørgensen [106] reviews "what we do and don't know about software development effort estimation." See also the friendly debate between Jørgensen and Boehm [107] about expert judgment versus formal models.

19 Diagrams similar to the Cone of Uncertainty were in use in the 1950s for cost estimation for chemical manufacturing [144]. Boehm [26, p. 311] introduced the Cone as a conceptual diagram for software estimation. Supporting data came much later; see Boehm et al. [32].

20 Results from numerous studies, going back to the 1960s, support the observation that there are order-of-magnitude differences in individual and team productivity. From early studies by Sackman, Erikson, and Grant [161], "one poor performer can consume as much time or cost as 5, 10, or 20 good ones." McConnell [132] outlines the challenges of defining, much less measuring software productivity.

21 Boehm and Valerdi's [33] review of the Cocomo family of formal models includes some historical perspective on models.

22 Walston and Felix [186] provide IBM data from the 1970s for estimating effort from program size. The data for the TRW effort-size curve is from Boehm [26].

23 Boehm and Valerdi [33] note that "although Cocomo II does a good job for the 2005 development styles projected in 1995, it doesn't cover several newer development styles well. This led us to develop additional Cocomo II-related models."

Notes for Chapter 5: Use Cases

1 Jacobson [96] provides a retrospective on use cases. He first presented them at OOP-SLA '87 [95].

2 The ATM use case in Example 5.6 is based on a fully worked-out use case in Bittner and Spence [22], which Ivar Jacobson, the inventor of use cases, called "THE book on use cases" [96].

3 As part of a discussion of user-interface design, Constantine and Lockwood discuss use cases at three levels: intentions, interactions, and interfaces [53].

4 The suggested order for evolving a use case is motivated by Cockburn [47, p. 17].

5 Jacobson, Spence, and Kerr [98] provide six principles for use cases: three for writing and three for using use cases to drive iterative development.

6 Petre [151, p. 728] conducted "interviews with 50 professional software engineers in 50 companies and found 5 patterns of UML use," ranging from no use of UML (70%) to selective use (22%) and wholehearted use (0%). Several participants mentioned informal usage of use cases. Only one of the 50 developers found use-case diagrams to be useful.

7 In a chapter entitled "Here There Be Dragons," Bittner and Spence [22] note that the behavior of most systems can be specified without inclusions and extensions.

8 For a discussion of use cases and user stories, see Cockburn [48] and the accompanying comments.

9 Beck [16] introduced user stories along with XP.

10 The description in Exercise 5.4 is adapted from the "Background and functionality" section of the Wikipedia entry for HealthCare.gov. https://en.wikipedia.org/wiki/HealthCare.gov . Text used under the Creative Commons CC-BY-SA 3.0 license.

Notes for Chapter 6: Design and Architecture

1 Based on the experience at the Software Engineering Institute (SEI), Kazman and Eden [110] observe, "In practice, the terms 'architecture,' 'design,' and 'implementation' appear to connote varying degrees of abstraction in the continuum between complete details ('implementation'), few details ('design'), and the highest form of abstraction ('architecture')." They propose the following: architecture is nonlocal and design is local, where nonlocal means that the specification applies "to all parts of the system (as opposed to being limited to some part thereof)."

2 Klein and Weiss [112] note: "Architecture is a part of the design of the system; it highlights some details by abstracting away from others."

3 The version of Conway's law [54] in Box 6.1, is from his website www.melconway.com/Home/Conways_Law.html .

4 From Vitruvius's *de Architectura*, Book 1, Chapter 3, Verse 2: "All these should possess strength, utility, and beauty. Strength arises from carrying down the foundations to a good solid bottom, and from making a proper choice of materials without parsimony. Utility arises from a judicious distribution of the parts, so that their purposes be duly answered, and that each have its proper situation. Beauty is produced by the pleasing appearance and good taste of the whole, and by the dimensions of all the parts being duly proportioned to each other." http://penelope.uchicago.edu/Thayer/E/Roman/Texts/Vitruvius/1*.html

5 Parnas [147] stressed the importance of modularity and implementation hiding.

6 Boklen [34] decoded the 1862 message by General Edmund Kirby-Smith of the Confederate army. The paper includes an image of the document with the message.

7 Stevens, Myers, and Constantine [174] introduce the concepts of coupling and "cohesiveness" (cohesion), which they attribute to Larry Constantine.

8 The first guideline for module design is from Parnas [147]. The remaining guidelines are based on Britton and Parnas [37, pp. 1–2].

9 Savor et al. [164] describe continuous deployment at Facebook and OANDA.

10 See [35] for a user guide by the original authors of UML. The preface includes a brief history of UML. Grady Booch and James Rumbaugh created an early draft of UML in 1994, by combining their object-oriented design methods. They were soon joined by Ivar Jacobson, and expanded the UML effort to incorporate his methods. UML 1.1 was adopted as a standard by Object Management Group (OMG) in 1997. The UML 2.0 standard was adopted in 2005.

In a 2006 interview, Jacobson observed, "UML 2.0 has become very large, it has become heavy, it's very hard to learn and study" [97]. UML has strong name recognition, but actual usage lags. A 2013 survey by Scott Ambler, an author of UML books, found that while all 162 respondents had heard of UML, "Only 13% found UML to be very useful, and 45% indicated that UML was useful but they could get by without it. A further 20% found it 'more trouble than it was worth'" [6].

11 According to a Wikipedia article, the parable of the blind philosophers and an elephant is an ancient Indian tale. A version appears in a Buddhist text, *Udana 6.4*, dated to about mid 1st millennium BCE.

12 Views have been incorporated into the standards IEEE 1471 and ISO/IEC/IEEE 42010.

13 The 4+1 grouping of architectural views is due to Kruchten [114].

14 The Greek philosopher Eratosthenes is credited with the sieve method for computing prime numbers. McIlroy [134] "cooked up" the prime-number sieve in Example 6.14 for a 1968 talk on coroutines.

15 The SEI list of definitions of software architecture has third modern, nine classic, and numerous bibliographic definitions [172].

16 The definition of software architecture is from Bass, Clements, and Kazman [14]. The authors were all at SEI when they published the first two editions of their book.

17 The approach to architecture description in Section 6.5 is adapted from Clements et al. [46]. View guides generalize the concept of module guides promoted by Parnas [37].

18 LaToza, Venolia, and DeLine [122] asked Microsoft architects, developers, and testers if they agreed with whether specific statements represented a "serious problem" for them. From the results, seven of the top eight concerns related to software architecture. Architecture cannot help with the number two concern: "Having to switch tasks often because of . . . teammates or manager. [62% agreed.]"

19 Example 6.16 is based on the work of Geppert and Roessler [78].

Notes for Chapter 7: Architectural Patterns

1 For Alexander's work on patterns, see [5]. In their book on software design patterns, Gamma et al. acknowledge, "The Alexandrian point of view has helped us focus on design trade-offs – the different 'forces' that help shape a design." [74, p. 356]. Shaw [166] writes, "[Alexander's patterns] helped shape my views on software architecture." Beck [16] notes the influence of Alexander's writings on Extreme Programming, especially the belief that the occupiers of a building should design it.

2 The cross section of the Hagia Sophia is from Lübke and Semrau [127]; see https://commons.wikimedia.org/wiki/File:Hagia-Sophia-Laengsschnitt.jpg .

3 Johnson and Ritchie [102] describe the Unix portability project in 1977. At the time, "Transportation of an operating system and its software between non-trivially different machines [was] rare, but not unprecedented." The three main goals were: write a portable C compiler, refine the C language, and port Unix by rewriting it in C.

4 Reenskaug's May 1979 proposal for the Smalltalk user interface is entitled Thing-Model-View-Editor [156]. *Thing* referred to the application, "something that is of interest to the user," *model* to the objects that represent the thing, *view* to a "pictorial representation" of the model, and *editor* to "an interface between the user and one or more views." "After long discussions," the editor was renamed *controller*.

5 See Fowler [71] for the evolution and variants of model-view-controller architectures.

6 The humble approach is motivated by Feather [67].

7 Fowler [71] notes that the VisualWorks variant of Smalltalk put view-specific logic into a component called Application Model, which fit between the model and the relevant controller. Later MVC architectures merged the equivalent of the Application Model into the controller.

8 McIlroy's comments about a catalog of standard components are from [133].

9 For named pipes on Windows, see https://msdn.microsoft.com/en-us/library/windows/desktop/aa365574%28v=vs.85%29.aspx. Accessed July 13, 2015.

10 Example 7.15 is motivated by the Spotify music streaming service [130].

11 Akidau et al. [4] explore issues related to unbounded streams and describe the processing model of Google Cloud Dataflow.

12 For MapReduce, see Dean and Ghemawat [60].

13 For the evolution of the Spotify event-delivery architecture, see the three-part description by Maravić, starting with [130].

14 The definition of product family is due to Parnas [148], who credits Edsger Dijkstra with the idea of a program family. Dijkstra [61] refers in passing to "a program as part of a family" of versions.

15 See http://splc.net/hall-of-fame/ for the Software Product Line Conferences Hall of Fame.

16 The HomeAway example is based on Kreuger, Churchett, and Buhrdorf [113].

17 Northrop [146] relates SEI's experience with product lines.

18 See Weiss and Lai [188] for the economics of product-line engineering at Bell Labs. David Weiss led a group in Bell Labs Research that worked closely with a small dedicated group in the business unit to support product-line engineering across the parent company, Lucent Technologies.

19 Plato's theory of Forms (or Ideas) appears in many of the dialogues, including *The Republic*. The excerpt in Exercise 7.1 is from Book X.

20 Exercise 7.6 is motivated by the T diagrams for a Java virtual machine in Grove and Rogers [81].

Notes for Chapter 8: Static Checking

1 Maranzano et al. [129] is the primary source for Section 8.1. The authors were all at Bell Labs when they began conducting architecture reviews in 1988. From their 700 reviews through 2005, between 29% and 49% of the design issues were categorized under "The proposed solution doesn't adequately solve the problem." Between 10% and 18% came under "The problem isn't completely or clearly defined."

2 The guiding principles for architecture reviews are adapted from Maranzano et al. [129] They "estimate that projects of 100,000 non-commentary source lines of code have saved an average of US$1 million each by identifying and resolving problems early."

3 Fagan [65] describes the early experience with software inspections at IBM. See also his subsequent paper on inspections [66]. See also the surveys [116, 10].

4 The Infosys data in Example 8.1 is from a book by Jalote [99] on project management at the Infosys.

5 Porter, Siy, Toman, and Votta found that there "was no difference between two- and four-person inspections, but both performed better than one-person inspections" [152, p. 338].

6 Porter and Votta [153] report on a study that found reviewers who used checklists were no more effective at finding defects than reviewers who used ad hoc techniques. Reviewers who used scenarios were more effective at finding defects.

7 Eick et al. [64, p. 64] found that 90% of defects were found during individual preparation. This data was collected as part of a study to estimate residual faults; that is, faults that remain in a completed system.

8 Votta [185] suggests two alternatives to group meetings: (a) "collect faults by deposition (small face-to-face meetings of two or three persons), or (b) collect faults using verbal or written media (telephone, electronic mail, or notes)."

9 Rigby et al. [157] review the "policies of 25 [open-source] projects and study the archival records of six large, mature, successful [open-source] projects." The six are Apache httpd server, Subversion, Linux, FreeBSD, KDE, and Gnome.

10 Mockus, Fielding, and Herbsleb found that 458 people contributed to the Apache server code and documentation [137, p. 311]; 486 people contributed code and 412 people contributed fixes to Mozilla [137, p. 333].

11 Rigby et al. [157, pp. 35:11–35:13] counted a median of two reviewers for Review-then-Commit and one reviewer for Commit-then-Review.

12 Henderson [86] describes code reviews at Google.

13 Holzmann [88, 89] describes the development of the software for the mission to land a rover on Mars.

14 Johnson [101] separated Lint out of his C compiler to provide optional stricter checks when needed. The name is motivated by lint on clothing.

15 For the SSL bug in iOS and Mac OS, see Bland [23].

16 David Hovemeyer "developed FindBugs as part of his PhD research . . . in conjunction with his thesis advisor William Pugh." [11] Example 8.4 is based on [90].

17 Bessey et al. [21] describe the challenges in commercializing the static analyzer, Coverity.

18 The checklist questions in Exercise 8.1 are from a seminal book on testing by Myers [140, pp. 22–32].

Notes for Chapter 9: Testing

1 The defective code in Fig. 9.1 is from the clock driver for the Freescale MC 13783 processor used by the Microsoft Zune 30 and Toshiba Gigabeat S media players [193]. The root cause of the failure on December 31, 2008 was isolated by "itsnotabigtruck" [94].

2 The Section 9.1.3 version of Dijkstra's famous quote about testing is from the second 1969 NATO Software Engineering conference [40, p. 16].

3 Example 9.3 is based on Weyuker [189].

4 For Example 9.4, primality testing is the problem of deciding whether a number n is a prime number. In 2002, Agrawal, Kayal, and Saxena showed that there is a deterministic polynomial algorithm for primality testing [3].

5 SWEBOK 3.0 merges system and functional testing into a single level [36, pp. 4–5]. The levels of testing in Section 9.2 assign the validation and verification roles to system and functional testing, respectively. The classic text on testing by Myers separates system and functional testing [140].

6 Jones has published summary data from 600 client companies [104]: "Many test stages such as unit test, function test, regression test, etc. are only about 35% efficient in finding code bugs, or find one bug out of three. This explains why 6 to 10 separate kinds of testing are needed."

7 The xUnit family began with Beck's automated testing framework for Smalltalk. In 1997, Smalltalk usage was on the decline and Java usage was on the rise, so Beck and Gamma created JUnit for Java. They had three goals for JUnit: make it natural enough that developers would actually use it; enable tests that retain their value over time; and leverage existing tests in creating new ones [18].

8 Parnas [149] introduced the "uses" relation as an aid for designing systems "so that subsets and extensions are more easily obtained." Incremental bottom-up integration corresponds to building a system by extension.

9 Myers [140, pp. 99–100] notes that a comparison between top-down and bottom-up integration testing "seems to give the bottom-up strategy the edge."

10 Zhu, Hall, and May [196] survey test coverage and adequacy criteria.

11 The leap-year specification is from the US Naval Observatory]183].

12 Myers [140, pp. 46–47] provides heuristic guidelines for equivalence partitioning.

13 MC/DC is included in RTCA document DO-178C [192]. ISO standard 26262-2011 Part 6 Table 12 requires MC/DC for automotive software.

  FAA Advisory Circular 20-115C, dated July 19, 2013, recognizes DO-178C as an "acceptable means, but not the only means, for showing compliance with the applicable airworthiness regulations for the software aspects of airborne systems."

14 While discussing industry trends in 2017, Ebert and Shankar [63] recommend MC/DC for detecting security back-doors.

15 Jones and Harrold [105] use pairs tables for MC/DC testing.

16 The NIST ACTS tool for combinatorial testing is available through GitHub: https://github.com/usnistgov/combinatorial-testing-tools.

17 For a NIST study of interaction failures for web servers, browsers, medical devices, and a NASA application, see Hagar et al. [84]. Web servers and browsers had more complex interaction failures.

18 D. M. Cohen et al. [50] show that for fixed t, the size of a t-way covering array grows logarithmically with the number of factors. They also describe heuristics for designing tests. The covering array with 13 tests for 10 factors in Table 9.5 is from Kuhn's keynote [115]. It also appears in Hagar et al. [84]. Garvin, M. B. Cohen, and Dwyer [75] explore an extension of combinatorial testing called constrained combinatorial testing, where "some features cannot coexist in a configuration."

19 The development process in Fig. 9.10 is from Benington's description of the SAGE air defense system [20].

Notes for Chapter 10: Quality Metrics

1 Lord Kelvin's observations on measurement, Box 10.1, are from [177, pp. 79–80].

2 Example 10.3 is based on an account by Clint Covington, Principal Program Manager Lead, Microsoft Office [58].

3 Basili and Weiss [13] advocate the use of goals to guide data collection and measurement: "Without goals, one runs the risk of collecting unrelated, meaningless data." Basili et al. [12] describe an approach that they call GQM$^+$Strategies, which extends the Goals-Questions-Metrics (GQM) approach of [13]. GQM$^+$Strategies starts with high-level goals that are refined into what they call "measurement" or "GQM" goals.

4 Garvin [76] synthesized the various definitions of quality for physical products into five approaches: "(1) the transcendental approach of philosophy; (2) the product-based approach of economics; (3) the user-based approach of economics, marketing, and operations management; (4) the manufacturing based and (5) the value-based approach of operations management." Kitchenham and Pfleeger [111] applied Garvin's model to software. The model in Fig. 10.2 uses "aesthetic" instead of "transcendental," "customer satisfaction" instead of "value,"and splits the user-based approach into two: functional and operations.

5 The definition of product quality follows Shewhart [168, p. 38].

6 Example 10.6 is based on email to Audris Mockus, dated May 14, 2014.

7 Buckley and Chillarege [39].

8 Stanley Smith Stevens proposed four levels of scales in 1946. The system has been challenged by theoreticians, especially the Nominal and Ordinal levels. Nevertheless, the Stevens system continues to be widely used; see the Wikipedia page for more information.

9 Anda, Sjøberg, and Mockus [7] studied reproducibility in software development by seeking firm-price bids from 81 companies for developing a system to the same requirements. The data in Fig. 10.3 shows the 35 bids. (Four contractors were selected to develop systems that were studied for two years after delivery.)

10 Gantt charts are named after Henry Gantt, who initially used them to measure worker productivity. See the Wikipedia page for more information.

11 The medians in Table 10.2, are from summary data provided by Jones [103, 104], reportedly from 600 client companies. There is other anecdotal data to support the observation that a combination of reviews, static analysis, and testing is highly effective for defect detection; for example, see Hackbarth, et al. [83].

12 CQM was introduced by Mockus and Weiss [138] under the name Interval Quality. Hackbarth, et al. [83] describe the use of CQM to drive quality improvement at Avaya.

13 The two images of distributions in Fig. 10.14 are from Wikimedia Commons. The image of the normal distribution is in the public domain. The image of the Student's t-distribution is by Skbkekas (February 22, 2010); used under the Creative Commons Attribution 3.0 Unported license: https://creativecommons.org/licenses/by/3.0/deed.en.

14 The Wikipedia article on Student's t-distribution credits Helmert and Lüroth with first deriving the distributions in 1876. William Sealy Gosset published them in English in 1908 under the pseudonym Student.

15 Begel and Zimmerman [19] describe how they collected and ranked questions that Microsoft engineers have for data scientists.

Notes for Appendix A: A Team Project

1 The ACM-IEEE curriculum guidelines for both computer science [1, p. 174] and software engineering [93, p. 45] strongly recommend a significant team project.

2 The ACM-IEEE curriculum guidelines have a learning hierarchy with three levels of mastery: Familiarity, Usage, and Assessment [1, p. 34]. The four levels in Section A.1 split Usage and rename Assessment. The levels and their descriptions were developed by a Computer Science curriculum committee at the University of Arizona.

References

[1] ACM/IEEE-CS. *Computer Science Curricula 2013*. ACM Press and IEEE Computer Society Press (December 2013).
DOI: http://dx.doi.org/10.1145/2534860 .

[2] Agile Alliance. Agile 101. Accessed January 21, 2019 at www.agilealliance.org/agile101/ .

[3] M. Agrawal, N. Kayal, and N. Saxena. Primes is in *P. Annals of Mathematics*, Second Series 160, 2 (September 2004) 781–793.

[4] T. Akidau, R. Bradshaw, C. Chambers, et al. The Dataflow Model: A practical approach to balancing correctness, latency, and cost in massive-scale, unbounded, out-of-order data processing. *Proceedings of the VLDB Endowment* 8, 12 (2015) 1792–1803.

[5] C. W. Alexander, S. Ishikawa, and M. Silverstein, with M. Jacobson, I. Fiksdahl-King, and S. Angel. *A Pattern Language*. Oxford University Press (1977).

[6] S. W. Ambler. UML 2.5: Do you even care? *Dr. Dobb's* (November 19, 2013). www.drdobbs.com/architecture-and-design/uml-25-do-you-even-care/240163 702.

[7] B. D. Anda, D. I. K. Sjøberg, and A. Mockus. Variability and reproducibility in software engineering: A study of four companies that developed the same system. *IEEE Transactions on Software Engineering* 35, 3 (May–June 2009) 407–429.

[8] J. Aranda and S. Easterbrook. Anchoring and adjustment in software estimation. *ESEC/FSE-13: Proceedings of the 10th European Software Engineering Conference Held Jointly with 13th ACM SIGSOFT International Symposium on Foundations of Software Engineering* (2005) 346–355.

[9] Aristotle. *Politics*. Translated by Benjamin Jowett. (n.d.). http://classics.mit.edu /Aristotle/politics.html

[10] A. Aurum, H. Petersson, and C. Wohlin. State-of-the-art: Software inspections after 25 years. *Software Testing, Verification and Reliability* 12, 3 (2002) 133–154.

[11] N. Ayewah, W. Pugh, D. H. Hovemeyer, J. D. Morgenthaler, and J. Penix. Using static analysis to find bugs. *IEEE Software* 25, 5 (September–October 2008) 22–29.

[12] V. R. Basili, M. Lindvall, M. Regardie, et al. Linking software development and business strategy through measurement. *IEEE Computer* 43, 4 (April 2010) 57–65.

[13] V. R. Basili and D. M. Weiss. A methodology for collecting valid software engineering data. *IEEE Transactions on Software Engineering* SE-10, 6 (November 1984) 728–738.

[14] L. J. Bass, P. Clements, and R. Kazman. *Software Architecture in Practice* (3rd ed.). Addison-Wesley (2013).

[15] F. L. Bauer. Software engineering. In *Information Processing 71: Proceedings of IFIP Congress 71*, Vol. 1, *Foundations and Systems.* North-Holland (1972) 530–538.

[16] K. Beck. Embracing change with Extreme Programming. *IEEE Computer* (October 1999) 70–77.

[17] K. Beck with C. Andres. *Extreme Programming Explained: Embrace Change*, 2nd ed. Addison-Wesley (2005).

[18] K. Beck and E. Gamma. JUnit: A cook's tour. (circa 1998). http://junit.sourceforge.net/doc/cookstour/cookstour.htm .

[19] A. Begel and T. Zimmermann. Analyze this! 145 questions for data scientists in software engineering. *Proceedings of the 36th International Conference on Software Engineering (ICSE)* (2014) 12–23.

[20] H. D. Benington. Production of large computer programs. *Symposium on Advanced Programming Methods for Digital Computers*, Office of Naval Research Symposium (June 1956). Reprinted with a foreword by the author in *IEEE Annals of the History of Computing* 5, 4 (October 1983) 350–361.

[21] A. Bessey, K. Block, B. Chelf, et al. A few billion lines of code later: Using static analysis to find bugs in the real world. *Communications of the ACM* 53, 2 (February 2010) 66–75.

[22] K. Bittner and I. Spence. *Use Case Modeling*. Addison-Wesley Professional (2003).

[23] M. Bland. Finding more than one worm in the apple. *Communications of the ACM* 57, 7 (July 2014) 58–64.

[24] B. W. Boehm. Software engineering. *IEEE Transactions on Computers* C-25, 12 (December 1976) 1226–1241.

[25] B. W. Boehm. Verifying and validating software requirements and design specifications. *IEEE Software* (January 1984) 75–88. A 1979 version is available as technical report USC-79-501. http://csse.usc.edu/TECHRPTS/1979/usccse79-501/usccse79-501.pdf.

[26] B. W. Boehm. *Software Engineering Economics* (1981). Prentice Hall PTR.

[27] B. W. Boehm. A spiral model of software development and enhancement. *Computer* 21, 5 (May 1988) 61–72.

[28] B. W. Boehm. Anchoring the software process. *IEEE Software* (July 1996) 73–82.

[29] B. W. Boehm. *Spiral Development: Experience, Principles, and Refinements.* Software Engineering Institute Report CMU/SEI-2000-SR-008 (July 2000). www.sei.cmu.edu/reports/00sr008.pdf

[30] B. W. Boehm. A view of 20th and 21st century software engineering. *Proceedings International Conference on Software Engineering (ICSE '06)* (2006) 12–29.

[31] B. W. Boehm. The Incremental Commitment Spiral Model (ICSM): Principles and practices for successful software systems. ACM Webinar (December 17, 2013). https://learning.acm.org/techtalks/icsm

[32] B. W. Boehm, B. Clark, E. Horowitz, et al. Cost models for future life cycle processes: COCOMO 2.0, *Annals of Software Engineering* 1, 1 (1995) 57–94.

[33] B. W. Boehm and R. Valerdi. Achievements and challenges in Cocomo-based software resource estimation. *IEEE Software* (September–October 2008) 74–83.

[34] K. D. Boklan. How I broke the Confederate code (137 years too late). *Cryptologia* 30 (2006) 340–345.
www.cwu.edu/ boersmas/cryptology/confederate%20code%20paper.pdf

[35] G. Booch, J. Rumbaugh, and I. Jacobson. *The Unified Modeling Language User Guide*, 2nd Ed. Addison-Wesley (2005).

[36] P. Bourque and R. E. Fairley (eds). *Guide to the Software Engineering Body of Knowledge (SWEBOK), Version 3.0*. IEEE Computer Society (2014).
www.swebok.org .

[37] K. H. Britton and D. L. Parnas. *A-7E Software Module Guide*. Naval Research Laboratory Memorandum 4702 (December 1981).

[38] F. P. Brooks, Jr. No silver bullet – Essence and accident in software engineering. *Proceedings of the IFIP Tenth World Computing Conference*. Elsevier, Amsterdam (1986) 1069–1076. Reprinted in *IEEE Computer* (April 1987) 10–19.

[39] M. Buckley and R. Chillarege. Discovering relationships between service and customer satisfaction. *ICSM '95: Proceedings of the International Conference on Software Maintenance* (1995) 192–201.

[40] J. N. Buxton and B. Randell (eds.). *Software Engineering Techniques: Report on a Conference Sponsored by the NATO Science Committee*, Rome, Italy, October 1969 (published April 1970).
http://homepages.cs.ncl.ac.uk/brian.randell/NATO/nato1969.PDF.

[41] K. Cabulong and T. S. Fasulo. 4Kids by Kids. Independent study course CSC499 with R. Sethi, University of Arizona (Spring 2016).

[42] Y. Cao, M. Gomez, H. Du, M. Mitchell, and A. N. Tran. Remote Expert's Decision Support System. Project report for course CSC436 by R. Sethi, University of Arizona (Fall 2016).

[43] M. Carolin, J. Groh, D. Decina, and A. George. Pool Pow! Project report for course CSC436 by R. Sethi, University of Arizona (Spring 2017).

[44] J. J. Chilenski and S. P. Miller. Applicability of modified condition/decision coverage to software testing. *Software Engineering Journal* (September 1994) 193–200.

[45] D. Clegg and R. Barker. *Case Method Fast Track: A RAD Approach*. Addison-Wesley Professional (1994).

[46] P. Clements, F. Bachmann, L. Bass, D. Garlan, J. Ivers, R. Linde, P. Merson, R. Nord, and J. Stafford. *Documenting Software Architectures: Views and Beyond*, 2nd ed. Addison-Wesley Professional (2011).

[47] A. Cockburn. *Writing Effective Use Cases*. Addison-Wesley (2001).

[48] A. Cockburn. Why I still use use cases. (January 9, 2008). http://alistair.cockburn.us/Why+I+still+use+use+cases.

[49] A. Cockburn and L. Williams. The costs and benefits of pair programming. http://collaboration.csc.ncsu.edu/laurie/Papers/XPSardinia.PDF.

[50] D. M. Cohen, S. R. Dalal, M. L. Fredman, and G. C. Patton. The AETG system: An approach to testing based on combinatorial designs. *IEEE Transactions on Software Engineering* 23, 7 (July 1997) 437–444.

[51] M. Cohn. *Agile Estimation and Planning*. Prentice-Hall (2005).

[52] CollabNet VersionOne. *14th Annual State of Agile Report*. (2019). http://stateofagile.versionone.com.

[53] L. L. Constantine. Essential modeling: Use cases for modeling user interfaces. *ACM Interactions* 2, 2 (April 1995) 34–46.

[54] M. E. Conway. How do committees invent? *Datamation* (April 1968) 28–31.

[55] M. A. Cusumano and D. B. Yoffie. *Competing on Internet Time*. The Free Press (1998).

[56] N. Dalkey and O. Helmer. An experimental application of the Delphi method to the use of experts. *Management Science* 9, 3 (April 1963) 458–467.

[57] A. Dardenne, A. van Lamsweerde, and S. Fickas. Goal-directed requirements acquisition. *Science of Computer Programming* 20, 1–2 (April 1993) 3–50.

[58] A. De Bonte and D. Fletcher. *Scenario-Focused Engineering*. Microsoft Press (2013).

[59] J. Dean. Software engineering advice from building large-scale distributed systems. Talk to Stanford Class CS293 (Spring 2007). https://static.googleusercontent.com/media/research.google.com/en//people/jeff/stanford-295-talk.pdf.

[60] J. Dean and S. Ghemawat. MapReduce: Simplified data processing on large clusters. *Communications of the ACM* 51, 1 (January 2008) 107–113.

[61] E. W. Dijkstra. Structured programming. In the report from the 1969 NATO Conference in Rome [40]. (April 1970) 84–88.

[62] G. T. Doran. There's a S.M.A.R.T. way to write management's goals and objectives, *Management Review* 70, 11 (1981) 35–36.

[63] C. Ebert and K. Shankar. Industry trends 2017. *IEEE Software* (March–April 2017) 112–116.

[64] S. G. Eick, C. R. Loader, M. D. Long, L. G. Votta, and S. Vander Wiel. Estimating software fault content before coding. *14th International Conference on Software Engineering (ICSE)* (May 1992) 59–65.

[65] M. E. Fagan. Design and code inspections to reduce errors in program development. *IBM Systems Journal* 15, 3 (1876) 258–287.

[66] M. E. Fagan. Advances in software inspections. *IEEE Transactions on Software Engineering* SE12, 7 (July 1986) 744–751.

[67] M. Feathers. The Humble Dialog Box (2002). https://martinfowler.com/articles /images/humble-dialog-box/TheHumbleDialogBox.pdf.

[68] N. Fenton and J. Bieman. *Software Metrics* CRC (2015).

[69] G. Ford. *1990 SEI Report on Undergraduate Software Engineering Education.* Software Engineering Institute Technical Report CMU/SEI-90-TR-003 (March 1990).

[70] M. Fowler. *UML Distilled 3rd ed.: A Brief Guide to the Standard Object Modeling Language*. Addison-Wesley (2003).

[71] M. Fowler. GUI architectures (July 18 2006). http://martinfowler.com/eaaDev/uiArchs.html .

[72] M. Fowler. Yagni. (May 26, 2015). https://martinfowler.com/bliki/Yagni.html .

[73] M. Fowler. The State of Agile Software in 2018: Transcript of a Keynote at Agile Australia. (August 25 2018). https://martinfowler.com/articles/agile-aus-2018.html .

[74] E. Gamma, R. Helm, R. Johnson, and J. Vlissides. *Design Patterns: Elements of Reusable Object-Oriented Software*. Addison-Wesley (1995).

[75] B. J. Garvin, M. B. Cohen, and M. B. Dwyer. Evaluating Improvements to a meta-heuristic search for constrained interaction testing. *Empirical Software Engineering* 16, 1 (2010) 61–102.

[76] D. A. Garvin. What does "product quality" really mean? *Sloan Management Review* 26, 1 (Fall 1984) 25–43.

[77] W. H. Gates III. The Internet Tidal Wave. Internal Microsoft memo (May 26, 1995). www.justice.gov/atr/cases/exhibits/20.pdf .

[78] B. Geppert and F. Roessler. *Multi-Conferencing Capability*. United States Patent 8,204,195 (June 19, 2012).

[79] B. Glick. The BBC DMI project: What went wrong? *Computer Weekly* (Feb 5, 2014). www.computerweekly.com/news/2240213773/The-BBC-DMI-project-what -went-wrong.

[80] C. A. Gomez-Uribe and N. Hunt. The Netflix recommender system: Algorithms, business value, and innovation. *ACM Transactions on Management Information Systems* 6, 4 (December 2015) Article 13.

[81] D. Grove and I. Rogers. (2009) The strength of metacircular virtual machines: Jikes RVM. In Spinellis and Gousios [173, pp. 235–260].

[82] A. Griffin and J. R. Hauser. The voice of the customer. *Marketing Science* 12, 1 (Winter 1993) 1–27.

[83] R. Hackbarth, A. Mockus, J. D. Palframan, and R. Sethi. Improving software quality as customers perceive it. *IEEE Software* (July/August 2016) 40–45. www.computer.org/cms/Computer.org/ComputingNow/issues/2016/08/mso201 6040040.pdf

[84] J. D. Hagar, T. L. Wissink, D. R. Kuhn, and R. N. Kacker. Introducing combinatorial testing in a large organization. *IEEE Computer* (April 2015) 64–72.

[85] O. Helmer. *Analysis of the Future: The Delphi Method.* RAND Corporation, Report P-3558 (March 1967).

[86] F. Henderson. Software engineering at Google (January 31, 2017). https://arxiv.org/ftp/arxiv/papers/1702/1702.01715.pdf .

[87] F. Herzberg. *Work and the Nature of Man.* Cleveland World Publishing Co. (1966).

[88] G. J. Holzmann. Landing a spacecraft on Mars. *IEEE Software* (March–April 2013) 17–20.

[89] G. J. Holzmann. Mars code. *Communications of the ACM* 57, 2 (February 2014) 64–73.

[90] D. Hovemeyer and W. Pugh. Finding more null pointer bugs, but not too many. *7th ACM SIGPLAN-SIGSOFT Workshop on Program Analysis for Software Tools and Engineering.* ACM (June 2007) 9–14.

[91] M. Iansiti and A. D. MacCormack. Developing products on Internet time. *Harvard Business Review* (September–October 1997).

[92] IEEE. *Recommended Practice for Software Requirements Specifications.* IEEE Standard 830-1998 (reaffirmed December 9, 2009).

[93] IEEE-CS and ACM. *Software Engineering 2014: Curriculum Guidelines for Undergraduate Degree Programs in Software Engineering.* www.acm.org/education/se2014.pdf.

[94] itsnotabigtruck. Cause of Zune 30 leapyear problem ISOLATED! The original post is gone. See "Zune bug explained in detail," by D. Coldewey. *Tech Crunch* (December 31, 2008). https://techcrunch.com/2008/12/31/zune-bug-explained-in-detail/ .

[95] I. Jacobson. Object oriented development in an industrial environment. *Conference on Object-Oriented Programming, Systems, Languages, and Applications (OOPSLA)* (October 1987) 183–191.

[96] I. Jacobson. Use cases: yesterday, today, and tomorrow. *Software and Systems Modeling* 3 (2004) 210–220.

[97] I. Jacobson interview. Ivar Jacobson on UML, MDA, and the future of methodologies. InfoQ interview (October 24, 2006). www.infoq.com/interviews/Ivar_Jacobson/.

[98] I. Jacobson, I. Spence, and B. Kerr. Use-Case 2.0: The hub of software development. *ACM Queue* 14, 1 (January–February 2016) 94–123.

[99] P. Jalote. *Software Project Management in Practice.* Addison-Wesley (2002).

[100] R. Jeffries. Essential XP: Card, Conversation, Confirmation (August 30, 2001) http://ronjeffries.com/xprog/articles/expcardconversationconfirmation/.

[101] S. C. Johnson. *Lint, a C Program Checker.* Computing Science Technical Report 65, Bell Laboratories (July 26, 1978). http://citeseerx.ist.psu.edu/viewdoc/summary?doi=10.1.1.56.1841 .

[102] S. C. Johnson and D. M. Ritchie. Portability of C programs and the UNIX system. *Bell System Technical Journal* 57, 6 (July–August 1978) 2021–2048.

[103] C. Jones. Software Quality in 2013: A Survey of the State of the Art. *35th Annual Pacific NW Software Quality Conference* (October 2013). The following website has a link to his video keynote: www.pnsqc.org/software-quality-in-2013-survey-of-the-state-of-the-art/.

[104] C. Jones. Achieving software excellence. *Crosstalk* (July–August 2014) 19–25.

[105] J. A. Jones and M. J. Harrold. Test-suite reduction and prioritization for Modified Condition/Decision Coverage. *IEEE Transactions on Software Engineering* 28, 3 (March 2003).

[106] M. Jørgensen. What we do and don't know about software development effort estimation. *IEEE Software* (March–April 2014) 13–16.

[107] M. Jørgensen and B. W. Boehm. Software development effort estimation: Formal models or expert judgment? *IEEE Software* (March–April 2009) 14–19.

[108] N. Kano. Life cycle and creation of attractive quality. *4th International QMOD Quality Management and Organizational Development Conference*, Linköping University, Sweden (2001) http://huc.edu/ckimages/files/KanoLifeCycleandAQCandfigures.pdf .

[109] N. Kano, N. Seraku, F. Takahashi, and S. Tsuji. Attractive quality and must-be quality (in Japanese). *Journal of the Japanese Society for Quality Control* 14, 2 (1984) 147–156.

[110] R. Kazman and A. Eden. Defining the terms architecture, design, and implementation. *news@sei* 6, 1 (First Quarter 2003).

[111] B. Kitchenham and S. L. Pfleeger. Software quality: The elusive target. *IEEE Software* (January 1996) 12–21.

[112] J. Klein and D. M. Weiss. What is architecture? (2009) In Spinellis and Gousios [173, p. 3–24].

[113] C. W. Kreuger, D. Churchett, and R. Buhrdorf. HomeAway's transition to software product line practice: Engineering and business results in 60 days. *12th International Software Product Line Conference (SPLC '08)*. IEEE (September 2008) 297–306.

[114] P. B. Kruchten. The 4+1 view model of architecture. *IEEE Software* (November 1995) 42–50.

[115] D. R. Kuhn. Combinatorial testing: Rationale and impact (keynote). *IEEE Seventh International Conference on Software Testing, Verification, and Validation* (April 2, 2014) Presentation available at http://csrc.nist.gov/groups/SNS/acts/documents/kuhn-icst-14.pdf

[116] O. Laitenberger and J.-M. DeBaud. An encompassing life cycle centric survey of software inspection. *Journal of Systems and Software* 50, 1 (2000) 5–31.

[117] A. van Lamsweerde. Requirements engineering in the year 00: A research perspective. *International Conference on Software Engineering (ICSE)*. (2000) 5–19.

[118] A. van Lamsweerde. Goal-directed requirements engineering: A guided tour. *Proceedings Fifth IEEE International Symposium on Requirements Engineering* (2001) 249–262.

[119] A. van Lamsweerde. Requirements engineering: From craft to discipline. *Proceedings of the 16th ACM SIGSOFT International Symposium on Foundations of software engineering. Association for Computing Machinery* (November 2008).

[120] A. van Lamsweerde, R. Darimont, and P. Massonet. Goal-directed elaboration of requirements for a meeting scheduler: Problems and lessons learnt. *Second IEEE International Symposium on Reliability Engineering* (1995) 194–203.

[121] C. Larman and V. R. Basili. Iterative and incremental development: A brief history. *IEEE Computer* 36, 6 (June 2003) 47–56.

[122] T. LaToza, G. Venolia, and R. DeLine. Maintaining mental models: A study of developer work habits. *28th International Conference on Software Engineering (ICSE '06)*. ACM (2006) 492–501.

[123] H. F. Ledgard. Ten mini-languages: A study of topical issues in programming languages. *ACM Computing Surveys* 3, 3 (September 1971) 115–146.

[124] I. Leslie. The scientists who make apps addictive. *1843 Magazine* (October–November 2016). www.1843magazine.com/features/the-scientists-who-make-apps-addictive

[125] N. G. Leveson. Medical devices: The Therac-25. Appendix A of *Software: System Safety and Computers* by Nancy Leveson. Addison Wesley (1995). http://sunnyday.mit.edu/papers/therac.pdf.

[126] N. G. Leveson and C. S. Turner. An investigation of the Therac-25 accidents. *IEEE Computer* 26, 7 (July 1993) 18–41. http://courses.cs.vt.edu/professionalism/Therac_25/Therac_1.html.

[127] W. Lübke and M. Semrau. *Grundriß der Kunstgeschichte. 14 Auflage*. Paul Nevv Verlag (1908).

[128] W. A. Madden and K. Y. Rone. Design, development, integration: Space Shuttle primary flight software system. *Communications of the ACM* 27, 9 (1984) 914–925.

[129] J. F. Maranzano, S. A. Rozsypal, G. H. Zimmerman, et al. Architecture reviews: Practice and experience. *IEEE Software* (March–April 2005) 34–43.

[130] I. Maravić. Spotify's event delivery: The road to the cloud (Part I). (February 25, 2016). https://labs.spotify.com/2016/02/25/spotifys-event-delivery-the-road-to-the-cloud-part-i/.

[131] A. Mavin and P. Wilkinson. Big EARS: The return of "Easy Approach to Requirements Syntax." *2010 18th IEEE International Requirements Engineering Conference* (2010) 277–282.

[132] S. McConnell. Measuring software productivity. ACM Learning Webinar (January 11, 2016). http://resources.construx.com/wp-content/uploads/2016/02/Measuring-Software-Development-Productivity.pdf.

[133] M. D. McIlroy. Typescript (October 11, 1964). http://doc.cat-v.org/unix/pipes/.

[134] M. D. McIlroy. Coroutine prime number sieve. (May 6, 2015). www.cs.dartmouth.edu/doug/sieve/.

[135] M. D. McIlroy, E. N. Pinson, and B. A. Tague. Foreword: Unix time-sharing system. *Bell System Technical Journal* 57, 6 (July–August 1978) 1899–1904.

[136] G. A. Miller. The magical number seven, plus or minus two: Some limits on our capacity for processing information. *Psychological Review* 101, 2 (1955) 343–352.

[137] A. Mockus, R. T. Fielding, and J. D. Herbsleb. Two case studies of open source software development: Apache and Mozilla. *ACM Transactions on Software Engineering and Methodology* 11, 3 (July 2002) 309–346.

[138] A. Mockus and D. M. Weiss. Interval quality: Relating customer-perceived quality to process quality. *International Conference on Software Engineering (ICSE ?08)*. ACM Press (2008) 723–732.

[139] J. J. Moder, C. R. Phillips, and E. D. Davis. *Project Management with CPM, PERT, and Precedence Programming*, 3rd ed. Van Nostrand Reinhold (1983).

[140] G. J. Myers. *The Art of Software Testing*. John Wiley (1979).

[141] G. J. Myers, T. Badgett, and C. Sandler. *The Art of Software Testing*, 3rd ed. John Wiley (2011).

[142] National Audit Office. *British Broadcasting Corporation: Digital Media Initiative* Memorandum (January 27, 2014) www.nao.org.uk/wp-content/uploads/2015/01/BBC-Digital-Media-Initiative .pdf.

[143] P. Naur and B. Randell (eds.). *Software Engineering: Report on a Conference Sponsored by the NATO Science Committee*, Garmisch, Germany, 7th to 11th October 1968 (January 1969). http://homepages.cs.ncl.ac.uk/brian.randell/NATO/nato1968.PDF .

[144] W. T. Nichols. Capital cost estimating. *Industrial and Engineering Chemistry* 43, 10 (1951) 2295–2298.

[145] D. North. Behavior modification. *Better Software Magazine* (March 2006). See https://dannorth.net/introducing-bdd/.

[146] L. M. Northrop. SEI's software product line tenets. *IEEE Software* (July–August 2002) 32–40.

[147] D. L. Parnas. On the criteria to be used in decomposing systems into modules. *Communications of the ACM* 15, 12 (December 1972) 1053–1058.

[148] D. L. Parnas. On the design and development of program families. *IEEE Transactions on Software Engineering* SE-2, 1 (March 1976) 1–9.

[149] D. L. Parnas. Designing software for ease of extension and contraction. *IEEE Transactions on Software Engineering* SE-5, 2 (March 1979) 128–138.

[150] D. L. Parnas. Software engineering: Multi-person development of multi-version programs. In *Dependable and Historic Computing*, C. B. Jones and J. L. Lloyd (eds.), *Lecture Notes in Computer Science* 6875 (2011) 413–427.

[151] M. Petre. UML in practice. *International Conference on Software Engineering (ICSE '13)*. (2013) 722–731.

[152] A. Porter, H. P. Siy, C. A. Toman, and L. G. Votta. An experiment to assess the cost-benefits of code inspections in large scale software development. *IEEE Transactions on Software Engineering* 23, 6 (June 1997) 329–346.

[153] A. Porter and L. G. Votta Jr. What makes inspections work? *IEEE Software* 14, 6 (November–December 1997).

[154] Project Management Institute. *A Guide to the Project Management Body of Knowledge (PMBOK Guide)*. Project Management Institute (2008).

[155] D. Rabinowitz. www.aiga.org/inhouse-initiative/intuit-quickbooks-ipad-case-study-app-design/.

[156] T. Reenskaug. The original MVC reports (February 12, 2007). http://folk.uio.no/trygver/2007/MVC_Originals.pdf.

[157] P. C. Rigby, D. M. German, L. Cowen, and M. Storey. Peer review on open-source software projects: Parameters, statistical models, and theory. *ACM Transactions on Software Engineering and Methodology* 23, 4 (August 2014) 35:1–35:33.

[158] C. R. Rogers and F. J. Roethlisberger. Barriers and gateways to communication. *Harvard Business Review* (July–August 1952). Reprinted, *Harvard Business Review* (November–December 1991). https://hbr.org/1991/11/barriers-and-gateways-to-communication.

[159] W. W. Royce. Managing the development of large software systems. *Proceedings IEEE WESCON* (August 1970).

[160] J. Ruberto. Design for Delight applied to software process improvement. *Pacific Northwest Software Quality Conference* (October 2011). www.pnsqc.org/design-for-delight-applied-to-software-process-improvement/.

[161] H. Sackman, W. J. Erikson, and E. E. Grant. Exploratory experimental studies comparing online and offline programming performance. *Communications of the ACM* 11, 1 (January 1968) 3–11.

[162] E. B. Sanders. Converging perspectives: Product development research for the 1990s. *Design Management Journal* 3, 4 (Fall 1992) 49–54.

[163] E. B. Sanders. From user-centered to participatory design approaches. In *Design and the Social Sciences*, J. Frascara (ed.). Taylor & Francis Books (2002) 1–7.

[164] T. Savor, M. Douglas, M. Gentili, et al. Continuous deployment at Facebook and OANDA. *IEEE/ACM International Conference on Software Engineering (ICSE)*. (2016) 21–30.

[165] B. Schneier. Attack trees. *Dr. Dobbs' Journal* (1999). www.schneier.com/academic/archives/1999/12/attack_trees

[166] M. Shaw. Patterns for software architectures. *First Annual Conference on Pattern Languages of Programming* (1994) 453–462.

[167] K. Schwaber and J. Sutherland. *The Scrum Guide* (November 2020). https://scrumguides.org/ .

[168] W. A. Shewhart. *Economic Control of Quality of Manufactured Product*. D. Van Nostrand (1931). Reprinted by American Society for Quality Control (1980).

[169] F. Shul, V. R. Basili, B. W. Boehm, et al. What have we learned about fighting defects. *Proceedings Eighth IEEE Symposium on Software Metrics (METRICS '02)* (2002) 249–258.

[170] H. P. Siy and D. E. Perry. Challenges in evolving a large scale software product. *International Workshop on Principles of Software Evolution* (April 1998).

[171] G. Smith and A. Sidky. *Becoming Agile: . . . in an Imperfect World.* Manning Publications (2009).

[172] Software Engineering Institute. *What Is Your Definition of Software Architecture?* Carnegie Mellon University, 3854 01.22.17 (2017). https://resources.sei.cmu.edu/asset_files/FactSheet/2010_010_001_513810.pdf.

[173] D. Spinellis and G. Gousios (eds.). *Beautiful Architecture.* O'Reilly Media (2009).

[174] W. P. Stevens, G. J. Myers, and L. L. Constantine. Structured design. *IBM Systems Journal* **13**, 2 (June 1974) 115–138.

[175] S. Taylor and K. Schroeder. *Inside Intuit.* Harvard Business School Press (2003).

[176] TeXShop. https://pages.uoregon.edu/koch/texshop/ .

[177] W. Thomson (Lord Kelvin). *Popular Lectures and Addresses, Volume I, 2nd Edition.* MacMillan (1891).

[178] A. N. Tversky and D. Kahneman. Judgement under uncertainty: Heuristics and biases. *Science* 185 (September 27, 1974) 1124–1131.

[179] US Department of Defense. *Military Standard: Technical Reviews and Audits for Systems, Equipments, and Computer Software* MIL-STD-1521B (June 4, 1985). www.dtic.mil/dtic/tr/fulltext/u2/a285777.pdf.

[180] US House of Representatives. Ways and means of effecting economies in the national space program. Hearing before the Committee on Science and Astronautics, 87th Congress, Second Session, No. 17 (July 26, 1962) 75–193.

[181] US House of Representatives. PPACA implementation failures: Answers from HHS? Hearing before the Committee on Energy and Commerce, 113th Congress, Serial No. 113-87 (October 24, 2013).

[182] US House of Representatives. PPACA implementation failures: Didn't know or didn't disclose? Hearing before the Committee on Energy and Commerce, 113th Congress, Serial No. 113-90 (October 30, 2013).

[183] US Naval Observatory. Introduction to calendars. http://aa.usno.navy.mil/faq/docs/calendars.php .

[184] USA Today. Microsoft banks on anti-Clippy sentiment (February 6, 2002). http://usatoday30.usatoday.com/tech/news/2001-05-03-clippy-campaign.htm.

[185] L. G. Votta Jr. Does every inspection need a meeting? *1st ACM SIGSOFT Symposium on Foundations of Software Engineering (SIGSOFT '93).* Distributed as *Software Engineering Notes* 18, 5 (December 1993)107–114.

[186] C. E. Walston and C. P. Felix. A method of programming measurement and estimation. *IBM Systems Journal* 16, 1 (March 1977)54–73.

[187] P. Weaver. The origins of modern project management. Originally presented at the Fourth Annual PMI College of Scheduling Conference (2007). www.mosaicprojects.com.au/PDF_Papers/P050_Origins_of_Modern_PM.pdf.

[188] D. M. Weiss and C. T. R. Lai. *Software Product Line Engineering: A Family-Based Software Development Process*. Addison-Wesley (1999).

[189] E. J. Weyuker. On testing non-testable programs. *The Computer Journal* 25, 4 (1982) 465–470.

[190] J. A. Whittaker. What is software testing? And why is it so hard? *IEEE Software* (January–February 2000) 70–79.

[191] J. A. Whittaker, J. Arbon, and J. Carollo. *How Google Tests Software*. Addison-Wesley (2012).

[192] Wikipedia. Modified condition/decision coverage. https://en.wikipedia.org/wiki/Modified_condition/decision_coverage.

[193] Wikipedia. Zune 30. https://en.wikipedia.org/wiki/Zune_30.

[194] S. Wray. How pair programming really works. *IEEE Software* (January–February 2010) 51–55. See also: Responses to "How pair programming really works." *IEEE Software* (March–April 2010) 8–9.

[195] P. Zave. Classification of research efforts in requirements engineering. *ACM Computing Surveys* 29, 4 (1997) 315–321.

[196] H. Zhu, P. A. V. Hall, and J. H. R. May. Software unit test coverage and adequacy. *ACM Computing Surveys* 29, 4 (December 1997) 366–427.

Index